D1373942

MONEY MATTERS

Also by A. James Meigs
FREE RESERVES AND THE MONEY SUPPLY

Contents

PART THREE: THE MECHANICS OF CONTROLLING MONEY

PART FOUR: WHY MONEY MATTERS

Charts

Preface

It is time to help spread both the good news and the bad about how and why money matters. This book combines observations made from vantage points ranging from that of a central-bank economist—at the Federal Reserve Bank of St. Louis; to visiting academic—at the Workshop in Money and Banking, University of Chicago; to capital-market economist—at the New York Stock Exchange and First National City Bank.

If the rise of Keynesian ideas can be called the Keynesian Revolution, the reemergence and reformulation of the Quantity Theory of Money since the mid-1950s can surely be called a counterrevolution. Nevertheless, it would be a gross betrayal of the spirit of this restoration to say "Money alone matters." It is enough merely to recognize again that money matters in the continually evolving body of economic thought.

Events of 1971 dealt a severe blow to monetarists' hopes that they might have made some headway in moving public policy in their direction. In the United States, monetarist tenets sank from view in President Nixon's New Economic Program. In the world at large, the setback to the new way of thinking about monetary policy was visible in some official reactions to the international monetary crisis.

But at the same time, monetarism gained with the U.S. decision to float the dollar on the foreign-exchange markets and to sever its formal link with gold. This experiment may well bring down the curtain on the system of fixed-exchange rates, buttressed in recent years by controls, that was ushered in at the Bretton Woods Conference of 1944.

Monetarist setbacks in the policy disputes of 1971 may never-theless be laying the groundwork of future gains in the wider areas of analytical debate. The ultimate test of a set of scientific ideas is their power to predict. If excessive growth in the U.S. money supply is allowed to persist, it will be the unpleasant duty of mon-etarist economists to predict the consequences: a rekindling of inflation and the threat of new international monetary crises. It is the confident, though depressing, expectation of monetary econ-omists that these predictions will prove out because all the discrim-inating evidence that can be gleaned from economic history supports the validity of the monetarist view of money, prices, and exchange rates.

In business forecasting, by contrast, the monetarist approach has been rapidly gaining acceptance. The rejection of monetarism by the monetary authorities makes the position of monetarist fore-casters in business all the more secure because their forte is pre-dicting the effects of money-supply changes on business profits, interest rates, and stock prices.

It may seem that the practical applications of the new monetary economics have been undertaken with reckless haste, in view of the disorderly state of opinion within the economics profession re-garding the role of money. More research is needed, to be sure, and much is under way. But, in the meantime, decisions must be made in business, whether or not we are entirely comfortable with the state of our knowledge.

Early results of applying the monetary approach to business forecasting have been so promising that there now are powerful market incentives for trying more. But another compelling reason for reviewing the practical applications at this early stage stems from a view of research expressed by Milton Friedman:

A fascinating aspect of scientific research is the unexpected connec-tions that are always turning up. Work on one problem turns out to have implications for a very different problem; the purest of theories has unexpected practical applications; and the most practical activities turn out to enrich pure theory.

Defense of free markets as means for accomplishing economic ends is a subordinate theme throughout the book. This theme has not just been dragged in by the heels but is directly related to the main one. For much of the current popular disenchantment with the performance of markets can be traced to instability of the monetary environment here and abroad. Many of the controls now spreading like jungle vines through the world economy thus have sprouted from misconceptions about how and why money matters. Moreover, by diverting attention from the real problem, these market interventions make it more and more difficult to regain the monetary stability in which markets function best.

It would be impossible for me to single out everyone who has contributed in some way to this book. Moreover, it has been possible to present only a sketchy introduction to their ideas. For the reader who wants to go deeper than I have in the text, therefore, the notes at the end give leads to the sources that have been especially helpful to me. The references were not chosen to present all sides of every debatable point; this book is frankly intended as an introduction to monetarist thought.

The two individuals who did the most to inspire the writing of this book are Milton Friedman and Homer Jones. They were chiefly responsible for establishing the tie between the academic world and the Federal Reserve Bank of St. Louis that has so enriched the field of monetary economics. Both have commented on the manuscript at various stages.

I owe a large debt to the Federal Reserve Bank of St. Louis— my alma mater; to Darryl Francis, President; to Leonall C. Andersen, Senior Vice President and Director of Research; and to Gerald T. Dunne, Vice President and gentleman scholar in residence. They run a graduate school in economics and central banking that cannot be matched in any university I know of. I also want to thank many friends elsewhere in the Federal Reserve System, the Bank of England, the Banque de France, the Deutsche Bundesbank, and the Banca d'Italia for the time they spent trying to explain central banking to me.

Dr. Bruno Brovedani, of the Banca Nazionale del Lavoro, led me to early applications of monetarism at the International Monetary Fund that I might well have missed. And, I want to thank Fritz Machlup for his own voluminous works in international monetary economics and for the splendid series of publications he instituted at the International Finance Section, Department of Economics, Princeton University.

David Fand, David Meiselman, Phillip Cagan, Beryl Sprinkel, and George Morrison have helped me in many ways ever since we were graduate students at the University of Chicago. They and other veterans of Milton Friedman's workshop should recognize their contributions even where not footnoted. Karl Brunner and Allan Meltzer commented on the manuscript and made many other contributions too numerous to list. Harry G. Johnson, Herbert Stein, and Paul W. McCracken also made helpful suggestions.

At First National City Bank I enjoyed the opportunity to participate in a lively, free center of research in applied monetary economics and banking. What made it challenging was the chance to see economic analysis at work in a profit-making institution. The Bank also gave me a three-month leave of absence to work on this book. Meeting hundreds of customers and guests of the Bank from every corner of the world has given me a view of the world economy that I could not have gained in any other way. Consequently, I now view the conventional analysis of closed economies as hopelessly inadequate.

Everyone in the Citibank Economics Department helped in some way. Many of the ideas in the book were hammered out in what amounts to a continuing departmental seminar and I also benefited from the special knowledge and skills of individual members of the staff. For a complete acknowledgment, therefore, I should print the roster of the Department. However, I have a special debt to the following people who performed the computations and checked the entire manuscript: Mrs. Leila Vieta, Mrs. Mary Turner, Nancy Newcomb, Frances Field, Mrs. Judith Meola, and Mary Mongibelli. If there is an error of fact anywhere in the book, it must be in something I put in after they had finished checking. Frances Brown of the Financial Library and her staff saw to it that I never lacked for books, no matter how unreasonable my requests. The charts were done by the Chart Section under the direction of George J. Suran. Lorraine Bouquet typed the entire manuscript more times than she likes to remember. But she never displayed the exasperation she must have felt when flawless copy came back all marked up with changes. In times of crisis, she had the generous help of Lorraine Rerisi and others.

Two great editor-economists, Harvey Segal of First National City Bank and William Wolman of Argus Research Corporation gave me many good lines and kept me from straying off the point. The final chapter, in particular, benefited from William Wolman's collaboration with me on a joint article, "Central Banks and the Money Supply" (Federal Reserve Bank of St. Louis *Review,* August, 1971).

My wife and children sacrificed countless hours of family projects that would have been much more fun than listening to a slow typewriter. Finally, I want to thank my father and the other Panama Canal diggers who taught me craftsmanship.

one

INVITATION TO THE DEBATE

1

SCIENCE AND POLITICS

. . . even the theorems of Euclid would be challenged and doubted if they should be appealed to by one political party as against another. At any rate, since the "quantity theory" has become the subject of political dispute, it has lost prestige and has even come to be regarded by many as an exploded fallacy. The attempts by promoters of unsound money to make an improper use of the quantity theory—as in the first Bryan campaign—led many sound money men to the utter repudiation of the quantity theory. The consequence has been that, especially in America, the quantity theory needs to be reintroduced into general knowledge.

Irving Fisher, *The Purchasing Power of Money*, 1911[1]

In writing their memoirs, men who have achieved high status as economic advisers to government are inclined to assign their successes to the power of the theories that they apply and their failures to a *deus ex machina* called politics. But it is the thesis of this book that defective theory—especially that which neglects money in general and the growth of the money supply in particular —is the rock on which economic policy founders, that it brings governments of diverse ideologies to grief by engendering either inflation or high unemployment. Although the thesis will be argued mainly with evidence from U.S. experience, it applies the world over.

THE POLITICS OF IT

After they were pushed off the stage by President Nixon's economists in 1969, the economic advisers of Presidents Kennedy and Johnson protested that they had not had time to finish their act. They claimed to have revived the U.S. economy from the comatose state in which they found it in 1961. And they claimed to have done so through skillful use of fiscal policy—changes in taxes and government expenditures. As a matter of fact, the new economists, as the Kennedy-Johnson advisers were called, regarded fiscal policy as the principal instrument for stimulating or cooling the economy; and they assigned to monetary policy only a minor supportive role until late in their tenure. But they had not had time to demonstrate the versatility of their fiscal approach by solving the problem of inflation as well. President Johnson had not taken their recommendation of a tax increase seriously in 1965 when signs of inflation began to appear.

Arthur Okun, the last chairman of President Johnson's Council of Economic Advisers, rested the case for the new economics in his book, *The Political Economy of Prosperity*:

The January 1966 budget marked the first defeat of the new economics by the old politics since Kennedy's decision in August 1962 to delay a tax-cut recommendation. Even more important, the new economics could not pass its crucial test because of the defense upsurge and the political paralysis of tax rates. The new economists had insisted repeatedly to their critics that the policy of fiscal stimulus would be turned off in time and would be amended to head off inflation when the economy did reach full employment. For political—not economic —reasons the skeptics won the debate.[2]

But politics does not excuse all—or even very much. It was not politics that caused the new economists to underestimate the contribution of monetary policy to their success in restoring high employment in the good years of 1961 through 1964; nor to overestimate the effectiveness of wage-price guideposts as curbs on inflation; nor to grossly overestimate the impact of the tax increase and expenditure ceiling in mid-1968, when President Johnson and the Congress finally provided the fiscal restraint they had recommended. They seemed unaware of the inflationary consequences to come when the Federal Reserve poured money like gasoline on the fire they were trying to curb with fiscal policy in 1968. As we shall see, however, the Federal Reserve authorities were only slightly, if any, more aware of the potency of money-supply changes during these years than were the Administration economists.

In its "pure form" the new economics had a short reign in the United States—1960–1968. Its high point was the tax cut of 1964. Its undoing was the inflation that began in 1965. But eight years were enough to reveal its inadequacy. Something was badly wrong with the theory underlying the new economics.

One hard fact of politics is that it is much easier for a new government to make fundamental changes in strategy and policy than for an established government to correct its own mistakes. No abject confession of error is required of an incoming government. Therefore, the Nixon advisers could do what would have been extremely difficult, perhaps impossible, for the Johnson advisers to do.

When they took office the Nixon economic advisers, some of whom had been openly skeptical of the new monetarism, elevated monetary policy to an eminence that it had never been given before in the history of the United States, or perhaps of any other country for that matter. The adoption of monetarism provided the Nixon advisers with a strategy that was a clear alternative to that of the Democrats, just as expansive fiscalism had provided a strategy for the Kennedy advisers in 1961. It would be all too easy to conclude from such turnovers of governments and their advisers that political viability is the ultimate test of economic theories.

Harry Johnson, of the University of Chicago and the London School of Economics, argues that the influence of the new monetarism will soon wane, partly because it is a theory designed to cope with one problem—inflation.

. . . I believe [Johnson says] the Keynesians are right in their view that inflation is a far less serious social problem than mass unemployment. Either we will vanquish inflation at relatively little cost, or we will get used to it. The odds at present are that we will accept it as a necessary price of solving other pressing domestic issues—this seems to be the current view of the present [Nixon] Administration—and in that case monetarism will again be reduced to attempting to convince the public of the importance of the problem it is equipped to solve before it can start arguing about the scientific superiority of its proposed solution to the problem.[3]

However, with commendable evenhandedness, Johnson called Keynesianism a one-problem theory as well:

The "New Economics" was favoured by the opportunity to sell Keynesian policies to meet a Keynesian problem [unemployment]; it encountered disaster when it tried to sell reverse Keynesian policies to meet a non-Keynesian problem [inflation].[4]

Unfortunately, he did not go on to say, as I believe he should have, that excessive reliance on the fiscalists' one-problem theory had contributed to the inflation that monetarist policies were later called upon to stop.

The Johnsonian dichotomy between a theory to serve those who are concerned about unemployment and a theory for those who are concerned about inflation may endure for a long time in the political arena. No less a person than President Nixon appeared to observe it when he explained a turn to more expansive policies in early 1971 by saying, "I am now a Keynesian." But the convenient evasion of responsibility for explaining inflation as well as unemployment should not go unchallenged by economists. The better theory will be the one that leads to the most effective policies for solving *both* problems—unemployment *and* inflation. I will argue that monetarism outperforms fiscalism in both roles.

Although the Nixon Administration disavowed its earlier faith in monetarists' prescriptions when it imposed the wage-price freeze in August, 1971, it by no means abandoned the goal of curbing inflation. Instead, Administration leaders evidently considered inflation such a crucial liability that extreme measures were justified. Nevertheless, monetarists believed the freeze—based as it was on a nonmonetary theory of inflation—was more likely to accelerate inflation than to slow it down. Underestimating the potency of money could undo Republicans as it had undone Democrats before. But that gets ahead of our story. It is time now to try to reintroduce the quantity theory into general knowledge.

ESSENTIALS OF THE NEW MONETARISM

At the outset we should settle the question of what we mean by *money*.[5] Money, in the sense used here, is a widely acceptable means of payment. It is an asset of consumers and businesses. It is not credit or loanable funds as the term is commonly used in financial markets. Although the cost and availability of credit play prominent roles in some theories of the business cycle, emphasis in the monetarist approach is placed instead on money as one of many types of assets held by the public. Money is something people own, not something they owe; although, of course, they may borrow to get it, as they may borrow to buy an automobile or a house.

By monetary policy, furthermore, we mean policies designed to influence the quantity of money, not policies designed to influence interest rates or the availability of credit for financing expenditures of businesses or consumers. Unfortunately, the term "monetary policy" in some discussions covers a wide variety of actions by the monetary authorities, many of which have little or nothing to do with money.

Changes in the supply of money and the supply of credit affect total spending in the economy quite differently. For example, if someone lends $100 to his son-in-law, the volume of credit is expanded. But the increase in potential spending by the son-in-law is offset by the decrease in the father-in-law's spending power. The credit transaction in this case is a shift in the ownership of part of the money stock.

If the stock of money is increased—by the issue of paper notes by a government or central bank or by a bank loan that establishes a new deposit—there is a first-round credit effect, as in the in-law case, but there is also a new factor. The stock of money is now larger in relation to the total stocks of goods and securities in the economy and in relation to the total flow of real income, than it was before. A change in the supply of money relative to everything else will influence people's choices between holding money or goods and securities. And their reactions will show up as changes in spending, while they try to get rid of cash or to acquire more.

Many different commodities, including gold, silver, seashells, and cigarettes, have been used for money. In modern economies, money consists of currency—hand-to-hand money—held by the public plus deposits in commercial banks—checkbook money—excluding deposits of the government and deposits held by banks in other banks. Some discussions of money restrict the definition only to whatever is used for conducting transactions and on which no interest is paid. According to such definitions, time deposits in banks would be excluded. I do not believe these distinctions based on inherent characteristics are crucial.

The crucial characteristics of money for our purposes are its convenience for carrying out transactions (the medium-of-exchange function), its use as a means for holding purchasing power (the store-of-value function), and the fact that the quantity in existence is subject to change by governments and other "outside" influences, such as the discovery and exhaustion of gold mines. This last characteristic is especially important because for centuries men have observed that when the quantity of money changes for any reason prices and incomes change, too.

Possibly the earliest formal statement of the quantity theory of money was by Jean Bodin in 1568, when he demonstrated by careful observation and analysis that the flood of gold and silver from the mines of the New World was the principal cause of the Price Revolution in Europe.[6] Prisoners in prisoner-of-war camps during World War II similarly observed that when the arrival of Red Cross parcels increased the supply of cigarettes in a camp the prices of haircuts and other goods and services, in terms of cigarettes, went up. As the stock of cigarettes was consumed between shipments, prices went down.[7]

At the beginning of the twentieth century, Irving Fisher analyzed the relationships among money, prices, and other magnitudes in more detail than had been done before. The quantity equation, $MV = PT$, was one of his many substantive refinements. The equation itself is not a theory; it merely groups in a convenient way the important variables to be explained: M, the quantity of money; V, velocity or rate of turnover of money; P, prices; and T, volume of transactions per unit of time. Real income or output could be substituted for T. According to Fisher's theory, velocity was regarded as stable (but not constant) and was determined independently of the other terms in the equation. Consequently, changes in M, the quantity of money, would be reflected in prices or output or both.

Fisher and other early monetarists focused most of their attention on the influence of money on prices. Indeed, one of Fisher's best known books was *The Purchasing Power of Money*. This history may explain why, even today, monetarism and the quantity theory are commonly believed to be concerned primarily with what causes inflation and how to cure it.

In common with the classical economists, early monetarists believed that prices and wages adjusted rapidly while adjustments in physical output and quantities of goods proceeded slowly. However, they by no means neglected the effects of money-supply changes on output; they expected output changes to be triggered by price changes. During the "transition periods" in which an economy adjusts to changes in prices caused by changes in money supply, Fisher said, the initial price changes touch off reverberations in interest rates, profits, and business activity that could culminate in booms and crises.[8] The business cycle was largely a "Dance of the Dollar."[9] Fisher and other early monetarists believed that the way to stabilize business activity, therefore, was to stabilize prices through controlling the money supply.

The Keynesians, as we shall see, reversed the emphasis, arguing that output and employment react quickly and that prices and wages are sticky. The new monetarists, while continuing to emphasize the importance of price changes, have devoted more attention to explaining the processes of short-run adjustment of income and employment.

Like Keynesians, the new monetarists expect monetary policy to affect income and employment before affecting the price level. Fisher himself gave more weight to direct effects of money-supply changes on economic activity after the depression caused the quantity theory to fall into disrepute. In his *100% Money,* he said, "a shortage of money such as the recent shortage of 8 billion dollars of checkbook money, *slows down trade at once without waiting to do so through a falling price level* [his italics]."[10] The strong point of the new monetarism, as compared with the old, is the new emphasis on explaining recessions as well as inflations.

As a Federal Reserve economist in the early 1950s, I accepted the quantity theory as an explanation of long-run price behavior. But I was blissfully ignorant of the possibility that money-supply changes might do much more than influence prices and interest rates. If my colleagues were more knowledgeable, they concealed their understanding well. We were the children of our time and had been well indoctrinated in Keynesian economics.

When disturbing rumors reached us that Milton Friedman, at the University of Chicago, and his colleague, Anna J. Schwartz, at the National Bureau of Economic Research, were linking business recessions, as well as price inflations, to money-supply changes, the natural reaction within the central bank was one of indignant incredulity.[11] We should not have been surprised, for, as Friedman and Schwartz said at the time, the idea that monetary disturbances are the principal sources of major fluctuations in business activity was by no means new.

When virtually the whole economics profession had adopted the Keynesian view of business fluctuations in 1946, Clark Warburton, former director of research for the Federal Deposit Insurance Corporation, pointed out that economists "have neglected an important phase of the relation of changes in the quantity of money to prices and business profits and prospects which had been recognized by eighteenth-, nineteenth-, and early twentieth-century economists."[12] He demonstrated, as did Friedman and Schwartz, that sharp decelerations in money-supply growth in the United States were followed by recessions.

Although difficult for some central bankers and many academic economists to accept, the monetarists' explanation of business fluctuations has been a great boon to business forecasters, for it has much improved their prospects for forecasting business-cycle turns. It should be instructive to note that the 1970 recession in the United States, for which Keynesians castigated the Nixon Administration, was accurately forecast by monetarists in 1969 from the behavior of the money supply. Keynesian forecasters, following different stars, missed the turn. I will have more to say about that later.

The other great strength of the new monetarism is its increased emphasis on explaining why and how money-supply changes influence output, employment, and prices. The key assertion of the new monetarism is that people want to hold some command over real purchasing power in the form of money. How much money they want to hold, furthermore, depends in a stable way upon what their income is, what other assets they have, interest rates, and how much they expect prices of goods and services to change. As such, this theory of the demand for money has much in common with explanations of the demand for automobiles, bonds, houses, and machinery.

The public, however, cannot change the total nominal amount of money, or number of dollars, pounds, marks, francs, rupees, or yen, existing in the economy at a given time. The size of the nominal money stock is determined by the banks and the monetary authorities in most countries today.

If the money stock grows faster than does the amount people want to hold, they individually try to hold down their balances to their desired levels in two general ways: (1) they make adjustments in their balance sheets by purchasing assets or paying off debts; or (2) they use current flows of income and expenditures to add to assets or to reduce indebtedness. In effect, they try to convert excess cash into goods and services of many kinds and securities, such as stocks and bonds. If one believes people will passively hold whatever cash comes their way without trying to adjust, he should remember the old saying, "Money burns a hole in the pocket."

Because one man's expenditure is another man's receipt, individuals' attempts to adjust their cash balances put other people out of adjustment, causing repercussions throughout the economy. These attempts to adjust increase the flows of expenditures and income and tend to raise the price level. The adjustments will continue until the real value of the money stock is again equal to what people want to hold.

If the money stock does not grow as fast as the demand for it, individuals trying to build up balances tend to reduce flows of expenditures and income and thus put downward pressure on prices. In this way, changes in money supply affect income and prices. This is a relationship that is potent for good; but also for evil.

By changing the rate of growth of the money supply, the monetary authorities could induce individuals and businesses to make portfolio adjustments that influence consumption as well as investment spending and purchases of financial assets and in this way produce desired and desirable changes in these magnitudes. This is the most hopeful way of putting it.

Unfortunately, money-supply changes have not, most of the time, been well calculated to produce desirable changes. It is a matter of historical fact that substantial changes of money supply in either direction have been a source of disturbance to business activity and prices, rather than offsets to disturbances arising elsewhere.

The principles of the portfolio-adjustment process initiated by money-supply changes, once grasped, are simple; but they explain a lot. As Milton Friedman has described the quantity theory, it is:

. . . the empirical generalization that changes in desired real balances (in the demand for money) tend to proceed slowly and gradually or to be the result of events set in train by prior changes in supply, whereas, in contrast, substantial changes in the supply of nominal balances can and frequently do occur independently of any changes in demand. The conclusion is that substantial changes in prices or nominal income are almost invariably the result of changes in the nominal supply of money.[13]

To sum up the monetarist credo:[14]

1. A change in the rate of growth of the money supply will cause a change in the rate of growth of nominal income (income in money terms) in the same direction about six to nine months later, on the average. However, the lag between a change in money-supply growth and the income response may at times be longer or shorter.

2. The change in rate of growth of nominal income usually shows up first in real output and hardly at all in prices.

3. The effect of a change in money-supply growth on prices comes about six to nine months after the effects on income and

output. Therefore, the average delay between a change in monetary growth and a change in the rate of inflation is about 12–18 months. This is why inflations, once started, are slow to stop. This also explains why a government can enjoy a temporary illusion that inflationary policies are not inflationary.

4. Monetary changes influence output in the short run by initiating fluctuations in business activity. Over decades, however, the rate of monetary growth primarily affects prices. The long-run rate of growth of output is determined by real factors; such as population growth, changes in technology, willingness to save, and the ingenuity and industry of people.

5. A change in monetary growth affects interest rates in one direction at first and in the opposite direction later on. Therefore, an increase in money-supply growth will at first reduce interest rates—the liquidity effect. The effect of the higher money-supply growth on income will later tend to raise the rates to their original level or a higher one. If, still later, the increased monetary expansion causes price inflation, and people expect the inflation to continue, market interest rates will go higher still. This is why countries with high rates of money-supply growth have high interest rates.

6. Central banks and governments can control the rate of growth of the money supply if they want to do so.

7. The effects of government spending on national income depend on how the spending is financed. If an increase in spending is financed by creating money, it will, at first, stimulate a rise in income and then an increase in prices that will divert real goods and services away from private use and into government use. If the increase in government spending is financed by taxes or by borrowing from the public, the main effect is that the government spends the funds instead of the taxpayer or the lender or the person who would otherwise have borrowed the funds. Fiscal policy, therefore, is extremely important for allocating resources between private and government uses but is ineffective for economic stabilization (for any given monetary policy).

The policy implications of monetarism are simple and straightforward. To avoid recessions or inflation, large and sudden changes in the rate of growth of the money supply should be prevented. The best monetary policy, given the current state of our knowledge, therefore, is to keep the money supply growing at a steady rate that is roughly equal to the long-run rate of growth of real output. That is all.

The proper role of monetary policy, in the monetarist view, is to provide a stable framework in which markets can function, not to direct the markets. This is small beer to those who expect the government to be continually swinging its weight around in order to offset perverse tendencies of private economies to run too fast or too slow. But it will work if we give it a chance.

ESSENTIALS OF FISCALISM

Nicholas Kaldor, long-time adviser to the government of Britain and Fellow of King's College, Cambridge, restated the Keynesian Manifesto in 1970:

> The Keynesian Revolution of the late 1930s has completely displaced earlier ways of thinking and provided an entirely new conceptual framework for economic management. As a result, we think of day-to-day problems—of inflationary or deflationary tendencies, unemployment, the balance of payments or growth—on different lines from those of economists of earlier generations. We think of the pressure of demand as determined by autonomous and induced expenditures, and we seek to regulate the economy by interfering at various points with the process of income generation: by offsetting net inflationary or deflationary trends emanating from the private sector or the overseas sector by opposite changes in the net income generating effect of the public sector. Previously, economists had thought of the level of demand—the volume of spending—as being directly determined by the supply of money and the velocity of circulation; and thought of regulating the level of expenditure mainly by monetary controls.[15]

John Maynard Keynes, also an adviser to the government of Britain and Fellow of King's College in his time, had shifted attention away from the classical focus on the quantity of money and toward flows of income and expenditure. In place of $MV = PT$, the Keynesian banner carries $Y = C + I + G$.

Total spending, Y, is equal to consumer spending, C, plus invest-

MONEY MATTERS

ECONOMICS, MARKETS, POLITICS

A. James Meigs

66111

HARPER & ROW, PUBLISHERS

NEW YORK, EVANSTON, SAN FRANCISCO, AND LONDON

To my wife, Lester

ment, I, plus government spending, G. Like $MV = PT$, this is not a theory but is merely a listing of items to be explained.

In the quantity theory, it is misbehavior of money, M, that causes business fluctuations and inflation. In the Keynesian system, investment, I, is the main source of disturbance. Paul Samuelson said in the 1970 edition of his influential textbook, *Economics:*

> Economists are agreed that an important factor in causing income and employment to fluctuate is fluctuation in investment. Whether we are to face a situation of inflationary bidding up of prices or shall live in a frigid state of mass unemployment can depend . . . upon the level of investment.[16]

The fundamental difficulty for economic policy, in the Keynesian view, is that saving and investing in industrial societies are generally done by different people and for different reasons. Saving (or its obverse, consumption) is determined primarily by income and, therefore, is conventionally regarded as "induced" rather than "autonomous." This is because the "propensity to consume" is supposed to be stable.

> The fundamental psychological law, upon which we are entitled to depend with great confidence both *a priori* from our knowledge of human nature and from the detailed facts of experience [said Keynes], is that men are disposed, as a rule and on the average, to increase their consumption as their income increases, but not by as much as the increase in their income.[17]

Investment, however, is believed by Keynesians to be highly variable. "Investment," says Paul Samuelson, "depends largely on the *dynamic* and relatively unpredictable elements of *growth* in the system, on elements outside the economic system itself: technology, politics, optimistic and pessimistic expectations, 'confidence,' governmental tax and expenditure, legislative policies, and much else [italics in original]."[18] If businessmen do not want to invest as much as consumers are willing to save, according to the Keynesian analysis, income will fall, thus reducing savings, until desired saving and desired investment are equal. If businessmen want to invest more than people are willing to save, income rises until desired saving and desired investment are again equal. In short, investment determines income and saving.

Unfortunately, there is no assurance that there will automatically be enough investment to ensure full employment or that there will not be so much as to cause inflation.

As far as total investment or money-spending power is concerned [says Samuelson], the laissez-faire system is without a good thermostat.

For decades there might tend to be too little investment, leading to deflation, losses, excess capacity, unemployment, and destitution. For other years or decades, there might tend to be too much investment, leading to periods of chronic inflation. . . .[19]

With a system in which income, employment, and prices are buffeted about by autonomous fluctuations in investment, another autonomous power must be called in as a stabilizer—government. The Keynesian view of an inherently unstable economy implies the need for discretionary changes in fiscal policy, hence the name "fiscalism" that I have applied to this school. Monetary policy, furthermore, is called upon by Keynesians to moderate swings in investment expenditures through changing interest rates.

Changes in government expenditures or taxes have a multiple effect on total income, as do changes in investment spending, according to the Keynesian multiplier principle (attributed by Keynes to R. F. Kahn).

It follows, therefore [said Keynes], that, if the consumption psychology of the community is such that they will choose to consume, e.g., nine tenths of an increment of income, then the multiplier k is 10; and the total employment caused by (e.g.) increased public works will be ten times the primary employment provided by the public works themselves, assuming no reduction of investment in other directions.[20]

Other key tenets of fiscalism are these:

1. Prices, in the short run, are assumed to be fixed. That is, they are determined essentially by outside forces; prices are determined by costs, which are mainly wages, and wages are determined by past history. This explains the advocacy by Keynesians of wage-price guideposts and incomes policies.

2. Prices, in the long run, are determined by the difference, or "gap," between actual output and potential full-employment output. If the vagaries of investment and government fiscal policies cause actual output to fall short of the full-employment level, there will be a deflationary gap and the price level will tend to fall. If

investment and fiscal policy drive total output above the full-employment level, there will be an inflationary gap that causes the price level to rise. This was the predicament in which President Johnson's advisers saw themselves in 1966.

3. Monetary velocity, instead of being stable as in the monetarist model, passively adjusts in the Keynesian system so that whatever quantity of money happens to exist can accommodate the volume of transactions that is determined by investment and fiscal policy. The notion that velocity is unstable has two important implications for monetary policy. The first is that money-supply changes will not influence income or consumption spending directly. The second is that money does not influence prices either. Therefore, it would be safe to use money-supply changes to influence interest rates.

4. According to the liquidity-preference theory of interest advanced by Keynesians, interest is the cost of holding money. If the money supply increases, people will buy bonds, thus reducing interest rates until rates are so low that someone will be willing to hold the additional money. Effects of money-supply changes, therefore, are transmitted to investment and other expenditures through changes in interest rates.[21] Monetarists, on the other hand, would expect excess cash balances to be exchanged for consumption goods and other real assets, as well as for securities.

This is an oversimplified description of the Keynesian system, just as the earlier discussion of monetarism was oversimplified. Latter-day Keynesians have been showing increasing respect for the role of money. However, this simple description does, I believe, fairly convey the flavor of the cultural heritage that millions of people in the world have absorbed from the most widely used economics textbooks and from the popular press. Furthermore, it is not much different from the rationalizations for policies that were published by the Council of Economic Advisers in the United States between 1961 and 1968.

TESTING, ANYONE?

If politics is the art of the possible, it would seem logical for politicians and those who advise them to be vitally interested in finding out which of these two schools of economics—monetarism or fiscalism—works best. Until the 1960s, however, surprisingly little was done to test them against one another to find which one had the strongest claim to scientific validity. Although a lack of scientific curiosity can be pardoned among politicians, it should not be excused on the part of economists.

It strikes me as significant that Keynes did not derive his theory from careful observation of the way the economy actually operates, as Irving Fisher and his predecessors did. Keynes accepted the popular verdict that the Great Depression demonstrated the ineffectiveness of monetary policy. But this was not careful observation; although the Federal Reserve claimed to have done all that was humanly possible, a vigorous counterrecessionary monetary policy actually was not tried. The depression was, instead, chilling evidence of the terrible consequences that can flow from gross mismanagement of money.

Keynes developed his *General Theory of Employment, Interest and Money* to support the fiscal measures that he was already advocating in England as cures for the depression, as Lawrence R. Klein of the University of Pennsylvania and Herbert Stein of President Nixon's Council of Economic Advisers have pointed out. "It was not his theory which led him to practical policies [said Klein], but practical policies devised to cure honest-to-goodness economic ills which finally led him to his theory."[22]

The idea of manipulating government expenditures and tax rates to revive the economy was firmly established in the United States, furthermore, well before the *General Theory* crossed the Atlantic in 1936. President Hoover recommended fiscal measures early in the depression. New Deal economists were happy to have the intellectual support of the *General Theory* for their "pump-priming" policies. But in their case practice came before theory.

Fiscal policy certainly had strong common-sense appeal, for it was perfectly plausible that if unemployed people were put to work by the government total income would be increased and probably be more than the amount of the government expenditure. Tax reduction, the fiscal measure consistently preferred by conservatives, also had strong practical appeal, although it was more difficult to see during the thirties how a tax reduction would benefit someone who did not have any income.

The *General Theory* was the intellectual fountainhead of the Keynesian revolution, the book that led economists to believe in powers of government spending and taxing that they actually had not observed directly. By 1961 the *General Theory,* as interpreted by the faithful, had hardened into orthodoxy. In *The Fiscal Revolution in America,* however, Herbert Stein observed:

> The evidence upon which economists have based their confidence in the power of fiscal policy has not consisted mainly of direct observation of fiscal policy. Rather it has consisted of certain observations about the nature of the economy which, if correct, would strongly imply the power of fiscal policy. Two propositions were particularly important. The first was that the amount of income currently being earned has a relatively large effect on spending. The second was that the amount of money people have—as distinct from their flow of income—has a relatively small effect on spending.[23]

The weaknesses of both of these propositions have been exposed in an explosion of research. Milton Friedman and David Meiselman produced one of the most devastating critiques of the conventional Keynesian faith in a study for the Commission on Money and Credit that had a disarmingly technical title: "The Relative Stability of Monetary Velocity and the Investment Multiplier in the United States, 1897–1958."[24]

What Friedman and Meiselman did was to perform a series of statistical tests to find out whether changes in money supply or changes in the Keynesians' "autonomous" expenditures (net private domestic investment plus the government deficit plus the net balance of exports over imports) have been the most closely correlated with changes in "induced" expenditures (consumer spending) in the United States. In their tests, money won hands down. Therefore, better forecasts of consumer spending (and total income) could be made from money-supply changes than from changes in investment and fiscal policy.

Published in 1963, but available in preliminary form two years earlier, the Friedman-Meiselman study was a galling challenge—some might say rash, as well—to throw down when Keynesian influence was at its peak in the government and universities of the United States. Spiced with an appropriate, but undiplomatic, comment on the "flabbiness of the profession," it scourged economists for having discarded the quantity theory and for having adopted the Keynesian income-expenditure theory on the basis of essentially no evidence.

. . . the simple version of the income-expenditure theory to which we have deliberately restricted ourselves in this paper [they said] is almost completely useless as a description of stable empirical relationships, as judged by six decades of experience in the United States.[25]

A rise in government spending or investment or exports, therefore, could not be counted on to have a large multiplier effect on total spending. In short, the Emperor had no clothes.

At the same time, Friedman and Meiselman brought money back into the center of the action. "On the evidence so far," they said, "the stock of money is unquestionably far more critical in interpreting movements in income than is autonomous expenditures."[26]

The Friedman-Meiselman charge that the high priests of Keynesian theory had invoked its power before determining whether the power existed called forth outraged replies that have already filled the journals and will continue to do so for years to come. But the critics have not shaken the monetarist case.

Econometric analyses—the use of statistical methods to test theories—like those of Friedman-Meiselman and their critics are valuable. But they cannot settle the doubts of decision makers in business and government or the general public. They cannot even satisfy many economists. The relatively new scientific discipline of econometrics is in such an unsettled state that its practitioners are vulnerable to the skeptics' charge of being able to find whatever they want to find. The debate between fiscalists and monetarists, therefore, cannot be restricted to the chosen ground of the econometricians, essential as their evidence is.

Here politics proves to be the partner of science, for it provides experiments the economist cannot perform in his own laboratory. Messy and apparently inconclusive though they sometimes are, economic-policy experiments in many countries are priceless sources of data for testing economic theories. To find evidence that is credible to decision makers in government and business, it will be necessary to review policies recommended, policies applied, and the results. That is what we will do in the next three chapters. For just as theories are drawn from experience, subsequent experience is the acid test of theories.

For the rest of Part One, economic prescriptions and predictions in the United States of the sixties and early seventies will be compared with results. Where possible, predictions based on the Keynesian income-expenditure theory will be compared with those based on modern monetary theory. These years are a rich period for such an examination because they reveal how the neglect of money and a misplaced confidence in fiscal policy can cause both inflation and unemployment.

2

FISCAL ILLUSION: 1960–1964

The Kennedy economists were, in the main, of
that generation which had been most moved
intellectually and emotionally by Keynes' General
Theory. They were neither so old as to have
learned it grudgingly and with qualifications nor
so young as to have first met it as an already
well-established doctrine. They had enlisted as foot
soldiers in the Keynesian army at the beginning
and risen through the ranks to become marshals.
. . . Although the meaning of Keynesianism
as a doctrine had changed substantially, the
esprit de corps of the school remained. Now its
leaders were coming victoriously to Washington
to practice what they had been teaching. They
had no reason to doubt that they knew what to do.
Herbert Stein, *The Fiscal Revolution in America,*
1969[1]

As they clattered into Washington that cold January of 1961, the
marshals of the Keynesian army had no way of knowing that their
revolution was soon to falter. Instead, they saw their advent to
power as the sweet fruition of the Keynesian revolution. It had been,
until then, largely an intellectual revolution. Now they would have
a chance to act. But much of what they thought they knew proved
not to be so when challenged by the tests of experience. And they
were to be held responsible for the results of economic policies,
whether or not the policies were what they prescribed. Worst of
all, for them, the instability and inflation that eluded their control in
the Soaring Sixties were to produce recruits and ammunition for
the monetarist counterrevolution.

DAWNING OF THE AGE OF ECONOMISTS

They were to have their day—an eight-year day. For eight years, they educated two Presidents and the people of the United States in what they were proud to call the new economics. Although, like staff advisers everywhere, they occasionally had to conceal their anguish when proposals were rejected or were distorted in translation, many of their ideas for getting the country moving again were tried.

During the Kennedy-Johnson years economists infiltrated high government policy-making positions on a wide front. Among the posts overrun were Director of the Bureau of the Budget; under-secretaries of the State, Treasury, Agriculture, and Commerce Departments; Director of the Agency for International Development; several ambassadorships, staff posts in the White House and the Pentagon; a clear majority of the members of the Federal Reserve Board of Governors; and more than half of the presidencies of the Federal Reserve banks. And each of these economists sat at the peak of a large or small pyramid of more junior economists, many of whom were on leave from university posts. A tour of duty at any level in an active agency was virtually guaranteed to raise an economist's price in either the academic market or the newly burgeoning market for business economists and consultants.

While economists were acquiring more influence in Washington than ever before, there was a parallel rise in the influence of economists in business. Moving closer to the seats of corporate power, economists tried to keep their employers and clients from being surprised by unforeseen turns in what had formerly been called the business cycle.

Business economists were perhaps more conservative in some respects than their professional colleagues in government and the universities; but, for the most part, they were Keynesians too in their approach to forecasting. This should be no surprise, for most had been trained in the same schools as the government and academic economists. Some of them had studied with future marshals of the Keynesian army; they shared in the excitement of being bearers of a new revelation. Many of the new business economists, furthermore, had served apprenticeships in federal agencies or the Federal

Reserve System, where they had acquired a deep and abiding respect for the power of government.

Climbing rapidly in the corporate hierarchy were the postwar business school graduates, all of whom had taken courses in modern economics. Whatever the doubts nursed by managers old enough to have been seared by the depression, the new generation of executives took it for granted that flexible management of the federal budget would make their five-year plans come true. The younger financial analysts and institutional investors in Wall Street were similarly buoyed up by the new economics. Guaranteed annual growth was the name of their game and growth would be assured by government.

As Walter Heller, chairman of President Kennedy's Council of Economic Advisers, put it, the first task of the Council was education:

No matter how inescapable the logic of the Keynesian idea may have been, and how apparent it was to economists as long as 20 or 25 years ago, it was not an "idea whose time had come" until it could be put in a form and framework which made it acceptable to the public and attractive to Presidents. That may not be economic optimality, but it *is* political democracy.[2]

So, finally, there was the press. Journalists admire activism, especially an activism that rests on a theory that they can convey in a paragraph or two. Walter Heller gave it to them, elegantly and with fervor. In Arthur Okun's approving view, "The press served as the textbook for the biggest course in elementary macroeconomics ever presented."[3] Not until 1966, when results departed widely from expectations, did more than a handful of financial writers begin to question the underlying rationale of the policies they had warmly embraced earlier in the 1960s.

SIMPLE MEASURES OF POLICY

Before reviewing the economic history of the 1960s we need a scoreboard and the names and numbers of the players. The accounts of what was happening were more than a little confusing at the time. Even today, it is difficult to distinguish facts about that period from some of the lingering illusions.

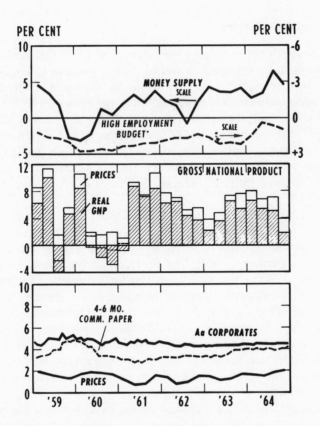

Chart 2-1. The 1960–1961 recession followed a contraction in the money supply and an increase in "fiscal drag" (surplus in the high-employment budget). Prices and interest rates were stable after the recession while real GNP grew at a high rate. The new economists say fiscal policy spurred the upsurge in output, although fiscal drag was not reduced much until taxes were cut in 1964. Monetarists say faster money-supply growth got the economy moving again.

NOTES: Money supply—quarterly change in M₁ (demand deposits and currency) at seasonally adjusted annual percentage rates (left-hand scale). High-employment budget—quarterly surplus or deficit in the high-employment, national-income-account budget estimated by Federal Reserve Bank of St. Louis; expressed as percent of high employment GNP; plotted on inverted scale (right-hand scale) so that surpluses are below zero line and deficits above. GNP—quarterly changes in seasonally adjusted annual percentage rates; shaded portions represent changes in real GNP; unshaded portions represent the part of change in current dollar GNP attributable to price changes. Aa corporates—monthly-average new-issue yield on long-term Aa utility bonds; First National City Bank series. 4–6 mo. Comm. Paper—monthly-average market yields on 4–6 month-maturity commercial paper; Federal Reserve series. Prices—quarterly change in GNP deflator at annual percentage rates; smoothed with a three-quarter weighted moving average. *Chart by First National City Bank.*

In order to aid in judging the relative merits of the fiscalist and monetarist interpretations of events, the top panel of Chart 2-1 displays one economic policy measure to represent each of the contending schools. To represent fiscal policy we have the high-employment budget surplus. To represent monetary policy we have changes in the money supply (demand deposits and currency). The next two panels contain measures of the economy's performance: changes in gross national product (in both current dollars and dollars adjusted for price inflation), changes in prices, and interest rates.

The high-employment surplus (or deficit) is a measure of the thrust of fiscal actions that was much used by the President's Council of Economic Advisers during this period and later was used by the Nixon advisers as well. The concept had been developed soon after World War II by the Committee for Economic Development and Milton Friedman, working independently.[4] Because government expenditures and revenues are influenced by changes in economic activity, the actual surplus or deficit at a particular time is not considered to be the best measure of the influence of the government's budgetary program. The high-employment surplus is an estimate of the surplus that would be produced by actual tax rates and expenditure programs if the economy were operating at high employment, say with a 4 percent unemployment rate in the United States.

During a recession—1970, for example—revenues fall below their high-employment level because personal incomes and corporate profits are lower. Expenditures are higher than they would have been at high employment because of higher payments for unemployment compensation and other welfare expenditures. The budget that would have produced a surplus at high employment, therefore, actually produces a deficit. In this situation, however, a fiscalist would consider *fiscal policy,* as distinguished from *fiscal actions,* to be still restrictive, or at least more restrictive than the actual deficit would suggest. High-employment surpluses, or movements toward surplus, are interpreted as fiscal-policy restraint or shifts toward restraint. Deficits, or movements toward deficit, are interpreted as expansionary fiscal policy or shifts toward expansion.

For easier comparisons of the two curves, the budget graph

is inverted so that deficits are plotted above the zero line and surpluses are below it. Therefore, *when the budget line and the money-supply line are both moving upward, fiscal and monetary policies are both moving in the direction of expansion. When the lines move downward, fiscal and monetary policies are becoming more restrictive.* Occasionally, as in 1962, 1966, and 1968, the lines move in opposite directions. These are the most significant periods for our purposes because they tell us something about which policy is the most powerful. We shall refer to this chart often in this and the next two chapters.

RECESSIONARY PROLOGUE

In the final year of the Eisenhower Administration the recovery from the 1957–1958 recession was choked off by the untimely beginning of the 1960–1961 recession. The recovery, if indeed it can be called a recovery, thus was one of the shortest on record. This dismaying turn of events took the nation by surprise, for there had been widespread agreement with President Eisenhower when he said in his State of the Union message that "1960 promises to be the most prosperous year in our history."[5]

To fight inflation and to correct the balance-of-payments deficit that had recently become embarrassingly large, the Administration had been driving hard to achieve a budget surplus. Proposals for tax cuts had been firmly rejected during the 1957–1958 recession. In the calendar year 1960 there was a $3.5 billion surplus in the budget on a national income-and-product-account basis. But if the economy had been at full employment the tax rates then in effect would have brought in enough revenue to produce a surplus of more than $13 billion. As judged by the high-employment surplus shown on the chart, fiscal policy was even more restrictive in 1960 than it later became in 1969 when the problem of inflation was much worse.

In his book, *Six Crises,* Richard Nixon has recorded that Arthur Burns warned him in March that a recession was imminent.[6] He tried to get the Administration to supply some fiscal and monetary stimulus but was unsuccessful. A sharp rise of unemployment in

October undoubtedly contributed to Nixon's loss in the November presidential election.

Monetary policy had also been extremely restrictive. The money supply had been contracting since the previous summer, causing monetarists—there were very few in those days—to become alarmed in the fall of 1959. However, the monetary authorities apparently believed an increase in velocity made the smaller money supply sufficient. This was in harmony with the Keynesian view mentioned in Chapter 1 that velocity passively adjusts so that any given quantity of money can accommodate the flow of income and spending. In any case, they thought inflation was a more clear and present danger than recession. The Federal Reserve was braced in January, 1960, to resist a strong rise in credit demand that was expected to accompany business efforts to rebuild inventories depleted by the 1959 steel strike. The long-heralded Soaring Sixties were expected to begin with a boom.

Nevertheless, some members of the Federal Open Market Committee—key policy-making group in the Federal Reserve System— recommended that the money-supply contraction be stopped. This warning, too, failed to have the desired effect. Although the Open Market Committee decided at its March 1 meeting to ease the degree of monetary restraint, the money supply continued to decline until after the recession began in May.[7] However, contraction of the money supply did not seem to alarm or to offend most outside observers in early 1960, possibly because interest rates were plummeting downward from their December, 1959, peaks.

The prevailing state of opinion among economists is well conveyed by the February, 1960, issue of First National City Bank's *Monthly Economic Letter*. In discussing complaints about a scarcity of money, the *Letter* said:

. . . people have more money and other liquid resources than ever before; their spending is rising and demands in the markets are sufficient to produce some measurable upward movement in price averages. The evidence from this side is that the supply of money is fully adequate.[8]

In its first Report, President Kennedy's Council of Economic Advisers attributed the 1960–1961 recession to the restrictive fiscal policy of the Eisenhower Administration.

The analysis of the budget program in terms of the full-employment surplus points to a probable major cause of the incomplete and short-lived nature of the 1958–60 expansion. The most restrictive fiscal program of recent years was the program of 1960. Its full-employment surplus exceeded any from 1956 to date. . . . Thus, whereas the Federal budget contributed to stability during the contraction phase of the cycle [the 1957–1958 recession] and during the first year of expansion, it was altered abruptly in the direction of restraint late in 1959 at a time when high employment had not yet been achieved.[9]

Writing several years later, Herbert Stein, who was to become a member of President Nixon's Council, said it was still impossible to say whether the fiscal policy of 1958–1960 was a mistake. He posed, without pursuing it further, what I believe is the most significant question about the policies of that period.

Would a more expansive fiscal policy have strengthened the recovery after 1958 and prevented the recession which began in 1960, *or were these developments so rigidly determined by the slow growth of the money supply during this period that they could not have been changed by fiscal policy* [italics added]?[10]

Paul McCracken, who was on the Council during those years and was to become chairman of President Nixon's Council, attributed the recession to "the unwise decision in 1958 against tax reduction. This and the glacial pace of monetary expansion caused the subsequent failure of the economy to regain full employment in 1960."[11]

According to Stein, if there was a mistake in fiscal policy in the 1958–1960 period it was not because the Eisenhower Administration did not "accept the modern view of the way in which the government's fiscal policy affects the economy."[12] The difficulty rather was that more aggressive pursuit of full employment would have endangered other objectives of the Administration, such as tax revision, checking the growth of federal spending, economic growth, international confidence in the dollar, and fighting inflation.

I believe, however, that President Eisenhower's advisers underestimated the restrictiveness of monetary policy at the time, if not when they looked back on their experience. Consequently, the economy was more depressed by the combined fiscal and monetary policies than they had any reason to expect. Their mistake was a natural one, given the prevailing attitudes of the Federal Reserve.

The monetary authorities shared fully in the general neglect of money. In fact, they hardly bothered to measure it in those days.

In its Annual Report for 1959 the Board of Governors noted that,

The money supply, which increased substantially in 1958 and early 1959, was limited to little further growth after last spring. The public's holdings of other liquid assets, however, expanded sharply throughout the year.[13]

This Federal Reserve suggestion that growth in other liquid assets might compensate for the lack of growth in money supply (actually a contraction) reflected a swing of majority professional opinion toward the idea that the proper concern of monetary policy was not money but "total liquidity" and a broad spectrum of interest rates. This new view was one of the products of a great upsurge of interest in the role of central banks that had been aroused by the worldwide inflation that followed World War II. Although some of the new monetarists had been heard in the inquiries of the Joint Economic Committee of the U.S. Congress and in other forums, central bankers found much more to their liking the conclusions of the Radcliffe Committee in England that were reported in 1959 and the "Gurley-Shaw thesis" that came to light at about the same time in the United States.

The Radcliffe Committee was an official inquiry into the financial system of Britain and the "Gurley-Shaw thesis" was a shorthand name for some conjectures about the role of financial intermediaries that were developed by two Stanford University economists, John G. Gurley and Edward S. Shaw.[14] Both put considerable weight on the availability of "near moneys," or substitutes for money, that they said could be created by many institutions in addition to banks.

Because other liquid assets, such as savings and loan shares and short-term government securities were considered to be close substitutes for conventionally defined money, money itself was not supposed to matter much. An unwary central banker, therefore, could easily be lulled into the comfortable belief that he would not be held responsible for either inflation or unemployment if the money supply failed to behave as monetarists thought it should. Nevertheless, the U.S. economy followed the monetarists' script in this instance, not the one of Radcliffe, Gurley, and Shaw. Recession followed the money-supply contraction of 1959, liquidity-growth notwithstanding. And a warning had been sounded in advance.

Milton Friedman, for example, had attributed the 1957–1958 recession to a mistake in monetary policy in a paper he prepared for the Joint Economic Committee in 1958. There he referred to "the tight money policy of 1956 and 1957 which coexisted with rising prices but whose delayed effects are with us in the current recession."[15] The delayed effects of the 1959 tight money policy similarly appeared as a recession in the following year, an election year to boot.

The restrictive policies applied during the Eisenhower Administration left to its successor an economy with high unemployment and a stable price level.

> Thus [said Stein], the austerity of the Eisenhower administration left the Kennedy administration able to practice the happy side of a modern fiscal policy—to cut taxes and increase expenditures, stimulating employment and economic growth, without transgressing conventional limits of fiscal soundness or reawakening the dragon of inflation.[16]

We shall see, however, that just as the misbehavior of money meant more unemployment than the Eisenhower advisers had expected from their restrictive fiscal policies, misbehavior of money was to mean more inflation than the Kennedy-Johnson advisers expected from their expansive fiscal policies.

GAPS, DRAGS, MIXES, TWISTS, AND GUIDEPOSTS

When the Kennedy Administration came in, it was widely agreed that counterrecessionary policies were called for. Monetary policy had turned around in the fall of 1960, the earliest reversal for any postwar recession. There was a sharp increase in the rate of growth of the money supply, as can be seen on the chart. However, a nagging deficit in the U.S. balance of payments seemed to rule out the possibility of an aggressive monetary policy, which, in those days, was considered to be a low-interest-rate policy. Low interest rates in the United States might make the deficit worse by increasing the outflow of dollars in search of higher returns in other countries.

Fiscal policy would have to do the job. But there was more fiscal talk than fiscal action in the first year. The budget began to move in the direction of expansion in 1961, largely because of a $3 billion increase in expenditures over those projected in the Eisenhower budget and because the Berlin crisis that summer increased defense expenditures by several billion more. These expenditure increases, however, were fortuitous rather than the results of conscious fiscal-policy decisions. But the Council of Economic Advisers did not let the windfalls go unsung. According to the 1962 Report, an increase of $8 billion over the original budget estimates for expenditures in fiscal 1962 (which began July 1, 1961) was "itself responsible for a rise in the gross national product that can be estimated conservatively at $15 billion."[17] This would mean a government-expenditure multiplier of about two. Nevertheless, the high-employment surplus remained very large because revenues rose rapidly also.

Before the fiscal-policy stimulus was applied, however, the rate of growth of real gross national product jumped to nearly a 9 percent annual rate in the second quarter of 1961. It grew for the year as a whole at a 6 percent annual rate. The recession was decisively and unmistakably at an end before the new economists had even warmed up. With inflation fears rising again, the new President veered toward fiscal firmness. This temporarily checked his advisers' hopes for more expansive policies, which they viewed largely in terms of increasing expenditures. The Administration had promised programs for improving education, rebuilding cities, and other expensive welfare efforts.

A low point was reached in the summer of 1961 [said Walter Heller] when Kennedy, flying in the face of modern economics, tentatively decided on a tax increase of $3 billion to finance the Berlin defense buildup in spite of the still-yawning gap between the economy's actual and potential performance.[18]

In the campaign to win President Kennedy and the Congress to a more activist, more expansionary fiscal policy, Walter Heller and his colleagues proved to be extremely resourceful in devising new terms or reviving old ones to make their points. One of the old ones brought up to date was the "gap" between actual and potential output. In its earlier run, during World War II, it had been the "inflationary gap" because estimated total demand then exceeded the economy's capacity. In the new incarnation the "output gap" measured how far actual performance was below potential.

In 1961, once recession had turned into recovery [said Heller], nothing was more urgent than to raise the sights of economic policy and to shift its focus from the ups and downs of the cycle to the continuous rise in the economy's potential. Policy emphasis had to be redirected from a *corrective* orientation geared to the dynamics of the cycle, to a *propulsive* orientation geared to the dynamics and the promise of growth [italics in original].[19]

This may have been modern economics, but it was a sharp departure from Keynesian theory, which was an explanation of *short-run* effects of investment and government expenditures on income with prices and the stock of capital held fixed. Keynesian theory did not purport to explain the forces determining *long-run* growth, a very different problem.

Another persuasive concept was "fiscal drag." As GNP grows, argued the Council, tax revenues rise, causing the high-employment surplus to rise, thereby putting a brake on income growth. This fiscal drag might even choke off an expansion before full employment was reached, as in the incomplete recovery from the 1957–1958 recession. It was necessary, therefore, to be always on guard against the automatic tendency for drag to develop. Fiscal drag was a depressant on economic growth comparable to the deficiency in investment opportunities, or "secular stagnation," that American economists had worried about in the late 1930s. The antidote for fiscal drag was a "fiscal dividend," which could take the form of an expenditure increase or a tax cut.

The combination of fiscal and monetary policies became known as the fiscal-monetary "mix." "There is, in principle," said the Council in its 1962 Report, "a variety of mixtures of fiscal and monetary policies which can accomplish a given stabilization objective."[20] In 1961, however, the balance-of-payments deficit was considered to be a constraint on the Federal Reserve's ability to fight recession by the traditional method of reducing interest rates, as we saw earlier. Consequently, the "mix" of antirecession policies would have to consist more of fiscal policy and less of monetary policy than it otherwise would have.

To derive the maximum domestic expansion from interest-rate policy without making the balance of payments worse, the Kennedy advisers introduced another innovation—"operation twist." The "twist" was intended to support investment spending and home building with lower long-term interest rates while keeping short-term rates high to minimize the flow of short-term capital to other countries.[21] There were two parts to the operation. One, called debt management, was carried out by the Treasury, which issued more short-term securities with one hand while buying long-term U.S. government securities with the other for various government investment and trust accounts. The other part was carried out by the Federal Reserve, which bought Government securities of longer maturities than it had done in the previous several years. By increasing the amount of short-term public debt relative to long-term debt in the hands of the public, these combined operations were expected to raise short-term rates and to reduce long-term rates.

The final major innovation in the new economists' armory was the "wage-price guidepost." Fearing that inflation would resume when the economy approached full employment, the Kennedy Council wanted to head it off by persuading industries and unions to exercise voluntary restraint in wage-price decisions. If industries and unions were to do something they would not otherwise have done, some sort of guidance was needed. So was born the guidepost concept. As Walter Heller said of the guideposts, "In essence they pit the power of public opinion and Presidential persuasion against the market power of strong unions and strong businesses."[22]

The guides were spelled out in the first Report of the Kennedy Council:

The general guide for noninflationary wage behavior is that the rate of increase in wage rates (including fringe benefits) in each industry be equal to the trend rate of overall productivity increase. General acceptance of this guide would maintain stability of labor cost per unit of output for the economy as a whole—though not of course for individual industries.

The general guide for noninflationary price behavior calls for price reduction if the industry's rate of productivity increase exceeds the overall rate—for this would mean declining unit labor costs; it calls for price reduction if the industry's rate of productivity increase exceeds the overall rate—for this would mean declining unit labor costs; it calls for an appropriate increase in price if the opposite relationship prevails; and it calls for stable prices if the two rates of productivity increase are equal.[23]

In later reports, 3.2 percent per year was proclaimed as the productivity-growth standard around which the massed phalanxes of big labor and big business were to rally. Furthermore, the approach was a congenial one to economists who held the Keynesian, essentially nonmonetary, view of how wages and prices are determined.

TO CUT OR NOT TO CUT

With their panoply of shining new rhetoric and policy instruments girding them about, the Kennedy advisers set confidently out in 1962 to reach the peak of full employment. Everything pointed to activist fiscal policy as the route to follow: the output gap made it desirable; fiscal drag made it necessary; fiscal dividends would make it effective; and operation twist and the guideposts would make it safe by covering their rear against a balance-of-payments crisis or an upsurge of cost-push inflation. But they lacked a convinced President and a malleable Congress at first.

They had, it is true, been able to persuade President Kennedy not to raise taxes to finance the defense buildup in 1961. Furthermore, saying that "the time to repair the roof is when the sun is shining," he asked the Congress in January 1962 for standby powers to cut individual income taxes temporarily and to initiate public works spending in case of recession—powers Congress was unlikely to grant. However, in his annual Budget Message to the Congress at the same time, he fulfilled his pledge of the previous July to submit a budget "strictly in balance" for fiscal 1963 (to begin July 1, 1962).

Although they would have preferred expenditure increases, Kennedy's advisers made a strategic decision to shift to tax reduction. From then on, tax proposals were in the direction of net reduction despite strenuous efforts, led by the Treasury, to close various "loopholes" in the internal revenue code.

After business activity faltered in the first half of 1962 and after the stock market plunged downward in May, the President spoke out for an expansive fiscal policy at Yale on June 11. "President Kennedy's landmark speech at Yale," said Walter Heller, "stands as the most literate and sophisticated dissertation on economics ever delivered by a President (and he wrote much of it himself)."[24]

Hopes for a "quickie tax cut" in 1962 to counter the unexpected near-recession soon died during the summer. In August the President announced he would seek tax reduction in 1963 instead. In December, however, he wavered again, according to Heller, partly because the economic outlook for 1963 was improving and partly because of resistance from members of the Administration who preferred expenditure increases to tax cuts.

. . . the long shadow of our Ambassador to India, John Kenneth Galbraith [said Heller], had fallen across the White House with a renewed call for expenditure increases rather than tax cuts in the face of vast unmet needs for public services.[25]

Important department heads in the Kennedy Cabinet also opposed tax cuts that might restrict their programs.

A few days later the President was again enthusiastic about tax cuts when his speech to the Economic Club of New York was well received. "I gave them straight Keynes and Heller," he told Heller, "and they loved it."[26]

The major tax actions of 1962 were on the corporate tax front. An investment tax credit and liberalization in tax treatment of depreciation went into effect in 1962 (both recommended in 1961). Designed to spur business investment, they increased annual cash flow of corporations by over $2 billion per year and increased the after-tax rate of return on new machinery and equipment. In a sense, these two moves were part of the interest-rate strategy of the Administration, for they were a way to reduce the cost of capital to corporations without driving interest rates down and thus getting into more trouble with the balance of payments.

Despite the moves toward expansiveness on the revenue side,

the budget swung abruptly toward restraint again in 1963 when the growth of expenditures slowed. In terms of the high-employment budget, therefore, fiscal policy appeared to be only slightly less restrictive in 1963 than it had been in 1960, the last year of the Eisenhower Administration. A sharp upswing of business activity at the same time weakened the Kennedy Administration's case for a tax cut. Not until President Johnson finally put the tax cut through in 1964 was the fiscal drag lifted.

The purpose of recounting the political difficulties the new economists encountered even in their most triumphant period of 1961 through 1964 is simply to remind us that the practical problems of carrying out an activist fiscal policy are immense. Furthermore, this account hardly scratches the surface; the fuller accounts by Heller, Okun, and Stein contain much more evidence of how difficult it is to get a government to change direction. Moreover, the Kennedy economists were pushing in what should have been a popular direction—toward prosperity with lower tax burdens, low interest rates, and no inflation. The political difficulties became far greater when the new economics called for higher taxes after 1965.

Two questions should be raised here. Did the new economists get the policies they wanted? Did the fiscal policies they did get perform as well as they expected?

In answer to the first question, they did not get as much expenditure growth as they would have liked. But the substitution of tax reduction was not a crucial weakness in their program to increase employment. As Paul Samuelson had said in the edition of his economics textbook that was current at the time:

. . . dollars of tax reduction are almost as powerful a weapon against mass unemployment as are increases in dollars of government expenditure. Such a program may involve a larger deficit than would an expenditure program. But it also means that there is no expansion of the government's sector of the economic system.[27]

In Arthur Okun's view, the "heavy reliance on tax reduction reflected neither an economic judgment on the relative efficacy of the two types of fiscal stimuli nor the administration's assessment of national priorities, but rather the political constraints of the day."[28] But Walter Heller saw in tax reduction the way to achieve expenditure increases as well.

The upsurge of tax revenues flowing from economic expansion [he said] would finance higher levels of local, state, and Federal spending than we would have had without the tax cut's stimulus—a stimulus that the country was unwilling to provide by deliberately enlarging the Federal budget.[29]

It is fair to say that the Kennedy-Johnson advisers got much of what they wanted in the first five years of their tenure. As Walter Heller said, "the Federal government deployed $48 billion of fiscal dividends (at annual rates) between the second half of 1960 and the second half of 1965." The dividends consisted of $16 billion in net tax reduction and $32 billion in expenditure increases, according to his calculations.[30] But did the "deployment of dividends" work?

On the whole, the performance of the economy in the early 1960s left little to be desired. Except for a brief pause in late 1962 and early 1963, output grew at more than 5 percent per year on average, which was far better than the performance of the 1950s. Unemployment declined from about 7 percent of the labor force in early 1961 to less than 5 percent in late 1964 and prices were stable.

Long-term interest rates on corporate and municipal securities were lower at the end of 1964 than they had been in the recession year 1960. At the time the decline of long rates was attributed to the skillful execution of "operation twist" by the Treasury and the Federal Reserve. As we will see later, however, the effectiveness of the "twist" was greatly exaggerated. Other explanations for the drop in long rates, such as a moderation in expectations of inflation, fit better.

Despite all the emphasis in Washington on fiscal policy during the period, I believe these years actually provided good demonstrations of the potency of monetary policy. One of these was the early period of recovery from the 1960–1961 recession. Business investment spending was slow to revive and there was a large surplus in the high-employment budget. Therefore, the two most important autonomous variables in the conventional income-expenditure theory gave little reason for predicting a vigorous rebound. Yet consumer spending and GNP were expanding rapidly by early 1961.

Fiscalists attribute the unusual strength of the expansion in the first half of the 1960s to the tax cuts and expenditure increases, although the main tax cut did not come until 1964. Monetarists, on the other hand, would attribute much of the early rise of consumer spending to the increase in money-supply growth that began in 1960. The monetary stimulus was clearly at work before tax rates were reduced.

The most interesting test occurred in 1962, when GNP growth slowed so much that a new outbreak of recession was feared by midyear. A stock market break in May severely jolted the aplomb of the new economists. Inasmuch as the budget was moving in the direction of expansion at the time, the 1962 business slowdown and the collapse of stock prices could hardly be attributed to a change in fiscal policy. The Council of Economic Advisers, in its 1963 Report, traced the slowdown to a shortfall of business investment of about $8 billion below the level that had been expected for the year 1962.

Five years of persisting slack in the economy had dampened businesses' willingness to invest, the Council said:

> With respect to both fixed investment and inventory investment, in short, the disappointing 1962 performance was a reflection of inadequate demand—not only of a current inadequacy but of one that had been accumulating for half a decade.
>
> . . . Business investment had taken on a character that was likely—in the absence of strong expansionary forces elsewhere in the economy —to cause the economy to stabilize at less-than-full employment levels more or less indefinitely.[31]

This was a textbook case of Keynesian "underemployment equilibrium" that would require a strong lift from government—a lift the President's 1963 tax program was designed to supply.

Nowhere in the Report does the Council suggest that the Federal Reserve might have been responsible for the economy's change of course. On the contrary, the Fed was praised for maintaining "adequate liquidity and favorable credit conditions." Interest rates generally declined. Nevertheless, the money supply had stopped growing at the end of 1961 and actually contracted during the third quarter of '62.

The Federal Reserve in its Report for the same period stressed the danger of an increase in the balance-of-payments deficit if short-term interest rates were allowed to fall too low. In any case, said the Board of Governors, "As shown in the record of the Federal Open Market Committee, open market policy remained stimulative throughout the year."[32] Although the Federal Open Market Committee noted the decline in money supply, committee members believed its effect should be counteracted by growth in public holdings of other liquid assets—the Radcliffe view again. After the stock market break in May, the Committee was concerned about "signs that economic expansion would not continue long."[33] Nevertheless, the Committee decided not to change policy, because of concern over the balance of payments. Not until the fourth quarter, after the Cuba missile crisis, did the money supply begin to grow again, and in the next quarter it shot upward at an extraordinarily high rate that persisted through the following year.

Monetarists would attribute the 1962 business slowdown to the sudden deceleration of money-supply growth in the first three quarters of 1962, when fiscal policy was believed by fiscalists to be expansive. After monetary expansion resumed in late 1962, the economy surged up again, although the budget had swung back to restraint again. Fiscalists have to call upon expectations of fiscal action to explain this recovery in the face of a large high-employment surplus.

Over most of the 1961–1964 period both fiscal and monetary policies were considered to be expansive. Therefore, it is difficult to say which should get the credit for the economic expansion of those years. But I repeat my belief that monetary policy played much more than a simple, accommodative role, with fiscal policy taking the lead. The expansion of money supply was the main source of stimulation. Although the interruption of 1962 also can be explained by monetary influences, the test did not last long enough to be conclusive. But more convincing tests were soon to come.

3

THE FAILURE OF FISCALISM

To the Congress of the United States:
I am pleased to report
—that the state of our economy is excellent;
—that the rising tide of our prosperity, drawing
new strength from the 1964 tax cut, is about to
enter its fifth consecutive year;
—that, with sound policy measures, we can look
forward to uninterrupted and vigorous expansion
in the year ahead.

President Lyndon B. Johnson, *Economic Report
of the President,* January 28, 1965[1]

As 1965 began, President Johnson was soon to find that price inflation would engage his Keynesian army in a war for which it was as ill-equipped by training and doctrine as his other army was for the jungle war in Vietnam. Advisers who had spent most of their adult lives thinking about how to keep the economy from sinking suddenly found themselves having to prescribe measures to hold it down. The ensuing swings in monetary and fiscal policies, as the Administration and the Federal Reserve grappled with unforeseen problems, proceeded almost like laboratory experiments.

A DECEPTIVE CALM: 1965

Looking back over the turbulent years since 1965 it is difficult to remember how calm most of 1965 was. In January, President Johnson launched his Great Society programs at home. In March, the first U.S. Marine combat units waded ashore near Danang,

South Vietnam. Federal expenditures, which had risen by about
6 percent per year from 1957 to 1965, were to rise at the annual
rate of nearly 15 percent for the next three years. But the problems to follow such a sharp change of direction in federal spending
policies were not even dimly perceived as the year began.

Early in the year there was widespread concern about the supposedly debilitating effects of fiscal drag. The 1964 tax cut had
briefly reduced the high-employment surplus, it is true; but personal incomes and corporate profits grew so rapidly that federal
tax revenues poured into the till faster than they could be spent
under President Johnson's lean first budget. It was feared that the
economy might go into a "high level stall" unless there was a
"fiscal dividend," another tax cut, or an increase in expenditures.

The Council of Economic Advisers explained the fiscal plan
for 1965 in the January, 1966, Annual Report:

> As 1965 opened, the remaining lift from the Revenue Act of 1964
> was not sufficient to assure a sustained reduction in unemployment.
> Consequently, a good opportunity was presented for a long-awaited re-
> duction in excise taxes and a liberalization of Social Security benefits.
> . . . These actions were proposed in the fiscal 1966 budget presented in
> January 1965. In combination with expected modest increases in other
> expenditures, they more than offset the normal growth of Federal
> revenues, and thus provided a net fiscal stimulus for calendar 1965.
> The stimulus was planned for the second half of the year.[2]

Money-supply growth, too, had slowed temporarily from the
unusually high rate reached in the second half of 1964. A nervous
stock market broke downward briefly following a June 1 speech
of Chairman Martin of the Federal Reserve Board in which he
cited disquieting similarities between 1965 and the late 1920s.[3]
His suggestion that a more restrictive monetary policy might be
needed to help correct the U.S. balance-of-payments deficit was
expected to meet stiff resistance in many official quarters.

After several years of price stability, the danger of price inflation seemed remote. Sophisticated investors in those halcyon
days were willing to buy high-grade corporate bonds yielding only
4½ percent. President Johnson had said in his *Economic Report*
in January:

Long-term interest rates, in particular, will continue to be held down by the vast flow of savings into private financial institutions. Long-term borrowers now reasonably plan on the essential stability of long-term interest rates in 1965.[4]

The Council of Economic Advisers believed in January that prospects for extending the recent record of price stability in 1965 were good. "The size of the existing gap [between actual and potential GNP] and the prospects for GNP suggest that widespread pressures on the supply capabilities of the economy are not likely to emerge this year," their Annual Report had said.[5] Moreover, President Johnson had pointed out that "reasonable price and wage guideposts are again spelled out" in the Report of the Council; and he said he counted *"on the sense of public responsibility of our labor leaders and our industrial leaders to do their full part to protect and extend our price stability* [italics in original]."[6]

Early 1965 probably was the high point in confidence that the wage-price guideposts could be an effective instrument for restraining inflation. The general pattern of wage and price decisions had closely approximated the Administration's guideposts ever since they were enunciated in 1962, and the Council believed the guideposts may have had a useful influence.[7]

After President Johnson announced a commitment of all-out support to the government of South Vietnam in July, it slowly became evident that the fiscal drag had been replaced by a fiscal catapult. As so often happens, however, fiscal actions were leading reported fiscal figures by a wide margin. Military orders had impacts in many industries months before they appeared in actual government outlays. Even so, the high-employment budget swung from the surplus that had worried some fiscalists early in the year to the first deficit since 1954. Fiscal policy, therefore, was viewed as becoming more expansive and was so at least partly by design. Moreover, businessmen had finally decided that prosperity was here to stay and were accelerating their spending for plant and equipment, much of it to increase military production. Once again, therefore, the two most important autonomous variables in the income-expenditure theory were indicating that rapid growth of income was ahead. After July, talk of a U.S. recession possibly to

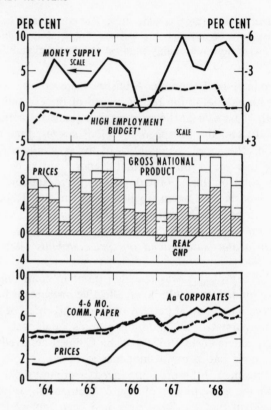

Chart 3-1. A sharp cutback in money-supply growth offset fiscal ease in 1966 to bring on the 1967 minirecession. Easy money in '65, '67, and '68 failed to keep interest rates from rising but more than doubled the inflation rate.

NOTES: See Chart 2-1.

begin in the winter moderated, as the economy continued to display strong forward momentum.

What did money supply do? It spurted upward after midyear, as can clearly be seen on Chart 3-1. One of the seeming mysteries of 1965 is why the Federal Reserve permitted the growth of money supply and bank credit to accelerate after the Vietnam buildup got under way and unmistakable symptoms of inflation began to appear. This acceleration, furthermore, followed four years of unusually rapid monetary expansion, so that a curb on money-supply growth might have been expected.

The principal reason for the 1965 burst of money-supply growth was that the monetary authorities tried to resist a rise of interest rates through buying government securities. These purchases added to the cash reserves of the banks and thus enabled them to expand bank credit and deposits—the main component of the money supply. Chairman Martin later testified:

. . . But generally speaking we were up against this fetish that the Federal Reserve ought to be able to control interest rates regardless of what the forces in the economy were and that any increase in interest rates would be a disaster. Even though those of us who have worked in this field know that the thing that really makes high interest rates is inflation getting out of control, we nevertheless delayed, the banks delayed, and the Board delayed, and it was not until December of 1965 that the Board finally acted.[8]

Even after the December, 1965, discount-rate increase, the System continued to try to moderate upward pressures on interest rates until February, 1966, when the first steps were taken to restrict the banks' lending power through reducing their reserves.

Looking back on it later, Walter Heller said the need for a change of direction in economic policy—from expansion to restriction—was quickly recognized in late 1965 once the costs of the Vietnam War became apparent. Nevertheless, it was the Federal Reserve that made the first move.

Close and friendly cooperation between monetary and fiscal authorities was the order of the day in the 1961–1965 expansion. But in December 1965, as overexpansion increasingly threatened, the Federal Reserve Board slipped out of the harness of monetary-fiscal coordination to raise the rediscount rate and touch off a wave of interest-rate increases. The Administration, although wincing at the timing and the "go-it-alone" nature of the action, did not seriously contest its substance.[9]

The "go-it-alone" Federal Reserve was soon to demonstrate that it could decisively overpower the expansive effects of a war, a soaring federal budget deficit, and a business capital-spending boom.

THE 1966 CRUNCH

Setting a Navy jet down on the deck of a carrier in one piece is not a landing but a controlled crash. The same thing could be said about the way the U.S. economy responded in 1966–1967 to monetary restraint. There was no recession, or at least not enough of one to win certification by the National Bureau of Economic Research. But the slowing in economic expansion and in the rate of rise of prices shown on the chart was almost unbelievably prompt. Many businessmen, as their 1967 profits told them, realized they had just survived something out of the ordinary. Some wished they had been warned early enough to have avoided the glut of unsold goods that piled up in their warehouses in early 1967.

In the 1966 fall forecasting season some monetary economists had argued that if the money supply continued to contract there would be a recession in 1967. Other forecasters, impressed with the Vietnam escalation and the growth of business investment spending, expected 1967 to be a year of strong expansion. Thus the scene was set for a showdown between the monetarists and the fiscalists. However, the Federal Reserve halted the experiment before the end of the year in perhaps its sharpest policy reversal on record. The ability of the economy to take off again so quickly after mid-1967 says more for the basic strength and resilience of the machine than it does for the skill of the pilots.

The 1966 experiment, although incomplete, clearly demonstrated the power of a restrictive monetary policy to offset an expansive fiscal policy. There was no general tax increase in 1966, although the President's economic advisers had told him at the end of 1965 that one would be desirable. There were some cuts in domestic expenditure programs; some excise tax cuts were rescinded; graduated withholding on individual income taxes was instituted; and the collection of corporate income taxes was accelerated. But these were no match for the escalating war costs and the early payments on the President's Great Society programs. As Arthur Okun said, "The economists in the administration watched with pain and frustration as fiscal policy veered off course."[10] The

Administration economists cannot be fairly criticized for failing to win the President to their policies. But their interpretation of what followed can be faulted.

According to Keynesian theory, the sharp swing of the budget into deficit should have had strongly expansive effects on the economy. Monetary policy, on the other hand, became extremely restrictive. Even though federal orders and expenditures grew far more than had been expected in 1965–1967, monetary restraint was so effective in slowing economic activity that the Federal Reserve spent much of 1967 trying to restore the lost momentum.

What remains to be explained is how monetary policy brought about the slowdown. The explanation most widely accepted by Administration economists, and most others by the way, was that Federal Reserve restrictions on credit growth first killed home building and then, with the aid of the suspension of the investment tax credit, eventually had some dampening influence on business fixed investment spending as well.

All in all, it seems reasonable—perhaps even conservative [according to the Council of Economic Advisers]—to estimate that credit-financed expenditures may have been held down directly by as much as $8 billion at year end as a result of tight money, compared with what would have happened had monetary policies continued supportive, as during 1964 and most of 1965. This direct impact of $8 billion GNP is roughly as great as the estimated direct impact from a 10 percent surcharge on personal and corporate tax liabilities.[11]

But this view fails to account for some important developments by stressing credit effects and overlooking money-supply effects of Federal Reserve policies.

There is no doubt that the Administration and the Federal Reserve tried to concentrate pressure on business-capital spending, while making futile efforts to shield home building through use of interest-rate ceilings to restrain competition between commercial banks and savings and loan associations for funds. Guided by an income-expenditure theory explanation of what was happening, the authorities tried to curb capital spending, one of the two main forces they thought were driving the economy while they were powerless to influence the other—the federal budget.

"Unsustainable" growth in spending for plant and equipment and for inventories was identified as a prime source of inflationary pressures. Business borrowing to finance this spending was officially regarded as the chief cause of high interest rates. The Administration asked business for voluntary restraint in capital programs and asked the Congress to suspend the investment tax credit. The Federal Reserve applied an array of selective measures designed to reduce bank lending to business and loosed a cascade of admonitory speeches and off-the-record interviews, capping the program on September 1 with an open letter to all the member banks of the System. Whatever the Board may have intended it to say, the September 1 letter was interpreted by many banks as a threat to restrict their privilege of borrowing from Reserve banks unless they slowed down their business lending. This cultural revolution spread confusion inside and outside the Federal Reserve System and brought the money markets to a state of near panic.

Most important of all, System open-market operations contracted bank reserves, leading to the contraction in money supply shown on the chart. Regulation Q ceilings on the interest paid on time deposits were held fixed in the face of rising market rates, thus causing a sharp contraction of time deposits. Money-center banks, whose negotiable certificates of deposit (CDs) could not be sold in the domestic market because of Regulation Q ceilings, borrowed funds from abroad, from the Eurodollar market, through correspondent banks or their own branches. The language of Shakespeare and Milton was enriched by a new word, "disintermediation," as people withdrew savings from commercial banks, mutual savings banks, and savings and loan associations—the so-called intermediaries in the saving and investing process—to buy government and corporate securities offering much higher yields.

LESSONS OF ADVERSITY

The experiment of 1966 was considered by some to have demonstrated the ineffectiveness of monetary policy, for the most restrictive policy that anyone would want to see produced only small and long-delayed effects on business investment, with disastrous side effects on the level of new housing starts. This was the verdict of early post-mortems reported by the Department of Commerce and Sherman Maisel, a member of the Board of Governors of the Federal Reserve System.[12]

The Council of Economic Advisers, which had earlier viewed monetary policy as playing a minor supportive role while fiscal policies took the lead, shifted in 1967 to a view of it as a powerful, but dangerous, instrument.

> The credit squeeze of 1966 had an impressive and beneficial restraining effect on overall demand. Its side effects were equally impressive but far less beneficial. . . . The cause of equity was not served by the arbitrary redistribution of income produced by very high interest rates or by the adversity experienced in the homebuilding industry . . . the liquidity of portfolios was impaired by rapidly rising interest rates.
>
> Last August, monetary policy was probably as tight as it could get without risking financial disorder. Any further increase in overall demand could not have been effectively countered by general monetary policy.[13]

I agree that 1966 certainly did demonstrate that monetary policy is a poor instrument for producing prompt and finely metered changes in business investment—if that is what the policy is supposed to do. However, recent attempts to measure monetary-policy effects on investment probably underestimate even the direct impacts because they neglect cash-balance effects. An even greater source of bias is the common neglect of monetary influences on consumption spending, which are then transmitted to business investment through increases or decreases in business sales.

This brings us back to the choice between the alternative fiscalist and monetarist frameworks for interpreting the policy results. A monetarist would argue that the 1966 program of restrictive measures was directed at too narrow a target, or, rather, the wrong target. Success, or lack of it, in curtailing business investment over the short run is not a relevant test of the effectiveness of monetary policy. Indeed, if the monetary authorities gauge operations by their effects on investment, they may badly underestimate the overall restrictiveness of their policy, as they did in 1966 and were to do again in 1969.

While the Federal Reserve was concentrating attention on business loans of banks, it inadvertently produced a sharp slowdown in growth of total bank credit and money supply. There are numerous indications in the policy record of the Federal Open Market Committee that the extent of the contraction of bank credit and money during the late summer and fall of 1966 surprised the Federal Reserve.[14] The contraction finally became one of the reasons for reversing the policy in November. The reversal came none too soon, for comparable decelerations in monetary expansion in the past had caused recessions.

Whether intended or not, the slowing of money-supply growth depressed growth of consumer spending, especially for automobiles and other durable goods. The change in consumer spending then laid the groundwork for inventory adjustments and the slowdown in plant and equipment spending that carried over into the minirecession of 1967, long after monetary policy had again turned around.

That is the monetarists' explanation. Others may find this difficult to accept. Commenting on studies of the impact of 1966 monetary policy on business investment spending, Arthur Okun has said:

Nor has anyone found dramatic effects on outlays for consumer durables as a result of the reduced availability and higher cost of installment credit. Tight money may, however, have contributed to the marked weakening of consumer spending in relation to income that developed late in 1966. This shift in behavior remains a puzzle. It may have reflected, at least in part, the reduced value of household assets, as both common stocks and bonds dropped sharply in price during the monetary squeeze.[15]

Conveniently for the monetarists' argument, the monetary policy changes in 1966 were so pronounced that their effects were more easily discernible than usual, particularly in the household sector. Peter Crawford, of First National City Bank, reported striking evidence of money-supply effects on consumer behavior in an article for the January-February 1967 issue of *Financial Analysts Journal*. He found that total liquid assets of households rose only a little more than half as fast in the first half of 1966 as they had in the second half of the previous year.

The substantial reductions in the rates of growth of liquidity and wealth in 1966 [he concluded] seem to go a long way toward explaining the softening of individuals' demands for durable real assets in 1966 and to suggest that these demands could remain weak in 1967.[16]

The disagreement about the impact of monetary policy in 1966 stems from a basic difference in the two bodies of theory discussed in the first chapter. The Keynesian income-expenditure model assumes that business investment spending and government spending are the prime movers of the economy and that consumption spending follows tamely along after the other two. Monetary policy is thus assumed to work through the influence of interest rates on the volume of investment. What puzzled Okun was the slump in consumer spending while government and investment expenditures were rising.

The monetarist model, on the other hand, assumes that changes in money supply have a direct impact on consumer spending, as well as on investment, because consumer goods are included among the assets that consumers can buy, or refrain from buying, when they want to adjust their cash holdings. In the Keynesian model, they would adjust cash holdings only through buying or selling bonds and other securities, thereby pushing interest rates up or down.

A powerful advantage of monetarism, therefore, is that it does not concentrate on a single segment of the total stream of expenditures. Moreover, the effects of money-supply changes can be expected to be more pervasive than changes in the cost of credit, or in the volume of autonomous expenditures, both of which directly affect a relatively small part of the public. Money, after all, is held by everyone in the economy.

This stress on the effects of money-supply changes on consumption certainly does not mean that monetary policy has no direct influence on business investment, for corporations as well as households respond to changes in their cash balances. Anyone who knows corporate treasurers very well would expect their cash positions to have some influence on investment decisions. However it was achieved, there was a remarkable change in business spending for plant and equipment. After running ahead of rates anticipated in the SEC-Commerce Department Surveys since early

1964, spending fell below anticipations in the third and fourth quarters of 1966 and declined in 1967.

FOOTNOTE ON CONTROL OF INTEREST RATES

Partly because of the dominance of the income-expenditure theory and partly because of even older ideas about central banking, it has long been taken for granted that the control of interest rates is one of a central bank's main tools. Therefore, it was natural for the Council of Economic Advisers and other outside observers to concentrate on what they believed were the interest-rate effects of Federal Reserve policies both when they were expansive, or "supportive," and when they were restrictive.

This idea that interest rates are a policy tool is now being questioned, for central-bank efforts to influence interest rates lead to money-supply changes that cannot safely be ignored. What happened in the 1960s demonstrates that money-supply changes resulting from efforts to influence interest rates, in fact, produce effects within a few months in the opposite direction from the one intended. "Easy" money then brings high interest rates and "tight" money brings low rates, just the reverse of the orthodox view. We will have more to say about the evidence for this proposition later on.

Although the Federal Reserve was castigated for producing high interest rates in the United States and in the Eurodollar market with its restrictive policies during 1966, it can be argued that the highly expansive policies of the previous year had much to do with the high rates of 1966. The 1965 policies certainly stimulated a rise of income that could be expected to increase demands for credit and thus to raise rates. They also aroused expectations of inflation, which would tend to raise rates, as Chairman Martin testified in the passage quoted earlier.

The abrupt slowing of credit expansion in the spring of 1966 raised rates further but only for a short time. Some interest rates had passed their peaks and were on the way down again more than two months before there was any indication in the policy record that the Open Market Committee wanted to ease.[17] This fall in rates is a good example of the tendency of a restrictive monetary policy to reduce interest rates.

In 1967 there was in some ways a repetition of the 1965 experience except that when interest rates again began to push upward Federal Reserve efforts to moderate the rise caused the money supply to grow even faster than it had in 1965. In actions reminiscent of Mark Twain's story of the Pope who issued his bull against the comet, both the President in his 1967 State of the Union message and Congress by statute had asserted a power to bring interest rates down by exhortation. In the contest of declamation, however, the papal bull wins handily, for it rests its claims on a jurisdiction over miracle and mystery that is foreclosed to the government of the United States by the First Amendment to the Constitution.

There had been a movement toward international disarmament in interest rates at the same time. Meeting at Chequers in England on January 21, the finance ministers of France, Germany, Italy, the United Kingdom, and the United States agreed that

They would all make it their objective, within the limits of their respective responsibilities, to cooperate in such a way as to enable interest rates in their respective countries to be lower than they otherwise would be.[18]

Unfortunately, exhortation was not enough.

The attempt to hold interest rates down, or to retard their rise, was made enormously more difficult in the United States by a massive federal budget deficit. Corporations and others who expected the government to be a big borrower rushed to the well, fearing it might go dry. The expansiveness of the 1967 fiscal and monetary policies, moreover, led people in the money and capital markets to expect strong economic activity, higher prices, higher interest rates, and a renewed tightening of monetary policy in the future. All these forces combined to put interest rates clearly beyond the control of the Federal Reserve unless the System was willing to risk an intolerable degree of price inflation.

The first member of the Federal Open Market Committee to go on record as opposing the policy of resisting the rise of interest rates was Darryl Francis, President of the Federal Reserve Bank of St. Louis, the most outspoken advocate of monetarism on the

Committee. The policy record of the meeting of May 23 reports that in dissenting from the policy action

Mr. Francis expressed the view that monetary policy had been highly stimulative thus far in 1967, that fiscal policy was providing an increasing stimulus, and that the economy was responding relatively quickly. On the grounds that a marked increase in demands for goods and services was likely later in the year and that monetary policy actions had their main effects after some time lag, he thought some firming in the money market should be sought now to guard against the development later of excessive demands and associated inflationary pressures.[19]

He proved to be far and away the best prophet on the Committee.

The natural resilience of the U.S. economy, rising government expenditures, and a highly expansive monetary policy caused a strong resurgence from the minirecession of the first half of 1967. However, growth of money supply in the third quarter ran at more than three times its average rate for the years 1957 through 1966. Such a rapid increase in money supply could be expected to induce some increase in real output for a time, but it was also certain to cause price inflation in 1968. It did.

ONCE MORE WITH FEELING: 1968

After their shaky performance in 1965–1967, the U.S. economic policy makers got down to work in dead earnest in 1968. The mistakes of the first attempt had been understandable, if not entirely pardonable, because it had been a long time since curbing inflation had been included in the program and everyone was out of practice. Furthermore, like a brass section playing Berlioz while the rest of the orchestra struggled with Mozart, fiscal policy had been wildly distracting. This time the performance should go more smoothly; at least the authorities and an anxious public hoped so.

The year 1968 got off to a good start. The Federal Open Market Committee had decided to seek firmer conditions in the money markets at its final 1967 meeting. The discount rate had been increased in November after the devaluation of the British pound. Money-supply growth slowed to less than half its mid-1967 rate.

The Congress was considering the President's request for the 10 percent income-tax surcharge that he had asked for in July of the preceding year. However, Wilbur Mills, Chairman of the House Ways and Means Committee, had been understandably reluctant to accept all he was told by economists at hearings the preceding September. He was unwilling to raise taxes at that time on the strength of their forecast of an acceleration in economic activity. Their insistence on the need for suspending the investment tax credit in 1966, he reminded them, had been followed by urgent requests to restore it before a year was out. The Federal Reserve, he noted, painted the need for a tax increase in somber colors, but had, nevertheless, flooded the country with money in 1967. As a matter of fact, however, he and his Committee were negotiating with the Administration in early 1968 to provide more budgetary restraint than had been asked for by coupling expenditure reductions with the tax increase.

The debate over the tax and expenditure proposals featured a parade of financial leaders and economists who predicted disaster in the money and capital markets unless taxes were increased. Underlying their predictions was a belief that there was a simple trade-off between monetary policy and fiscal policy. According to the trade-off, or "fiscal-monetary-mix" view, increasing fiscal restraint would permit an easing of monetary restraint and lower interest rates, something devoutly desired by everyone. Having been brought to the brink of panic by a militant Federal Reserve in 1966, the financial leaders did not want the Federal Reserve to be so provoked again.

The Federal Open Market Committee had long believed that monetary policy was being asked to do too much and fiscal policy was not doing enough. There were many plaintive comments regarding the slow progress of tax legislation during 1966, 1967, and 1968 in its Record of Policy Actions.

As the Revenue and Expenditure Control Act of 1968 neared enactment, staff estimates for the third quarter presented at the Committee's June 18 meeting "suggested that growth in real GNP would slow sharply if the pending fiscal legislation were enacted."[20] A decline of interest rates since the preceding meeting of the Committee was attributed to growing expectations that fiscal restraint legislation would be enacted soon, and additional declines were expected if the legislation passed. The Committee agreed that, if Congress acted affirmatively, System open-market operations "should seek to accommodate any resulting declines in short-term interest rates and to cushion any upward pressures on such rates that might emerge subsequently."[21]

Alfred Hayes, President of the Federal Reserve Bank of New York, said later:

> This euphemism seemed to place the Federal Reserve in a somewhat more passive and less aggressive role than if we had made an affirmative decision to ease because of fears that continued restraint plus the fiscal package would constitute too restrictive a program for the economic circumstances. But, semantics aside, the consequences were much the same as a decisive move toward ease. Money and credit grew in the last half of 1968 at a disturbingly fast pace.[22]

Some economists who emphasized the importance of money supply cautioned against an easing of monetary policy. In June, 1968, for example, the *Monthly Economic Letter* of First National City Bank pointed out that

> A tax increase and expenditure cuts should reduce the deficit and consequently reduce Treasury borrowing. But this would not permit the Federal Reserve to ease its policy suddenly and to bring about substantially lower interest rates.[23]

And in July, immediately after the bill was enacted, the *Letter* said:

> . . . if the rapid expansion in narrowly defined money supply is sustained through the summer months, it could well result in continuing strong expansion in the economy, growing credit demands, and higher interest rates in 1969.[24]

As the long summer wore on, Federal Reserve operations were "directed at accommodating the tendencies for short-term interest rates to decline," even though committee members were concerned about the rapid rates of increase in bank credit that were experienced in July and projected for August (at the August 13 meeting).[25] Interest rates, moreover, proved to be less inclined to fall than had been expected. As a matter of fact, they showed a disturbing tendency to rise in spite of the growth in bank credit and money supply. Consequently, several committee members "noted that a cut in the discount rate might have the effect of moderating further upward pressures on short-term rates without requiring reserve injections of the size that might otherwise be needed for that purpose."[26] This was clear recognition of the link between operations to influence interest rates and the growth in the supply of money.

On August 15, discount rates were reduced from 5½ percent to 5¼ percent in what the Board called a technical adjustment to bring them into alignment with market rates. At the August 19 meeting of the Open Market Committee, as at the preceding meeting, the desirability of cushioning upward pressures on short-term rates was noted. By the time of the October 8 meeting, however, the staff had revised upward its estimates of GNP for the third quarter, mainly because consumer spending had proved stronger than expected.[27] Committee members began to fall away from the policy of holding interest rates down. Some of them believed that rates of bank-credit growth were excessive in the light of persisting inflationary pressures and the unexpected strength in the economy. Three members voted in dissent on October 8, one on October 29, and four on November 26.

At their final meeting of the year, December 17, the Committee faced up to the fact that "The current rate of expansion in overall economic activity was significantly higher than had been projected earlier."[28] The boards of directors of nine of the twelve Reserve banks had acted, subject to Board approval, to raise discount rates. The Board planned after the meeting to act on discount rates and also to consider an increase in member-bank reserve requirements. Accordingly:

> The Committee was unanimously of the view that greater monetary restraint was required at this time in light of the unexpected strength of current economic activity, the persistence of inflationary pressures and expectations, and the recent rapid rate of growth in bank credit.[29]

The Manager of the Open Market Account was instructed to operate "with a view to attaining firmer conditions in money and short-term credit markets."[30] Thus ended one of the most embarrassing episodes in recent Federal Reserve history.

REPLAY OF A FUMBLE

The economic policy debacle of 1968 should lay to rest for all time the easy generalizations about trade-offs, or fiscal-monetary policy mixes, that had misled policy makers and confused people who toil in the money and capital markets. And it tested the predictive abilities of the two main theoretical frameworks we have been considering—the income-expenditure theory and the quantity theory. Unfortunately, we can do little more than skim this bouillabaisse here; but several main issues stand out.

First is the use of economic forecasting. Economic policy activists—or perhaps adventurists is a better word—outside the Federal Reserve System have chided the System for not improving its timing through more explicit use of forecasts. However, on this occasion in which forecasts unquestionably influenced policy, the forecasts were far wide of the mark.

Although the Board's own large econometric model, about which more later, was not yet on stream for forecasting, others were consulted. Two of the best known whose predictions were widely publicized—the Wharton School Model at the University of Pennsylvania and the Michigan Model at the University of Michigan—undershot the actual cumulative change in GNP for the year ending in June, 1969, by 42 percent and 50 percent, respectively.[31]

The System would have been better advised simply to have assumed that the Revenue and Expenditure Control Act would have no influence on total spending in the first year after its enactment. But it would have required steely determination to ignore the cries of "fiscal overkill" that were heard from every side, including the Council of Economic Advisers. As a matter of fact, the growth of GNP did begin to slow at once but certainly not by enough to justify the panic that gripped Washington. The rate of price inflation leaped upward.

As we will see later, the basic source of the forecasting error was the reliance on a naïve elementary textbook version of the

income-expenditure theory that placed excessive weight on fiscal influences and virtually ignored the effects of earlier money-supply
growth on consumption expenditures in the second half of 1968.
Despite their complexity and the vast amounts of work that went
into them, the econometric models could be no better than the
income-expenditure theory on which they were based. Poor theory,
poor forecast.

The fact that fiscal action came later, and was larger, than they
had expected also frightened many forecasters, probably leading
them to make pessimistic assumptions about other so-called autonomous variables in their models.

The most puzzling development to many forecasters was a jump
in consumption expenditures in the third quarter, immediately after
the surcharge was applied.

On my own work sheets as of mid-1968 [said Arthur Okun], the
surcharge, which began to affect pay checks through withholding on
July 15, was expected to reduce the increment of consumption in the
third quarter by $2 billion. [The gain actually increased from $9.7
billion in the second quarter to $14.6 billion in the third.] We do not
know and cannot tell whether or not the surcharge had such an effect,
compared with the increase that would have otherwise occurred. We
do know that the main reason consumption exceeded the forecasts was
not that we were wrong about the impact of the surcharge but that we
were wrong about the emerging strength of consumer demand, quite
apart from the surcharge.[32]

It seems to me that the answer to the puzzle is the same as it was
in 1966, money. The deceleration of money-supply growth caused
a slowdown in consumer spending that puzzled fiscalists in 1966.
The high rates of money-supply growth in 1967 and 1968 caused
an increase in consumer spending that the surcharge could not offset in 1968.

A second major issue is the degree of the central bank's influence
on interest rates. Much of the discussion that preceded enactment
of the Revenue and Expenditure Control Act assumed that, if the
bill were enacted, the Federal Reserve would keep interest rates at
lower levels. The bill was enacted and the Federal Reserve did what
it could; but interest rates, after dipping briefly, rose higher than
ever.

The most interesting issue is the relative potency of fiscal and monetary policy. In the 1966 test, the fiscal controls were set for expansion while monetary policy was restrictive. Monetary policy won. In 1968 fiscal policy made a massive shift toward what was conventionally considered to be restraint. Monetary policy became expansive. Again, monetary influences decisively overpowered fiscal influences.

The possibility that monetary policy might overpower fiscal policy is not peculiar to the United States. Britain has had a remarkably similar experience. The money supply of Britain grew very rapidly in 1967 and 1968. At the same time, the Chancellor introduced tight budgets, with increases in indirect taxes and cuts in government spending. In November, 1967, and April, 1968, the corporation tax, purchase tax, Selective Employment Tax, and many other duties were increased. Nevertheless, there was a consumer spending boom from the autumn of 1967 on.

The economy experienced a mixture of expansionary monetary policy and tight budgetary constraints [said A. A. Walters]; superficially it is clear that the monetary stimulant was more powerful than the budgetary depressant. The consumer boom certainly caught the authorities by surprise—but such behavior is entirely consistent with a monetary interpretation of these events.[33]

Why did U.S. economists who had confidently preached the virtues of fiscal policy succumb to fears of overkill when the government did what they had so earnestly recommended? That is too big a question to answer here, but part of the answer lies in the old article of faith that fiscal policy is more powerful and influences the economy more quickly than does monetary policy.

After two years of work with its large econometric model, the Board of Governors of the Federal Reserve System reported in its 1968 Annual Report:

The current version of the model, like the preliminary version completed last year, suggests that both monetary and fiscal policies have powerful effects on the economy, though the time lag between a change in policies and the economic effect of the change is longer for monetary policy than for fiscal policy.[34]

Leonall Andersen and Jerry Jordan, of the Federal Reserve Bank of St. Louis, came to very different conclusions with a much simpler model in the same year.[35] Their results indicate that tax changes have a negligible or unpredictable influence on income; expenditure changes have a small, prompt, but temporary, influence; and money-supply changes have a powerful influence that works more quickly than many monetary economists had believed. The experience of 1968 was much kinder to the findings of Andersen-Jordan and Friedman-Meiselman than to those of the Board of Governors' econometric model.

What happened in 1968 will no doubt be exhaustively analyzed for years to come. But consumers and businessmen, not to mention the Congress, saw what they had been told was a restrictive fiscal policy washed away on a wave of money. This left the Federal Reserve with a staggering problem in reestablishing its credibility when it renewed the fight against inflation in 1969.

In its 1968 operations, moreover, the Federal Reserve had risked offending the Joint Economic Committee of the U.S. Congress. For in reviewing the monetary explosion of 1967 in March, 1968, the Committee had said:

> All of this brings us to a reiteration of the recommendation in last year's report that in increasing the money supply monetary policy should move in the direction of a moderate and steady jog instead of in alternate sprints and rests. Sudden changes in the money supply have clearly given rise to instabilities in the economy. . . .
>
> We are thus convinced that a steady rise in the money supply more or less consistent with the projected rate of economic growth—generally within a range of 3 to 5 per cent per year—would be a healthy longrun ideal. But the very essence of such a policy is to avoid large and sudden changes or reversals. The present situation is no exception.[36]

The Committee had thought enough of these recommendations to set them in bold type in its *Report* so they would not be missed.

It was not only the Federal Reserve's credibility that was tarnished by the upsurge of inflation in 1967 and 1968. The luster of wage-price guideposts was dimmed almost to the vanishing point, as well. Although in January, 1969, the outgoing Johnson Council of Economic Advisers intoned once again its ritual incantation of faith in the guideposts, the chant lacked the old-time resonance and fervor.

Between 1961 and 1965, according to the Council's swan song, decision makers with discretionary power generally conformed to the guideposts, which had recommended that the rate of increase in wage rates (including fringe benefits) not exceed the trend rate of over-all productivity growth—estimated at 3.2 percent for most of these years. In its 1967 and 1968 Reports the Council continued to urge maximum possible restraint in wage and price decisions but did not suggest adherence to the productivity-growth standard Wages and prices had risen faster than the standard in 1966 and went up even faster in 1967 and 1968.

The blemished price-wage record of the past three years reflects primarily an excessive growth of demand. . . . Once consumer prices started to move up sharply, increases in compensation no larger than the productivity trend would not have led to any improvement in real income. Workers could not be expected to accept such a result, particularly in view of the previous rapid and consistent rise in corporate profits.[37]

In wages and prices, as with interest rates, exhortation was not an effective substitute for control of the money supply. Correcting this oversight, therefore, was the first order of business for the incoming Nixon advisers.

4

COSTLY REPAIRS: 1969–1971

In 1970, we are feeling the postponed pinch
of the late Sixties. If responsible policies had
been followed then, the problems of 1970 would
be much easier. But we cannot undo the errors
of the past. We have no choice but to correct
them, and to avoid repeating them.
   President Richard M. Nixon, *Economic Report
   of the President,* February 2, 1970[1]

The Nixon Administration had a program for gradually slowing
the inflation with, it hoped, minimum cost in unemployment. But,
as is often the case in the United States, important parts of that
program had to be entrusted to powerful groups whose cooperation
would have to be won through persuasion, not compulsion. One of
these was the Congress, in which the opposition party had a majority and thus had the advantage of controlling the committees
that can make or break a President's budget. The other was the
Federal Reserve System. There was no question that the Congress
and the Federal Reserve wanted to moderate the inflation, but there
was little agreement about the means to that end.

FISCALISTS BY ANY OTHER NAME

Considering where President Nixon received his education in economics, it was entirely natural for him to reach back to the Eisenhower Administration of the fifties for key economic advisers:
Arthur F. Burns, first for the White House and later for the Board
of Governors of the Federal Reserve; Paul W. McCracken, Chair-

man of the Council of Economic Advisers; Henry Wallich, Special Consultant to the Secretary of the Treasury; and Charls Walker, Under Secretary of the Treasury.

In addition to these Eisenhower advisers, he appointed to the Council of Economic Advisers Herbert Stein, a distinguished authority on fiscal policy, and Hendrik Houthakker, a Harvard professor with impeccable credentials in theoretical and quantitative economics who had served on the staff of President Johnson's Council of Economic Advisers. To be Secretary of Labor and later to head the new White House Office of Management and Budget, the President selected George Shultz, an authority on labor markets and Dean of the Business School at the University of Chicago. Paul Volcker, who had served in the Treasury during the Kennedy Administration, filled the sensitive post of Under Secretary of the Treasury for Monetary Affairs.

Except for Phillip Cagan of Columbia University and Leonall Andersen of the Federal Reserve Bank of St. Louis, who served briefly as monetary advisers on the staff of the Council of Economic Advisers, known monetarists were conspicuously absent from the upper ranks of the Nixon Administration, although a few young ones may have infiltrated lower levels of the bureaucracy. Milton Friedman—like Paul Samuelson, his fiscalist counterpart before him—stayed out of the government but was reputed to be an unofficial adviser.

Although the leaders of the monetarist counterrevolution did not come victoriously to Washington to practice what they had been teaching, some of their ideas were brought in by President Nixon's advisers. During their eight-year exile from Washington, the advisers who had served President Eisenhower read the economic policy lessons of the 1960s and also benefited from the explosion of monetary research that occurred during those years. Arthur Burns was President of the National Bureau of Economic Research while some of the best of the monetary research was performed there. Paul McCracken said of himself soon after becoming Chairman of the Council that he was not a Friedmanite but had become somewhat "Friedmanesque." When they came back to Washington they were wary of the wide swings in money-supply growth that their Democratic predecessors had considered unimportant, if not necessary. In their plans and statements they gave monetary policy, and the money supply in particular, far more weight than their predecessors had.

The Nixon turn in U.S. economic policies might be seen as a half-turn rather than an about-face, however. Money was elevated in importance but fiscal policy was not turned out. According to Herbert Stein, Republicans had been vigorous advocates of fiscal policy during the Hoover Administration and all through the Eisenhower Administration. But the advisers of the new Administration saw themselves as a very different breed of fiscalist than were the Kennedy-Johnson advisers whom they replaced. They did not believe in alternating deficits and surpluses in the high-employment budget, and other fiscal devices, to goad a sluggish economy or to guide the private sector. They wanted the budget to provide a stable framework for the economy rather than a heavy-footed driver. As President Nixon said in his first Economic Report to the Congress:

... *we must achieve a steadier and more evenhanded management of our economic policies.* Business and labor cannot plan, and consumers and home-buyers cannot effectively manage their affairs, when Government alternates between keeping first the accelerator and then the brake pedal to the floor [italics in original].[2]

President Nixon explained that the purpose of his Administration's economic policies was "to slow down the rapid expansion of demand firmly and persistently, but not to choke off demand so abruptly as to injure the economy."[3] To the Council this meant regulating growth of demand through a combination of fiscal and monetary policies so that a gap would open up between potential total real output and actual output. "Such a GNP gap," the Council said, "places a downward pressure on the rate of inflation. Businesses find themselves selling in markets less receptive to price increases. This forces greater resistance to cost increases, including wage increases."[4]

In another sharp break with the policies of the previous administration, the Nixon Administration announced that it would not use wage-price guideposts. The Council of Economic Advisers argued that the results of U.S. experience and numerous trials of such policies in other countries did not justify confidence that attempts to exert direct influence on wages and prices would help to curb inflation in 1969.

Noting the disagreement between fiscalists and monetarists on prescriptions for 1969, the CEA argued the need for covering both fronts.

The Government could not prudently let the control of inflation depend on the choice of one of these strategies to the neglect of the other. Many uncertainties exist about the relative power of fiscal and monetary actions taken separately. There is much less doubt about the power of fiscal and monetary actions taken together. A reliable policy had to turn away from both the rising deficits and the rapid monetary expansion.[5]

The fiscal-policy plan for 1969 called for keeping a budget surplus as large as the one that had been achieved by the Revenue and Expenditure Control Act of 1968, which was about $3 billion to $5 billion. A ceiling of $192.9 billion was to be held on fiscal 1970 expenditures. The expenditures were held within the ceiling during calendar 1969 despite increases in costs of certain "uncontrollable items," such as interest on the public debt, Medicare, and public assistance, and some Congressional actions that raised expenditures. Compensating cuts were made in other expenditures, particularly defense.

On the revenue side, the Administration asked the Congress to extend the 10 percent surcharge for an extra year and to defer some scheduled reductions in excise taxes. It also asked the Congress to repeal the 7 percent investment tax credit that had been enacted in 1962, suspended in 1966, and reenacted in 1967. Although the Congress took a long time in considering these proposals, it eventually did extend the surcharge (at a 10 percent rate during 1969 and a 2½ percent rate during 1971), postponed the excise tax cuts, and repealed the investment tax credit. Consequently, a budget surplus was maintained throughout calendar 1969.

Having put its game plan together, the Council stressed the need for time and patience; hence the label "gradualism."

It takes time for changes in policies to work through their effects on the economy [said Paul McCracken]. Economic processes do not operate in ways that produce instant results. This is a difficult matter for impatient people, and Americans have never been criticized for excessive patience.[6]

GRADUALISM IS NOT FOR THE FED

Unfortunately for the game plan, some of the most impatient Americans were in the Federal Reserve System at the time. As 1969 began, the System was just recovering from its embarrassing overreaction to the fears of "fiscal overkill" that seized Washington when the Revenue and Expenditure Control Act of 1968 was passed. The Johnson Administration economists who shared in that unseemly little panic had by early '69 withdrawn for rest and recuperation to privileged sanctuaries in friendly universities and foundations. But the Federal Reserve people were left to face the flak. Furthermore, some of them were troubled by the thought that if they had stuck to their guns a little longer in 1966 or had not been so concerned about recession and high interest rates in 1967 they could have beat back inflation before it became so well entrenched. The task looked to be more difficult in 1969.

William McChesney Martin decided to serve another year as head of the Board of Governors to lead one last battle. The Federal Reserve dug in like a batter who has just missed two easy pitches and intends to knock the next one out of the park.

The swing of the federal budget from large deficit to surplus in 1968 provided the monetary authorities with a priceless opportunity to conduct their policies in 1969 without the frustrating conflicts over accommodating large Treasury borrowings in the money markets that they believed marred their performance in 1967 and 1968. The Administration, furthermore, was determined to avoid a swing of the budget back to deficit which might draw monetary policy off course.

The Council of Economic Advisers said later that it was difficult to tell at the time what rate of growth in the money supply would achieve Chairman Martin's intention "to disinflate without deflating." But it certainly was necessary for the money supply to grow more slowly than the 7.1 percent increase of 1968.[7]

Spectators on the sidelines urged a policy of monetary gradualism to match the fiscal gradualism of the Administration. In January, the First National City Bank *Monthly Economic Letter* said, for example:

Just as the inflationary implications of money supply growth should not have been overlooked in 1967 and 1968, the restrictiveness of an abrupt reduction in monetary growth should not be underestimated in 1969. In the past, sharp reductions in the rate of growth of the money supply have been followed by economic recessions. It would appear prudent, therefore, to move to a less expansive monetary policy gradually.[8]

Milton Friedman recommended that money-supply growth be slowed down in small steps at intervals of several months to minimize the risk of recession.[9]

The monetary authorities, however, were not as much convinced that money matters as were the Council of Economic Advisers and the nagging monetarists. They were more concerned with availability of credit, or *credit* policy. When they embarked on their new campaign their tactics were much the same as those that had caused trouble in 1966.

The System tried to control the availability of credit to certain users, particularly businesses, and did not pay much attention to the money supply. This was a conventional central-bank approach and was much like the policies sometimes applied by European and other central banks. But we shall see that selective control over credit availability is an inefficient way to control inflation.

Where other central banks attempt to restrict bank loans to business by imposing quotas or ceilings on the amounts that banks can lend, the Federal Reserve relied on limiting the supplies of funds to those banks that specialize in lending to large businesses. Regulation Q—the ceiling on rates banks can pay for time deposits—became the "cutting edge" of policy as it had been in 1966. But in 1969 the distortions and repercussions in U.S. money markets and the Eurodollar market abroad were much more severe than they had been in 1966.

As in 1966, furthermore, money-supply growth fell to a much lower rate than monetarists considered safe. When the money supply appeared to be growing at less than a 2 percent annual rate in the first half, some monetary economists forecast a recession for 1970 to follow a business cycle peak sometime in the second half of 1969, unless money-supply growth picked up.

In late May, Milton Friedman sounded a warning in his *Newsweek* column against letting monetary policy become too restrictive.

It would be a major blunder for the Fed to step still harder on the monetary brakes. That would risk turning orderly restraint into a severe economic contraction. If anything, the Fed has already gone too far [italics in original].[10]

Soon thereafter, revised figures indicated that money-supply growth had actually been higher than the rate on which the monetarists' warnings were based, although it was sharply lower than the 1968 rate. From the middle of the second quarter, however, money-supply growth was held virtually to zero. By September, monetarists were convinced that there would be a substantial slowdown in business activity, a sharp fall in corporate profits, and a rise in unemployment in late 1969 and early 1970. Consumer spending had already responded to the slowing in monetary expansion.

In retrospect, it is surprising that more economists in 1969 did not forecast a recession for 1970. The historical record of the United States and other countries indicates that it is extremely difficult to slow an inflation without bringing on a recession. Therefore, the probability of at least a mild recession was high if there was to be a serious attempt to curb the inflation.

With the consumer price index rising at more than 5 percent per year, inflationary expectations were well rooted. However, it was difficult for many economists to conceive of a recession taking place when business spending for new plant and equipment was booming along.

The 1969 policies of the Federal Reserve did not appreciably affect business investment spending right away and so fostered an illusion, particularly among businessmen, that monetary policy was ineffective. Their 1966–1967 experience had convinced many of them that the monetary restraint would not persist long enough to make it worth their while to cut back. Despite sharp increases of interest rates and other costs of capital programs, corporations kept on borrowing and building at a frenetic rate. Surveys of their intentions indicated continuing strength in business investment spending into 1970.

In explaining why businessmen "broke the economists' rules" and continued to spend in the face of excess capacity and deteriorating profitability in 1967–1969, one advocate of corporate planning attributed their lemming-like persistence to planning. According to Dean S. Ammer of Northeastern University:

> When a business is run according to plan, there is no reason to cut back on planned capital spending unless something happens that drastically changes the premises on which the plan rests. For the typical corporation, nothing unexpected happened.[11]

They did not know it when they answered Ammer's questionnaire, but the unexpected recession was soon to have a drastic impact on the premises of many corporate planners.

Major banks, blocked from their usual sources of time-deposit funds by Federal Reserve restrictions on the rates they could pay (Regulation Q ceilings), aggressively tapped alternative sources. They borrowed from smaller banks (federal funds); they attracted Eurodollars through their branches abroad; they sold assets; and some issued commercial paper through holding-company affiliates. They used these funds mainly to meet loan commitments to their corporate customers.

Although home building and consumer spending for durable goods eased, upward pressures on prices were strong throughout the year, as can be seen in the price measures on Chart 4-1. Frustrated as they were, with their battle apparently going so poorly, some Federal Reserve officials were nettled by suggestions from monetarists that the slowdown in money-supply growth might cause a recession. Notwithstanding the fact that control of the money supply had become a central part of the Administration's economic strategy, high Federal Reserve spokesmen launched scathing criticisms of monetarism in general and Milton Friedman in particular.

One line of argument in Federal Reserve replies to the mone-

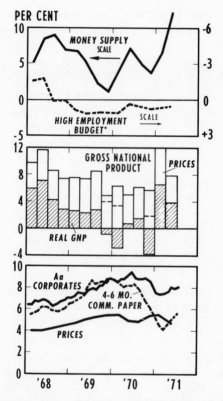

Chart 4-1. Monetary and fiscal restraint in 1969 and the recession of 1969–1970 combined to slow the inflation. After holding monetary expansion to a moderate rate for a year, the Federal Reserve jeopardized hard-won gains in the inflation battle in a futile attempt to hold down interest rates in 1971. The resulting monetary explosion left the future of prices and interest rates very much in question at midyear.

NOTES: See Chart 2-1.

tarists was that the System cannot, or does not, control the money supply. We shall examine that one in detail later. Another was that the monetarists had not proved that money-supply changes cause business fluctuations. And the third, often combined with either or both of the others, was that anyone who recommended less restraint in 1969 was not sufficiently concerned about the danger of inflation.[12] This last argument is ironic in view of the common belief that monetarists are concerned only with curing inflation. In this case they were much concerned with avoiding recession and unemployment.

There was a crucial question: Would a halt in money-supply growth like the one in the second half of 1969 cause a recession? From his position as Chairman of the Council of Economic Advisers, Paul McCracken of course could not answer that question publicly. But, while stressing the need for some restraint in expansion of bank credit and money supply in August, he suggested the need for moderation in the degree of restraint.

The data do suggest, however, that the rate of monetary and credit expansion in 1969 has actually been somewhat short of what would be required for on-going full employment even with a reasonably stable price level. *A stop-go monetary policy is always to be avoided*—and particularly at a time, such as the present, when the economy and financial markets are subjected to more than the normal quota of uncertainties [italics added].[13]

He also said that formidable data problems were making it difficult to quantify the pace of monetary expansion.

J. Dewey Daane, member of the Board of Governors, said in September:

. . . the monetarists contend, as they do so vehemently today, that too slow a growth rate [for money supply] will plunge the economy into a recession. . . . Judging by the press coverage he has received, there can be little doubt that he [Friedman] has won converts to his view that changes in the money supply are the most important determinant of changes in GNP. But there also are many people, both professional economists and laymen, who seriously doubt whether the simple causal relationship popularized by Friedman between changes in the money supply and GNP really exists. . . . I have always been highly skeptical of the simple causality case.[14]

When the time came for outlook talks at the beginning of 1970, the 1969–1970 recession had already begun, although this was not yet apparent to everyone. Alfred Hayes, president of the Federal Reserve Bank of New York, in arguing against an easing of policy, said:

. . . there are some economists who argue that a serious recession is already assured by reason of the weak performance of the money

supply over the past six months. I hope I have already made it clear
that I see no merit in any such mechanical view. The biggest dangers
I see on the horizon are (1) the danger that fiscal policy will be a
weaker and weaker ally of monetary policy in the anti-inflation effort,
and (2) the danger that pressures from outside the Federal Reserve and
inside the System itself will prevent our maintaining a sufficiently restrictive policy for a long enough time to turn the trick.[15]

The most crushing rebuke to the efforts of monetarists to arouse
the sleeping populace at the very end of 1969 came not from the
Federal Reserve itself, but from an alumnus, Robert V. Roosa,
long-time officer and gifted articulator of monetary-policy issues at
the Federal Reserve Bank of New York, and Under Secretary of the
Treasury for Monetary Affairs in the Kennedy Administration:

> Among those who foresee depression, there are some, notably Pro-
> fessor Friedman and his group, [he said] who have such sublime
> confidence in the validity of their one-track explanation of economic
> phenomena that they seem to think the basis has already been laid for
> controlling inflation. They believe that a return to easier money, along
> the straight line path that they would draw across the chart of time,
> will eventually restore balance and avert the slump which, otherwise,
> they view as inevitable.
>
> As one who has never been able to share in the mysteries of the
> Friedman monetary school—though I yield to no one in saluting the
> crucial importance, year in and year out, of monetary policy—I can
> only consider the current edition of Friedman as another episode in
> his long record of nimble escapes from reality.[16]

Without arguing about who may be escaping from reality here,
I would merely point out that by the time those words were spoken
monetarists were no longer arguing about how to *avert* a slump.
They had turned their attention to the problem of how to get out
of one without sacrificing the ground that had been won in the fight
against inflation. Furthermore, the Federal Reserve rebuttals were
addressed more to some monetarists' idea of a steady-growth monetary rule than they were to the specific monetarist forecast that a
recession would result from the sharp monetary deceleration of
1969. They were less than convincing on the second point, if not
on the first.

At its final meeting in 1969, on December 16, the Federal Open

Market Committee heard from its staff that growth in real GNP might be coming to a halt in the fourth quarter. Although the latest Commerce-SEC survey of business plans, taken in November, suggested that outlays on new plant and equipment would rise sharply in the first half of 1970, "the strengthening of the outlook in this sector did not appear sufficient to change materially the prospect for little or no growth in real GNP in the first half."[17] In other words, the FOMC staff had virtually forecast a recession.

Despite the forbidding outlook, "The Committee agreed that no relaxation of monetary policy would be appropriate at this time, in view of the persistence of inflationary pressures and expectations and the high degree of uncertainty with respect to the extent to which fiscal policy might be relaxed."[18] The Committee was worried about pending legislation regarding federal taxes and social security benefits that might relax fiscal restraint by more than had been assumed in the staff projections.

Monetarists feared in '69 that too restrictive a policy then would lead to an overly expansive policy in 1970 when the Fed would turn to fighting recession. If 1969 was like 1966, would another 1967 follow? This time the climate of opinion among economists and policy makers was quite different than it had been in 1966. The experience of the earlier 1960s and the research done by the growing number of monetarists made it difficult for the Federal Reserve to ignore the money supply any longer.

At its first meeting in 1970, the Federal Open Market Committee decided to seek moderate expansion of the monetary aggregates and to give lower priority to the control of interest rates. This was a revolutionary step, for the Federal Reserve had never before tried deliberately to control the money supply. Monetarists were overjoyed because they saw this change as the beginning of a fruitful experiment. Unfortunately, as we will see, the experiment continued for only one year.

MONEY RULES AND SLOWING PAINS IN 1970

The Federal Reserve System, which is nominally independent of the Administration, might well have changed its ways in any case because the evidence of harm done by excessive volatility in monetary expansion was accumulating too rapidly to be ignored. And monetarists were receiving a respectful hearing in several of the Reserve banks. Furthermore, the Joint Economic Committee of the Congress had been pushing the Fed to control the money supply since 1967, as we saw in Chapter 3. But bringing the money supply under control would have been much less likely had the Administration not wanted it done.

When Arthur F. Burns became Chairman of the Board of Governors in February, 1970, the Federal Reserve settled down to applying the new strategy of controlling money supply. By then, unfortunately, the recession had already begun. The anti-inflation program, therefore, proved to be more painful than I believe it would have been had the Federal Reserve been more careful in 1969.

There was much confusion about the Fed's new approach at first, although the new Chairman of the Reserve Board, Arthur F. Burns, explained the new policies more clearly than Federal Reserve policies had been explained in the past. He implied that there was not to be a sudden swing to rapid expansion in bank credit and money supply as there had been in 1967.[19] Nevertheless, the money supply did not grow smoothly, partly because of technical problems that we shall discuss in Chapters 9 and 10.

When the Federal Reserve announced that it intended to hold money-supply growth to a moderate rate, many observers thought this meant adoption of the constant-growth rule that Milton Friedman had been recommending for years. For a few weeks in the second quarter, however, the money supply grew much faster than the expected rate, which led some observers to conclude that monetarism had been discredited. Joseph Slevin, writing in the Washington *Post,* said, for example:

. . . the most fashionable economic theory of the past decade has been knocked out of the ring and may be out of contention for all time to come.

The theory is the highly touted "black box" monetarist approach of University of Chicago economist Milton Friedman. It got its come-uppance from a national crisis and a very plain showing that it does not work.[20]

His confident announcement was based on misinterpreting the welter of voices from inside the Fed. Increasing the emphasis on monetary aggregates as guides had not committed the Federal Reserve System to a constant-growth rule for money supply. Therefore, a change in the growth rate of money supply did not mean that money had been abandoned as a guide. The increase in money-supply growth in the second quarter of 1970 was a temporary one brought on by unusual events, such as a postal strike and a state of extreme nervousness in the securities markets after announcement that U.S. forces were entering Cambodia.

Financial institutions were disturbed about what they viewed as arbitrary changes in the rules of the money-market game that might cause interest rates to fluctuate more widely than in the past. They believed one of the main Federal Reserve functions had been to maintain "orderly markets," and they feared what might happen if this role was neglected. With widespread speculation about a liquidity crisis and serious recession running through the markets, the Federal Reserve supplied reserves to assist a large Treasury financing operation in May, as it had done many times before. After the Penn Central Railroad filed for bankruptcy in June, the monetary authorities again supplied reserves liberally to banks and suspended the Regulation Q ceilings on 30-89-day bank negotiable certificates of deposit (CDs).

For a time, holding money-supply growth to a moderate rate was considered to be less important than the task of calming fears of breakdown in the financial markets. Nevertheless, the Federal Reserve could no longer be casual about large increases in money supply and was soon trying to moderate the expansion.

After growing at a 7.2 percent annual rate from the first quarter to the second, the money supply grew at a 5.3 percent annual rate on average for the third quarter and a 3.8 percent rate in the fourth quarter. The U.S. monetary authorities seemed to have learned the lesson of the 1960s when large increases in money supply brought on the inflation that still bedeviled them in 1970.

It would be pleasant to say that the adoption of moderate money growth as a target speedily resolved the problems of the U.S. economy. But this did not happen. Instead, the United States felt the pains of recession and of inflation hangover at the same time. Profits and stock prices fell; unemployment and the cost of living rose.

By midyear, total real output in the U.S. economy had been showing little or no growth for three successive quarters. In the third quarter there was a slight improvement in business activity; but in the fourth quarter a long strike at General Motors caused a contraction of real GNP and industrial production. Consumers were coolly unresponsive to the advertising that is commonly supposed to keep them marching in lockstep as dutiful members of the affluent society. Businessmen, who had seemed as determined as Admiral Farragut at the Battle of Mobile Bay, cut back sharply on their expansion plans and reduced their employment rolls.

Crises, real or imaginary, threatened on all sides: an urban crisis, a housing crisis, a confidence crisis, and a liquidity crisis, to name just a few. Among the few redeeming features of the situation was that interest rates fell like a rock in the second half of the year and stock prices rose.

Because the word "recession" means something different to everyone who uses it or hears it, there was an understandable reluctance in Administration quarters to apply the term to the 1970 situation. But if we put some of the more sensational details aside for a moment, we can see in Chart 4-1 that the U.S. economy was in a mild business recession.

The tremendous resilience of the U.S. economy was well demonstrated by the fact that the 1969–1970 recession was so mild. In addition to having been subjected to one of the sharpest monetary decelerations in many years, the economy had to adjust to a sharp contraction in defense employment as the Nixon Administration moved to end the Vietnam War. Employment attributable to defense spending fell by nearly 1.8 million from its peak in fiscal 1968 to fiscal 1971. During calendar 1970 the armed forces were reduced by about 400,000; civilian employment for the Department of Defense declined by nearly 100,000 more; and private defense employment was reduced by about 600,000, for a total reduction in defense employment of 1.1 million.

Business managers, who may have paid a lot of money in 1969 to be told that there was not going to be a recession in 1970, did not really care whether or not the National Bureau of Economic Research ever would award its seal of approval to the current whatever-it-was. They just wanted to know when, if ever, the economy was going to recover from what was not supposed to happen. They had been taken by surprise and were more than a little shaken by the experience.

One classic fiscal remedy for a dragging economy—a tax cut—was mentioned by hardly anyone. It was a season for preoccupation with sores on the body politic—poverty, decaying cities, crime, and a new one, pollution of the environment. It was taken for granted that these would absorb massive amounts of federal tax revenues if and when the Vietnam War ended. Nevertheless, the Tax Reform Act of 1969 did provide some tax reduction in 1970 and the surcharge expired at the end of June.[21] Tax revenues, furthermore, were about $7 billion lower than they would have been at full employment.

A long strike throughout the far-flung plants of the General Motors Corporation was the final blow in a disheartening year. According to estimates of the Council of Economic Advisers, that one strike reduced the nation's gross national product by $14 billion in the fourth quarter (at an annual rate), completely masking from view any signs of a turn from recession. More strikes threatened in the year ahead, raising the specter of "cost-push" inflation that would overwhelm the conventional instruments of monetary and fiscal policy. The unemployment rate hit 6 percent in December.

When the score for the year was finally tallied, 1970 proved to be the first since 1957 to show a *net decline* in real gross national product. It was a minute decline, to be sure—0.5 percent—but it was a far cry from the 4.3 percent annual rate at which potential real GNP was estimated to be growing. During two years of Nixon Administration stewardship, unemployment had risen and the output gap had widened, but only close readers of the statistics could find any compensating benefit in a slowing of the rise in cost of living. In the push-button, quick-relief idiom of American politics, it was easy to argue that the economic malaise was the fault of a do-nothing Administration.

With appropriate solemnity, the Senate Democratic Policy Com-

mittee placed in the *Congressional Record,* in September, 1970, a
report on the state of the economy prepared by the three previous
chairmen of the President's Council of Economic Advisers, Walter
Heller, Arthur Okun, and Gardner Ackley. To no one's surprise,
their examination yielded:

. . . a disturbing picture of accelerated and unduly prolonged inflation;
soaring interest rates and financial disruptions; a stagnation of production and jobs, the cost of which continues to grow; policies that have
remained long on hopes and short on achievements.[22]

The irony of asking the advisers who had helped to lead the country
into its sad predicament to draw up a bill of indictment of their
successors was not lost on everyone. But, to repeat a Walter Heller
statement cited earlier, "That may not be economic optimality, but
it *is* political democracy."[23]

The main charges were that inflation had accelerated and "the
economic outlook is for only sluggish growth as far ahead as one
can see."[24] On fiscal policy, the report said, "The new Administration made only modest changes in the fiscal posture that it had inherited from President Johnson." The Federal Reserve, however,
with the active support of the Administration, had "pursued an extremely restrictive monetary policy during 1969, allowing the
money supply—currency and demand deposits combined—to increase only 2 percent during the year."[25] The most withering
language, however, was reserved for the charge that the Nixon Administration had foresworn attempts to influence specific wage and
price decisions.

An important source of the intensified inflation [the report said] was
the President's [Nixon's] prompt and unequivocal assurance that prices
and wages were no longer considered to be the Government's business
—which means the public's business. This was widely read as an invita-
tion for business and labor to cease the self-restraint practiced under
the Kennedy and Johnson Administrations.[26]

The guideposts which the Johnson advisers had virtually abandoned
in the last two years of their tenure had become, in retrospect, the
sine qua non of a successful strategy for combating inflation.

In the elections of November, 1970, the Republican party failed
to gain majorities in the House of Representatives or the Senate;

and the number of state governorships held by Republicans fell from 32 out of 50 to 21. Inevitably, political analysts singled out the economic issues as the major stumbling blocks for Republican candidates. And, almost immediately, there was press speculation about Administration pressure on the Federal Reserve to give up the fight against inflation and to swing into restoring full employment before the 1972 elections.

In December, for example, Leonard S. Silk, of the *New York Times,* said, "we are witnessing the emergence of what should go down in the history books as the Accord of 1970."[27] From speeches of President Nixon and Arthur Burns, Silk and other commentators concluded that Dr. Burns must have exacted a promise from the President to adopt an incomes policy for influencing wages and prices in exchange for a more expansionary monetary policy on the part of the Fed. Or perhaps the President had persuaded Dr. Burns to swing the Fed around in exchange for an incomes policy.

WRINGING DEFEAT FROM THE JAWS OF VICTORY IN '71

In the January, 1971, Budget Message, the Administration included a "policy forecast" of a $1,065 billion GNP for 1971. This stirred a storm of denunciation from former advisers of the Kennedy-Johnson Administrations, including Paul Samuelson, Walter Heller, Arthur Okun, Otto Eckstein, and Gardner Ackley. In hearings held by the Joint Economic Committee in February some of these economists and others went fearlessly and unforgettably on record with their own lower forecasts of $1,045 billion to $1,050 billion.[28] Businessmen, furthermore, were so depressed by their 1970 setbacks that they were quite prepared to believe recovery would be slow and painful.

Sam Nakagama of Argus Research Corporation argued, however, that the Joint Economic Committee hearings and an overly excited press corps had caused a great deal of confusion.

. . . the contrast between the Administration's "policy forecast" of a $1,065 billion GNP and the "standard" private forecast of $1,045 billion [he said] has been played up to the point where it might seem a shocking crime had been committed. The fact is, however, that the "standard" forecast is almost always wrong and usually by a wide margin.[29]

Nakagama also pointed out that the forecasting record of the Kennedy-Johnson advisers had not been especially outstanding for accuracy. On two occasions, he said, their forecast of annual change in GNP had erred by more than 7 percent. In view of their record, their criticism must be regarded as a counsel of perfection. Administration spokesmen quite properly argued that the standard private forecast often underestimated the strength of recoveries and that the difference between their forecast and the standard forecast was only slightly greater than the normal range of forecast error of 1 to 1½ percent.

Under the swirling political controversy lay scientific disagreement about the relative potency of monetary and fiscal policy. Economists of a fiscalist persuasion argued that a much more expansive fiscal policy would be necessary to propel the economy out of the doldrums. Price inflation was at last slowing down, but the moderately expansive monetary policies of the Federal Reserve would not be enough to get the economy going again.

In February, *Time* ran an article called "Milton Friedman: An Oracle Besieged" in which "a top official" of the Federal Reserve Board was quoted as saying, "We've been putting out money for some time at about the rate Friedman said, and we still have a sick economy."[30] Richard F. Janssen, in the *Wall Street Journal* the same week, went even further in reporting "Nixon's Flight from Friedmanism."

So with the experience of the late 1970s [*sic*] reviving the old adage that the Fed "can't push on a string," Mr. Nixon and his men are muting their Friedmanism in favor of the basic Keynesian credo: When the Government really wants to make sure that more money is spent in a sluggish economy, it had better start by spending more itself.[31]

Despite the great expectations of many observers, the President's budget for fiscal 1972 (to begin July 1, 1971) did not represent a switch to a more expansionary fiscal policy. It continued to focus on a spending ceiling. Budget outlays were slated to rise by $16.4 billion, or about the same as in fiscal '71.

Economic recovery was expected to increase revenues by enough to *reduce* the estimated deficit in the unified budget from $18.6 billion in fiscal '71 to $11.6 billion in fiscal '72. On the high-employment basis plotted on Chart 4-1, the budget was held approximately in balance. No wonder fiscalists challenged the Administration forecast. They had petitioned for fiscal relief but none was promised in the budget. To make matters worse, in their view, business investment spending was flat and consumers were unlikely to take up the slack as long as unemployment remained high.

Monetarists, furthermore, did not, and could not, offer the Administration a prescription for quickly and easily returning the economy to high employment without risking a reacceleration of inflation. The dynamics of GNP growth, monetary expansion, prices, and price expectations were simply not well enough understood for anyone to do that. But there was the compelling recent experience of 1966–1967 to cite in advising against a departure from the moderate approach of the Administration's original game plan.

Administration economists had the 1966–1967 experience well in mind. In its first "inflation alert" in 1970, the Council of Economic Advisers had argued that 1966–1967 "represented a major lost opportunity to regain a more stable price level."[32] The swing to massive monetary expansion in 1967 had been followed by a resurgence of price inflation. Four years later, with inflation finally slowing down again, monetarists could only urge that the 1967 mistake not be repeated.

While fiscalists worried about the lack of fiscal stimulus, monetarists soon had reason to fear that the economy would be overstimulated by monetary policy. The Federal Open Market Committee decided in January to aim for something like a 7½ percent annual rate of growth of the money supply in the first quarter, in order to compensate for a shortfall in money-supply growth in fourth quarter 1970. By the Federal Reserve's method of measurement—change from December monthly average to March monthly average—the actual growth was at an 8.9 percent annual rate. By the method used for Chart 4-1—change from the quarterly average of the fourth quarter to the quarterly average of the first quarter—the increase was a more tolerable 6.5 percent annual rate. In the second quarter, however, the growth rate rose to an intolerable 12 percent annual rate. By any measure, the first half money-growth rate was much too high to be long sustained without reviving price inflation again. The overreaction to recession that monetarists had feared might happen in 1970 happened in 1971 instead, when it was even more likely to revive inflation than it would have been in 1970.

The monetary explosion in the first half was all the more startling in view of what Chairman Burns had told the Joint Economic Committee on February 19:

> I can assure this Committee that the Federal Reserve will continue to supply the money and credit needed for healthy economic expansion. But I wish to reaffirm the assurance that I gave to this Committee and the nation a year ago—namely, that the Federal Reserve will not become the architects of a new wave of inflation. We know that the effects of monetary policy on aggregate demand and on prices are spread over relatively long periods of time. We are well aware, therefore, that *an excessive rate of monetary expansion now could destroy our nation's chances of bringing about a gradual but lasting control over inflationary forces* [italics added].[33]

Most disconcerting to monetarists was the thought that the Federal Reserve, if not the Administration, had abandoned control of the money supply.[34] The Federal Reserve had evidently reduced emphasis on money-supply control and increased emphasis on attempts to influence interest rates.

Interest rates had gone through their largest cyclical decline since World War II by March, 1971. But with an economic recovery under way they were sure to rise. If the monetary authorities were to resist the rise of rates, as they had in 1967 (see Chapter 3), money-supply growth would soar and the battle against inflation would be lost again. Monetarists had the dismaying sensation of seeing an old movie come flickering onto the screen for the fourth time in a theater with no exits.

The Federal Reserve's evident preoccupation with interest rates in early '71 was one of the principal sources of the monetarists' sense of *déjà vu*. "Operation twist"—the 1961 attempt to reduce long-term rates while permitting short-term rates to rise—had been revived. As in 1961, the recession had driven short rates so low that the authorities thought they should be raised to curb the U.S. balance-of-payments deficit. At the same time it was hoped that long-term rates, which had also fallen, could be reduced even more in order to facilitate a revival of home building and business investment. The Federal Reserve, or at least important parties within it, seemed determined to attempt again what experience of the 1960s had demonstrated could not be done. It seemed incredible that the lessons of 1965, 1967, and 1968 could have been forgotten so soon.[35]

The process of rooting out monetarist tenets from U.S. economic policy councils, which began in the Federal Reserve, appeared complete when President Nixon announced the wage-price freeze and other economic policy measures on August 15. In his television address to the nation, much of which was devoted to the control of inflation, the President did not mention the Federal Reserve or monetary policy. In an hour-long press conference devoted to the new program on the following day, Treasury Secretary Connally did not mention monetary policy either. Nor was he asked by a roomful of alert, critical Washington reporters what the monetary authorities might be going to do.

Observing that the monetarist "plague" was ebbing fast, Paul Samuelson had reported on August 1, "Not a single member of the Federal Reserve Board has succumbed to monetarism."[36] No monetarist would contradict that statement; all deeply regretted their failure to win even one member of the Board as a convert. If the Board was unwilling to continue the experiment begun in January, 1970, the chances for getting a fair test of monetarism in the United States were bleak indeed. The prospects for success in curbing inflation had already been direly imperiled by the monetary explosion of first-half 1971, but a return to a moderate rate of monetary growth might not yet have been too late. Prices respond to changes in money supply with a very long lag and the effects of the '69 and '70 restraints were still showing up in a slowing of the inflation rate in '71.

It is much too early to assess the prospects of the President's new economic program or even to guess at what the parts of it that require Congressional action will look like when finally put in place. But one thing seems clear to me: the United States economy will have an upsurge of output in the rest of '71 and all of '72 the like of which has rarely been seen except in Japan or perhaps Germany.

Before the President announced his program, some monetarist forecasters looked for real GNP to increase over the six quarters ending in fourth quarter '72 at about a 6–6½ percent annual rate. This projection was based largely on the potential for growth built up by highly expansive fiscal and monetary policies of the past and on an assumption that the Federal Reserve would not move abruptly to choke off the expansion. The new policies, therefore, should accelerate a recovery process already well under way.

The expansion in aggregate demand was clear to see in the first half of '71, when consumer spending rose at a 10 percent annual rate and home building soared, despite the highly publicized reports of low consumer confidence. But the impact of this increase in demand on U.S. production was muted by the diversion of demand into imports. Had this not happened, GNP in current dollars would have risen by a stunning $27 billion in the second quarter, staying right on course toward the $1,065 billion annual goal the Administration had set in January. The President's program will, by design, shift some of this demand back into U.S. products through changes of exchange rates and the import surcharge. At the same time, however, these measures will reduce the dampening effect of imports on U.S. prices, requiring even more vigilance on the price front than would have been required before, if the U.S. inflation is to be curbed.

The wage-price freeze and whatever anti-inflation measures follow it will have to contend with enormous price pressures. But there is nothing in the experience of other countries with income policies and other direct controls to justify the widespread approval with which they were greeted in the United States. To me, this was a clear instance of hope overwhelming reason.

SCIENCE AND POLITICS AGAIN

It would be misleading to conclude from the review of U.S. economic experience in the last three chapters that insidious politics will doom the world to eternal inflation. Although widely held, that is too simple a view. As we saw, the Eisenhower Administration sought price stability and economic growth in the 1950s. It achieved price stability and recession. The Kennedy-Johnson Administrations sought economic growth and price stability. They achieved growth and inflation. The Nixon Administration sought price stability and economic expansion. It achieved, first, recession, then a turn toward price stability, and in 1971, the beginning of a strong economic expansion. I believe the expansion and the approach to price stability could have continued indefinitely, if, with victory in sight, the temptation to do too much had been resisted.

It would be good politics in any country to maintain high employment and price stability at the same time. Politicians want that and so do the voters. I believe it can be done. In the quotation used at the beginning of Chapter 2, however, Herbert Stein said of President Kennedy's economists, "They had no reason to doubt that they knew what to do."[37] That has been the main problem all along; economists have not felt they had reason to doubt that they knew what to do. Unfortunately, their advice at times has been appallingly bad. Governments have been led again and again to adopt policies that have had disappointing results. And if businessmen, the press, and the general public occasionally applaud bad policies, one need only remember from whom they learned their economics.

U.S. economic policies, in particular, would have turned out much better since the 1950s if the Federal Reserve and the economic advisers of both political parties had not underestimated the power of inappropriate money-supply changes to thwart their plans.

The rest of this book, therefore, will discuss contributions of the new monetarism to economic science and political economics. In Part Two, for example, lessons in how to predict the results of economic policies will be drawn from the experience of business forecasters. There we will see how monetarist forecasters predict the consequences for businesses and investors of economic policy makers' mistakes. How central banks could avoid such accidents by properly controlling the money supply is the subject of Part Three. Monetary research is covered in Part Four and international implications of monetarism are discussed in Part Five. The final section presents suggestions for establishing a stable monetary framework for the world economy.

two
_____

BUSINESS FORECASTERS FIND A NEW TOOL

5

PERILS OF THE MONEYLESS FORECASTER

MR. ACKLEY. This morning the Department of Commerce released the second quarter figures for corporate profits. The first quarter figure, which we previously had, was $79 billion. The preliminary estimate for the second quarter shows an increase—a modest one—$79.2 billion. And our economic projections do call, as the Secretary said, for further increases over the year ahead.

THE CHAIRMAN. You better get that information out pretty quickly because it is a little more optimistic than some of the statements made to me by corporate executives.

Hearings Before the Committee on Ways and Means, House of Representatives, August 14, 1967[1]

Because corporate earnings are eerily responsive to even small changes in the rate of growth of GNP, the most carefully drawn corporate plan or security analysis can be brought low by an unforeseen change in economic conditions. Therefore, the ability to forecast turns in economic activity, if only by a few months, substantially enhances anyone's prospects for exerting influence and achieving affluence. Every business decision aimed at a future payoff and every Wall Street investment recommendation is based consciously or unconsciously on some sort of forecast of the economic environment.

The famous remark of Keynes, "In the long run we are all dead," is an understatement. A business or an investment fund that makes a mistake in predicting the timing or the effects of a business turn on sales, costs, and profits can be dead, or at least critically ill, in the short run. That prospect should marvelously concentrate the thoughts of forecasters, as the prospect of hanging affected the thinking of Samuel Johnson's doomed friend.

MISSING THE TURNS

Unfortunately, it is precisely at the turning points that business forecasters in the United States have earned their lowest marks. In *An Appraisal of Short-Term Economic Forecasts,* Victor Zarnowitz found that

... the record of the numerical forecasts of GNP (like that of qualitative turning-point forecasts) does not indicate an ability to forecast the turn several months ahead. Not only were actual turns missed but also turns were predicted that did not occur.[2]

The standard forecast had an undistinguished record in calling the turns over the 1960–1971 period reviewed in Chapters 2–4. This was unfortunate because it was a time of high hopes and extravagant claims for the power of the new economics and the contribution of economists to decision making in government and business. However, the inadequacy of the performance was not widely apparent because there were few turns to be predicted in the long expansion between the recessions of 1960–1961 and 1969–1970.

Most forecasters missed the 1960–1961 recession, expecting a boom instead. The 1967 minirecession was a moot case; monetarists expected a recession while most standard forecasters expected, at most, "a mild slowdown in the second half." The '67 minirecession was too mini to merit certification by the National Bureau of Economic Research, but it nevertheless was a significant, thoroughly unpleasant, event to many business firms.

In 1968, as we saw in Chapter 3, the standard forecasters and the large econometric models expected the surtax to produce a sharp slowdown in the second half. There may well have been one because of the deceleration of money-supply growth in the second half of 1967, but the forecast itself prodded the Federal Reserve into flooding the country with money. Although standard forecasters did generally expect a mild slowdown for 1970, few expected a recession. Some announced in positive terms that there would *not* be a recession.

Perhaps the worst miss was the underestimation of the 1971 recovery, when standard forecasters expected a slow, sluggish expansion that would keep the economy below par for years. This forecast undoubtedly influenced the Nixon Administration to change course in August, 1971. But it was a bad forecast. It was so out of character for the U.S. economy that the forecasters had to discover or invent special explanations for it, such as a change in economic structure or a "shift in liquidity preference." With regard to calling the turns, it can truly be said of forecasters, "Many are paid but few deliver."

The mild 1969–1970 recession had an unsettling effect on many businessmen because it was such a surprise. They had been led by the new economics to believe recessions were a thing of the past and so they confidently rejected the signs of trouble ahead in 1969. When recession did hit, many became overly pessimistic about prospects for recovery.

Despite missing the turns, however, Zarnowitz says economists have been able to make annual forecasts of GNP and the industrial production index that are, on the whole, more accurate than any simple extrapolation of the preceding year's level or change.[3]

This chapter traces some of the reasons for the failures and the successes of the "standard" forecast. One of the main conclusions is that leaving money out of his calculations can cause a forecaster to miss turning points even though his longer-run projections of the major economic aggregates may be good. Suggestions are therefore made for improving the conventional GNP forecasts by using changes in growth of the money stock as a leading indicator of cyclical turns in business activity.

PROPERTIES OF THE STANDARD FORECAST

Although this account may be unjust to a few of the more sophisticated standard forecasters, it is also a fair representation of the approach adopted by most business managers, market researchers, and security analysts in the 1960s. By a "standard" forecast I mean a gross national product forecast obtained by projecting the principal components—such as consumer spending, government spending, and investment—separately and then summing them to a total. Zarnowitz reported that this was the approach used by many of the business forecasters covered in his study.

There are, it seems to me, three main sources of error in the standard forecast. First, forecasts of GNP three or four quarters ahead are seldom better than simple extrapolations—extension of trend lines. This is hardly an accident, for more than half of the standard forecast is usually based on simple extrapolation of state and local government expenditures and of consumer spending for services and nondurables. Moreover, it is a rare forecaster who expects cyclical changes to originate in these sectors of the accounts.

Second, even the forecasts of avowedly non-Keynesian economists are much influenced by income-expenditure theory, which, as experience of the sixties indicates, is a poor predictor. The national-income-and-product-accounts framework and the availability of anticipatory data on the federal budget, business plans for plant and equipment expenditures, and construction contracts lead naturally to placing heavy weight on government and investment spending as critical elements in the forecast. There also is a tendency to assign prime causal importance to those types of expenditure that fluctuate most widely.

The forecaster typically focuses on surveys of investor intentions and such measures as inventory-sales ratios, capacity-utilization rates, and manufacturers' orders in his search for clues that would indicate impending changes in expenditures and output. He then generally adjusts consumer spending upward or downward from its growth trend in light of his estimates of investment and government expenditures.

Estimates of consumer spending place great weight on the effects of fiscal policy changes on personal disposable income. Consequently, too much can be expected of a tax increase, as we saw in 1968, when standard forecasters and sophisticated econometric modelers alike expected the income tax surcharge to have a prompt, substantial depressing effect on consumer spending. The upward influence of increases in social security benefits and government pay increases in 1970 was similarly overestimated. This over-emphasis on short-run income effects on consumer spending comes straight out of the simple textbook version of Keynesian economics. discussed in the first chapter.

Because it is a common practice of standard forecasters to assign some prominent explanation for each expansion—such as auto sales, home building, inventory rebuilding, or tax reduction—some forecasters begin to lose heart when their favorite source of motive power appears to be playing out before they have found a replace-ment for it. This is why they tend to underestimate the strength and the persistence of recoveries. For example, early in the 1960s there was widespread concern about the lack of precedents for having more than "two good auto years back to back."

The weakness of the standard recovery forecast is even greater in the early forecasts made before some prominent source of ex-pansive force has become visible. The forecast recovery, therefore, is likely to be late and weak. This tendency to worry about the sources of expansion comes from the Keynesian idea that the economy does not naturally tend to reach full employment.

Third, the standard forecast is usually based on a model of an inherently unstable economy in which disturbances originating in government or investment cause fluctuations in GNP unless checked by monetary and fiscal policy. Money plays no role in the model as an originator of fluctuations but may come in later as part of a contracyclical policy. To a monetarist, the standard forecaster seems usually to be looking in the wrong sectors of the economy for the signals of an approaching turn.

Forecasts for 1970 made during 1969 illustrate these practices very well. The bullish forecasters relied heavily on the Commerce-SEC plant and equipment expenditures survey, which indicated con-tinuing strong growth in capital spending. Some rashly asserted there could be no recession if business spending continued to grow. These forecasts, in turn, added to the fears of the authorities and contributed to the widespread notion that anti-inflation policies were not working.

Forecasts for 1971 illustrate the tendency for reliance on projections of business investment spending to cause standard fore-casters to underestimate the strength of recoveries. As we saw in Chapter 4, the Administration's "policy forecast" of a $1,065 billion GNP was ridiculed by "standard" forecasters who were huddling around a figure of $1,045 billion when the Administration forecast was announced in January. The standard forecasters were expecting the recovery from the 1969–1970 recession to be an exceptionally sluggish one, largely because business plant and equipment expenditures evidently were not going to do much more than move sideways for a year or more, if they would do even that well. The cuts in defense spending also appeared to have a more depressing effect on business forecasters than on the economy.

I believe it is fair to say that most of the multi-equation econo-metric models developed in recent years use basically the approach sketched here. The operators of such models must assume, or fore-cast, future values of numerous exogenous variables, such as tax rates and government expenditures, in order to generate a GNP forecast. Furthermore, they depend upon interest rates to transmit the effects of monetary policy changes through long roundabout processes to a few activities such as home building and business investment spending.

The consumer, in these models, is the last to feel the effects because these come to him through higher or lower income when the interest-sensitive activities pick up or slow down. Although these models can spew out a splendid array of numbers, therefore, they are slower to turn than an underpowered supertanker with a full load of oil. Coming of age with the computer in the early 1960s as they did, the econometric models had no turns to miss until 1966. Therefore, they predicted the economy's position quite well through the years of steaming on a steady course.

On the other hand, as they demonstrated in 1968, the large econometric models tend to be overly sensitive to changes in gov-ernment taxing or spending. Fiscal policy, as in the simple text-book Keynesian model and in many of the standard forecasts, is assumed in these models to have prompt, direct effects on consumer spending. However, if in the real world money-supply changes can overpower fiscal-policy changes, as they did several times in the 1960s, a forecasting model that is too sensitive to fiscal policy and not sensitive enough to monetary policy will mislead the policy maker in business or government just when he needs it most. Business cycle turns do not come very often; but when they do they can have drastic effects on unwary corporate executives, politicians, and investors. Some of these models have been giving increasing weight to monetary influences in recent years, which should improve their performance.

One obvious merit of the econometric models is the consistency with which the implications of the various assumptions can be worked out. Nevertheless, judgment and intuition in forecasting the exogenous variables still have much to do with the quality of the final forecast. Furthermore, operators of the big models that are actually used for forecasting frequently make ad hoc adjustments in their equations as they go along, if results do not seem plausible. For example, if home building appears to be increasing more rapidly than the construction sector equations have been predicting, some of the constants or coefficients in these equations may be adjusted arbitrarily in hopes of improving subsequent forecasts. Some critics call these adjustments "fudge factors." Consequently, much larger amounts of judgment and intuition are involved in applying these models than many outsiders realize.

MONETARISM FOR FUN AND PROFIT

While the makers of U.S. economic policies were absorbing hard lessons in the 1960s, and reliance on earnings projections was growing in business planning and budgeting and security analysis, a quiet revolution was going on in the ranks of business forecasters. Establishment seers, who had been hovering for years over steaming kettles of indicators to discern the shape of things to come, were challenged by two groups of upstarts: the econometric model builders and the monetarists. It will be the monetarists who concern us here.

Early in those years, forecasting conferences held by the American Statistical Association, the National Industrial Conference Board, and the then-infant National Association of Business Economists would occasionally include a known monetarist on a program, perhaps more to appease a captious minority than out of any desire to encourage the propagation of heresy. By 1969, however, a NABE seminar devoted entirely to monetary forecasting attracted several hundred people.[4] They were attracted by rumors that the monetarists must be doing something right.

The business economist who probably did more than anyone else to make the new sect respectable was Beryl Sprinkel. His 1964 book, *Money and Stock Prices,* won a large and enthusiastic audience.[5] As often happens in rapidly developing industries, however, the technology of forecasting was changing faster than it could be written up and disseminated. As late as 1966, *How Business Economists Forecast,* a massive compendium of "vivid essays revealing the trade secrets of the leading economist-forecasters in today's business world," did not include any section on the monetarist approach to forecasting.[6]

Business economists who adopted the monetary approach drew heavily on the research work of three main groups: the Friedman-Schwartz-Cagan-Meiselman group—at the University of Chicago, Columbia University, and the National Bureau of Economic Research—the Karl Brunner and Allan Meltzer group at their various universities and conferences; and the Federal Reserve Bank of St. Louis—which is by all odds the most productive center for monetary research in the world today. All three centers, furthermore, have former students and associates in missionary outposts throughout the known world, who have also contributed to the growing stock of monetary lore.

While the researchers developed and tested theories, a few business economists diligently monitored the flow of unpublished papers and research reports for ideas that could be applied in forecasting. As we shall see later, some of these applications may have been made too quickly; but, on the whole, the results have more than justified the effort.

THE MONETARY APPROACH

Paradoxically, two of the most important assertions underlying what I would call the monetary school of forecasting say nothing about money. These two statements, or empirical generalizations, are: First, private enterprise economies are inherently stable. Second, they have a persistent tendency to grow. The key to forecasting in this approach, therefore, is to identify the occasional disturbances that can cause significant departures from the norm. In short, the fluctuations to be forecast are considered to be the results of external shocks to an otherwise stable system, rather than an inherent characteristic of the system.

The notion of an essentially stable system that is implicit in most monetarists' forecasting is diametrically opposed to the Keynesian idea that the economy is basically unstable. As Paul Samuelson said in a passage quoted in the first chapter, Keynesians—and many standard forecasters—believe "the laissez-faire system is without any thermostat."[7] Therefore, business fluctuations are caused by swings in the willingness of businessmen to invest; there can be alternating periods of too much investment and not enough investment. To forecast business fluctuations, standard forecasters keep a sharp eye on the forces they believe influence business investment.

The monetarist position [says Karl Brunner] . . . denies the proposition that the dynamic process governed by the private real sector is unstable over some major ranges, or that anticipations of the business community are subject to large swings independent of major policy events or actions pursued by the authorities. The private sector absorbs shocks and transforms them into a stabilizing motion. . . . The monetarist position argues further that the major instabilities and uncertainties of the economic process result from the behavior of the government sector.[8]

A helpful way to visualize the monetarist concept of a stable system that is subjected to occasional shocks is Milton Friedman's "plucking model."[9] In this approach, real output usually is viewed as bumping along just under the ceiling of maximum feasible output. Irregularities in the surface of the ceiling and its upward slope, which corresponds to the potential growth rate, are determined by the available resources and methods of organizing them. Occasionally, however, output is plucked down by a cyclical contraction. It returns to the ceiling again when recovery sets in. For series on prices and money values there is no physical ceiling, so there is noth-

ing to prevent the series from being pulled up—in price inflations—as well as down.

Modern Keynesian analysis also uses the concept of an output
ceiling but with an important difference. The Council of Economic
Advisers through the early sixties used estimates of the ceiling to
show how far the economy was operating below its potential or,
rather, how far the economy should be pushed by policy measures
to reach the full-employment goal. In the Keynesian system the
economy is assumed to stay below the ceiling unless pushed up to
it. In the monetarist system the economy is assumed to be at the
ceiling unless pulled away temporarily by a monetary disturbance.
This difference of view obviously makes a big difference in forecasting methods.

The monetary research to be reviewed in later chapters provides
a good theoretical base and much evidence for expecting that
cyclical disturbances sufficiently severe to win National Bureau
certification seldom, if ever, occur unless there has been a substantial disturbance in the rate of money-supply growth. Consequently, one major implication for the business forecaster is that
the standard forecast, with its usual large element of extrapolation,
could do well over periods in which there are no pronounced
changes in money-supply growth.

In such periods, however, there is some possibility that the nonmonetary approach will forecast downturns or reductions in output
growth that do not materialize, especially if growth of expenditures
for business plant and equipment appears excessive to the forecaster or if the federal budget threatens to develop a surplus. The
"fiscal drag" theory is a good example. In the early sixties, and
even in 1965, there was a great deal of worry about a supposed
automatic tendency of the budget to develop a surplus and thus to
thwart recoveries before full employment could be reached.

The characteristic lead of money-supply changes over the responses of output and prices is convenient to the forecaster for
obvious reasons. Furthermore, as the experience of the 1960s indicated, money-supply changes induce changes in consumer spending, which in turn influence business expenditures for inventories
and plant and equipment through effects on business sales. It thus
seems highly probable that investment responds more slowly to

money-supply changes than does consumer spending, although money-supply changes undoubtedly have some direct effects on investment expenditures as well.

A forecasting approach or model that relies upon changes in investment to trigger changes in other kinds of expenditure, while neglecting the direct effects of money-supply changes on consumption, will be slow in responding to monetary disturbances. Surveys of plant and equipment expenditure intentions, for example, generally indicate continuing strength as cyclical peaks are approached but then show significant downward revisions after a peak has been passed. This may explain some of the misses in forecasting downturns that Professor Zarnowitz has reported. The plant and equipment surveys certainly contributed to the reluctance of most forecasters in 1966 and 1969 to believe a slowdown was coming. And they delayed recognition by many forecasters that a recovery was coming in 1971. Similarly, the common tendency for forecasters to underestimate growth of output during the early stages of recoveries probably results in part from their waiting to find confirmation in the behavior of capital investment. This is like waiting to see the caboose before announcing that a train is coming.

There is one more implication of the evidence on the money-supply theory that is of great significance to forecasters. This is that money-supply changes have little or no influence on long-run rates of growth in real output, although they do influence prices. We will see why this is so when we discuss how money works in later chapters. In terms of the plucking model, the main effect of a monetary contraction is to pull the economy away temporarily from the feasible output ceiling.

If several periods of monetary restriction occur in quick succession, as they did in the 1950s, however, growth of output may be held down for longer than one cycle because recoveries are checked before output has had time to return to the capacity ceiling. Money-supply growth, however, cannot push output up through the ceiling for more than a short time. At some point, excessive money-supply growth merely raises prices. We found this out in 1965 and 1968.

The standard forecaster comes into his own in long-term forecasting because real factors—population changes, technology, tastes, and the amounts of machinery and other capital available—

instead of monetary factors determine the course of the economy in the long run. In effect, the problem of the long-term forecaster is to discover the slope and other features of the feasible output ceiling. The chief contribution of money here is in determining the rate of rise of the price level so that forecasts can be expressed in current dollars or pounds or yen or whatever currency the forecaster is dealing with. Money matters a great deal in the short run but has little influence on output in the long run.

6

ADDING MONEY TO THE PALETTE

Throughout the near-century examined in detail
we have found that:
1. Changes in the behavior of the money stock
have been closely associated with changes in
economic activity, money income, and prices.
2. The interrelation between monetary and
economic change has been highly stable.
3. Monetary changes have often had an
independent origin; they have not been simply
a reflection of changes in economic activity.
Milton Friedman and Anna Jacobson Schwartz,
*A Monetary History of the United States, 1867–
1960,* 1963[1]

Picasso has radically changed his style more than once without
suffering any loss of creativity or popular esteem. The Beatles, too,
drew a faithful audience with them through a remarkable evolution
in style, until the tragic day they dissolved the group in 1970.
Economists, however, seem passionately devoted to the modes of
expression they learned in their youth. The standard forecast,
therefore, will surely continue to flourish.

Contrary to the fears of some traditionalists, nevertheless, recognition of money-supply effects in business fluctuations does not
require a helter-skelter leap into a new forecasting style. Judiciously
done, the incorporation of money-supply effects can heighten per-
ception at crucial points without sacrificing the richness of detail
that provides aesthetic satisfaction to many forecasters and to the
buyers of their work.

MONEY LEADS

The simplest way to add money to the standard forecast is to use it as a leading indicator, as a statistical series that consistently turns upward or downward before the GNP or other comprehensive measure of economic activity. Much of the early monetary research by Milton Friedman, Anna Schwartz, Phillip Cagan, and Clark Warburton was directed at finding out the length of the lags between peaks or troughs in money-supply growth and the corresponding peaks and troughs in the business cycle. They accumulated mountains of evidence on the cyclical timing of changes in money supply, economic activity, money income, prices, and interest rates.[2] It was natural, then, for the early users of money supply in business forecasting in the 1950s, such as Beryl Sprinkel, to follow this approach.

Only four out of the 36 leading indicators listed by the National Bureau of Economic Research in 1966 scored higher for regularity and length of lead than did changes in the growth of the money supply (demand deposits and currency).[3] The indicators that scored higher than money were stock prices, initial claims for unemployment compensation, new orders for durable goods in general, and new orders for machinery and equipment. Of the four, two had a median lead of six months over business-cycle peaks and troughs and two had a median lead of four months, as compared with a median lead of 14 months for the money supply. Changes in the stock of money, therefore, give much earlier warning signals than do any of the other high-scoring leading indicators on the list.

The extra lead time provided by money-supply changes is extremely important because the data for most leading indicators are at least one month old before they are published. In addition, it is difficult to conclude that a peak or trough has been passed until this has been indicated by at least two months of data. Therefore, an indicator with a median lead of six months actually provides only about three months of warning, which may not be enough time for a business or an investor to take precautionary action.

The National Bureau study, however, noted that the long lead of money-supply changes does raise the question of whether the series is positively or inversely related to the cycle—that is, whether it leads or follows the cycle.[4] I would consider that question of causation already settled by the research to be discussed later.

As can be seen from Chart 6-1, money-supply growth declined before each recession and before the minirecession of 1967. There were especially clear indications of trouble ahead in 1947–1948, 1959, 1966, and 1969. Changes of such magnitude in the behavior of the money supply should at least be taken as cautionary signals if they occur when the standard GNP forecasts are indicating strong expansion. The forecasters would be well advised to go back and take another look in such circumstances, especially at their estimates of consumer spending. As a matter of fact, this is what most monetary forecasters do. None look *only* at money.

A more explicit means for adding money to the standard forecast is what could be called the Applied Pathology Method. Assume, for purposes of illustration, that there is an abrupt fall in the growth of the money supply, as in 1959 or 1969. Although the economy may appear so exuberant that the monetary authorities are trying desperately to curb it, the forecaster can assume he is a doctor whose patient has been exposed to measles. It should be only a matter of time until the spots begin to appear. By taking a particular recession from the past, or perhaps a composite of several, as a pattern for the possible recession to come he can sketch the rough outlines not only of the coming downturn but of the upturn beyond it.

The timing and dimensions of the forecasted recession can be adjusted as the magnitude of the monetary disturbance becomes clearer. Milton Friedman and Anna Schwartz have found that the severity of a business recession is roughly proportional to the magnitude of the monetary deceleration that precedes it.[5] The key point is that the forecaster who has noticed a pronounced change in the rate of monetary expansion is alert to the possibility of a business cycle turn ahead and so is looking for the symptoms. A fall in interest rates, as in January, 1960, September, 1966, and January, 1970, is a clinching bit of evidence that a cyclical peak has been reached or is very near. We will look at that indicator in more detail later.

When a turnaround in monetary growth becomes evident, as it did

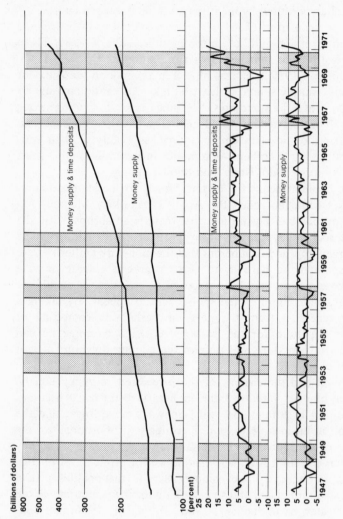

Chart 6-1. The rate of growth of the money supply is a good leading indicator for business forecasters.

NOTES: Money supply—monthly-average demand deposits and currency; money supply and time deposits include time deposits of commercial banks; all seasonally adjusted. Rates of change—monthly at annual rates, smoothed with three-month weighted moving average. *Chart by FNCB.*

by February, 1970, an upturn in business should be expected two or three quarters later. That misleading figure of speech about "pushing on a string" should be cast into outer darkness. Remember instead that the U.S. economy is extremely buoyant and will bob up again of its own accord soon after monetary forces stop pulling it down. This may well be true also of other predominantly private-enterprise economies.

FILLING IN THE DETAILS

It should be evident by now that incorporating money-supply effects in forecasting still leaves much to be done. A monetary disturbance sets off a long and complex process of adjustments throughout the economy. We have a great deal to learn about these processes. Econometric models should be useful for this work. So should the vast collection of business-cycle observations of the National Bureau of Economic Research and others. Furthermore, we have by no means ruled out the possibility that business fluctuations can also be caused by nonmonetary disturbances. Government is certainly a source of disturbance to be reckoned with by the forecaster. And there are others.

In respect to short-term forecasting, Professor Zarnowitz has pointed out that the traditional method of estimating principal components and then adding them up to total GNP does not do so well for individual components.[6] Yet some of these components may be more significant than total GNP to the business forecaster. The forecaster who works for an auto company is unlikely to get a bonus for being right on total GNP if he misses on consumer expenditures for durable goods.

This suggests that it might be useful to turn the forecasting procedure around; that is, to forecast changes in the total from the influence of money-supply changes on aggregate income, for example, and then to work out the implications for individual components. As we learn more about the effects of money-supply changes, furthermore, we should be able to apply this knowledge to forecasts of the components as well. Leonall Andersen, for example, has found strong relationships between money-supply changes and most of the principal components of GNP.[7]

A MONEY MODEL

Up to this point we have considered money-supply changes simply as a leading indicator that could be used to modify the standard forecast. Unfortunately, however, there is no simple rule for relating the date of a turn in monetary growth to the date of the next cyclical peak or trough. Furthermore, the rate of growth of money supply is such an erratic series that, even when it is smoothed with a three-month moving average like the one used in Chart 6–1 or the six-month moving average like the one used in the U.S. Commerce Department publication *Business Conditions Digest,* one may be in doubt for several months whether or not a peak or trough has occurred in the series.

In addition, the business forecaster is interested in more than the major recessions. A change in economic activity that is almost imperceptible in current dollar GNP, such as the 1967 slowdown or the one of 1962, could be highly significant to the prospects for profits in many businesses. These objections have led some economists to exclude money from their forecasting kits, although they may not have applied such strict tests to other leading indicators.

Many of the models being experimented with for business forecasting, like the ones illustrated here, are lineal descendants of the equations Friedman and Meiselman used to compare the effects of money-supply changes with those of changes in the autonomous expenditures of the Keynesian system.[8] The Friedman-Meiselman study was published in 1963. By 1967 their equations had been adapted for forecasting purposes. One of the first of this genre of monetary forecasting models was the work of Michael Keran at the Federal Reserve Bank of St. Louis.[9]

In money models the quarterly change in GNP, or other variable to be forecast, is related to changes in money supply in earlier quarters. Sometimes changes in other variables such as interest rates and government expenditures are also included. Incorporating a government expenditure variable was an innovation introduced by

$ BILLIONS

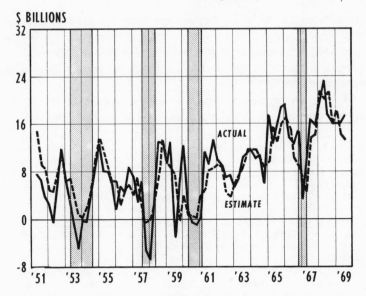

Chart 6-2. A simple monetary forecasting model explains changes in GNP growth.

NOTES: Quarterly changes in seasonally adjusted current-dollar GNP. Estimated changes from equation 6-1 (Table 6-1) with actual changes in money supply and high-employment-budget Federal expenditures. *Chart by FNCB.*

Leonall Andersen and Jerry Jordan in 1968.[10] Differences from model to model consist largely of differences in techniques for treating time lags and in the selection of periods over which to estimate the relationships.

The best discussions of this general family of monetary models yet in print are to be found in the Federal Reserve Bank of St. Louis *Review* and in papers presented by Leonall Andersen and other economists of the St. Louis Fed. The forecasting equation they discussed in the November, 1968, issue of the St. Louis *Review* produced better forecasts for the second half of 1968 than did the large econometric models that contributed to the Federal Reserve's decision to ease monetary restraint at the time of the tax increase in 1968. The St. Louis model also performed well in 1969 and 1970.

Chart 6-2 compares actual changes in current dollar GNP with estimates of an early St. Louis–type equation used at First National City Bank in 1969. In this equation (Equation 6-1 in Table 6-1), most of the change in estimated GNP is accounted for by changes in money supply in the same quarter and in the two preceding quarters.

Changes in high-employment federal expenditures in the same quarter and in the three preceding quarters also have some in-

Table 6-1. GNP Forecasting Model

Equation 6-1
First Differences
2Q 1951–3Q 1969

$$GNP(t) = 2.1054 + 2.3148\ M(t) - 0.5438\ M(t\text{-}1) + 2.7933\ M(t\text{-}2)$$
$$+ 0.2236\ E(t) + 0.3673\ E(t\text{-}1) - 0.2018\ E(t\text{-}2) - 0.6613\ E(t\text{-}3)$$
$$+ 0.3517\ GNP(t\text{-}1) - 0.1300\ GNP(t\text{-}2)$$

	Std. Error	t Stat.	Beta Coeff.	Part Corr.
M(t)	.6840	3.3841	.3839	.3896
M(t-1)	.9171	− .5930	−.0901	.0739
M(t-2)	.7738	3.6098	.4596	.4113
E(t)	.2394	.9340	.0871	.1160
E(t-1)	.2405	1.5273	.1467	.1875
E(t-2)	.2364	− .8539	−.0810	.1061
E(t-3)	.2196	−3.0119	−.2695	.3523
GNP(t-1)	.1150	3.0577	.3484	.3570
GNP(t-2)	.1108	−1.1737	−.1277	.1452

R^2 adj. = .64
D.W. = 2.03

Note: Data represent quarterly changes in gross national product in current dollars as a function of quarterly changes in money supply (demand deposits plus currency in the hands of the public); quarterly changes in high-employment budget expenditures; and lagged quarterly changes in gross national product in current dollars.

fluence but less than that of the money-supply changes. Incidentally the coefficients indicate that an increase in federal expenditures will push up the rate of GNP growth in the quarter in which it occurs and the following quarter. After that it tends to slow GNP growth, contrary to what the multiplier effect of the income-expenditure theory would predict. Over a year the net effect on GNP of a federal expenditure increase is approximately zero. This result suggests that an increase in government spending in a high-

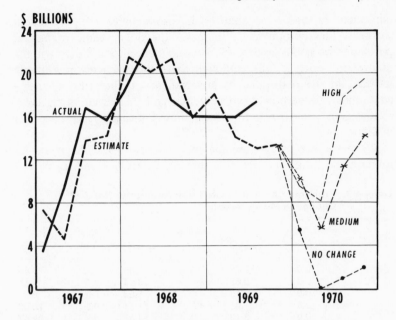

Chart 6-3.   GNP forecasts for 1970 depended upon assumptions about money-supply growth.

NOTES: See Table 6-2 for assumptions. *Chart by FNCB.*

employment economy is soon offset by reductions in private expenditures, the "crowding-out effect." Not even the federal government can call nonexistent resources into being.

It is evident that the equation tracks swings in GNP growth quite well, although it accounts for but 64 percent of the variance of GNP change over the whole period. Furthermore, some of the apparent misses were the results of major labor disputes, such as the steel strike in 1959 and the auto strike in 1964. Strikes cause actual GNP to be lower than would be estimated from money supply and federal expenditures in the quarters in which they occur and cause higher-than-predicted GNP in subsequent quarters.

The uptick of GNP growth in the third quarter of 1969 can be attributed mainly to a pay increase for federal employees. According to the conventions of national income accounting, a federal pay increase is treated entirely as a price increase and no allowance is made for changes in productivity of government workers. This automatically increases the dollar value of federal purchases of goods and services—and hence total GNP—in the quarter in which it falls, although there has been no measurable increase in the real value of government expenditures. Quarters containing a government pay increase, and there were some large increases in 1969–1971, therefore, show unusually large increases in GNP.

When we step away from the past and try to use the model to forecast the future, the ice gets thinner. Chart 6-3 and Table 6-2

Table 6-2. Projected Changes in GNP with Alternative Rates of Change in Money Supply

		No Change ΔM_1	Δ GNP	Medium ΔM_1	Δ GNP	High ΔM_1	Δ GNP
1969	4	0.0	12.99	0.4	13.46	0.4	13.46
1970	1	0.0	5.65	4.0	10.34	3.5	9.65
	2	0.0	.15	4.0	5.84	6.3	8.31
	3	0.0	1.06	4.0	11.55	10.2	18.03
	4	0.0	2.12	4.0	14.41	5.7	19.67

Note: Money-supply changes are percent changes at annual rates; GNP changes are in billions of dollars. In all cases, high-employment budget expenditures were assumed to grow at a 3 percent annual rate.

illustrate how the model was used in October, 1969, to project five quarters ahead, using the data available through third quarter 1969. For each of the projections, it was assumed that federal high-employment expenditures would continue to grow at a 3 percent annual rate. This was consistent with administration estimates of the budget at that time. The high projection was based on an assumption that the Federal Reserve would sharply reverse its policies, as it did in the fourth quarter of 1966 through fourth quarter 1967, and would thus produce a peak 10.2 percent annual rate of money-supply growth in the third quarter of 1970. For the medium projection it was assumed that money supply would grow at a 0.4 percent rate in the fourth quarter of 1969 and then at a 4 percent annual rate through the end of 1970. For the low projections, a zero rate of money-supply growth for the rest of 1969 and all of 1970 was assumed.

The most difficult problem of the monetary forecasting approach is apparent at once. To give his employers or clients a most likely forecast the forecaster must not only forecast the effects of monetary and fiscal policies, he must forecast what those policies will be. All of these assumptions were made before it was known what the Federal Reserve, the Administration, and the Congress were going to do in 1970 with the money supply and federal expenditures. This problem, of course, is not peculiar to monetarists; it plagues all forecasters. Most other forecasting methods, as a matter of fact, require making many more assumptions about autonomous variables.

By October of 1969 it was evident that the monetary deceleration of that year was likely to cause a recession, no matter what the Administration and the Federal Reserve would decide to do in 1970. All three of these projections, therefore, were recessions or minirecessions. The main question to be answered in the assumptions was how the Federal Reserve and the Administration would react to the symptoms of recession.

The low assumption was ruled out at once because it was almost inconceivable that the Federal Reserve would continue to be so restrictive during a recession, regardless of what prices or the balance of payments might be doing. Thus the Federal Reserve would surely permit money supply to grow again in 1970, but by how much? The 1967-type response, shown by the high projection, would not have significantly moderated the depth of the second-quarter trough in GNP growth but would have returned GNP growth to inflationary levels in the third and fourth quarters.

Because the highly expansive policies of 1967 caused inflation to accelerate again, thus more than canceling out all benefits of the 1966 restraints, it seemed highly likely that the monetary authorities would try to avoid that mistake in 1970. In 1967, moreover, the Federal Reserve helped the Treasury to market massive amounts of new federal securities. In the course of these operations in support of the Treasury, the Fed bought government securities, thereby increasing the reserves of the banks and expanding the money supply. Consequently, the Fed was more expansive in 1967 than it would otherwise have been. In 1970 the Treasury would not be borrowing as much as in 1967 because the budget

$ BILLIONS

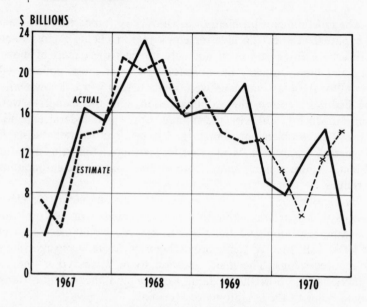

Chart 6-4. Forecasts and actual GNP changes diverged in 1970.

NOTES: See Table 6-2 for actual and predicted GNP changes. *Chart by FNCB.*

could be expected to be under much better control. This expectation was reflected in the assumption of a 3 percent growth rate for expenditures. All of these considerations made it unlikely that money supply would grow as rapidly in 1970 as it had in 1967. Therefore, some approximation of the medium assumption seemed the most useful for 1970 forecasts.

As it turned out, the medium forecast was not bad, even though the money-supply growth and federal expenditures did not conform exactly to the assumptions. Federal expenditures proved to be larger than had been assumed, and money-supply growth rates ranged from a low of 3.8 percent in the fourth quarter to a high of 7.2 percent in the second, with an average rate of 5.1 percent for the year 1970, slightly higher than the rate assumed for the best forecast.

On Chart 6-4 are plotted the model's "best" forecast from October, 1969, and the actual changes in GNP for the five forecast quarters though fourth quarter 1970. Table 6-3 compares the

Table 6-3. Actual versus Projected Changes in GNP, Money Supply, and High-Employment Budget Expenditures

		Actual GNP	Actual Δ GNP	Est. GNP	Est. Δ GNP	Actual Δ M₁	Est. Δ M₁	Actual Δ E	Est. Δ E
1969	4	951.7	9.1	956.1	13.5	1.2	0.4	7.0	3.0
1970	1	959.5	7.8	966.4	10.3	4.0	4.0	2.5	3.0
	2	971.1	11.6	972.2	5.8	7.2	4.0	27.9	3.0
	3	985.5	14.4	983.8	11.6	5.3	4.0	− 9.0	3.0
	4	989.9	4.4	998.2	14.4	3.8	4.0	4.6	3.0

Note: Money supply and high-employment budget expenditures are percent changes at annual rates, GNP figures are in billions of dollars.

actual changes of GNP in the five forecast quarters with the forecast and compares the assumed changes in money supply and the assumed high-employment budget expenditures with the actual changes.

On a quarter-by-quarter basis, there are several large errors between forecast and actual GNP changes. The largest of these, in fourth quarter of 1970, however, can be explained by the General Motors strike, which reduced GNP by about $14 billion, according to estimates of the Council of Economic Advisers. Without the strike the actual growth of GNP in that quarter would have been much closer to the forecast.

A more important error appears in the second quarter, which the model indicates should have been the lowest point in the recession. This one affects the timing of the turn from recession to recovery. Actual GNP increased much more than the forecast in the second quarter. Again an extraneous event, another large pay increase for federal employees, made reported federal purchases of goods and services, as well as GNP, larger than they would have been if the pay increase (and retroactive salary payments) had fallen in some other quarter. The pay increase appears as a 27.9 percent annual rate of increase in high-employment expenditures in the second quarter. Without that pay increase the second quarter would have been the lowest in terms of rate of growth of reported GNP.

On a cumulative-change basis, however, the quarterly errors tend to offset one another. The cumulative change for the five forecast quarters was $55.6 billion, as compared with an actual cumulative change of $47.3 billion. If an adjustment of $14 billion is added to the actual GNP change for the auto strike, the difference between the cumulative forecast and the actual is only $5.7 billion, or an error of about 9 percent.

If we add the forecast cumulative changes to actual third quarter 1969 GNP, we have a forecast GNP of $983.8 billion (annual rate) in third quarter 1970, as compared with an actual of $985.5 billion. On this basis, the forecast error is 0.2 percent. The forecast for fourth quarter 1970 is $998.2 billion, as compared with an actual of $989.9 billion. On a strike-adjusted basis, GNP was $988.5 billion in the third quarter and $1,003.9 billion in the fourth, indicating forecast errors of 0.5 percent and 0.6 percent, respectively.

In the annual forecasting derbies the main event is usually the picking of a number for gross national product for the year. The 1970 GNP forecast of our low-cost monetary model—made in October of 1969—was $980.2 billion, compared with an actual of $976.5 billion, or a strike-adjusted actual of $980.7 billion. Luck you say? But of course—in part.

The key was the assumption of a 4 percent money-growth rate, which put the projections in the right neighborhood. Had we known the money-growth rates that the Federal Reserve was actually going to provide, the model would have slightly overestimated GNP. If we could have assumed the federal expenditure rates that actually occurred, this too would have led the model to err on the high side.

In the forecast that First National City Bank actually used in 1970 the estimated current dollar GNP was $965.0 billion, or roughly $11.5 billion under the actual for the year and $15 billion under the strike-adjusted actual.[11] In the working forecast—the "judgment model"—the pure money model GNP estimates were adjusted downward to allow for a tendency of the model to underestimate the depth of recessions that can be seen on Chart 6-2. This would have been about right if the Federal Reserve and the government had behaved more nearly in accord with the policy assumptions.

The projections for 1971 and 1972 that are shown on Chart 6-5 were made with a slightly revised forecasting equation (Table

$ BILLIONS

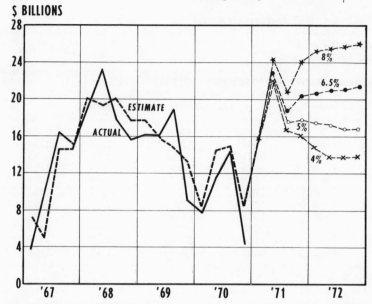

Chart 6-5. Various assumptions about money produced 1972 forecasts that ranged from recession to inflation.

NOTES: See Table 6-5 for assumptions and forecasts. *Chart by FNCB.*

6-4) and the assumptions listed in Table 6-5. This equation has a built-in adjustment for strikes, called a "strike dummy." The dummy improves the fit in strike years, although it is only a crude adjustment. For third quarter 1971, a four-week steel strike was assumed in all of the projections. Whether we like it or not, models such as these do not eliminate the need for using judgment in adjusting for special circumstances.

The projections marked 5 percent and 4 percent (for assumed money-growth rates) would have been disappointing to the Administration, unless there was a substantial slowing of the inflation rate because they would not mean a high enough growth of real GNP in 1971 to reduce unemployment. An average increase of $30 billion per quarter would be required to reach the Administration's forecast of $1,065 billion for the year. The rebound from the GM strike generated such an increase in the first quarter but not even the 8 percent track would consistently produce a $30

Table 6-4. GNP Forecasting Model

First Differences
2Q 1951—4Q 1970

$$GNP(t) = 2.0892 + 1.7776\ M(t) + .1332\ M(t-1) + 2.1016\ M(t-2)$$
$$+ .2936\ E(t) + .2663\ E(t-1) - .3017\ E(t-2) - .3700\ E(t-3)$$
$$- 2.0097\ S(t) + .3738\ GNP(t-1) - .1553\ GNP(t-2)$$

	Std. Error	t Stat.	Beta Coeff.	Part Corr.
M(t)	.6109	2.9098	.3185	.3328
M(t-1)	.8291	.1606	.0238	.0195
M(t-2)	.6848	3.0689	.3714	.3488
E(t)	.1726	1.7014	.1308	.2021
E(t-1)	.1760	1.5136	.1212	.1805
E(t-2)	.1767	−1.7073	−.1325	.2027
E(t-3)	.2017	−1.8345	−.1498	.2172
S(t)	.4658	−4.3147	−.2999	.4636
GNP(t-1)	.1007	3.7133	.3743	.4106
GNP(t-2)	.0953	−1.6293	−.1548	.1938

R^2 adj. = .69
D.W. = 1.95

Note: Data represent quarterly changes in gross national product in current dollars as a function of quarterly changes in money supply (demand deposits plus currency in the hands of the public); quarterly changes in high-employment budget expenditures; quarterly changes in a strike variable representing auto and steel strikes, derived from a man-days idle series; and lagged quarterly changes in gross national product in current dollars.

Table 6-5. Projected Changes in GNP with Alternative Rates of Change in Money Supply

		$\triangle M_1$	$\triangle$ GNP	$\triangle M_1$	$\triangle$ GNP	$\triangle M_1$	$\triangle$ GNP	$\triangle M_1$	$\triangle$ GNP
1971	1	6.5	15.67	6.5	15.67	6.5	15.67	6.5	15.67
	2	5.5	21.89	5.5	21.90	6.5	22.79	8.0	24.21
	3	4.7	16.57	5.5	17.46	6.5	18.75	8.0	20.81
	4	4.0	15.94	5.5	17.77	6.5	20.29	8.0	24.05
1972	1	4.0	14.64	5.0	17.41	6.5	20.71	8.0	25.18
	2	4.0	13.62	5.0	17.20	6.5	21.01	8.0	25.50
	3	4.0	13.61	5.0	16.75	6.5	21.06	8.0	25.66
	4	4.0	13.77	5.0	16.79	6.5	21.42	8.0	26.05

Note: Money-supply changes are percent changes at annual rates; GNP changes are in billions of dollars. In all cases, high-employment budget expenditures were assumed to grow at a 6 percent annual rate and a four-week steel strike was assumed.

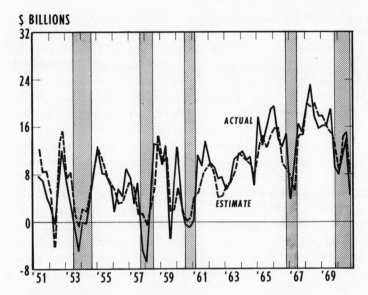

$ BILLIONS

Chart 6-6. An adjustment for strikes improves the money model.
NOTES: See Table 6-4 for forecasting equation. *Chart by FNCB.*

billion per quarter growth in nominal GNP. But an 8 percent growth rate for money supply would seem inflationary, if past experience is any guide—and that is what we have to rely on.

Just as the model tends to underestimate the depth of recessions, however, it tends to underestimate rates of expansion in recoveries. Therefore, the judgment model used for working purposes probably should adjust GNP estimates upward from those yielded by the pure money model. The economy should do better in 1971 and 1972 than this model indicated in early 1971. Actual money-supply growth in the second quarter of '71 rose to a 12 percent annual rate, far above what we had assumed was the most inflationary rate the authorities were likely to permit.

Here is where it pays to look at more than models and money and government spending. An assessment of the Administration's $1,065 billion forecast by Phillip Cagan of Columbia University in April, 1971, in effect tested the forecast for consistency by comparing it with the behavior of GNP in earlier recoveries. "It has been so long since the last recession in 1961," he said, "that we may forget that we do know something about the special character of cyclical movements."[12] In his judgment the $1,065 billion GNP would not require an exceptionally rapid expansion, as judged by the first year of other cyclical recoveries. The standard forecasters in early 1971 seemed to have forgotten the track record of the U.S. economy, for they had announced that it could not be done, as we saw in Chapter 4. The monetary authorities were far too pessimistic about the outlook in early '71. If they had not been, they would have been more careful to guard against overexpansion of the money supply.

In addition, Cagan said, the growth rate of current dollar GNP should decline after 1971, as it usually does in the second year of a cyclical recovery. Especially this time, when it was hoped that a larger and larger part of the reported GNP growth would be real rather than price change. The explosion of money-supply growth in first-half 1971 was ominous in that it pointed to a resumption of inflation.

NO MAGIC KEY

Obviously, the monetary approach to forecasting is not simple; but neither is any other forecasting method. For those who accept the initial premises that the economy is inherently stable and that money-supply changes are a principal source of disturbance, money models like the ones illustrated here have the great advantage of being sensitive to what really matters. Furthermore, they are inexpensive to build and to use, at least in comparison with the large econometric models. The simple St. Louis model, for example, has been called "our low-cost competitor" by Edward Gramlich, who works with the FRB-MIT econometric model at the Board of Governors.

Nevertheless, there are some problems that may discourage forecasters who are thinking of adopting a monetary approach:

1. Milton Friedman has often warned that the lags in money-income or money-consumption relationships are long and variable. The lags incorporated in these equations are in effect averages

of lags that may have varied considerably from period to period. Nevertheless, the conformity of the peaks and troughs in the estimated and actual GNP changes in the charts is impressive. Not only are the major recessions and expansions clearly indicated but even minor slowdowns, like the ones in 1955, 1962, and 1967, appear.

2. Numerous definitions of money or other monetary aggregates have been used by various investigators. The choice among them is more crucial to the Federal Reserve than to business forecasters, who can experiment with the readily available versions until they find the one that works best for them. Until 1966, M_2—which includes time deposits—seemed to yield slightly better results than M_1—which excluded time deposits. Unfortunately, the impact of Regulation Q ceiling rates on time deposits in 1966 and 1969 made it impossible to rely on M_2 relationships that had been estimated when the ceilings were not influencing deposit growth.

Most monetary forecasters have turned to M_1 since 1966, even though it, too, may have been distorted by the influence of the rate ceilings. The fact that both 1966 and 1969 were crucial years for forecasters made the problem even worse. Needless to say, monetarists are keenly interested in any changes the Federal Reserve may make in its methods of collecting and processing money-supply data and, to a man, they devoutly hope the Federal Reserve will never again allow rate ceilings to obscure visibility.

3. A change in monetary policy that causes money-supply growth to depart from the forecaster's earlier assumptions may ruin his forecast. This is terribly inconvenient for the forecaster whose employer has a strong revealed preference for a single-valued, 12-month forecast to cover the company's planning and budgeting period. However, there are ameliorating considerations.

Because of the lags in effects of monetary policy, and of fiscal policy too, already-observed data substantially determine the outlook for about six months; assumptions about future monetary policy become critical for the following six months. Therefore, the forecaster has a six-month grace period in which to warn his management of a change in the outlook. As information comes in suggesting that the monetary authorities are changing course, he can try new assumptions on his computer. Holding fast to a 12-month forecast just because there are 12 months in the company's fiscal year is to risk becoming irrelevant, if not unemployed.

4. The short-run effects of money-supply changes are divided between effects on real output, or income, and effects on prices. There is no easy way to sort these out, although the distinction is obviously important. For example, most economists, whether of monetary or other persuasions, badly underestimated the rate of price inflation in 1969 and some overestimated the price inflation rate for 1970.

One rule-of-thumb approach to forecasting inflation rates is to forecast current-dollar GNP changes and then to assume that an indicated growth of more than 4 percent per year means price inflation. Real GNP rarely grows at much more than 4 percent per year in the United States, nor do I believe it is likely to do so in the future. However, when nominal GNP is growing at less than a 4 percent annual rate, this does not mean falling prices. As we have seen in the post–World War II period, prices continue to rise during recessions. However, a sustained period of nominal GNP growth at less than 4 percent per year gradually reduces the inflation rate. Researchers at the Federal Reserve Bank of St. Louis and elsewhere are now incorporating sophisticated versions of this simple notion—the difference between potential and actual GNP—in price-forecasting equations.

For the typical business forecaster, however, being able to forecast the rate of price inflation accurately is not crucial to success. Working usually about one year ahead, he is most concerned with being able to tell his employers whether business is going to get better or worse and by roughly how much. A simple monetary model can do well in answering that vital question. Businesses do business in current dollars in any case. To deflate current-dollar GNP estimates, those who care to do so can use the inflation rate of the current year, modified by judgment as to whether inflation is accelerating or slowing down.

The forecasters who do need to pay close attention to their price forecasts are those who must forecast interest rates, as we shall see in the next chapter.

It is ironic that if the monetary authorities believed more strongly that money matters they could put monetarist forecasters out of business. All that monetarist forecasters do is to forecast the results of monetary policy errors, if you believe that fluctuations in money-supply growth are errors.

The business-cycle turns that are so hard for forecasters to spot are put there by the monetary authorities. If central banks were to follow a steady-growth rule in controlling the money supply, monetarists would see no signs that cycle turns were ahead. More to the point, there might be no cycle turns to pick.

MONEY AND INTEREST RATES

. . . in order to estimate the possible variation
in the rate of interest, we may, broadly speaking,
take account of the following three groups of
causes: (1) the thrift, foresight, self-control,
and love of offspring which exist in a community;
(2) the progress of inventions; (3) the changes
in the purchasing power of money. The first
cause tends to lower the rate of interest; the
second, to raise it at first and later to lower it;
and the third, to affect the nominal rate of interest
in one direction and the real rate of interest in
the opposite direction.
Irving Fisher, *The Theory of Interest,* 1930[1]

Of Irving Fisher's three causes, monetarists have learned to
concentrate on the third—the changes in the purchasing power of
money. But the educational process has not stopped with monetarists. People who earn their bread by lending in the capital
markets have rediscovered in an excruciatingly painful way a truth
that Irving Fisher had clearly explained in 1896.[2] This truth is
that changes in the purchasing power of money have powerful
effects on market interest rates—the nominal rates to which Fisher
referred.

THE REAL RATE AND THE MONEY RATE

As Fisher explained it, we should distinguish between two kinds
of interest rates: real rates and money (or nominal) rates. The real
rate is the interest rate measured in terms of goods. When some-

one lends $100 this year in order to get $105 next year, he gives up $100 worth of goods and services for what he hopes will be $105 worth of goods and services next year. We have no direct measure of this real rate. The money rate is the one we can see in the markets, where loans are measured in dollars, not goods.

If lenders and borrowers all believed that the purchasing power of money would remain constant, the real rate and the nominal rate would be the same. But people seldom, if ever, do believe that the purchasing power of money will remain constant. Therefore, the money rate of interest will be higher than the real rate if people believe prices will rise; and it will be lower than the real rate if people believe prices will fall. With prices expected to rise 5 percent per year, lenders will demand the real rate plus 5 percent so that they will be protected against the expected loss in the purchasing power of money. Borrowers will be willing to pay this 5 percent inflation premium because they expect to repay their loans with dollars worth 5 percent less per year than the dollars they borrow.

The revived Fisherian emphasis on the purchasing power of money directly contradicted a central proposition of the conventional approach to interest-rate forecasting used before 1965 because it implied that an easy-money policy would cause interest rates to rise. Most forecasters and money-market practitioners considered it an obvious fact instead that an easy-money policy would cause interest rates to fall. They accepted the traditional view that central banks could control interest rates through increasing or decreasing the supplies of credit and money and by changing the central banks' own discount rates.

The business cycle was important, in the conventional view, for two reasons: it influenced the demand for credit and it influenced credit policy and thereby influenced credit supply. The first step in anyone's interest-rate forecast, therefore, was a forecast of economic activity or GNP. After the introduction of the Federal Reserve's Flow-of-Funds Accounts in the mid-fifties, many forecasters in the United States began to project supplies of credit and demands for credit that they believed were implied by their own or other GNP forecasts. Expected federal budget deficits or surpluses played a key role in the flow-of-funds projections as well as in the GNP forecasts. The interest-rate forecasts would then depend largely on how the Federal Reserve was expected to react to the projected economic and credit-market conditions. Would the Federal Reserve allow a projected gap beetween credit demand and credit supply to be filled with bank credit? Or would it not? As a matter of fact, this flow-of-funds approach is still widely used.

The conventional approach to interest-rate forecasting had two parts of the problem right. That is, it was correct in expecting business fluctuations to push interest rates up or down. In the United States after World War II, interest-rate peaks roughly coincided with business-cycle peaks and interest-rate lows followed recession troughs by two to five months (see Chart 7-1). And the approach was correct in assuming that efforts of the Federal Reserve to counteract recessions and expansions would also push interest rates down or up, at least for a time. But even those few economists who were aware of the effects of price expectations on interest rates thought they worked so slowly that they could be safely overlooked in forecasting.

As we saw earlier, however, the Federal Reserve and other central banks struggled mightily but unsuccessfully to curb the rise of interest rates in the second half of the sixties. Interest-rate forecasts of all types, therefore, proved to be spectacularly wrong.

In 1965, on the very eve of the inflation that still bedevils the United States, prudent, farseeing portfolio managers of financial institutions bought long-term corporate bonds yielding 4½ percent or less. Investors were glad to get them because corporations were so well supplied at the time with retained earnings and depreciation allowances that they were not borrowing much. Little did these expert portfolio managers know that by mid-1970 their actual return on these bonds would prove to be less than zero because of a depreciation in the purchasing power of money that they had not foreseen. Viewed in the glaring light of hindsight, lending decisions of banks and other institutions were also costly.

It is, of course, an ill wind that blows nobody good; the corporations that had the prescience or the good luck to borrow in 1965 were handsomely rewarded for the care they took of the institutions' money over the next five years. The same thing could be said of the homeowners who had bought houses in 1965 with mortgages yielding less than 6 percent to lenders. The government borrowed well, too.

Fisher had anticipated just such a possibility when he pointed out that the influence of changes in the purchasing power of money on the money rate of interest will depend on whether or not the changes are foreseen. "If it is not clearly foreseen," he said, "a change in the purchasing power of money will not, at first, greatly affect the rate of interest expressed in terms of money."[3]

One of the most remarkable aspects of capital-market behavior in the period since 1965 is that the inflation that was not foreseen in 1965 was very quickly reflected in market interest rates. When the price level was rising less than 1½ percent per year in the early sixties (as measured by the GNP deflator), long-term bond yields were about 4½ percent or lower. In mid-1970, shortly after the rate of rise of prices approached 5½ percent, corporate bond yields hit 8½ percent. A 4 percentage-point increase in the rate of price inflation had been roughly matched by a 4 percentage-point rise in corporate bond yields. This was a more rapid adjustment than Fisher would have expected. Reverent Fisherians, consequently, underestimated the rise of rates along with nearly everyone else.

FROM THEORY TO DOGMA

For more than sixty years, Fisher's idea about the effects of inflation on interest rates had been an esoteric proposition familiar only to a few economists. The painful experience of lenders in the 1960s, however, made it a matter of dogma in the capital markets in less than five years. Now, everyone knows that price inflation means high interest rates. This suggests that the grading system used in the markets must be quite effective in eliminating slow learners.

By 1971, however, forecasters were in some danger of forgetting that changes in the purchasing power of money affect market interest rates in both directions. Most of the people who were courageous enough, or foolhardy enough, to publish their views on the future of interest rates in early 1971 agreed that inflation had much to do with pushing rates to the peaks reached in 1969 and 1970. From there on they seemed to me to divide into four main camps. One group expected rates to remain high because inflation would never be curbed. Another expected rates to remain high even if inflation were to slow down—because of real forces, such as an expected capital shortage and a decline in the propensity to save. The third group expected rates to come down because of a slowing in the inflation rate. And a fourth expected rates to be driven down by the Federal Reserve. Membership of this group grew considerably during 1970.

We should not expect to keep these forecasters confined to the camps I just mentioned. There were certain to be migrations from camp to camp. For example, the forecasters who expected rates to be driven down by the Federal Reserve were likely to join the perpetual-inflation group in expecting high and rising rates after 1972. As a matter of fact, if the Federal Reserve were to try very hard to do what they expected in 1971, we might all join those who expect perpetual inflation and high rates.

The views of all these forecasters, and of the people who inhabit the markets as well, incorporated in various ways expectations about future prices, what determines future prices, and the effects of price changes. Fisher believed that people's expectations about prices were drawn from their own experience. Furthermore, in his day most people could remember periods in which prices fell as well as periods in which prices rose. Consequently, they did not jump quickly to the conclusion that a year of rising prices meant perpetual inflation or that a short period of falling prices meant perpetual deflation.

" . . . when prices are rising," Fisher said, "the rate of interest tends to be high but not so high as it should be to compensate for the rise; and when prices are falling, the rate of interest tends to be low, but not so low as it should be to compensate for the fall."[4] Between 1965 and mid-1970, however, long rates rose higher and more quickly than can be explained by Fisher's view that price expectations and money interest rates are adjusted slowly in the light of actual price behavior.

One possible explanation for the apparent speeding up of interest-rate reactions to price inflation is that a long and accelerating rise of prices has a more powerful impact on expectations than an inflation that moves at varying speeds. We all must admit that the price rise from 1964 on was strong and convincing. Another is that expectations are influenced by other information than the actual past behavior of prices. The new ingredient is economic policy or, rather, expectations about economic policy. Instead of looking just at prices, people analyze the speeches of the monetary authorities and read the election returns to decide whether or not inflation will continue.

Whatever caused the change, the lags in interest-rate reactions to changes in prices have shortened since Fisher's day. I should amend that to say the lags in reaction to a speeding up of inflation have shortened. We cannot be sure that the lag in reaction to a slowing of inflation has shortened as much, for in 1971 we had not yet had much opportunity to observe the effects of a slowing in the rate of inflation.

LESSONS FOR THE SEVENTIES

The outlook for U.S. interest rates in the seventies, therefore, depends upon what policies the Administration and the Federal Reserve will follow, how soon and how much those policies will influence the rate of inflation, and finally, how soon and how much the change of inflation rates will influence price expectations and interest rates. To take these possibilities in turn, if the Administration and the Federal Reserve stay on the 1970–early 1971 strategy of moderation in fiscal and monetary policies, the slowing of price inflation, which had been so elusive, should become more noticeable in 1972, unless the monetary explosion of 1971 causes inflation to reaccelerate.

By 1975 the purchasing power of money could be approximately stable, as it was in the early 1960s. After all, four years of extraordinarily expansive monetary and fiscal policies were required to get the inflation started. In the absence of such policies, inflation will not continue indefinitely. Even if the price stability of the early sixties is not regained, however, the inflation rate should be considerably lower than it was when interest rates reached their peaks in 1969 and 1970.

I have already indicated that interest rates should react to a slowing of inflation by drifting gradually downward after 1971. Whatever investors may say about inflation, many have been acting for some time as though they at least do not expect the inflation rate to increase. Judging by the tremendous volume of bonds purchased by households and institutions in 1970 and 1971, the inflation premium in bond yields seemed to have eased investors' fears of future injury from inflation. If they were to see inflation actually slowing down, therefore, their appetite for fixed-income securities might increase even more.

The painful lesson to lenders in the 1960s was that unforeseen inflation brings depreciation in the bond account. The more pleasant lesson of the 1970s may be that unforeseen slowing of inflation brings capital gains for the bond buyer. Either way, the slow learners are penalized, which may account in part for the shortening of the lags that I mentioned earlier.

The Financial Research Center of Princeton University found in a survey of 137 large institutional investors in 1971 that they expected an average annual inflation rate of nearly 4 percent for the next decade.[5] A bond yielding 8 percent or more at the time of the survey would, therefore, provide them a real rate of return of 4 percent or more, if they correctly predicted the rate of inflation. If the inflation rate were to fall below 4 percent, as I expect it will, the 8 percent bond of 1971 would produce more than a 4 percent real rate of return.

If inflation were to go well above 4 percent per year, however, the investors who bought 8 percent bonds would suffer capital losses, as did those who bought 4½s in 1965. It is no wonder then that American investors have learned to keep one ear or both on Washington at all times. In interest-rate forecasting, as in forecasting the GNP, the most difficult problem is to forecast what the government and the central bank will do. In early 1971 an alarming upsurge in money supply raised the odds on another acceleration of price inflation that would drive rates higher.

Before escaping into the euphoric, less inflationary, long run, interest-rate forecasters in early 1971 had some troublesome details to clear up about the rest of the year. The U.S. economy had been below par for more than a year. Interest rates had fallen since June, 1970, as they always do in recessions. As economic activity improved in 1971, therefore, rates could be expected to rise. Nevertheless, the downward influence of the slowdown in price inflation on rates should tend to counteract the upward influence of the increase in activity. This suggested that although rates would rise again during 1971, the rises would stop far short of the previous peaks.

Another widely held view at the time, however, was that the recovery from recession would be slow, in fact, so slow that interest rates would continue to decline for much or all of 1971. The continuing decline of rates in this view would result from weakness of credit demand and from efforts of the Federal Reserve to get the economy moving again by expanding bank credit and the money supply.

Economic stagnation was the least likely outcome of the Administration's policies of curbing inflation and ending the Vietnam War. Both of these policies had contributed to unemployment by reducing demand for the products of some of this country's most important industries, including durable goods manufacturing in general and the aerospace industry in particular.

But it should not have been forgotten that the war and the space program had diverted enormous amounts of manpower and other resources from the production of many other things that Americans wanted, and still want—including millions of new houses and the community facilities required for a high-quality life. Inflation was one of the ways in which the U.S. government had extracted from an unenthusiastic electorate the real resources for the Vietnam War and the phenomenal expansion of nondefense programs that accompanied the war from 1965 through 1968. High interest rates also played a part in the diversion of capital resources from home building and from state and local governments.

The resilience and flexibility of the economy could be counted on to complete the difficult transition from war to peace speedily. Unfilled demands would not long be neglected after resources became available for filling them. There was good reason to expect a recovery that would be a revelation to those forecasters who had allowed the pressing problems of the day to rob them of historical perspective. But there was a danger that the Federal Reserve might help that recovery with too much zeal and reawaken the sleeping dragon of inflation.

THE MONETARISTS' KIT FOR INTEREST-RATE FORECASTING

The revival of Fisher's view of interest-rate determination certainly improved the forecasting of interest rates but did not make it simple or foolproof. His contribution was the emphasis on the influence of price expectations, which had been a glaring oversight on the part of most forecasters. The new monetarists have added the improvements in forecasting fluctuations in business activity that were covered in the preceding chapter.

Monetarists' forecasting models now try to capture three different effects of money-supply changes on interest rates. The first is the familiar liquidity effect, the short-run tendency of an increase in money-supply growth to reduce interest rates. This one turns out to be surprisingly weak as compared with the others.

The second is the income effect, the tendency of an increase in money-supply growth to increase income six to nine months later and thereby to increase demands for credit and money and to raise rates. The projections of a GNP model like the one in the preceding chapter are used by some forecasters as the income variable in interest forecasting equations.

Some forecasters, myself included, were so pleased to have discovered the tendency of the income effect of money-supply changes on interest rates to offset the liquidity effect that they were led to forecast too early a turnaround of interest rates in 1969, when monetary policy became restrictive. Earlier periods of monetary restraint in the United States, such as 1959 and 1966, had resulted in slowdowns of economic activity and declines in interest rates well before the monetary authorities relaxed the restraints.

From early 1969 on, therefore, monetarist forecasters watched

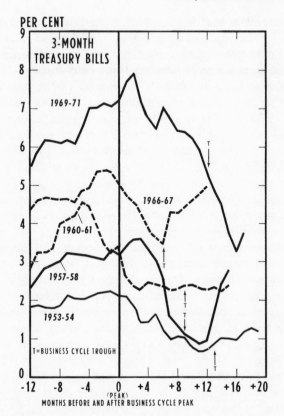

Chart 7-1. Interest rates peak near business-cycle peaks and turn up soon after cycle troughs.

NOTES: Monthly average yields on three-month Treasury bills. Dating of cyclical peaks and troughs by National Bureau of Economic Research and First National City Bank (1966–1967). *Chart by FNCB.*

and waited for a downturn in interest rates that did not come. Short-term interest rates peaked in December of 1969 and long-term rates did not peak until the following June. When interest rates finally did fall, however, the decline was greater than everyone expected.

The most plausible explanation for expecting the interest-rate turnaround in 1969 too early was that expectations of price inflation continued to carry rates on upward even after the 1969–1970 business recession had begun. The monetarist forecasters were correct in forecasting a recession that would cause rates to fall. But they made two mistakes. The first was to underestimate the amount and persistence of inflation from 1965 through 1970 and the second was to underestimate the impact of the inflation and possible other factors upon expectations and rates. As I said earlier, the 1965–1970 adjustment of interest rates to price inflation was in the direction predicted by Irving Fisher but was much more rapid than he would have expected. Needless to say, forecasters have been working feverishly since 1969 to improve their ability to forecast price-inflation rates and to learn more about how price expectations are formed. Although we believe major improvements have been made, we will not know for sure until we have observed more cycles of inflation and recession.

What causes the stability of the anticipated real interest rate is still, to me, largely a mystery. The real rate seems to be influenced by slow-moving forces of population changes, technological changes, and the willingness of people to defer consumption today for greater consumption in the future. Some economists who study the determinants of economic growth argue that the real rate is equal to the long-run rate of growth of real output, for it is the yield of the total stock of real capital in all forms. In any case, forecasters probably will not be too badly misled if they assume the real rate to be nearly stable while they focus on the forces that make nominal rates fluctuate around it.

The forecaster's problem is compounded also by the obvious fact that there is no such thing as "the" interest rate, whether real or nominal. What he faces is a vast array of particular market rates on short-term and long-term instruments ranging from commercial paper to home mortgages. Demand-supply analyses, such as the flow-of-funds approach, will still be necessary for moving to the rates for particular instruments from the forecast levels of a few key rates that can be provided by monetarist models.

There is no danger of a collapse in the real rate, in my opinion. The world economy is certainly not heading into another depression that would paralyze saving and investment. Nor do we have much reason to expect the real rate to be substantially higher than it has been in the past decade, despite the fears of a capital shortage. The real rate on high-quality corporate bonds should remain around 3 or 4 percent in the United States, as it has for many years. The more difficult questions concern how large an inflation premium will be included in the money rates that we can see in the markets and how savers and investors will react to the economic policies of governments.

The most damaging feature of the inflationary environment in which the capital markets labored after 1965 was not price inflation, although that was damaging enough. Given time, money interest rates could adjust to a steady rate of price inflation, as Fisher predicted, so that interest rates and the markets could do their work of allocating capital resources smoothly and efficiently. Far more damaging was the uncertainty about how much inflation there would be and what, if anything, would be done about it.

Fears of direct credit controls in the United States surely made interest rates higher in the sixties than they would otherwise have been. Fearing they might at some time be cut off from credit suppliers, especially banks, corporations borrowed more than they needed and were willing to pay commitment fees for funds they had not yet borrowed. Lenders, furthermore, were more reluctant to lend than they would have been if the monetary authorities had not been so determined to reduce bank lending to businesses. Large banks, effectively cut off from domestic time-deposit funds by Regulation Q ceilings on the rates they were allowed to pay, were afraid they would eventually be cut off from their alternative sources in the Eurodollar market. After Regulation Q was suspended on large negotiable certificates of deposit in June, 1970, the fears of borrowers and lenders were quickly dispelled and interest rates fell. Nevertheless, the interest-rate effects of controls imposed by governments in capital markets are extremely difficult to forecast.

The lingering uncertainty about economic policies delayed recognition in wage and price decisions of a movement toward price stability that should not be, but could be, aborted. Most helpful in dispelling uncertainty about the future purchasing power of money in the United States was the announced determination of the Administration and the Federal Reserve to avoid after 1968 the wide swings in fiscal and monetary policies that had brought confusion and disorder to the capital markets in the first place. The swing to highly expansionary monetary policy in early 1971 was disconcerting evidence that monetary instability had not yet been eliminated. But it was not yet too late to bring money under control. If the Federal Reserve eventually demonstrates through its actions that the prospect for stability can become more widely accepted, interest rates and the markets will behave as Fisher would say they should. Thrift, foresight, self-control, love of offspring, and the progress of inventions will replace changes in the purchasing power of money as the key determinants of money interest rates.

MONEY AND THE STOCK MARKET

Let the market bother me? Why of course not!
I go home at night and sleep like a baby. I wake
up every two hours and cry.
Anonymous stockbroker, May, 1970

The "see-through" theory that became popular in the late sixties
was the latest variant of the old Wall Street truism that stock
prices lead the business cycle. This new version, however, called for
a more robust faith, or perhaps more credulity, than did its predecessors. It was used in 1969 to predict an upturn in stock prices
that should precede a business recovery that should follow a business downturn that hadn't even begun at the time the prediction
became popular. But the prediction of a fall upturn in stock prices
in 1969 turned out to be wrong. So did the prediction of a spring
upturn in 1970. Not until the fall upturn in 1970 did stock prices
step out to lead an upturn in business.

THE "SEE-THROUGH" THEORY

If we look for the foundations of this now somewhat disheveled,
but still beguiling, faith, we find that beliefs about how the Federal
Reserve would react to inflation and unemployment were prominent among them. Monetarism may have made slow headway in
converting academic economists and the monetary authorities, but
Wall Street fell without even token resistance. The *Wall Street*

Journal, for example, reported from a typical daily sampling of brokers' opinions in November, 1969:

Another factor that buoyed prices somewhat, brokers stated, was news that industrial output fell in October for the third month in a row, the longest such downtrend period since early 1967; it raised hopes that it will prove persistent enough to damp the inflationary expectations among businessmen. Also, Kenneth Davis, Jr., Assistant Secretary of Commerce, said yesterday, "We are beginning to win our fight against inflation and we are confident that it will be brought under control without a recession."[1]

With the benefit of such on-line, real-time analysis, the Dow-Jones industrial average rose nearly three points that day.

On the following day, brokers cited Argus Research, a leading investment research firm:

A statement by Argus Research Corp. that "the accumulation of new figures seems to support the proposition that some kind of a recession is under way" was received with mixed feelings, brokers said. It intensified fears that the economy would sustain a severe setback, they explained, but it also raised hopes that the day was nearing when the Federal Reserve Board could relax credit restrictions.[2]

Despite the encouraging news about the onset of recession, however, the Dow-Jones average fell five points.

These examples may be exaggerated, but they do reveal some of Wall Street's respect for the awesome power of monetary policy. There appear to be the ingredients here of a perpetual motion machine for explaining stock price fluctuations: Changes in economic conditions change monetary policy, which changes stock prices and economic conditions, which change monetary policy and so on around again. In this chapter, therefore, the several links in this self-propelling cycle are examined to see if it does indeed furnish a good basis for predicting movements in stock prices.

The monetary authorities, too, have been impressed with their influence on stock prices. A confirmation of monetary-policy effects on stock prices and consumer spending was reported by J. Dewey Daane, member of the Board of Governors of the Federal Reserve

System. Describing the results of work with a large econometric model at the Board, he said:

The way monetary policy affects consumption is, in considerable part, through its impact on the value of equities. I suppose it will come as a surprise to no one that monetary policy is revealed to have a potent effect on the stock market. And it turns out, according to this research, that fluctuations in equity prices seem to have a measurable direct effect on consumption.[3]

The National Bureau of Economic Research includes an index of 500 common stock prices on its list of leading indicators for identifying business-cycle turns.[4] The stock-price index has a median lead of four months before both upturns and downturns and scores higher by National Bureau timing criteria than any other indicator on the list. In spite of the jokes about how the stock market has predicted five out of the last four recessions, stock prices are strongly related in some way to business fluctuations and monetary policy. The simplest way to use money supply for stock-price forecasting, therefore, is to use it as a leading indicator. Changes in money-supply growth lead changes in stock prices and changes in stock prices lead the business cycle, usually. But why?

MONEY, PROFITS, AND STOCK PRICES

In Chart 8-1 it can be seen that stock prices tend to lead corporate profits. That is, there usually has been a dip in stock prices before each dip in profits. Stock prices generally turn around and head upward again before profits even reach bottom. One might infer from this that investors are good forecasters of cyclical swings in profits. This I doubt because the consensus economic forecast, as we saw earlier, has had a dismal record at business-cycle turns.

The strength of business is generally exaggerated by the consensus view at cycle peaks and the strength of recoveries is underestimated at cycle troughs. Although I have no sample of profit forecasts to prove it, I suspect that investors and security analysts

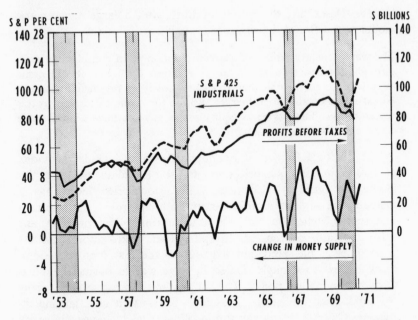

Chart 8-1. Money-supply changes lead stock prices and stock prices lead changes in profits over business cycle.

NOTES: S&P 425 Industrials—monthly-average, Standard and Poor's Index of 425 Industrials; Profits before taxes—quarterly averages, Department of Commerce series, seasonally adjusted, all U.S. corporations in billions of dollars; Change in money supply—quarterly changes in money supply (demand deposits and currency) at seasonally adjusted annual percentage rates. Shaded areas—recessions identified by National Bureau of Economic Research and 1966–1967 minirecession (dated by FNCB). *Chart by FNCB.*

have a similar tendency to extrapolate recent rates of earnings growth and thus to be slow in recognizing turns.

There is no doubt that the sharp fall of profits in 1970 surprised many analysts, largely because company managements were surprised also. According to the monetarist view, the swings in both stock prices and profits can be explained by changes in the rate of growth of money supply, which generally lead both on the chart. Monetary forecasters predicted a drop in profits for 1970 from the behavior of the money supply in 1969 and a rise in profits in 1971 from the behavior of the money supply in 1970.

Chart 8-2 presents the results of an attempt to estimate a rela-

INDEX POINTS

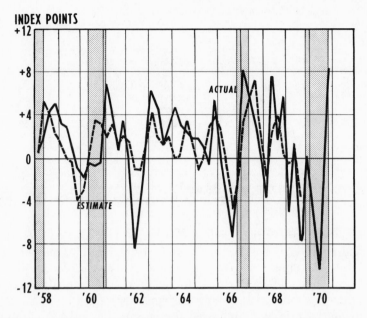

Chart 8-2. A simple money model predicts major swings in stock prices.

NOTES: See Table 8–1 for forecasting equation. Changes are quarterly changes of Standard and Poor's Index of 425 Industrials, in index points. *Charts by FNCB.*

tionship between quarterly changes in money supply and quarterly changes in Standard and Poor's Index of 425 Industrials. The objective here was to find a way to estimate not just when money-supply changes influence stock prices, but by how much. The equation is presented in Table 8-1. The solid line plots the actual quarterly changes in the index, and the broken line plots changes estimated by the equation from the money-supply changes that occurred over the period.

This equation explains 38 percent of the variance in stock price changes with money-supply changes over the year preceding the quarter being predicted. That is quite good when one considers how many different forces are believed to affect the stock market. An examination of the chart makes it clear that the estimating equation is wide of the mark in particular quarters but tracks

Table 8-1. Stock Price Model 1958 (1)–1969 (3)

First Differences

$SP(t) = .9981 + 2.0170\ M(t) - 1.6279\ M(t\text{-}2) - .3201\ M(t\text{-}4)$

	Std. Error	t Stat.	Beta Coeff.	Part Corr.
M(t)	.4156	4.8533	0.6227	.5949
M(t-2)	.4436	−3.6697	− .5201	.4884
M(t-4)	.4193	−0.7633	− .1002	.1156

R^2 adj. = .38
D.W. = 1.84

Note: Data represent quarterly changes in Standard and Poor's 425 Industrials Index as a function of quarterly changes in money supply (demand deposits plus currency in the hands of the public).

major swings in prices quite well, such as the cycles of 1960–1961 and 1966–1967 and the decline from 1968 into third quarter 1969.

In 1962, money-supply changes indicated a small decline in stock prices, but nothing like the market break that actually occurred. Folklore of the market now attributes the ferocity of that break to the historic eyeball-to-eyeball confrontation between President Kennedy and the steel industry over prices. Whether or not the Administration argument with the steel industry caused the break in stock prices, the break in stock prices helped to change Administration policy. The May market break apparently was a factor in turning the Kennedy Administration toward the major tax cut the President proposed in June. However, by August the shock of the market break apparently had faded because the tax cut was postponed.

This evidence implies that major turns in money-supply growth promptly influence stock prices. The main impact of a money-supply change on stock prices appears in the same quarter. Furthermore, much of the effect of a money-supply change on the rate of change in stock prices appears to wear off in about six months and the rest within a year. Thus, on average, if there is a large increase in the money supply in a quarter, the rate of rise in stock prices should increase in that same quarter and then fall back to its longer-run average rate over the next several months, even if the high rate of money-supply expansion persists. Another acceleration in monetary expansion would be required to keep stock prices rising faster than the average rate represented by the constant term of the equation (approximately one index point per quarter from 1958 through third quarter 1969).

From a forecaster's viewpoint, it would be far more convenient if a change in money supply in a quarter was followed in the next quarter, or even later, by a change in stock prices. Beryl Sprinkel's long survey of stock prices indicates that this was true years ago, before so many people believed in the influence of money on stock prices or had timely money-supply data.[5] Over the period covered by Chart 8-2 the lags appear to have shortened. Thus, the estimated changes led the actual in the early years and followed in the later years. This suggests that as investors learned to pay more attention to money supply they reacted more quickly to signs of monetary policy change. In fact until 1970 they appeared to have been anticipating policy changes even before changes occurred. This implies that to forecast a change in stock prices one must first correctly forecast a change in money supply, no mean task, as we saw in the preceding chapter.

Moreover, unless the change in money supply is a large one, it is likely to be offset by any of the many other forces affecting stock prices. As a matter of fact, the money-supply effect might be offset in any particular quarter. This can be seen from the instances on the chart in which there were large deviations between estimated and actual changes. Therefore, he who dares to call a turn in stock prices from money supply must not only forecast a substantial change in money supply but must also forecast one that will persist for several quarters. This is not easy, but it might be done once in a while. The Federal Reserve, after all, has sharply reversed its policies several times within the past decade.

WHAT HAPPENED IN 1970?

Having stated a few propositions about what is required to forecast stock prices with a simple money-supply model, it is time to get down to an illustration of how they might be applied. Chart 8-3 illustrates the problem with stock-price projections that were made

INDEX POINTS

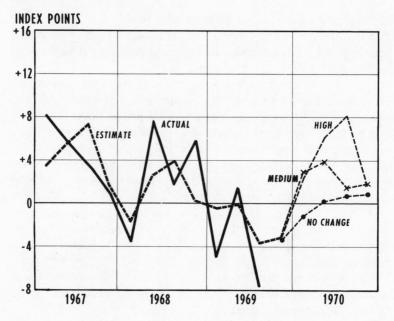

Chart 8-3. Stock-price forecasts for 1970 depended upon assumptions about money-supply growth.

NOTES: See Table 8-2 for assumptions and forecasts. *Chart by FNCB.*

in October, 1969, based on three different assumptions about monetary policy. The forecasting equation is the same one used in Chart 8-2. Under all three assumptions, stock prices would be expected to rise in 1970, as implied by the see-through theory. However, there would be wide variations in timing and magnitude.

For the high money-supply growth projections on Chart 8-3, it was assumed that the Federal Reserve would sharply reverse its policies, as it had in the fourth quarter of 1966 through fourth quarter 1967. This is the high assumption used in the GNP projections of Chapter 6. Something not much different from this assumption appears to have been behind some of the more bullish forecasts that circulated in the market in 1969. The bulls seemed to expect the Federal Reserve to respond strongly to the first hint of recession in the air.

For the medium projection it was assumed that the Federal

Reserve would permit the money supply to grow at just under a 1 percent annual rate in the fourth quarter of 1969 and then at a 4 percent annual rate through the end of 1970. For the low projection a zero rate of growth of money supply for the rest of 1969 and all of 1970 was assumed.

It is important to remember that these projections reflected only monetary influences on stock prices, and an ultra-simple version of the money-stock-price relationship at that. Before basing any decisions on them an investor should have tried to adjust them for the effects of other factors that could change profits expectations, such as progress, or lack of it, in settling the Vietnam War.

A virtual explosion in stock prices would have been produced by the turnaround in monetary policy assumed for the high projections. It is also interesting that this high-growth projection implied a continuing decline in stock prices in fourth quarter 1969 because the assumed turn toward monetary ease did not come until first quarter 1970. Some market forecasters in October, 1969, thought the turn in stock prices would lead the turn in money-supply growth simply because monetary policy was so restrictive at that time that an easing was sure to come soon.

What would happen if expectations of a monetary policy change were not soon validated by Federal Reserve action is a good question. The October, 1969, rally and the subsequent November-May slump in stock prices appear to have followed just such a scenario of high hopes for an easier monetary policy followed by disappointment.

The medium assumption of a 4 percent money-growth rate implied a moderate rise in stock prices. The zero-growth assumption implied a continuing fall in stock prices through the first quarter of 1970 and then a return to slowly rising prices by the fourth quarter. This rather surprising result stems from the constant term of the regression equation. In the absence of any money-supply effect, the equation would predict a rise of one index point per quarter, or four index points per year. However, there was no comparable, long-sustained period of zero money-supply growth in the years over which the equation was fitted. As indicated by the GNP projections in Chapter 6, such a long period without any growth in money supply would produce a severe recession. In that case, investors' earnings expectations probably would change, making it unlikely that stock prices would behave in the way projected here. The medium assumption thus seemed to be the most likely, for the reasons given in discussing the GNP projections in Chapter 6. (See Table 8-2 for the assumptions and projections.)

Table 8-2. Projected Changes in S&P425 Industrials with Alternative Rates of Change in Money Supply

		— No Change —		— Medium —		— High —	
		$\triangle$ M$_1$	$\triangle$ S&P425	$\triangle$ M$_1$	$\triangle$ S&P425	$\triangle$ M$_1$	$\triangle$ S&P425
1969	4	0.0	−3.45	0.4	−3.04	0.4	−3.04
1970	1	0.0	−1.07	4.0	2.96	3.5	2.36
	2	0.0	.29	4.0	4.00	6.3	6.22
	3	0.0	.77	4.0	1.55	10.2	8.09
	4	0.0	1.00	4.0	1.91	5.7	1.74

Note: Stock prices are Standard & Poor's 425 Industrials Index (1941−1943=10), money-supply changes are percent changes at annual rates.

The next chart (8-4) shows what actually happened to stock prices in 1970, compared with the "best" projection (Table 8-3). It can readily be seen that the performance of the equation left much to be desired.

Comparing the cumulative changes is no comfort either. If the estimated cumulative changes for the five forecast quarters are added to the actual level of the S&P Index for third quarter 1969, we would have a fourth quarter 1970 forecast level of 111.1. The

Table 8-3. Actual versus Projected Changes in S&P425 Industrials, and Money Supply

		Actual S&P	Actual $\triangle$ S&P	Est. S&P	Est. $\triangle$ S&P	Actual $\triangle$ M$_1$	Est. $\triangle$ M$_1$
1969	4	103.80	.12	100.64	−3.04	1.2	0.4
1970	1	97.36	− 6.44	103.60	2.96	4.0	4.0
	2	86.71	−10.65	107.60	4.00	7.2	4.0
	3	86.35	− .36	109.15	1.55	5.3	4.0
	4	94.72	8.37	111.06	1.91	3.8	4.0

Note: Stock prices are Standard and Poor's 425 Industrials Index (1941−1943=10), money-supply figures are percent changes at annual rates.

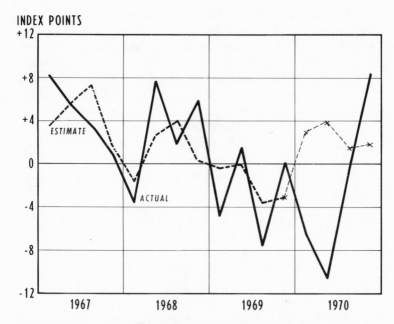

INDEX POINTS

Chart 8-4. The simple money model forecast an upturn for stock prices in first-half 1970, but prices actually went down.

NOTES: See Table 8-3 for actual and predicted stock-price changes. *Chart by FNCB.*

actual for the quarter was 94.7. Stock prices were finally moving in the right direction, but they were still a long way from where they would have been if the forecast had been accurate.

The error was not produced by mistakes in predicting monetary policy. Although monetary policy turned in the first quarter and was more liberal than assumed for the medium projections for most of the year, stock prices continued to fall at a sickening rate until the third quarter. Anyone who had speculated in stocks on margin in fourth quarter 1969 in expectation of a strong rebound in early 1970 would have felt as if he were suspended over hell on a spider-web through much of that year. That is, if his broker did not sell him out in the May-June panic. Let this be a lesson.

There are no projections for 1971 on the chart. This equation should go back to the drawing board. Michael Keran, of the

Federal Reserve Bank of St. Louis, has reported in an article in the Federal Reserve Bank of St. Louis *Review* that he tested a more sophisticated stock-price model, which also failed to perform well in 1970.[6] He believes that an important but basically random shock pushed stock prices down temporarily in the second quarter of 1970 and the normal relationships between stock prices and the variables he used were not restored until the fourth quarter. He singled out the Cambodian incursion and the campus riots of May, 1970, as events that may have depressed stock prices by increasing investors' uncertainty. The possibility that such events may recur should make us more cautious in attempting to forecast stock prices.

HOW MONEY AFFECTS STOCK PRICES

The theory of the demand for money, which we discussed in the first chapter, provides a plausible explanation of how money-supply changes affect stock prices. When there is a sudden increase, or contraction, in money supply, nominal cash balances in the hands of the public may be greater or less than the amounts people want to hold. In trying to adjust their cash holdings, therefore, people might first be expected to buy or sell financial assets, including stocks, thus influencing prices and yields.

In discussing the impact of an increase in monetary growth during a recession, Milton Friedman and Anna Schwartz have said:

... we should expect it to have its first impact on the financial markets, and there, first on bonds, and only later on equities, and only still later on actual flows of payments for real resources. This is of course the actual pattern. The financial markets tend to revive well before the trough. Historically, railroad bond prices have risen very early in the process. Equity markets start to recover later but still generally before the business trough. Actual expenditures on purchases of goods and services rise still later.[7]

In the later stages of this adjustment the influence on stock prices may be just the opposite of the initial effect. After having initially been induced by a money-supply increase to buy stocks, some investors might later sell stocks in order to buy other assets as they complete their adjustment to the change in monetary policy.

The first-round effect of a money-supply change could be called the liquidity effect and is the one relied upon by people who use the leading indicator approach to forecasting stock prices. It accounts for the positive first-quarter effect of money-supply changes in our equation. To put it another way, it is a change in the rate at which investors discount the expected flow of corporate earnings.

When interest rates are high, the present value of a dollar of future income is less than it would be if interest rates were low. The lower the rate of discount the greater is the present value of a given flow of expected future income. Therefore bonds, which are titles to future money payments, fall in price when interest rates rise and rise in price when interest rates fall. The same reasoning should apply to stocks, which also are titles to future payments. Any particular flow of expected future dividends, therefore, is worth less when interest rates (and the investors' rate of discount) are high than when they are low. With stocks, there is the additional complication that the amounts of future dividends are uncertain.

For a first approximation we might assume that investors' expectations regarding the earnings flow are not changed by the money-supply change. But, as more and more people are becoming aware, a monetary-policy change will also change corporate profits several months later. Thus there should be a secondary effect of a monetary-policy change on stock prices through a change of investors' earnings expectations. The greater attention being given to money-supply effects may well increase the impact of this profits-expectation effect in the future by making monetary forecasters out of more investors.

The equation illustrated here does not make explicit allowance for changing profit expectations. When we included corporate profits at quarter t (the quarter for which we are attempting to forecast stock prices) as a variable, the performance of the estimating equation was considerably improved. As a matter of fact, the R^2, or percentage of variance accounted for, rose to 45 percent. This suggests that the earnings expectations of investors are influenced by the current level of profits. To use it for forecasting stock prices, however, we would also have to forecast profits.

From Keran's work it is now apparent that people who believe an increase in money-supply growth will usually or always push stock prices up are making the same mistake as those who believe an increase in money-supply growth will usually or always push interest rates down. There is a short-run liquidity effect in both cases that is in line with the popular belief. But investors must be concerned with what happens after the immediate liquidity effect. Furthermore, the liquidity effect in a particular quarter can be offset by the delayed effects of money-supply changes in earlier quarters.

In the late 1960s excessive money-supply growth brought on inflation. As we saw in Chapter 7, expectations of future inflation caused interest rates to rise. Although many people believe that equities are a good hedge against inflation, this common belief overlooks the effects of inflation on interest rates. The rise of interest rates raised investors' rates of discount, thereby depressing the prices of outstanding bonds and stocks. Keran's estimates indicate that the depressing effect of rising interest rates on stock prices was more important than the liquidity effect of accelerating money-supply growth.

Inflation, furthermore, does not help corporate earnings, except for a brief time in the very early stages, when selling prices tend to rise faster than some important business costs. As the inflation matures, and this one certainly did, any costs that may have been lagging catch up and earnings growth slows down. This is when businessmen start worrying about "cost-push" inflation and profit squeezes. In the late 1960s and in 1970 the depressing effects of high interest rates on stock prices were reinforced by reductions in expected earnings.

More sophisticated models, such as the ones developed by Keran and others, undoubtedly will improve our understanding of movements in stock prices by identifying and measuring more of their determinants. We should not expect to see a push-button stock-price forecaster, however. The relationships are too variable.

What these models do demonstrate is the powerfully destabilizing influence of volatile monetary policies on a major part of the public's wealth and savings. Most Americans today have a stake in the stock market through direct investment, stock options, and stock-purchase plans where they work and through pension funds, most of which are heavily invested in equities. Stock ownership is spreading rapidly in other countries as well. It behooves the monetary authorities, therefore, to think of how they may be affecting this wealth when they swing from one extreme to another in their policies.

BEYOND 1971

Major swings in monetary policy undoubtedly have contributed to major swings in stock prices, but they have by no means been the only important source of price fluctuations. Although there are many pitfalls, as we have just seen, watching for monetary policy changes has made it possible to forecast some of these major changes in stock prices. A forecaster might well continue to rely on the familiar cycle of easy money—rising stock prices—price inflation—tight money—falling stock prices—recession—easy money—rising stock prices. However, I would like to suggest that this cycle might not persist indefinitely.

One way the pattern may change is through a return to the price stability that the U.S. economy enjoyed between 1959 and 1964. This may seem a strange thing to say at a time when much of the financial community is still learning how to cope with the inflation that began in 1965. Nevertheless, it could be a costly mistake for investors and portfolio managers to assume that inflation will not, or cannot, be brought under control.

What would a return to price stability mean to the stock market? Part of the answer lies in what it would do to corporate profits. Just as an unanticipated increase in price inflation temporarily increases corporate profits, an unanticipated slowdown in the rate of inflation can be expected to depress profits. This may have a tendency to slow the rise in stock prices while the inflation is decelerating. If investors begin to expect less price inflation, demand for equities as an inflation hedge will also be reduced. These effects should be temporary, however.

In 1970 the high level of bond yields was mentioned by many analysts as a reason for the failure of stock prices to rise when monetary policy eased in the first quarter. This was the first time in some years that bond yields had been given much attention in discussion of stock prices. But there is something to the argument when one compares the expected yields on stocks and bonds.

The realized yield (dividends plus price appreciation) between 1926 and 1960 on a random portfolio of common stocks listed on the New York Stock Exchange was about 9.7 percent, according to the Merrill Foundation study at the University of Chicago.[8] Between 1955 and 1960 the yield was 11.2 percent. The equity yield on a large pension fund from the beginning of 1957 through the end of 1969 was 10.1 percent.[9] The "gun-slingers" who offered their services as portfolio managers in the Soaring Sixties commonly promised considerably higher yields. Bond yields, until 1969, were obviously unexciting by comparison. Realized yields (coupon minus price depreciation) on bonds bought, say, in 1965, were even lower, in fact negative, as we saw in the preceding chapter. It is no wonder that institutional investors shifted heavily into stocks in the 1960s.

By the middle of 1970, however, current bond yields stood at 8.5 percent or higher, where they had roughly adjusted for an expected 4 percent to 5 percent rate of price inflation. They, therefore, were not much below the historic average yield on stocks. Furthermore, the 500 stocks in Standard and Poor's Composite Index had, as a group, produced a *negative* realized yield between the end of 1967 and mid-1970, just as bonds had done. If price inflation becomes no worse, the investors who bought bonds in 1969 and 1970 will realize at least the 8–9 percent coupon yields. If inflation slows down and interest rates fall accordingly, the bond investors of 1969 and 1970 will also have capital gains, making their realized yields somewhat higher than the coupon yields. Stocks, on the other hand, might have trouble making the long-run 9–12 percent yield, even with higher dividends, if many investors switch to bonds. Stocks should, however, do better than 9–12 percent while recovering from the abnormally depressed levels of mid-1970.

However, the effects of inflation on stock prices are more complicated than they might seem at first. For example, Al Burger, of the St. Louis Federal Reserve Bank, has found that stockholders as a group fared better in the four stable-price years, 1960–1964, than in the four inflation years, 1964–1968.[10] The Keran analysis makes it clear why this should be so. Therefore, it should be obvious that stockholders do not have a vested interest in inflation.

A second radical change to consider would be a shift by the Federal Reserve to paying more attention to money supply and less to interest rates as guides to monetary policy. If this were done, fluctuations in money-supply growth would be considerably reduced. The Federal Reserve made such a shift in January, 1970, and held to it rather well through that year. Although the Federal Reserve reverted to its preoccupation with interest rates in 1971, the results were so damaging to the U.S. economy that another try at controlling the money supply could be expected.

If, as I have argued, instability in money-supply growth is an important source of instability in stock prices, getting the money supply under better control would make the stock market more stable. This should increase price-earnings ratios and thus increase stock prices.

The volume of trading would probably be smaller in a less volatile market, for investors would presumably have fewer occasions for switching into or out of stocks. Security analysts and portfolio managers could concentrate more on problems of selecting issues and would be less likely to have their appraisals of earnings prospects upset by unforeseen cyclical disturbances.

The behavior of the money supply in the first half of 1971 was unsettling evidence that the era of steady money growth and stable securities markets had not yet arrived. Therefore, those who try to forecast stock prices from changes in the money supply may yet have a chance to improve on their 1970 performance.

three
_____

THE MECHANICS
OF CONTROLLING
MONEY

9

THE FEDERAL RESERVE AND THE U.S. MONEY SUPPLY

The first necessity of a Central Bank, charged
with responsibility for the management of the
monetary system as a whole, is to make sure that
it has an unchallengeable control over the total
volume of bank money created by its Member
Banks.

John Maynard Keynes, *A Treatise on Money,*
1930[1]

Money-supply changes cause inflation and recession, as the
1960s amply demonstrated. Central bankers, who may be blamed
when something goes wrong, could therefore be expected to follow
Keynes' advice to the letter. In particular, they could be expected
to learn everything they could about how to make their control
over money unchallengeable.

Until recently, however, more research into how central-bank
actions influence the money supply has probably been done by outsiders looking into the central banks than by insiders looking out.
There have been several apparent reasons for this. An early one
was the idea, now generally disavowed by central bankers, that
money does not matter. Another was a belief that although central
banks might control the money supply they have other, more important, things to do. This argument will be set aside for later
attention because it is still alive and well in several countries. A
final argument was the washing-of-hands plea that central banks
cannot control the money supply directly or could not do so well
enough to make the effort worthwhile. This one, too, has lost force,

as the costs of leaving money unmanaged have become ever more apparent. For, after all, there is no one else who can manage the money supply if the central banks do not. Their research departments are now making up for the earlier neglect of this important subject.

THEY SAID IT COULDN'T BE DONE

At some point or other most of us have been exposed to a classroom demonstration of the multiple-expansion process, or bookkeepers' alchemy, through which an addition to the reserve base of the banking system is said to result in a several-fold increase in bank deposits. A tough-minded student may reject the whole thing as implausible or come away with a smoldering distrust of institutions that appear able to create or destroy money with strokes of the pen or, in these days, by directing electric impulses through the ganglia of computers.

The Federal Reserve, too, has reacted against the classroom explanation of money-supply determination. Commenting on problems of attempting to control the money supply, Sherman J. Maisel, Member of the Board of Governors, has said:

> Many unsophisticated comments and theories speak as if the Federal Reserve purchases a given quantity of securities, thereby creating a fixed amount of reserves, which through a multiplier determines a particular expansion in the money supply.
>
> Much of modern monetary literature is actually spent trying to dispel this naïve elementary textbook view . . .
>
> The growth of the money supply in any period is the result of actions taken by the Federal Reserve, the Treasury, the commercial banks, and the public. Over a long period, the Fed may play a paramount role, but this is definitely not the case in the short run . . . —to the best of my knowledge—*the Fed has not attempted to control, within very wide limits, the growth of the narrowly defined money supply in any week or month* [italics added].[2]

There is an engagingly schizophrenic air about this discussion, for the Board of Governors of the Federal Reserve has assiduously propagated the "naïve elementary textbook view" for many years in some of its official publications. My thumbworn 1954 edition of *The Federal Reserve System: Purposes and Functions* contains a chapter which winds up with an apt summation:

Aside from [some] qualifications, what is significant from the standpoint of reserve banking operations is that the issuance of a given amount of high-powered money by the Federal Reserve may generate a volume of ordinary money which is several times as large as the amount issued, and that, on the other hand, Federal Reserve extinguishment of a given amount of high-powered money may result in a reduction of several times that amount in loans and investments and in demand deposits, that is, in ordinary money.[3]

By the time of the 1961 edition, faith in the multiple-expansion process had apparently risen. Where the writers of the 1954 edition had said "may generate" and "may result," their 1961 counterparts said "will generate" and "will result." Anyone who wants to refresh his memory of how the multiple-expansion process works as new reserve funds are diffused through the banking system can find a well-illustrated discussion of it in *Purposes and Functions*.

In any case, the Federal Reserve has tried occasionally since January, 1970, to do what it had not yet attempted at the time Governor Maisel wrote his paper. On January 15 the Federal Open Market Committee concluded that "in the conduct of open market operations increased stress should be placed on the objective of achieving modest growth in the monetary aggregates."[4] This was widely interpreted at the time as not merely a tactical decision for the ensuing three weeks but a fundamental change in open-market strategy that would place relatively more stress on controlling total bank credit and money supply and less emphasis on interest rates. The methods for achieving this, however, were not spelled out.

Dr. Maisel and the Federal Reserve tradition he reflects are correct in pointing out that there is no simple, unchanging mechanical link between bank reserves and the money supply. He is also correct in observing that actions of the Treasury, the banks, and the public also influence the money supply. But his reaction has gone too far. The classic explanation, drastically simplified as it is, contains an inescapable truth for central bankers: *Central-bank actions—such as buying or selling securities, or discounting bank-*

*ers' notes, or buying or selling foreign currencies or gold—can—
and usually will—change a country's money supply by an amount
larger than the central-bank transaction.* This will be true no matter
what the central bank may have intended to accomplish while
acting in the market.

At this stage we will not be concerned with why central banks
do what they do but instead will concentrate on tracing out how
their actions interact with those of the banks and the public to
determine the money supply. A convenient framework for doing
this is the one used by Allan Meltzer in his 1959 study of the
French money supply and by Milton Friedman, Anna Schwartz,
and Phillip Cagan in their historical studies of the U.S. money
supply.[5] Essentially an elaboration of the multiple-expansion
analysis, it has been used in various forms by many other investigators in the United States and other countries. It divides the
factors determining the money supply into two groups: those under
control of the central bank and those in the hands of the banks
and the public.

At the center is "high-powered money"—sometimes called the
"monetary base"—which consists of bank reserves plus currency
held by the public. In the United States the bank reserves are deposits of commercial banks at Federal Reserve banks (the monetary liabilities of the Reserve banks) and currency held by the
banks. Defining, issuing, and regulating the quantity of high-
powered money are governmental functions shared with, or
delegated to, the central banks. They are the source of the awesome
power and responsibility of the central banks.

The ratio of narrowly defined money supply (demand deposits
and currency) to high-powered money in the United States is about
2.55 to one, meaning that for every dollar of high-powered money
there are about 2½ dollars of money in the hands of the public.
This logically leads to the notion of the money multiplier, which
determines how much money would be generated by an additional
dollar of high-powered money. If the 2.55 ratio were constant over
time, the multiplier also would equal 2.55; and an increase of one
dollar of high-powered money would raise the money supply by
$2.55.[6]

If we use the broad definition of money preferred by Milton

Friedman and others—currency, demand deposits, and time deposits—the ratio is about five to one. An increase of $1 in the stock of high-powered money, therefore, would increase the broadly defined money supply (M_2) by $5 if the ratio remains unchanged.

If the money multiplier were always the same, changes in the money stock would be determined entirely by changes in the quantity of high-powered money. A 5 percent increase in high-powered money would produce a 5 percent increase in the money stock. But this multiplier is not constant; the banks and the public can change it and thus can change the money supply to some degree even if the quantity of high-powered money is fixed. (See Chart 9-1.)

As Leonall Andersen of the Federal Reserve Bank of St. Louis has aptly put it, money-supply determination can be visualized in the following way:

> Monetary authorities provide high-powered money which is viewed as a pool into which banks dip to meet reserve requirements and to obtain desired excess reserves. The public also draws on this pool for currency. Banks and the public thus compete for use of the limited amount of high-powered money provided by the monetary authorities.[7]

How the banks and the public use the available supply of high-powered money, therefore, determines the size of the money multiplier—the ratio of total money supply to high-powered money. Two ratios are crucial here in determining what the money multiplier is: the ratio of currency to total money that is maintained by the public and the ratio of reserves to deposits that is maintained by the banks.

Changes in three variables—the volume of high-powered money, the currency-money ratio, and the reserve-deposit ratio—therefore can account for all changes in the money supply. Money supply will be increased by an *increase* in high-powered money, by a *reduction* in the ratio of currency held by the public to total money supply, or by a *reduction* in the ratio of bank reserves to deposits, if the other two determinants remain fixed. These are, however, merely accounting statements at this point. The really interesting questions concern the reasons why high-powered money and the two ratios change.

If it is difficult for the central bank to control the volume of

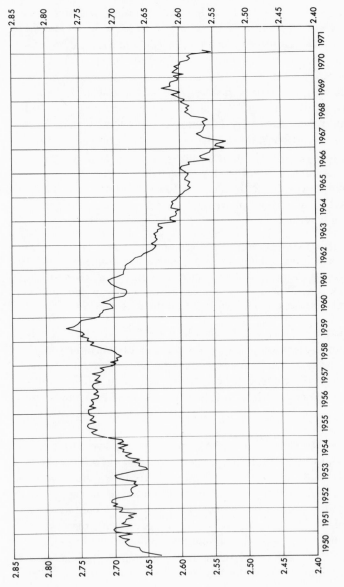

Chart 9-1. The monetary multiplier changes over time but is predictable
enough for money supply to be kept under control.

NOTES: Monetary multiplier is the ratio between money supply (demand deposits
and currency) and the monetary base (estimated by Federal Reserve Bank of
St. Louis). See Jerry L. Jordan, "Elements of Money Stock Determination,"
Federal Reserve Bank of St. Louis *Review*, October 1969, pp. 10–19. *Chart by
Federal Reserve Bank of St. Louis.*

high-powered money or if the ratios controlled by the banks and the public are highly unstable or unpredictable, the central bank will not be able to control the money supply effectively. This is a critical question because so much of the debate over the effectiveness of monetary policy turns on whether or not central banks can control the money supply. Researchers have demonstrated in the past few years that the quantity of high-powered money can be controlled and that the monetary reactions of the banks and public are stable and predictable. A central bank can *control the money supply, if it wants to.* On this point we have the agreement of Alan R. Holmes, senior vice-president of the Federal Reserve Bank of New York, who supervises the open-market operations of the Federal Reserve System:

. . . it may be worthwhile to touch on the extensively debated subject whether the Federal Reserve, if it wanted to, could control the rate of money supply growth. In my view, this lies well within the power of the Federal Reserve to accomplish provided one does not require hair-splitting precision and is thinking in terms of a time span long enough to avoid the erratic, and largely meaningless, movements of money supply over short periods.[8]

The reasons why Alan Holmes and other Federal Reserve officials do not want to control growth of the money supply directly will be taken up later.

Phillip Cagan found that increases in high-powered money accounted for nine-tenths of the growth in the U.S. money stock over the long period 1875–1955.[9] Most of the growth in high-powered money, furthermore, came from two sources—growth of the gold stock, and, after the Federal Reserve System was established, growth in credit extended by the Reserve banks. Increases in high-powered money were especially important in the two World Wars (average 16.3 percent annual growth rate) when Federal Reserve credit was used to finance part of the government's expenditures.

The Cagan data make it obvious that changes in high-powered money dominate the long-term movements of money supply that are so important in explaining changes in the price level. But how important is high-powered money in determining the short-period

changes in money supply that monetarists believe cause business
fluctuations?

Month-to-month changes in U.S. money supply since World
War II have been dominated by changes in high-powered money
just as were the long-run growth rates discussed earlier. Karl Brunner and Allan Meltzer have found, for example, that 85 percent
of the variation in the monthly change in narrowly defined money—
demand deposits and currency—is accounted for by changes in
the monetary base and by changes in Treasury deposits at commercial banks in the current and previous months.[10] The privately
held money supply is reduced when Treasury balances at commercial banks rise—as when people pay taxes—and is increased
when Treasury balances fall—as when the Treasury pays for federal purchases of goods and services. Changes in Treasury deposits
are a troublesome source of static, but changes in monetary base
are by far the most important determinant of the U.S. money
supply.

With a relationship estimated over the 200 months ending in
March, 1965, Karl Brunner and Allan Meltzer were able to predict
monthly changes in the non-seasonally adjusted stock of money
for the months of July, 1966, through September, 1969, with impressive results.[11]

What we have to find out, therefore, is why the volume of
high-powered money changes and why the Federal Reserve does
not keep it under better control. These are such important questions
that the whole next chapter will be devoted to them. Before turning to them, however, we should take a look at how those money
ratios in the hands of the public and the banks behave.

THE CURRENCY RATIO

If the public draws currency out of U.S. banks and if the Federal
Reserve does not add to the total supply of high-powered money,
total bank deposits would be reduced by about $10 for every
dollar in currency that is taken out. Although the average multiplier for narrowly defined money is only about 2.5, the multiplier
for total bank deposits is close to 10.

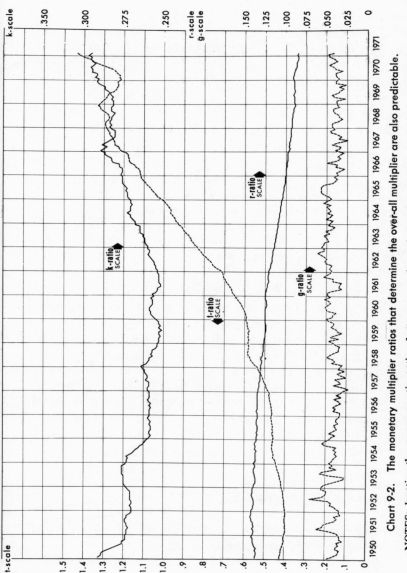

Chart 9-2. The monetary multiplier ratios that determine the over-all multiplier are also predictable.

NOTES: k-ratio—the currency ratio, ratio of currency to demand deposits; t-ratio—ratio of time deposits to demand deposits; r-ratio—reserve ratio, ratio of total commercial bank reserves to total deposits; g-ratio—ratio of Federal Government demand deposits to private demand deposits. See Jerry L. Jordan, "Elements of Money Stock Determination," for additional details. *Chart by Federal Reserve Bank of St. Louis.*

The public's ratio of currency to demand deposits is quite volatile, as can be seen from the line labeled k-ratio on Chart 9-2. It has a pronounced cyclical pattern, rising on the eve of recessions and falling during recessions. These changes in the currency ratio, therefore, strongly influence the size of the money stock that can be supported on a given volume of high-powered money.

It is curious that the currency ratio receives rather little attention in monetary literature, although currency drains during money panics—runs on banks—were among the main reasons for establishing the Federal Reserve System and the Federal Deposit Insurance Corporation. According to Phillip Cagan:

> Even in discussions of cyclical movements, high-powered money and the reserve ratio have generally received all the attention, while the currency ratio has been little noticed. One reason for the differential treatment is that sources of variation in high-powered money and the reserve ratio involve activities of the government and banks—both easy to discuss (and exaggerate)—whereas sources of variation in the currency ratio involve actions of innumerable holders of money and are, except in panics, obscure.[12]

The currency ratio, however, can be observed and predicted well enough that changes in it can be prevented from changing the total money supply. The Federal Reserve has good information on the flows of currency into and out of the hands of the public and so can promptly offset any change in the currency ratio that threatens to produce undesired changes in the money supply.

The long-term growth prospects of the commercial banking industry will be determined in part by the banks' efforts to persuade people to use deposits instead of currency. In the short run, however, the bankers simply must accommodate the long lines of people who fill their lobbies before each holiday or weekend.

RESERVE REQUIREMENTS

Assuming for the moment that the amount of high-powered money available for the banks is determined by actions of the monetary authorities and the public, the total volume of bank deposits will then be determined by the ratio of reserves to deposits that the banks maintain. Much of the literature on the difficulty of controlling the money supply assumes that this ratio is highly variable and unpredictable. This is not true.

There are two main sources of change in reserve-deposit ratios in the United States (other than changes in the reserve requirements set by the Reserve Board). The first is the fact that reserve requirements differ among classes of banks and by type of deposit. The second is variation in banks' demand for cash or excess reserves that will be discussed in the next section. If demand deposits are transferred from country banks, where the required reserve ratio was 13 percent in early 1971, to Reserve city banks, where the required ratio was 17½ percent, the average requirement ratio for the system would go up, and so the volume of deposits that could be supported on a given quantity of total reserves would go down. Similarly, if the share of time deposits (which have a low reserve-requirement ratio) in total deposits rises, the average reserve ratio goes down.

In 1969, the problem was made even more complicated by the imposition of reserve requirements on some of the liabilities of banks to their foreign branches—the so-called Eurodollar borrowings of U.S. banks—and on some of the loans of overseas branches of U.S. banks to U.S. residents. All of these requirements absorb changing amounts of the pool of high-powered money.

In his pioneering study, *The Supply and Control of Money in the United States,* Lauchlin Currie pointed out in the early thirties that shifts of deposits within the U.S. system would cause difficulties for money-supply management, if the System ever became interested in trying it.[13] In principle he was correct. In practice, however, shifts in the average reserve-requirement ratio are surprisingly small (except, of course, the occasional changes in the whole structure that the Board of Governors may make for policy reasons). George Benston found in a recent study, for example, that changes in distribution of demand deposits among classes of member banks between successive reserve settlement periods are small and predictable.[14] Long-term cumulative changes, however, have been produced by a steady drift of demand deposits from city banks, where reserve requirements are high, to country banks, where reserve requirements are low.

Shifts of deposits between member banks and nonmember banks are a minor source of uncertainty in predicting total demand deposits largely because the Fed has information on nonmember deposits only at June and December call dates. Between these dates the Fed must estimate them. As Benston and Clark Warburton point out, the nonmember banks do not escape Federal Reserve limits on their power to expand because they are required by state banking laws to keep reserves with larger banks, which usually are member banks.

Whether one is interested in predicting just demand deposits for the narrowly defined money supply or total deposits for the broadly defined money supply, transfers between demand and time deposits cause problems by changing the average reserve-requirement ratio. Nevertheless, this problem is manageable, too, according to George Benston's estimates. He thus concludes that "shifts into or out of time deposits need not adversely affect the Federal Reserve's control of money supply."[15]

In the short run, banks have little or no influence on the average reserve-requirement ratios. Over a longer time period, however, they can influence the ratios by inducing the public to hold more time deposits in relation to demand deposits, as they did during most of the sixties, for instance. But such changes are so gradual that they should not cause difficulties for money-supply management.

Although textbooks and some Federal Reserve statements describe changes in reserve requirements as an instrument for increasing or reducing bank credit and money supply, requirement changes are seldom so used. When reserve requirements are changed, furthermore, the reserve-supplying or reserve-absorbing effects of the change are nearly always offset by open-market operations.

THE GOLDEN RATIOS

In addition to the reserves they are required to hold, U.S. banks hold some cash "excess reserves" in the form of currency in their own vaults and deposits at Federal Reserve banks. In countries in which there are no reserve requirements, banks also hold some cash. Strange as it may seem, it is through this paper-thin margin of bank cash that central banks wield their greatest influence on bank decisions to buy or sell earning assets and thus to expand or contract deposits. For the central banks are the ultimate source of bank cash, which they create or extinguish. ". . . it is clear— or at least we must hope so—" said W. F. Crick long ago, "that the banks, so long as they maintain steady ratios of cash to deposits, are merely passive agents of Bank of England policy, as far as the volume of money in the form of credit is concerned."[16]

Volumes have been written in attempts to refute that simple statement, most of them relying on the theoretical possibility that the cash ratios are not steady. The ratios clearly are not constant, but how much do they vary? For the United States, the stability of the banks' reserve ratios is shown by the line labeled r-ratio, on Chart 9-2, which is the ratio of total reserves (required reserves plus excess reserves) to total commercial bank deposits. Jerry Jordan of the Federal Reserve Bank of St. Louis has found that this ratio is the least volatile of the ratios that determine the overall money multiplier, "although it is influenced by the banks' desired holdings of excess reserves and the distribution of total deposits among all the subclasses of deposits in the various classes of banks, which are subject to a large array of reserve requirements."[17]

Some attempts to explain the association between money-supply changes and business fluctuations reverse the direction of causation. Richard Davis of the Federal Reserve Bank of New York says that "the possibility of important influences running from business to money seem to weaken substantially the evidential value of the work done by Friedman and his collaborators in trying to establish a dominant *causal* role for money."[18] Generally it is argued that increasing interest rates stimulated by an increase in business activity will induce banks to reduce their ratio of reserves to deposits and thus to increase deposits and money supply. Davis, however, was unable to find much evidence that this actually happens. Nor has anyone else found such evidence.

My own opinion is that the main influence of business conditions on money supply does not come through changes in bank reserve ratios. In the United States, whatever influence business conditions have on the money supply results from slack in the Federal Reserve's grip on the supply of high-powered money, as we will see in the next chapter. In other countries, we will see later that the balance of payments has a troublesome influence on the supply of high-powered money. Nevertheless, movements in the base still dominate the changes in money supply.

Why should we expect the ratio of bank cash to bank deposits to be stable? One answer is the quantity theory—the theory of the demand for money—in microcosm. Banks behave like the general public in that they want to hold some cash for emergencies. Every day a bank has large inflows and outflows of cash—most of it in the form of balances at Reserve Banks—as its many depositors transfer money to it or draw money out. But bank managers keep their eyes on the risks and chances for profit that face them. They are not going to hold much more, or much less, cash than they think they need. Although an individual bank may be willing for a few days to tolerate a cash position that is lower or higher than its accustomed level in relation to total deposits, the bank will expand or contract its earning assets, and hence its deposits, if the discrepancy persists. Some U.S. banks are content to remain in a cash-deficit position, that is, to be borrowing daily from other banks or the Eurodollar market. But somewhere in the banking system there must be some cash to be passed around from bank to bank. In the United States, that free cash amounts only to about $200 million, compared with around $450 billion of total commercial bank deposits.

With bankers, as with the general public, cash burns a hole in the vault; and so when the central bank injects new cash (reserves) into the system it will induce a prompt increase in the money supply. Bankers simply cannot resist the impulse to add to their earning assets when cash flows in or to reduce them when cash flows out. This can be demonstrated for banks not only in the United States but in other countries as well. And, as we will see later, the same principle applies in the Eurodollar market.

W. F. Crick summed it up elegantly when he said:

What now is the moral of the story? It is just this: that the banker has his ideal of liquidity combined with profit-earning capacity. His ratios are a golden legend, inscribed in gleaming figures around the facts of yesterday's position . . . particularly [the ratio] of his cash to his deposits. But deposits are the adjustable item; cash is a matter of change or of policy outside his control. Through earning assets the banker contracts or expands his liabilities. Through the banker's balance sheet and the banker's judgment is exerted the ultimate power of cash to determine the scope of deposits. In this indirect but vital way it is cash that controls the deposits.[19]

HIGH-POWERED MONEY OUT OF CONTROL

To suffer either the solicitation of merchants, or the wishes of government, to determine the measure of bank issues is unquestionably to adopt a very false principle of conduct.

Henry Thornton, *An Enquiry into the Nature and Effects of the Paper Credit of Great Britain,* 1802[1]

When the Federal Reserve was established it was supplied under the original act with two quasi-automatic, but conflicting, criteria for deciding how much Federal Reserve money to create or retire. The first was a gold-standard rule that, had it been followed, would have obliged the System to add to the supply of high-powered money whenever gold flowed into the country and to reduce it when gold flowed out. The other was the "real-bills" doctrine, according to which the appropriate amount of money would be provided automatically if the Federal Reserve Banks were to accommodate the needs of commerce and trade by discounting notes, drafts, and bills of exchange arising out of actual commercial transactions—in short "to suffer . . . the solicitation of merchants."

The fledgling Reserve Banks quickly received a bruising introduction to the difficulty of controlling the quantity of high-powered money under those rules.[2] First, although not especially alarming at the time, there was a gold inflow during the period of American neutrality, 1914–1917, as the Allies bought supplies in the United States. The Reserve Banks allowed this inflow to expand high-powered money and the money supply. In actual fact they could not have offset the impact of this gold inflow on U.S. money supply if they had wanted to because they had no assets to sell and lacked statutory authority to raise reserve requirements. Then from mid-1917 to June, 1920, U.S. banks, in perhaps an excess of patriotic fervor, borrowed heavily from the new Reserve Banks to finance war production and to buy war bonds. The Reserve Banks helped them to do this by keeping their discount rates well below market interest rates. By the middle of 1920 the money supply was more than twice as large as it had been in November, 1914, when the Reserve Banks opened for business.

Belatedly trying to cap the gusher they had opened up, the Reserve Banks raised discount rates in 1920 to the highest levels ever imposed, before or since. A sharp contraction in money supply followed, as the banks struggled to pay off the indebtedness they had so blithely taken on when discount rates were lower. Between September, 1920, and January, 1922, the money supply fell by 9 percent and there was a severe business recession.

After their inauspicious beginning in trying to use the traditional discount-rate instrument to control member-bank borrowing and total Federal Reserve credit (the Federal Reserve's contribution to high-powered money), the Reserve Banks ran into another perplexing problem in 1922 when they tried to build up their earning assets through buying securities in the open market. When the Reserve Banks bought securities, the member banks reduced their borrowings from the Reserve Banks by about the amount of the securities purchased, leaving total Federal Reserve credit (and high-powered money) about unchanged. When securities were sold in 1923, member-bank borrowing increased, again leaving total Reserve bank credit approximately unchanged.[3] An alarming implication of this unexpected reaction of the banks to System open-market operations was that the volume of discounting must be independent of the discount rate in the U.S. banking system. The orthodox principles of central banking inherited from the Bank of England somehow did not seem to work in a system containing thousands of individual banks.

THE RESERVE-POSITION DOCTRINE

With truly ingenious theoretical arguments, early Federal Reserve economists concluded that the apparently perverse reactions of the banking system actually provided the System with powerful means for influencing bank credit and interest rates through buying and selling securities in the open market. Open-market operations were elevated to the commanding role played by the discount rate in other countries. Moving open-market operations to the center as they did is an interesting example of being right for the wrong reason—for their reason was the reserve-position doctrine that was to dominate Federal Reserve thinking for nearly half a century. Reserve-position doctrine, as we shall see, is a theory about how interest rates, not the monetary aggregates, can be controlled.

The two key assertions of what I will call U.S. reserve-position doctrine were: (1) reserve losses caused by Federal Reserve open-market sales of securities induce banks to increase their borrowings, and reserve gains caused by Federal Reserve purchases induce them to reduce borrowing; and (2) high levels of member bank borrowing cause short-term market interest rates to be high and low levels of borrowing cause market rates to be low.[4] Underlying both of these propositions was an assumption that banks are so reluctant to be in debt that they borrow only when they must and repay as soon as they can. Under this assumption, the volume of their borrowing would be affected very little, if at all, by changes in profitability or cost. Therefore, banks would not borrow from the Federal Reserve banks to take advantage of a favorable spread between market interest rates and the discount rate. If System open-market operations were said to control member-bank borrowing, other influences on borrowing, such as the profit motive, had to be assumed away. These assumptions have been a fatal flaw in the doctrine to this day.

Rules for conducting open-market operations flowed directly from the new doctrine, as explained by W. Randolph Burgess a few years later:

The principle of open market operations may be summarized by saying that purchases of securities by Reserve Banks tend to relieve member banks from debt to the Reserve Banks, and lead them to adopt a more liberal lending and investing policy. Money rates become easier; bank deposits increase. . . . Conversely, sales of securities by the Reserve Banks increase member bank borrowing and lead the banks to adopt a somewhat less liberal policy. Money rates grow firmer; bank deposits tend to decline.[5]

The reserve-position doctrine, as expressed in the 1920s and in its money-market conditions variant today, is superficially plausible. But its utter inadequacy as a guide for controlling the stock of high-powered money was demonstrated by the answer to a question of fact: Are open-market operations the principal determinant of member-bank borrowing? They were not in the 1920s and are not today. This was recognized early by such outside observers as C. O. Hardy, Seymour Harris, and John Maynard Keynes.[6] Keynes objected that, far from there being a tradition against borrowing in the United States, banks there were much more willing to borrow from the central bank than were London banks. Furthermore, he argued, the Reserve Banks kept discount rates too low in relation to other money-market rates. Consequently:

. . . whatever the cause, the result is plain—the Federal Reserve Banks have not the same control over the amount of their Member Banks' reserve resources that the Bank of England has. The history of the Federal Reserve System since the war has been, first of all, a great abuse of the latitude thus accorded to the Member Banks to increase the "advances" of the Reserve Banks, and subsequently a series of efforts by the Reserve authorities to invent gadgets and conventions which shall give them a power, more nearly similar to that which the Bank of England has, without any overt alteration of the law.[7]

It is noteworthy that the Federal Reserve authorities are still busy inventing or reintroducing gadgets and conventions for controlling member-bank borrowing.

Harris, Hardy, and Keynes also attacked the argument that changes in member-bank borrowing automatically offset System open-market operations. They pointed out that when open-market operations were large they were likely to be partially, but not entirely, offset by changes in borrowing. Because it was the supposedly automatic reaction of the banks that was said to give the Fed power to control borrowing through open-market operations, these were serious criticisms of the reserve-position doctrine. Unfortunately, by the time these studies appeared in the early 1930s, the depression had given the Federal Reserve more urgent problems to worry about.

The Federal Reserve view on borrowing, if consistently followed, led to perverse open-market operations. *Instead of simply offsetting undesired changes in member-bank borrowing through open-market operations, the System often allowed changes in borrowing to influence open-market operations in the wrong direction.* This was a major reason why the Federal Reserve at times tended to amplify cyclical swings in economic activity.

The mechanics are not difficult to grasp. When a pickup in business activity or a Federal budget deficit led to an increase in the demand for bank credit, banks would borrow more from the Federal Reserve. If the Federal Reserve had not decided to increase its degree of restraint, the increase in member-bank borrowing might be interpreted by those in charge of open-market operations as evidence of more restraint than was intended. Additional reserves would be supplied through open-market operations. An injection of high-powered money from open-market operations, therefore, was added to the increase that came at the initiative of the banks. Moreover, as the extra growth of the money supply worked through the economy, credit demands would increase further and the banks would go back to the discount window to borrow more. The same process would occur in reverse if demand for credit fell.

DID THE FED SWING THE 1960 ELECTION?

One of the best examples of the perverse effects of following reserve-position doctrine and one that may have influenced the course of world history, occurred in early 1960. As we saw in Chapter 2, Richard Nixon, then Vice President, tried unsuccessfully to get fiscal policy action to avert the recession Arthur Burns had warned him of in March of that election year. Federal Reserve economists had seen the danger signals too. Some members of the Open Market Committee expressed concern about a continuing decline in the money supply at the February 9 meeting.[8]

On March 1, the Committee instructed the Manager of the Open Market Account to ease the degree of monetary restraint. But the money supply continued to decline.[9] At the March 22 meeting Delos C. Johns, President of the Federal Reserve Bank of St. Louis, pointed to the discrepancy between results and what the Committee had wanted the Manager to do. He attributed this discrepancy to the way the instruction was expressed:

The time had come, in his opinion, for the Committee to subordinate its consideration of net borrowed reserves and other money market pressures to objectives expressed in terms of total bank reserves or the money supply. He did not mean to say that the Committee thereby would have adopted a system that would assure the avoidance of mistakes, but the use of such a technique would help to avoid doing things to total reserves and money that the Committee did not intend.[10]

By the April 12 meeting total reserves and money supply were still declining, despite the supposed easing of monetary policy. President Johns diagnosed the situation with a scholarly dissection of the reserve-position doctrine:

There has been for some time a conjuncture of forces operating to bring about a continuing reduction of total member bank reserves and contraction of the money supply. Parenthetically these resulting phenomena . . . have at times been obscured by other developments heralded in various quarters as indicators of lessening monetary restraint, namely, a sharp decline in interest rates . . . and a decrease in that widely accepted barometer of monetary policy, net borrowed reserves. . . .

Insofar as the Management of the System Account receives from the Committee a guide to open market operations, it is in terms of a net borrowed reserve target or range, subject . . . to latitude or leeway according to the way things develop and to the "feel of the market."

However, with Treasury bills yielding 3 per cent or below . . . and with the discount rate at 4 per cent, profit-minded bankers may generally be counted on to prefer liquidating bills for purposes of adjusting to reserve drains, rather than borrowing from their Reserve Banks. . . .

The Committee's staff has been pointing out for some time that liquidation of short-term Government securities has been occurring at a rapid rate. Nevertheless in order to induce [member-bank] borrowing at such levels as would bring about net borrowed reserves within the target range, the Management of the System Account has had to sell bills. Thus, a mechanism had been adopted by the Committee which, under the conditions existing, virtually assured a continuing contraction of total reserves, commercial bank credit, and the money supply.[11]

It may already have been too late when the Committee decided to ease on March 1 to have materially improved economic conditions by the time of the election in November. The money supply, as it was measured at that time, had been contracting since the previous July—seven months. *But the money supply continued to contract for four more months after the Open Market Committee decided to ease.* The election, furthermore, was so close that even a small improvement in business conditions could well have thrown it to Nixon rather than to Kennedy.

It is ironic that the agency that was trying to do something about the coming recession—and that had the power to do it—tripped over doctrine inherited from the twenties. A similar mistake on a more cataclysmic scale converted the 1929 Crash into the Great Depression. And it is ironic that in 1970 and 1971 the Federal Reserve System was still bemused at times by the same ideas under a new name, the "money-market strategy," and was still occasionally "doing things to total reserves and money that the Committee did not intend."

WHY TAKE THE ROUNDABOUT WAY?

This excursion through history was not intended as a session in psychoanalyzing the Federal Reserve. But it should help to explain why System open-market operations have never followed the naïve elementary textbook approach for controlling high-powered money and the money supply that is explained so clearly in *Purposes and Functions*. It is not inconceivable that the System might at least have experimented with a more straightforward approach in its formative years if it had not been captivated so early by reserve-position doctrine.

Although central banks had traditionally been more concerned with interest rates, writers on banking had shown a lively interest in the causes of fluctuations in the supply of money and bank credit long before the Federal Reserve was established. When C. A. Phillips published his classic exposition of the multiple-expansion process in 1920 he pulled together ideas that had been discussed in banking literature for a century or more.[12] However, E. A. Goldenweiser, who was in a good position to observe the Board for many years—as director of its Division of Research and Statistics—said the idea that the Federal Reserve System would create high-powered dollars was not in the minds of the founders of the System nor was it clearly understood by the Federal Reserve for some time after its creation.[13] Furthermore, there was no precedent in the operations of other central banks for trying to control bank reserves or high-powered money through open-market operations. Other central banks depended mainly on discounting.

HIGH-POWERED MONEY TODAY

Some practical aspects of the Federal Reserve's problems in controlling the quantity of high-powered money can be seen in the reserve changes reported in Table 10-1 for the month of March, 1971. Three sources of change in total bank reserves are distinguished: (1) operating transactions over which the Federal Reserve has little or no control, (2) member-bank borrowing, which is nominally under control of the banks in the short run but is determined, to a near approximation, by the Federal Reserve, and (3) open-market operations, through which the Fed would have to supplement or offset the other two sources in order to produce any desired change in the total.

In this particular month the operating transactions as a group would have reduced total reserves by $689 million if the banks and the Federal Reserve had done nothing to offset the drain. This figure appears on the first line of the net changes column at the far

Table 10-1. Factors Tending to Increase or Decrease Total Member-Bank Reserves, March 1971

In millions of dollars; (+) denotes increase, (−) decrease in total reserves

Factors	Mar. 3	Mar. 10	Mar. 17	Mar. 24	Mar. 31	Net Changes
			Changes in daily averages— week ended on			
Operating transactions (subtotal)	−653	+137	−238	+ 89	− 24	−689
Federal Reserve float	−749	+183	−392	+348	−337	−947
Treasury operations*	− 99	−105	+508	−186	− 60	+ 58
Gold and foreign account	+ 17	+ 2	− 5	+ 20	− 41	− 7
Currency outside banks	+220	+ 92	−628	−177	+421	− 72
Other Federal Reserve accounts (net)+	− 42	− 35	+280	+ 85	− 9	+279
Member-bank borrowings	+ 8	+163	−131	+ 43	− 76	+ 7
Open-market operations (subtotal)	+271	−438	+892	−559	+578	+744
Outright holdings:						
Government securities	+327	−310	+132	+122	+158	+429
Bankers' acceptances	− 5	− 2	—	+ 6	− 1	− 2
Repurchase agreements:						
Government securities	− 41	−104	+604	−554	+372	+277
Bankers' acceptances	− 1	− 15	+ 66	− 43	+ 13	+ 20
Federal agency obligations	− 9	− 7	+ 90	− 90	+ 36	+ 20
Total	−374	−138	+523	−427	+478	+ 62
Memorandum Item:						
Change in member-bank req. reserves	+227	+ 50	−371	+255	−121	+ 40
Change in excess reserves	−147	− 88	+152	−171	+357	+103

Note: Because of rounding, figures do not necessarily add to totals.
* Includes changes in Treasury currency and cash. + Includes assets denominated in foreign currencies.
Adapted from Table I, Federal Reserve Bank of New York Monthly Review, April, 1971, p. 76.

right side of the table. Notice, also, that in the second and fourth weeks of the period, operating transactions added to bank reserves but not by enough to offset the drains in the other three weeks. The main operating factor tending to contract reserves was a decline in Federal Reserve float of $947 million.[14] The member banks made up an insignificant part of the loss by increasing their borrowings by $7 million.

Federal Reserve open-market operations were the final determinant of the stock of total bank reserves, offsetting the drain from the operating transactions and supplementing the small increase in member-bank borrowing. The net effect of the various open-market transactions of the Fed during the month was to increase reserves by $744 million. Total reserves, therefore, increased by $62 million.

The arithmetic is straightforward, but there are some problems of interpretation. In the first place, there is no reason to believe that the Fed intended to produce a $62 million increase in total reserves, although, as we saw in Chapter 4, the Federal Reserve had been trying specifically to control growth of the monetary aggregates since January of the year before. The manager of the Open Market Account had instead been instructed by the Federal Open Market Committee to conduct open-market operations "with a view to maintaining prevailing money market conditions while accommodating any downward movements in long-term rates." Furthermore, money-market conditions were to be modified if monetary and credit aggregates appeared to be deviating significantly from the growth paths expected.[15]

This arcane language meant essentially that he was to try to keep member-bank borrowings and a collection of short-term market interest rates about where they were in February. He was also to try to bring long-term rates down. Therefore, open-market operations during the period were not specifically directed at offsetting the effects on total reserves of the operating transactions and of changes in member-bank borrowing at all. Interest rates were the primary target and were to be shifted only if the aggregates strayed too far off course.

The "money-market strategy" used in conducting Federal Reserve open-market operations takes short-run changes in bank deposits and required reserves as something to which open-market operations and total reserves must adjust, rather than something to be directly controlled by them. Paul Meek and Rudolf Thunberg of the Federal Reserve Bank of New York have called the strategy an accommodative one:

The System's weekly strategy [they say] insulates the banking system reasonably well from swings in nonborrowed reserves due to market factors, but it accommodates week-to-week changes in required reserves at the same time. This approach enables the banking system to respond very flexibly to the volatile short-run demands of its customers for money and credit, since the System supplies and absorbs reserves on demand in an effort to keep the Federal funds rate within its prescribed range. Under this accommodative posture, the week-to-week changes in the money supply clearly stem from shifts in demand rather than from reserve injection. These shifts do, in fact, produce large variations in the money supply. The absolute change in the narrowly defined money supply, before seasonal adjustment, averaged $2 billion from week to week in 1970. This compares with long-term growth that averaged about $200 million per week for the year as a whole.[16]

An additional complication, which was introduced in 1968 by a rule change, is that the amount of daily-average required reserves the banks must maintain in each statement week is based not on that week's deposits but on the deposits of two weeks earlier. As a result:

In the real world [says Alan Holmes], banks extend credit, creating deposits in the process, and look for the reserves later. The question then becomes one of whether and how the Federal Reserve will accommodate the demand for reserves. In the very short run, the Federal Reserve has little or no choice about accommodating that demand; over time, its influence can obviously be felt.[17]

Furthermore, says Holmes:

. . . the suggestion that open-market operations should be used in the short run to prevent a rise in total reserves through member bank borrowing is completely illogical. Within a statement week, the reserves have to be there; and in one way or another, the Federal Reserve will have to accommodate the need for them.[18]

By compelling the banks to meet some of their needs at the discount window, he said, the Federal Reserve can gradually induce the banks to make asset adjustments. "As pressure on the banks is maintained or intensified, the banking system as a whole is forced to adjust its lending and investment policies with corresponding effects on money and credit—and eventually on the real economy."[19] The Federal Reserve thus reacts to influence the stock of high-powered money *after* the banks have expanded or contracted deposits, rather than taking the initiative in supplying a stock of high-powered money to which the banks must adjust.

This is like imposing a rule in football that a defensive back must let a runner get two steps ahead before tackling him. Of course, the defense man could try to tackle so hard that the runner would not want to come that way on the next play. In effect, this is what the Federal Reserve does in making it more or less difficult for the banks to obtain the reserves they must have in a reserve period. But this is a slow approach that may confuse the banks and other participants in the money markets.

The epic absurdity of the lagged reserve requirement was revealed by a series of sharp increases of demand deposits in certain weeks of 1970 and 1971 that showed up like blips on a radarscope (see Chart 10-1). One of the worst of these was the week ending April 1, 1970, when the demand deposit component of the money supply increased by $7.5 billion before seasonal adjustment and $6.4 billion seasonally adjusted, which was more than the expected growth for a whole year at the moderate growth rate the System was pursuing at the time. Revision of the data later scaled the unadjusted increase to $4.0 billion and the seasonally adjusted increase to $1.6 billion, but by any measure this was an extraordinary increase for one week.

The initial cause of the April 1, 1970, increase of deposits was a postal strike which interrupted the normal flow of checks. With fewer checks being presented for payment, the banks saw an increase in deposits on their books. They put this money to work in making more loans and buying securities, thus creating still more deposits, although this is not what the process looked like to an individual bank. Under the old arrangement the banks' reserve requirements would have gone up at the same time, which would

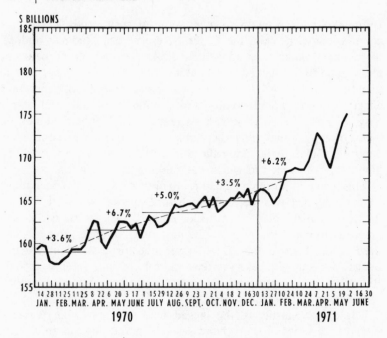

Chart 10-1. Demand deposits in 1970 and 1971 behaved erratically at times.

NOTES: Weekly plottings. The percentage rates refer to quarterly changes at seasonally adjusted annual rates. *Chart by FNCB.*

have caused them to be more cautious in expanding loans and investments.

Two weeks later, when the banks had to meet the higher requirements based on deposits of the April 1 week, the Federal Reserve supplied the necessary reserves through open-market operations. The reserves were supplied somewhat grudgingly because the jump in bank deposits and money supply was by then embarrassingly visible. Nevertheless, the open-market operations effectively validated the deposit expansion and left the Federal Reserve with a difficult problem of gradually shrinking deposits and money supply in order to get back on the normal growth course later.

Perhaps the banks should have anticipated in the April 1 week the higher reserve requirements that were going to hit them two

weeks later, but they had become conditioned to expect that reserves somehow would be available at about the Federal funds rate
then prevailing. (The Federal funds rate is the rate paid by banks
for reserves borrowed from other banks. It was between 7 percent
and 8 percent in early April.)

The Federal Reserve was not exactly writing on a blank slate
when it adopted the lagged-reserve-requirement rule. Harry Johnson and John W. L. Winder had concluded several years earlier
that a similar rule made it difficult for the Bank of Canada to regulate deposit expansion of the chartered banks of Canada. An obligation of the central bank to avoid shocks to the system by not
making it too difficult for the banks to obtain the cash they are
legally required to hold they said:

. . . clearly weakens its control by permitting the chartered banks
some freedom in determining the quantity of bank credit, to the extent that they act on the expectation that the central bank will tacitly
accept an expansion of credit that they initiate by providing the necessary cash after the event.[20]

As Alan Holmes testified, the Federal Reserve, like the Bank of
Canada, attempts to regulate the banks by making it more or less
difficult for them to obtain the cash they are legally required to
hold as a consequence of lending and investing decisions they made
weeks earlier. This arrangement puts an unnecessary layer of complications in the way of good money-supply control that would
not be there if the required reserves of a period were based on the
deposits of the same period.

One extenuating feature of the lagged reserve requirement is
that it does give the Federal Reserve effective control over the
volume of member-bank borrowing in the short run. In any given
week the volume of required reserves is predetermined (by the
deposits of two weeks earlier). Cash that can be counted as reserves
is also predetermined. The Federal Reserve controls the volume of
unborrowed reserves, leaving a balance that must be met by borrowing. Excess reserves for the system are so small that they provide
little or no latitude for the banks in meeting their reserve requirements. Nevertheless, the banks still have the initiative in determining the volume of required reserves, as Alan Holmes points out.

The ability to control member-bank borrowing, therefore, merely simplifies the problem of "punishing" the banks by forcing them to borrow.

MONEY-MARKET CONDITIONS INSTEAD OF MONEY SUPPLY

The money-market strategy for conducting open-market operations is the reserve-position doctrine of the 1920s by another name but with the same old warts.

Essentially, [say Meek and Thunberg] this strategy involves using open-market operations to accommodate week-to-week changes in required reserves by varying nonborrowed reserves *so that member bank borrowings at the discount window and/or the Federal funds rate remain within the desired range* [italics added].[21]

Since its genesis in the 1920s, the use of open-market operations to control member-bank borrowing has been explained by Federal Reserve spokesmen as a means for gradually putting pressure on banks to change their lending and investing policies. Thus, Randolph Burgess in 1936: ". . . purchases of securities by Reserve Banks tend to relieve member banks from debt . . . and lead them to adopt a more liberal lending and investing policy . . . sales of securities by the Reserve Banks increase member bank borrowing and lead the banks to adopt a somewhat less liberal policy."[22] Alan Holmes in 1969: "As pressure on the banks is maintained or intensified, the banking system as a whole is forced to adjust its lending and investing policies with corresponding effects on money and credit."[23]

These Federal Reserve explanations of open-market operations dwell *on indirect effects of levels of borrowings and money-market rates on banks' lending policies.* But they neglect the *direct effects of changes in total reserves on banks' ability to lend and invest.* These direct effects, however, are far more important than the indirect effects.

The conventional Federal Reserve view implies that the banks, as a group, have a considerable degree of latitude with respect to the volume of assets and deposits they choose to have. This is true of any one bank, but it is not true for the system. In fact, the total volume of deposits for the system is closely constrained by the amount of reserves the Federal Reserve puts into the system or takes out, either by lending to the banks or through buying or selling securities. Therefore, no matter what the banks might want to do in the way of lending and investing policies, the Federal Reserve can induce them to expand or contract total deposits promptly and at any time.

The pressure of any given set of money-market conditions actually should be seen as bearing not on the banks' policies *but on the Federal Reserve itself, for it determines when, and by how much, the Fed will expand the reserves of the banking system or contract them.*

If the Open Market Committee expresses a target in terms of volume of member-bank borrowings—the original 1920s concept— *or free reserves*—the target used through much of the 1950s—[24]*or "money-market conditions"*—the target of the 1960s and early '70s—*it is in effect attempting to peg the price of credit.* This is more explicit now that the money-market condition target specifically includes the federal funds rate, in addition to the traditional discount rate; but control of interest rates was viewed from the beginning as the purpose of open-market operations. The reserve-position theory developed in the 1920s was not a theory of how the money supply is controlled. It was instead a theory to explain central-bank control over interest rates.

Winfield W. Riefler, who was the chief articulator of the Federal Reserve doctrine, said in 1930:

Whether central banks confine themselves to protecting the exchanges and forestalling panics, or under a broader conception of these functions undertake to stabilize business and control price levels, their chief instrument of action is the price charged for credit, and they must endeavor to accomplish these objectives mainly by bringing their influence to bear on money rates.[25]

By controlling interest rates directly it would be possible, according to the doctrine, to control quantities of credit and money indirectly. Other central banks could do this with their discount rates;

the Federal Reserve must rely on open-market operations. The theory implies that at any given time there is a certain quantity of bank credit demanded and that this quantity will (or must) be supplied by the banking system. Given the reserve balances provided by currency flows, gold flows, and the other "operating transactions" of Table 10-1, and by the open-market operations of the Federal Reserve, therefore, the banks will borrow whatever additional reserves are required in order to supply the quantity of credit demanded.

Open-market operations of the Federal Reserve then influence market interest rates by determining the size of the residual "need" for reserves that must be met by discounting. This is what Alan Holmes and other Federal Reserve spokesmen mean when they speak of easing, maintaining, or intensifying pressure on the banks. Because the banks are reluctant to borrow, according to the doctrine, they raise the interest rates they charge as their indebtedness increases. This in turn influences the quantity of credit demanded in future periods by changing its cost. Therefore, the Fed should be able to control both the price and—with a lag—the quantity of credit. One must admit that this is a breathtakingly ingenious doctrine and it appears to be logically correct. But, in the real world, it does not work.

Like a commodity stabilization board that is trying to peg the price of corn, the Fed finds that under some conditions it has to feed money into the market to make its price effective and at other times it has to draw money out. If it happens to set its price a little below what the market price would be if it did not intervene it will find that it is supplying dollars to the market through Reserve bank discount windows and through open-market purchases of securities. If it happens to set its price a little higher than the free-market price, it will find that the banks are paying back their borrowings at the discount windows and it will be selling securities to mop up funds that would otherwise push the market price of credit down.

The key to understanding how the Federal Reserve's money-market strategy works, therefore, is to recognize that *the Federal Reserve sets the price of bank reserves but the market determines the quantity supplied.* What happens when price-stabilizing machinery is used to control not just the price but also the rate of flow of corn or dollars into the market? For this is what the Federal Reserve has been trying to do.

In theory, the authorities could predict the price at which the market would demand the quantity of corn or dollars per week, or month, or year that the authorities want to provide and then peg the price at that level. I tested this idea twelve years ago and concluded that the relationships between price and quantity of bank reserves supplied are so weak and unreliable that they should not be the basis for managing total reserves, bank credit, and the money supply.[26] Numerous other researchers have confirmed that finding.[27]

Another approach would be to adjust the peg price whenever the flow of corn or dollars becomes too large or too small. The Open Market Committee does this now by setting a target price ("range of money-market conditions") at each meeting that is to be maintained by open-market operations until the next Committee meeting. However, the meetings are three or four weeks apart. More often than not, furthermore, the Committee instructs the manager at each meeting to maintain for the next period about the same market conditions as those that prevailed in the preceding period, whether or not actual market conditions were what the Committee had specified for that period. Discount rates are adjusted even less frequently.

Even though the manager of the Open Market Account has some discretion in adjusting money-market conditions between meetings of the Committee, the strategy of slowly adjusting the target price in order to control the flow of reserves into the banking system means that the Federal Reserve perennially *follows* developments in credit markets rather than *leading* them or even being reasonably current. When credit demands change rapidly, as at the beginning of a recession or during an international monetary crisis, the Fed's credit-price peg may lag behind. Until the market-conditions target is adjusted, the flow of reserves into the banking system may be too small or negative, as in early 1960, or much too large, as in early 1971.

Our hypothetical corn-price stabilizers have the advantage of using in their pegging operations the commodity whose price they want to manage. In trying to manage the price of credit, the Federal Reserve, however, uses high-powered reserve dollars, a very different commodity, whose influence on the price of credit is by no means so clear and direct as many people think. The immediate impact of a reserve injection on interest rates and the ultimate impact—after the new reserves have supported a multiple expansion of bank credit and money supply—are likely not even to be in the same direction.

Still a third approach would be to decide the amount of new reserves to be supplied in a particular period and let the market determine the price. This is the approach preferred by monetarists, who believe the present system is archaic and accident-prone.

In a sophisticated and vigorous defense of the Federal Reserve's money-market strategy in 1969, however, Governor Sherman Maisel argued that the approach of trying to control the money supply through changes in total reserves would be seriously vulnerable to three major sources of error.[28] First, although not first in his ranking, was a group of technical factors (the operating factors of Table 10-1), which the Federal Reserve now tries to offset. Second, reactions of the banks—such as borrowing from the Federal Reserve or from one another or buying or selling assets—and reactions of the public—such as shifting deposits from one type to another—would be difficult to allow for. Third, irregular movements would arise, he said, from errors in estimating seasonal forces and in estimating special transitory needs of the economy (like the short-run changes in public demands for cash mentioned in the Meek-Thunberg article cited earlier).

The first two sources of error account for a small part of the variability in money supply. Unless one requires "hair-splitting precision" in control over short periods as Alan Holmes says, they are by no means an insuperable problem. Lionel Kalish, George Benston, Allan Meltzer, Karl Brunner, and others have shown how they might be overcome.[29] All that is lacking is a trial.

The third problem, what Governor Maisel calls the "irregular movements in money supply," would be much more serious than the others, according to the estimates he presented. But this would be true only if one accepts the implicit assumptions that there are erratic short-run swings in the demand for money and that the Federal Reserve should accommodate such swings by increasing and contracting the money supply. No monetarist worth his salt is willing to accept those assumptions. Instead, I believe it would be highly desirable, and possible, to reduce the short- and long-run variability in rates of money-supply growth. The way to do this is to *improve the control of high-powered money through reversing the System's approach to open-market operations, that is, to control the quantity instead of the price.*

The degree of Fed control over the money supply could be sharply increased by preventing short-run changes in the demand for credit by businesses and government from having so much influence on the supply. Attempting to accommodate them, as the Fed has done for years, injects a set of influences that are extremely difficult to predict or to control. In fact, it establishes a much more difficult target for open-market operations than one of achieving a desired average growth rate in reserves or money.

If these short-run accommodations of credit demands canceled each other out over longer periods, as the defenders of the money-market-conditions strategy seem to assume, they would not seriously affect total money supply. But there is no assurance that this is so. Instead, there is much evidence that *these short-run changes have accumulated into long-run errors in the control of high-powered money* at turning points in the business cycle and at other times as well, often despite recognition of a turning point by the Federal Open Market Committee. The relentless arithmetic of the multiple-expansion process runs on no matter what the central bank does.

The 1960 downturn we discussed earlier was a clear example of cumulative errors in the control of high-powered money that frustrated the Committee's purpose of countering an incipient recession. The summers of 1965 and 1967 and the first eight months of 1971 were, it seemed to me, examples of cumulative errors in accommodating changes in demand for credit that led to more expansion of bank credit and money supply than the Open Market Committee thought was appropriate. The latter case is especially discouraging because it occurred after the Federal Reserve decided to shift its strategy toward more deliberate control of the money supply.

In 1970, the Federal Reserve attempted to maintain better control over the money supply than it ever had before. When the procedures for doing this were explained in early 1971, they proved to be an uneasy compromise between the old practice of accommodating short-run changes in demands for credit and the new objective of moderate expansion in monetary aggregates. The results obviously were not always what the Committee intended.

In the third and fourth quarters of 1970, these procedures led to a shortfall for some weeks between the 5 percent per year money-supply growth target and actual money growth. The Federal Open Market Committee attempted to specify at each meeting a set of money-market conditions (interest rates and level of member-bank borrowings) that staff estimates indicated would produce the desired expansion of money supply. The money market conditions then were the operating target for day-to-day purchases and sales of securities. With short-term interest rates falling rapidly, however, in the fourth quarter of 1970, staff estimates consistently overestimated the rates of money-supply growth that would occur with the money-market conditions that the Open Market Committee sought to maintain. The money supply grew *less* than they intended, principally because the Committee at that time was fearful that short-term rates would fall too far and would increase the balance-of-payments deficit. This was the early-1960 problem all over again.

In the first eight months of 1971 the problem was just the opposite. When interest rates began to rise again in February because of the economic recovery that had begun in December, and to soar during the international monetary crisis in May, the Committee was hesitant about letting them rise too quickly. The effort to moderate the rise of rates through purchasing government securities expanded bank reserves and money supply. Staff estimates of the money-supply growth that would result from any given set of money-market conditions were then consistently on the low side. Money supply grew *more* than the Open Market Committee intended. This was the 1967 problem all over again.

The greater emphasis on controlling high-powered money and money supply in 1970 was a giant step in the right direction. The experience gained should be valuable not only to the Federal Reserve System but also to other central banks that face the same problems. And it surely should lead to a radical revision of Federal Reserve procedures for controlling high-powered money. The Open

Market Committee, the Administration, and the general public were running out of patience with accidental changes in the money supply and were about to insist on a higher standard of performance. The reversion to attempting to control interest rates again in 1971 was regrettable, but its consequences should eventually force the authorities to go back to the 1970 policy of controlling the aggregates.

The defense of reserve-position doctrine or its offspring, the money-market strategy, cannot rest on the argument that it is the best way to control high-powered money, the money supply, or other monetary aggregates, for it is not. Its supposed advantage is as a substitute for controlling the money supply, as its defenders imply when they argue that attempts at close control of the money supply would have intolerable side effects on interest rates. It remains to be seen whether the benefits of short-run stability in interest rates and other money-market conditions are great enough to offset the costs of instability in money-supply growth.

11

OTHER CENTRAL BANKS AND THE MONEY SUPPLY

I fully recognize that there are limits on the
ability of central banks to resist the depreciation
in the value of money. But they must use their
powers as fully as possible. This means that in
the operating model of central banks the money
supply must be taken as an independent variable;
otherwise there would be little reason to have
central banks at all.

   Dr. J. Zijlstra, speech delivered to the thirty-
   ninth Annual General Meeting, Bank for
   International Settlements, 1969[1]

Economists of many countries argue that confidence in the ability
of a central bank to control the nation's money supply is a luxury
that only the United States can enjoy. In many other countries
surpluses or deficits in international payment balances are said to
force expansion or contraction of domestic money supplies despite
what the central banks may try to do. This, it is argued, makes
countries vulnerable to "imported inflation"—especially inflation
imported from the United States.

As a large and nearly self-sufficient country, the United States
is much less dependent on international trade than are most other
countries of the world. Deficits and surpluses in the U.S. balance
of payments, therefore, seldom have much direct influence on the
U.S. economy, although concern over deficits does influence U.S.
policies.

Nevertheless, external influences, important as they are, cannot relieve the monetary authorities in other countries of responsibility for what happens to the money supply. We know they *can* control the money supply *because many of them have done it* from time to time. Italy, Germany, and Greece curbed inflations in the early postwar years by holding down money-supply growth. Japan frequently changes its rate of money-supply growth. Britain and France sharply reduced money-supply growth in 1969.

Many other central banks have demonstrated from time to time that they can control the money supply. Like the Federal Reserve System, however, they have not, until recently, given much attention to the problems of controlling the money supply as a regular policy. Their demonstrations of ability to control it have generally been in response to emergencies such as inflations or balance-of-payments problems.

It is important to get to the bottom of the charges that other central banks cannot control the money supply if we are to understand the problems of the international monetary system that will be taken up in later chapters. Two main sources of difficulty are most often mentioned. One is that institutions are so different in other countries that techniques that are effective in the United States would not work elsewhere. Another is that the balance of payments would overwhelm the monetary authorities even if they did have effective instruments for controlling the money supply. This latter argument is especially important, for, if it is true, the monetary policy problems of countries must be solved somewhere else than at home—the United States, for instance—or domestic economic stability must be sought only through fiscal measures and controls.

There is still a third source of difficulty that is not so often mentioned, although I believe it may be the most important of all. This one is the common practice of making the same mistakes the Federal Reserve System makes by trying to stabilize interest rates and credit-market conditions. High-powered money and the money supply get out of control when central banks try to avoid fluctuations in interest rates.

THE MULTIPLE-EXPANSION PROCESS IS AT HOME ANYWHERE

The idea that the multiple-expansion process works in the United States but might not work in other countries should be dismissed at the outset. We have evidence from many careful studies that changes of money supply in other countries are dominated by changes in high-powered money—or monetary base—just as they are in the United States. According to Karl Brunner:

No doubt the monetary base is not the only determinant of the money supply. The public's and the banks' behavior affects the money supply also. But the relative orders of magnitude are of crucial importance in this context. The monetary base dominates all the major movements of the money supply in all countries examined thus far.[2]

Allan Meltzer's study, "The Behavior of the French Money Supply: 1938–54," was an early classic of the monetarist counter-revolution.[3] Inspired in part by Karl Brunner's lectures in 1954–1955 and published in 1959, Meltzer's study demonstrated that a close and stable relationship existed between the monetary base (high-powered money) and the money supply of France between 1938 and 1954 despite substantial changes in the circumstances under which the monetary system operated. Meltzer found that the monetary base could be used to predict the money supply of France with an average error of less than 1½ percent.

The data indicate [he said] that the coefficient of multiple expansion [the multiplier] was largely unaffected by changes in social institutions but was markedly affected by particular monetary policies. This result and our ability to predict changes in the money supply indicate that the central bank—though legally empowered to control the money issue through open-market operations, rediscount rate changes, and a variety of postwar direct controls over banks—was primarily responsible for the increase in the money supply.[4]

At about the same time Meltzer was doing his study in France, economists of the International Monetary Fund were applying similar methods of analysis to the monetary expansion processes of numerous other countries. Bruno Brovedani reported on his work on Latin American monetary systems in lectures at the Centro de Estudios Monetarios Latinoamericanos in Mexico in 1960.[5] In an IMF Staff Paper in 1960, Joachim Ahrensdorf and S. Kanesathasan reported on a comparative study of the money multiplier covering twelve countries: Brazil, Canada, Ceylon, Colombia, Egypt, the Federal Republic of Germany, Italy, Japan, New Zealand, the Philippines, the United Kingdom, and the United States.[6]

Other studies of the interplay of high-powered money and the money multiplier have been made for Germany, Japan, South Korea, Argentina, Italy, Canada, and other countries.[7]

The multiplier is not a simple constant in any of the countries studied. But the fact that changes in the multiplier are a source of change in the money supply does not mean that the money supply cannot be controlled. Some of the studies have demonstrated that the reserve ratios and the currency ratios that determine the size of the multiplier are influenced by interest rates, income, and other variables and therefore behave in a predictable way. Furthermore, changes in the public's holdings of currency or the banks' holdings of cash reserves can be detected by the monetary authorities virtually as soon as they occur. It should be possible, therefore, to offset changes in the multiplier by increasing or decreasing the stock of high-powered money before money-supply growth diverges far enough from the authorities' desired rate to cause any harm to the ultimate objectives of price stability and high employment.

This review does not do justice to these studies and probably overlooks others, but I will simply argue that they provide compelling evidence that there is a multiple-expansion process in any country that uses commercial-bank deposits as part of its money supply. I believe, furthermore, that changes in the currency ratios and reserve ratios can be offset by central-bank actions. The ability or inability of central banks to control the money supply, therefore, depends mainly on how well they control the stock of high-powered money or monetary base.

There are two main problems in controlling high-powered

money. One is the balance of payments—the "imported inflation" problem—and the other is a whole collection of domestic reasons for the central banks to issue or retire high-powered money.

"IMPORTED INFLATION"

To illustrate the "imported inflation" problem, we will work outward from the United States to trace effects in other countries of changes in U.S. monetary growth rates. We will assume that exchange rates are fixed and that keeping them so is an important goal of the monetary authorities in the major industrial countries. This is one of the greatest sources of difficulty in controlling money supply, for if the authorities do whatever is required to keep exchange rates from changing, their countries may suffer unwanted fluctuations in money supply. If they concentrate on controlling money supply in order to maintain domestic price stability and high employment, they may be unable to prevent exchange rates from changing.

Suppose growth of the money supply of the United States were suddenly to accelerate to a much higher rate and to continue at this higher rate for several years, as it did from 1965 through 1968. Forecasters in the United States could confidently predict that incomes and prices would rise there. However, the effects of an inflationary U.S. monetary policy would not stop at the shoreline. In addition to increasing their spending for U.S. goods and services, U.S. residents would buy more foreign goods and services, including such capital goods as industrial plants, mines, or hotels in other countries. They would probably also buy more foreign securities.

Although the rise of U.S. spending abroad would be accelerated by a rise in U.S. prices relative to prices in the rest of the world, the spending increase would begin well before there was any noticeable change in prices. The increase in U.S. demand for foreign goods, services, and securities would merely be part of the process through which U.S. residents attempted to reduce the excess cash balances produced by the change in monetary policy.

The United States would therefore have a deficit in its balance of payments, that is, a net transfer of money to other countries, to pay for the difference in value between what the United States bought from other countries and what it sold to them. Perhaps we should say the United States would have a larger deficit than it had before the change in monetary policy.

Viewed from the other side, the increase in the U.S. balance-of-payments deficit would increase balance-of-payments surpluses, or reduce deficits, of other countries. Sellers of goods and services and securities to the United States would have more dollars in U.S. banks or in dollar accounts in banks of their own or other countries.

People of other countries, as well as residents of the United States, would find themselves holding more cash, or at least more dollars, than they prefer to hold in relation to their incomes and other assets. In attempting to reduce their excess balances of dollars, therefore, some residents of other countries would buy more U.S. goods and services and securities. Some would buy other currencies with dollars in order to buy goods and services at home or in other countries. Their offering of an increased supply of dollars on the foreign-exchange markets would then cause the price of dollars in terms of other currencies to fall. This is the point at which the central banks would face difficult choices.

Under the terms of the Bretton Woods Agreement, member nations of the International Monetary Fund are obliged to keep the dollar price of their currencies (exchange rate) within a band of 1 percent above and 1 percent below agreed par values. The United States, in turn, is obliged to maintain a par value for the dollar in terms of gold. Faced with a fall in the price of the dollar in terms of their own currencies or rises in their own exchange rates, central banks must buy enough dollars in exchange for their own currencies to keep exchange rates within the allowed range. This is not unlike a government program of buying wheat or corn to keep prices from falling when crops are unusually large.

Unfortunately, a central bank pays for anything it buys with high-powered money, as we saw in Chapter 9. Through the multiple-expansion process, the high-powered money exchanged for the dollars then causes a somewhat larger increase in the domestic money supply of the country whose central bank buys dollars. In this manner an increase in money supply engendered by a change in U.S. monetary policy spreads to other countries or is reluctantly "imported" by them. If the central bank did not buy the dollars, the price of dollars in terms of their currencies would fall—their exchange rates would rise. But the dollar inflow would not increase the domestic money supply.

Although our example described an increase in world money supply that originated in the United States, the United States is by no means the only source of world inflation. If some other country, France, for example, were suddenly to increase its money supply rapidly for some domestic reason, the consequences for world money supply would be much the same as if the United States had done so. People in other countries would find they had an excess supply of francs, which they would then sell for dollars or their own currencies. The price of the franc in terms of dollars (exchange rate) would tend to fall. The Banque de France would buy francs with dollars from its reserves to keep the exchange rate from falling. The people in other countries who had sold francs would then have an excess supply of dollars which they, in turn, might sell to their central banks, thus increasing the money supplies of other countries.

Incidentally, other central banks, including the U.S. Federal Reserve System, might also buy francs with dollars or other currencies in order to help the Banque de France stabilize the franc exchange rate. Or they might lend dollars to the Banque de France so the Banque could continue buying francs even after its own dollar reserves were low. The end result would be the same—an increase in world money supply.

The key point is that the money supplies of these countries would increase not because the central banks decided to increase them but for reasons unrelated to domestic monetary policy and, indeed, often in conflict with the objectives of domestic monetary policy. This is similar to the conflict of objectives that arises when the Federal Reserve or some other central bank buys government securities in order to help the Treasury finance a deficit.

Dr. Heinrich Irmler, Member of the Directorate of the Deutsche

Bundesbank, described in June, 1970, how the dilemma appears to a practicing central banker:

Foreign exchange movements are in fact the most important determinant of money supply in Germany that eludes the control of the Bundesbank. Before the change of parity in the spring of 1961 and again before the next revaluation in the autumn of 1969 many billions of Deutsche Mark of central bank money had come into being simply because the Bundesbank, or prior to 1958 its predecessor, the Bank deutscher Länder, was obliged to convert the inflowing dollars into Deutsche Mark at the fixed parity . . . given a rigid exchange rate, the creation of central bank money or the destruction of central bank money is outside the control of the central bank.[8]

Wherever it originates, inflation caused by overexpansion of a country's money supply will be transmitted through the fixed exchange-rate system to other countries. Countries that choose to maintain fixed exchange rates, therefore, seem doomed to accept a world-average rate of price inflation. There is the rub.

HIGH-POWERED MONEY OUT OF CONTROL AGAIN

The mechanics of "imported inflation" were clear to see from 1958 on. It also was easy to attribute the creeping inflation on the Continent of Europe to two countries—the United States and Britain—that had persistent balance-of-payments deficits. In 1964, however, two American professors, Ira O. Scott and Wilson Schmidt, who had been enjoying an academic season in Bologna, Italy, questioned this comfortable wisdom.[9] They pointed out that the central banks of Europe had indeed been adding to the stock of high-powered money by buying dollars. But the central banks had also been buying domestic assets in the course of lending to their governments or lending to banks and others through their discount windows. Not all of the inflation was imported; some of it was homegrown. To prevent it, said Schmidt and Scott, the central banks should have offset their purchases of foreign exchange with sales of other assets.

Paolo Baffi, of the Banca d'Italia, made the same point in 1968. His summary review of changes in the holdings of foreign and domestic assets at European central banks between 1959 and 1967 revealed that

. . . the big countries, far from offsetting the expansionary effect of the foreign component, added to it by augmenting central bank credit to domestic borrowers, while the small countries accepted such expansion in the monetary base as was generated by their foreign surpluses without significantly adding to or subtracting from it.[10]

As Dr. Baffi and Scott-Schmidt suggested, the central banks might have been expected to offset the effects of the foreign-exchange inflows (mostly dollars) by selling domestic assets or reducing their purchases, if they had wanted to resist inflation. The U.S. Federal Reserve System routinely offsets foreign transactions that would otherwise increase or decrease bank reserves and money supply, as can be seen in Table 10-1.

One argument to explain why other central banks do not do more offsetting—or "sterilizing," as it is often called—is that matching central-bank purchases of dollars or other foreign exchange with sales of domestic assets might raise domestic interest rates relative to rates in other countries and thereby attract an even greater flow of funds from outside.

A strong preference for stable interest rates, whether or not international flows of funds are involved, helps to account for the changes in money supply that originate at home. For, as the Scott-Schmidt and Baffi papers argue, *domestic* influences have been important contributors to inflation in Western Europe since 1958. I take 1958 as a starting point because before then exchange controls in European countries interfered with the international flows of funds that later were said to cause "imported inflation." Furthermore, European central banks were more concerned about a "dollar shortage" than about a dollar surplus before 1958.

In truth, central bankers, including those in the U.S. Federal Reserve System, would rather concern themselves with conditions in the money markets than with the money supply. The money-market strategy of the U.S. Federal Reserve System and other central banks is an alternative to controlling money supply. But it is an ineffective approach for achieving stability of economic activity and prices because it permits high-powered money and money supply to get out of control. It is the source of homegrown inflation.

Central banks are preoccupied with interest rates and credit conditions partly because the central banks themselves evolved directly, or indirectly, from commercial banks; and their officials are steeped in the mores and mystique of the financial world. Consequently, as Milton Friedman has said of the U.S. monetary authorities:

> To them it seemed perfectly natural and understandable in trying to serve the public interest to place major emphasis on interest rates and credit conditions rather than on the aggregate quantity of money. From this point of view, I think, it has been an unfortunate thing that we have had a Reserve bank which has been as closely linked to the banking community and to the lending and investing process as it has, not at all because the individuals are trying to feather their own nests, not for that reason, but because they naturally interpreted the instrument they were dealing with in terms of the environment they knew best and were most familiar with.[11]

Professor Harry Johnson, of the London School of Economics and the University of Chicago, made a similar observation in explaining why the Bank of Canada might have a different view of economic policy than the government:

> . . . its routine activities bring it into intimate contact with one special sector of the economy, the financial system. It is only to be expected, therefore, that its . . . views on monetary policy . . . will be influenced in general by the habits of thinking about economic affairs prevalent in the financial community . . . and in particular by the financial community's assessments of the nature of contemporary national economic problems and the policies appropriate to deal with them, whether these assessments are grounded in thorough economic analysis or not.[12]

Central banks the world over strive to avoid disrupting the functioning of the financial system with interest-rate changes. Unfortunately, this may mean tolerating money-supply changes that disrupt the rest of the economy.

We saw in Chapter 10 that if a central bank tries to keep interest rates from rising by purchasing securities it will increase the stock of high-powered money and the money supply. Bank credit and money supply, therefore, tend to expand when credit demand is strong and to grow more slowly or to contract when credit demand is weak.

In most central banks, lending through the discount window is far more important than open-market purchases or sales of securities. But this too is likely to produce increases in money supply when credit demand is strong and reductions when credit demand is weak, for the initiative in changing the volume of central-bank credit rests with the commercial banks. Accommodating credit demands through either device—open-market operations or central-bank discounting—is far from ideal from the standpoint of money-supply control.

INSTRUMENTAL VARIATIONS

The Federal Reserve System, if it chooses to do so, can offset international payments or changes in credit demands with its open-market operations. Other central banks, however, are said to lack the tools for offsetting either of these influences effectively. Although it is impossible here to make a thorough review of central-bank instruments, it nevertheless would be desirable to examine the main types in use today.[13] It is important to recognize, of course, that neither these instruments nor the central banks were expressly designed for the task of controlling the money supply. They evolved for many other purposes. But they have, at times, been deliberately used to control money supply and surely will be used more for this purpose in the future.

These instruments break down into two principal types: those designed to control the stock of high-powered money—administrative control of discounting, for example—and those designed to control what the banks and public do with the high-powered money —reserve requirements or restrictions on the amounts of particular assets the banks can hold.

Supplying high-powered central-bank money through rediscounting notes brought to them by commercial banks or through lending (advances) to banks and others against collateral of various kinds is a practice inherited from the days when the first central banks were commercial banks.

In the traditional view of central banking it was the discount rate, not the volume of central-bank credit (high-powered money), that was important. The key task of early central banks, such as the Bank of England, was to "protect the reserve." That is, to prevent the nation's gold reserve from getting too low by keeping interest rates high enough to attract gold from abroad. The discount rate, therefore, was set mainly with an eye to the outside world and was expected to determine the whole structure of interest rates in the country. The volume of central-bank lending then would be determined by the willingness of banks and others to borrow at the official rate.

Under the "real-bills" doctrine, furthermore, the volume of central-bank credit was believed to be self-regulating and not excessive if the central bank confined itself to rediscounting short-term notes arising out of business and trade transactions. The "real-bills" doctrine has caused no end of trouble because, wherever it is followed, money supply grows rapidly during booms and contracts in business recessions.

If control of the volume of central-bank credit, rather than interest rates, were the objective, however, changes in discount rates might conceivably be used as a regulator. If the banks were borrowing too much, the rate could be raised. It could be lowered when the authorities wanted bank borrowings and money supply to grow more rapidly. Through frequent, small changes in rate, therefore, growth in high-powered money and money supply might be kept under close control. But the discount rate is rarely used for this purpose by the world's major central banks. George Garvy, of the Federal Reserve Bank of New York, has listed several reasons inhibiting the free and frequent use of discount rate changes since World War II:

(a) Fear that the signal would be overinterpreted.
(b) Fear that large rate fluctuations would produce disruptive effects on the market for government securities and, more generally, on capital markets.

(c) Fear that automatic linkage between the discount rate and bank lending and/or deposit rates would tend to produce levels of interest rates that would be politically unacceptable.

(d) Fear of inducing undesirable international capital flows that would offset intended domestic effects of rate changes.[14]

Discount rate changes tend in practice to be large (seldom less than one half percentage point) and infrequent. Consequently, they are useful only for making occasional gross adjustments in money-growth rates, not for continuous, close control. Furthermore, more often than not, changing the money supply is only a subordinate objective of a discount rate change.

Having, in effect, forsworn use of the discount rate for regulating the supply of high-powered money, those central banks that do try to regulate the volume of discounting employ a wide variety of nonprice rationing devices. The most highly developed and most flexible of these is the "window guidance" (*Madoguchi Shido*) used in Japan.[15] The Bank of Japan, in cooperation with the Ministry of Finance, can maintain close control over the supply of high-powered money by adjusting ceilings on the amounts it allows banks to borrow. Through direct consultation with the banks, furthermore, it can influence their lending policies and their foreign-exchange transactions.

Michael Keran, of the Federal Reserve Bank of St. Louis, concluded from his study of the Japanese monetary system that the Bank of Japan can readily offset the effects of fluctuations in international reserves and government transactions on the supply of high-powered money:

In order to have expansions and contractions in high-powered money consistent with monetary policy objectives [he says], the central bank must take substantial action to break the "natural" expansions and contractions in high-powered money from international and government transactions.

High-powered money is a homogeneous financial asset which the Bank of Japan can control to any degree of accuracy it wishes. This is because it can know the level of high-powered money at any time [all the sources of high-powered money are recorded on its balance sheet] and because it can change the level at any time by changing central bank credit.[16]

Outside of Japan, however, the discount mechanism generally is an inefficient instrument for controlling the supply of high-powered money. A major reason for this is that the lending function of many central banks has been burdened with conflicting responsibilities. For example, in some countries the central bank is supposed to accord privileged treatment to certain preferred institutions, such as public enterprises, or to certain types of investment or export credit. When a central bank tries to restrict the expansion of its credit, therefore, it may find it difficult to turn away the privileged borrowers.

The most common disability of the discount mechanism is a tendency to accommodate short-run fluctuations in demands for credit. As we saw in the discussion of the U.S. Federal Reserve's money-market strategy, short-run changes in credit demands can add up to long-run changes that should be offset if the money supply is to be kept under control. In his study of the discount mechanism in leading industrial countries, George Garvy found:

> Most central banks use the discount mechanism to minimize day-to-day and week-to-week fluctuations in money market rates and gyrations due to tax payments . . . and similar recurrent periods of stress. Usually, offsetting other recurrent influences on the money market, such as fluctuations in the Treasury balance with the central bank, equally belongs to the category of routine activities.[17]

Such routine activities may make for calm and orderly financial markets, but they can and do produce perverse changes in bank credit and money supply. They, therefore, have all the faults of the accommodative open-market operations conducted by the Federal Reserve System in the United States.

The open-market purchases and sales of securities that are the principal instrument of the Federal Reserve System in the United States are used much less in other countries. This is partly because, except for England and Canada, other countries do not have well-developed markets for short-term securities. Central bank purchases or sales on a scale large enough to be effective in controlling bank credit and money supply it is feared would cause large, disruptive fluctuations in interest rates. In some countries in which open-market operations are used on a small scale, such as Germany and France, these open-market operations are intended not as a means for controlling the quantity of money but as a means for stabilizing rates in the market for government securities.

George Garvy suggests, in addition, that reliance on central-bank discounting and the fact that banks are habitually in debt to their central banks for considerable amounts have tended to inhibit the development of open-market operations even where markets might be able to accommodate them.

When banks acquire excess cash [Garvy says], they tend to reduce their borrowing . . . so that the central bank does not need to sell securities in the open market to mop them up. Conversely, in countries where commercial banks are almost continuously borrowers from the central bank, they have little inducement to hold eligible securities, the yield on which is usually lower than the discount rate.[18]

Despite the "thinness" of the markets, open-market operations in government and other securities are being used more and more in other countries—Germany, France, and Japan, in particular. In countries that do not have a large and actively traded volume of outstanding government securities, it is conceivable that central banks could issue securities of their own that they could thereafter buy or sell whenever they wanted to influence the stock of high-powered money.

In his study, *Central Banking in Latin America,* Frank Tamagna, of the American University in Washington, D.C., reported that the Banco Central de la República Argentina demonstrated the possibilities of this technique in the late thirties and early forties when it sold certificates of participation in a portfolio of government bonds that otherwise would not have been marketable.[19] This action helped to develop a market that made the central bank more effective. Other central banks might do the same if and when they become seriously interested in controlling the money supply.

Although they do not conduct a large volume of open-market operations in securities, most central banks conduct large and frequent open-market operations in foreign exchange. Unfortunately, these operations are conducted primarily in obedience to a simple rule—buy or sell as much foreign currency as necessary to keep exchange rates from changing. One result of this operating rule is the "imported inflation" which is said to demonstrate the inability of many central banks to control the money supply.

SUBSTITUTES FOR CONTROLLING HIGH-POWERED MONEY

In struggling to maintain a semblance of control over the monetary base in the face of inflows of foreign exchange, central banks have developed many ingenious and complicated devices for inducing their banks not to convert foreign exchange into domestic central-bank money that would then support an increase in domestic money supply.[20] These devices provide incentives to banks and others to hold foreign currencies in other countries rather than to convert them into domestic currency. They are, in effect, devices for controlling international flows of funds. Skillfully and diligently applied as they are, however, they are only partially successful at best. If they were more effective, we would not hear so much complaint about imported inflation.

Being unable or unwilling to control the supply of high-powered money, many central banks turn to attempts to influence what banks and the public do with it. The simplest device for this purpose is the variable reserve requirement. In principle, a central bank could offset the money-supply effect of an increase in high-powered money by requiring the banks to increase the ratio of their idle cash reserves to deposits. This would reduce the money multiplier.

When the Federal Reserve raises or lowers reserve requirements, the Board of Governors usually announces that the step is equivalent to absorbing or releasing a particular amount of bank reserves, say, $750 million, for example. Other central banks that have the power to set reserve requirements could do the same. But if reserve-requirement changes were large enough to offset inflows of foreign exchange fully, they would have about the same impact on interest rates and other credit-market conditions the authorities hope to avoid by not resorting to open-market operations or discount-rate changes.

A much-used compromise approach is to require banks to immobilize part of any new high-powered money in a so-called secondary reserve of government securities. The logic of this is based on a very different theory of how a central bank influences economic activity and prices from the monetary theory we have been using. This alternative credit-availability approach assumes that central banks exert their influence through controlling the flow of new loan credit to businesses and consumers. If the banks use new cash to buy government securities, therefore, the increase in high-powered money is believed to be less inflationary than if the banks make loans.

From the standpoint of controlling the money supply, however, it is immaterial whether the banks make loans or buy securities when they receive new reserves. Their deposits, which are part of the money supply, increase just as much either way. As a matter of fact, imposition of a security reserve requirement might actually make the increase in money supply per unit of new high-powered money slightly greater than if there were no such requirement. This is because the banks, viewing their security reserve as a partial substitute for cash reserves, might reduce the ratio of their cash reserves to their deposits, thus increasing the money multiplier.

The ultimate weapon, if the supply of high-powered money is not controlled, is the imposition of ceilings and other administrative restrictions on the amounts of assets that banks are permitted to hold. Like the secondary reserve idea, this approach stems mainly from the credit-availability theory of central banking. If it worked, it would be the equivalent of an increase in cash reserve requirements because new cash reserves could not be used by the banks after total bank loans and investments reached the ceiling; the ratio of cash reserves to assets (and deposits) would rise.

In practice, ceilings on advances or other assets rarely are effective in restraining growth of the money supply when the supply of high-powered money increases. The banks have too much incentive for buying earning assets that are not proscribed by the regulations; deposits and money supply, therefore, grow in spite of the central bank's efforts to hold them down through exhortation, moral suasion, or fiat. It would be far better if new high-powered money were prevented from getting into the monetary system in the first place.

This review of central-bank practices and instruments for controlling money supply has been necessarily hypothetical because few, if any, central banks do in fact attempt systematically and regularly to control money supply. They usually are much more concerned with many other tasks. Nevertheless, the widely expressed skepticism about the ability of central banks to control the money supply does not seem to me to be warranted.

Efforts of the U.S. Federal Reserve System to control money supply are inhibited, as we saw in Chapter 10, by a strong reluctance to tolerate short-run fluctuations in interest rates. The same reluctance is a strong inhibiting influence in other central banks as well. And the other central banks have an additional, and powerful, deterrent in their unwillingness to do anything that might cause exchange rates to change. Furthermore, most of them lack the well-developed money markets that facilitate the use of open-market purchases and sales of securities as the principal instrument of the Federal Reserve System in the United States.

With all of these provisos, however, it cannot be said that the central banks of the world are unable to control the money supply. The root problem is that they have not yet resolved the question of what they should control—interest rates, exchange rates, or money supply. As long as they give higher priority to controlling interest rates and exchange rates they will be unable to control the money supply effectively.

12

THE STRANGE AND WONDERFUL EURODOLLAR

Just as most bankers fifty years ago indignantly
rejected the insinuation that they were fabricating
domestic money, most bankers in the Eurodollar
system today cannot bear the thought that they
are able to fabricate, and are in fact fabricating,
foreign money. How could one believe that
honest bankers in London, Zurich, Frankfurt,
and Milan were busy creating U.S. dollars? A
preposterous idea close to malicious libel—except
for those who have thought it through in a
classroom rather than in the board room of a
bank.

Fritz Machlup, "Eurodollar Creation: A
Mystery Story," 1970[1]

Eurodollars are dollar-denominated deposits in banks outside
the United States, including the foreign branches of U.S. banks.
These deposits range in maturity from one day to several months,
and interest is paid on all of them.[2] Their most interesting feature
is that many of these dollars, probably more than half of them,
were created *outside* the United States in a process that is not
controlled by the Federal Reserve System or by any other central
bank.

The prohibition of interest payments on deposits of less than
30-day maturities by banks in the United States has been a major
factor in the development of the Eurodollar market, for it permits
Eurobanks to offer an important service that cannot be offered by
banks in the United States. The Eurobanks rake in and lend out

these dollar deposits on a worldwide table with the dizzying dexterity and finesse of master croupiers.

Central bankers and governments have been uneasy about the Eurodollar market ever since it became visible about 1958. Its explosive growth baffles them; they know something is going on but they are seldom sure quite what. They do know that one of its main attractions for the players is that the Eurodollar market provides opportunities for avoiding many of the regulations and restrictions that they try to enforce in national money markets.

Of most interest to us here, however, is that the Eurodollar market adds to the world supply of dollars—and sometimes reduces it—as though it were an overseas branch plant of the U.S. monetary system. Not all of the dollars whirling around in the Eurodollar market are dollars that have been exported from the United States, although the flows of dollars from and to the United States play major roles in the market's processes. Therefore, if the money supply of a country is viewed as the volume of domestic currency held by its residents plus the volume of dollars they hold, part of the dollar component is generated by a market that is not under the effective control of any central bank or international agency. Furthermore, these dollars—aptly called "stateless money" by Professor Fritz Machlup—are not counted in the money supply of any country.

DEBATE OVER MULTIPLIERS

Although there is much disagreement about the size of the multiplier, I believe the Eurodollar market is a multiple-expansion banking system that can expand or contract the supply of dollars *outside* the United States, just as the U.S. banking system and the Federal Reserve can expand or contract the supply of dollars *inside* the United States. Many of the European banks that accept dollar deposits are not required to hold reserves against them, but individual banks do voluntarily hold some dollars either in other European banks or in banks in the United States as a cash reserve against unexpected withdrawals. They could not operate safely otherwise. Nor could they operate profitably if they held a dollar in a U.S. bank for every Eurodollar on which they pay interest. Therefore, the dollar deposit liabilities of the Eurobanks are some multiple of their deposit balances (reserves) in U.S. banks. Furthermore, if the ratio of Eurobanks' dollar liabilities to their cash reserves in U.S. banks is stable, a change in the size of their reserve base will be reflected in a change in total Eurodollars that is greater than the amount of the reserve change. This is exactly the same in principle as though a central bank were to change the supply of high-powered money in the banking system described in Chapter 9.

Persuasive arguments for the existence of a significant multiplier in the Eurodollar system have been presented by a number of writers.[3] Paolo Savona of the Bank of Italy and Michele Fratianni of Ohio State University have made this multiplier a major part of their explanation of world money-supply determination.[4]

Guido Carli, governor of the Bank of Italy, has estimated that it ranges between 3 and 7.[5]

Other students of the Eurodollar system, such as Fred Klopstock of the Federal Reserve Bank of New York, argue that the multiplier must be very small, if it exists at all.[6] Unfortunately, we cannot settle the matter with the data now available. Nevertheless, the similarity of the Eurobank system to the multiple-expansion system described in Chapter 9 is striking.

One of the major factors affecting the stock of Eurodollars on which all the experts agree is international trade. If a Paris wine merchant is paid by a New York importer for a shipment of Beaujolais with a check for $1 million drawn on a New York bank, this may increase the U.S. dollar reserves of the Eurobank system. Whether it does or not depends upon whether the Paris merchant holds the dollars in a U.S. bank or deposits them in a bank outside the United States. While the merchant holds the $1 million balance in New York, his deposit there is analogous to the currency component of domestic high-powered money or monetary base. It is part of what Savona and Fratianni call "International Monetary Base." If he then deposits the dollars in his Paris bank, the balance in New York is transferred to the account of his Paris bank in New York, where it becomes part of the dollar reserves of the Eurobank system and can support a multiple expansion of Eurodollar deposit liabilities. Where the experts disagree is on the question of whether this increase in reserves will in fact cause a larger increase in the volume of Eurodollars or just a one-for-one change.

In some discussions of this question chains of individual transactions are described in order to estimate what the multiplier is by accounting for "leakages" from the system. One such classroom exercise might assume that the Paris bank would lend most of the Eurodollars obtained from the Paris businessman to a bank in London, which would lend the dollars to a British firm to pay for wool from Australia. The Australian wool exporters might keep the dollars on deposit with another London bank which, in its turn, would lend most of them to a German firm to pay for electronic components from Japan. At each step a part of the original $1 million in New York is transferred to the account of the appropriate Eurobank in the same or another New York bank.

At the end of this series of transactions: (1) the Paris wine merchant would still have $1 million in a Paris bank; (2) the Paris bank would have, say, a $950,000 time deposit in a London bank and $50,000 in a New York bank; (3) the first London bank would have a $900,000 loan to the British wool importer and $50,000 in a New York bank; (4) the Australian wool exporter would have a $900,000 balance in the second London bank; (5) the second London bank would have perhaps an $800,000 loan to the German manufacturer and $100,000 in a New York bank; (6) the Japanese electronics manufacturer would have $800,000 in a Tokyo bank; (7) the Tokyo bank would have $800,000 in a New York bank.

After netting out the $950,000 interbank deposits (Paris-bank deposit in London), we can see that the original $1 million (U.S. dollars) transferred to the Paris wine merchant has expanded to $2.7 million (Eurodollars), which are held by the Paris wine merchant, the Australian wool exporter, and the Japanese electronics manufacturer. Furthermore, the expansion potential of the original $1 million has not been exhausted because the Tokyo bank is still holding $800,000 of idle cash in New York, which it is unlikely to do for very long. The balances held in New York by the various Eurobanks as reserves are "leakages" from the system that limit the expansion process.

The analysts who believe there is a very small, or no, Eurodollar multiplier would argue that the scenario outlined here is highly unrealistic. It is much more likely, they say, that the new dollars received by the Paris wine merchant would leak back to America, or into a central bank, almost immediately, thus stopping the expansion process. Borrowers of Eurodollars, according to this argument, want them either to pay for purchases from the United States or to convert them into other currencies, in which case central banks are likely to buy the dollars and withdraw them from the Eurodollar system.

Such exercises of the imagination in lieu of facts cannot be decisive. We do know, however, that thousands of individual transactions every day add to, or reduce, the cash reserves of the Eurodollar system in U.S. banks. These transactions can be classified and described like the factors affecting U.S. bank reserves in Table 10-1.

When a Frenchman with a Eurodollar account in a Paris bank wants to make a dollar payment to someone in the United States, his Paris bank must provide dollars in a U.S. bank, either by drawing down its own account in a U.S. bank or by arranging to get U.S. bank dollars from some other Eurobank that day. This obligation of the Paris bank flows from the distinction between Eurodollars—dollar deposits in banks outside the United States—and U.S. dollars—U.S. currency and bank deposits in the United States. As Charles Scanlon said in his study of definitions and mechanics of Eurodollar transactions:

. . . unlike the U.S. dollars held by foreigners, Eurodollars are not direct claims on the resources of the United States. They are only claims on foreign banks, and it remains for these banks to provide the dollars from their reserves when the claims are exercised.[7]

However it is done, the transfer of these Eurobank-owned dollars to the American reduced the dollar reserves of the Eurobank system, just as the payment by another American for wine from France increased Eurodollar reserves.

PER CENT

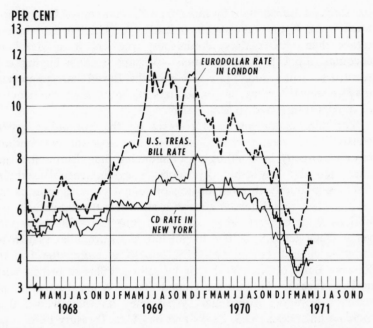

Chart 12-1. Eurodollar rates soar when U.S. banks are barred by Regulation Q ceilings on CD rates from obtaining funds domestically.

NOTES: *Chart by FNCB.*

Incidentally, this illustrates why the Eurobank system must keep some reserves in U.S. banks even though not every individual Eurobank has to keep any particular percentage of its Eurodollar liabilities on deposit in the United States. The size of the Eurodollar multiplier is determined by the ratio between the total Eurodollar liabilities of the Eurobanks to nonbanks and the total of Eurobank-owned deposits in U.S. banks. The reserve base is affected also by what amounts to the borrowing and lending of reserves. For example, when rates paid by Eurobanks on dollars rise above the rates attainable on short-term liquid assets in the United States, Americans and other holders of U.S. dollars may be induced to transfer dollars from their accounts in U.S. banks to Eurobanks. These transfers of deposits in U.S. banks to the accounts of Eurobanks add initially to Eurobank dollar reserves and may increase the stock of Eurodollars by more than the amount of U.S. dollars transferred. If the interest-rate incentive for holding Eurodollars, rather than U.S. dollars, diminishes, transfers from Eurobank accounts into U.S. bank accounts—perhaps through buying U.S. securities—will reduce the reserves of the Eurodollar system and may reduce the stock of Eurodollars by more than the amount of dollars transferred to U.S. banks.

The third major source of reserves for the Eurodollar system consists of the central banks. The central banks add or withdraw reserves directly by building up or reducing their Eurodollar balances just like any other depositors. They influence Eurodollar reserves indirectly through buying or selling other currencies for dollars when rate differences make it attractive for individuals and businesses to convert other currencies into Eurodollars, or vice versa. They get U.S. dollars to put into the Eurodollar system by reducing their balances with U.S. banks (including the Federal Reserve Bank of New York) or by selling dollar securities, such as U.S. Treasury bills, in the United States. When they withdraw reserves from the Eurodollar system they do the reverse; they increase balances in U.S. banks and buy U.S. Treasury bills.

Just before several of the European central banks revalued their currencies or allowed them to float in May, 1971, they were troubled by large inflows of dollars, some of which had been borrowed in the Eurodollar market to take advantage of higher interest rates in Germany or in expectation of upvaluations in the Deutschemark and other European currencies against the dollar. Germany, at the time, was keeping interest rates high to fight inflation, but the spread between German rates and Eurodollar rates was a powerful incentive for borrowing Eurodollars to convert them into German time deposits or other investments. It also provided incentive for German businesses to do their borrowing in the Eurodollar market rather than in Germany.

As we saw in Chapter 11, these inflows of dollars caused expansion of domestic money supplies when the central banks bought them with high-powered money in order to keep exchange rates from changing. Therefore, it was much to the interest of these central banks to stem the inflow. However, some of them apparently deposited some of the dollars they had just bought in Eurobanks, where they were promptly re-lent to others who exchanged them for marks and other currencies.

Some observers called this practice "double-counting" of central-bank reserves at the time because central banks count their Euro-dollar deposits as part of their exchange reserves. What is more to the point is that it probably increased the Eurodollar multiplier. When the central banks redeposited the Eurodollars they had bought in their exchange-pegging operations, there was no leakage of Eurobanks' dollar reserves out of the Eurobank system. Had the central banks instead transferred dollars to the Federal Reserve Bank of New York to be invested in U.S. Treasury bills as soon as they bought them, the Eurobank system would have lost reserves and the volume of Eurodollars would have contracted by some multiple of the reserve drain.

Although the central banks are not supposed to be run like profit-making institutions, some of them apparently contributed mightily to their own discomfort by feeding the Eurodollar machine for the sake of the slightly higher return they could earn on Euro-dollar deposits than on short-term liquid assets in the United States.[8]

It is frustrating to be unable to estimate the Eurodollar multi-plier as we would the multiplier in a national monetary system. Nevertheless, the Eurodollar system has all the earmarks of a fractional-reserve banking system, or rather, part of a larger world system if it is viewed as an extension of the U.S. monetary system. The cash reserves of the system amount to less than $17 billion (demand deposits of foreign commercial banks in U.S. banks) as contrasted with about $38 billion of Eurodollar liabil-ities at the end of 1969. Similar figures for the end of 1970 were $12 billion in cash reserves and $46 billion of Eurodollar liabilities, which suggests that the fraction of Eurodollars that is created in Europe has increased. If we include liabilities of U.S. banks to their foreign branches in the reserves of the Eurobank system, these reserves totaled $29.8 billion in 1969 and $19.7 billion in 1970. By either definition, the multiplier appeared to have increased between 1969 and 1970.

We know that the volume of these reserves changes, and we can identify some of the sources of the changes in the actions of the world's businessmen; the Eurobanks themselves; and the central banks, including the U.S. Federal Reserve System. Monetary theory tells us, furthermore, that changes in the reserve base of such a system should cause a much larger change in the total liabilities of the system, both in the Eurobank part of it and in the United States. Therefore, I believe Milton Friedman was right when he said:

The existence of the Eurodollar market increases the total amount of dollar balances available to be held by nonbanks throughout the world for any given amount of money (currency plus deposits at Federal Reserve Banks) created by the Federal Reserve System. It does so by permitting a greater pyramiding on this base by the use of deposits at U.S. banks as prudential reserves for Eurodollar deposits.[9]

THE MAGIC SPRING

The startling potential of the Eurodollar market was most clearly projected by its performance between early 1966 and the end of 1969. Within less than four years, U.S. banks dipped into the Eurodollar market for more than $12 billion. But the more dollars they bailed out, the more Eurodollars there were in the market. By the end of 1969 the volume of Eurodollars had more than tripled—to about $38 billion.

If dollars came only from America, and if U.S. banks were busily taking them home again through this period, how could there be three times as many Eurodollars at the end of the period as there were at the beginning? Furthermore, Eurodollar rates reached horrendous heights in 1969, eliciting anguished cries about a shortage rather than a surfeit of Eurodollars. This puzzle is a good example of the confusions that arise when we fail to distinguish between money and credit.

If one takes a monetarist's view of what happened, it can be argued that the methods chosen by the Federal Reserve for fighting inflation in the United States tended to inflate the rest of the world because the Eurodollar component of the world's money supply ballooned. If one takes credit availability and interest rates as measures of monetary policy, however, one would conclude instead that the U.S. policies produced excruciatingly restrictive effects in the rest of the world.

Walking in slow motion through what Professor Machlup has called the "square dance" may help to clear up the mystery. To simplify the bookkeeping, furthermore, we will concentrate on one year, 1969. In the United States that year major money-center banks suffered a loss of time deposits because they were prohibited by the Federal Reserve's Regulation Q from paying the market rate. At the same time they were faced with a strong demand for business loans. To offset the loss of time deposits they instructed their London branches or correspondents to bid for more Eurodollar deposits and to transfer dollars to the head offices in New York, Chicago, and other centers.

On the books of the U.S. money-center banks, time-deposit liabilities (mostly negotiable certificates of deposit, or CDs) contracted by about $12 billion, as investors transferred funds out of bank CDs and into other liquid assets offering higher interest yields. But as the branches raked in Eurodollars abroad, demand deposits were transferred from the balances of Eurobanks to an item called "liabilities to foreign branches," which grew by $7 billion.

Although not all of the loss of time deposits was offset by the increase in liabilities to foreign branches, the attraction of Eurodollars from abroad enabled the U.S. money-center banks to expand their business loans by more than they otherwise could have done. These transactions did not increase the U.S. money supply, but they did increase the supply of bank credit in the United States.

Outside the United States the immediate impact of the Eurodollar gathering by branches of U.S. banks was the transfer of $7 billion of U.S. dollar reserves from other Eurobanks to the U.S.-owned Eurobanks. If nothing else had happened, these other Eurobanks would have had to reduce their Eurodollar loans or sell other dollar assets in order to get dollars. This would have reduced the volume of Eurodollar credit (loans), although the volume of Eurodollar money (deposits) would not have been affected. This is because the U.S. branches were, in effect, lending the dollars to their head offices instead of using them to make Eurodollar loans outside the United States. It could be argued, however, that there should

$ BILLIONS

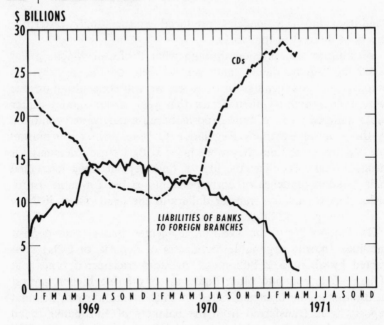

Chart 12-2. In 1969, large U.S. commercial banks borrowed Eurodollar deposits from their foreign branches. In 1970, when they were able to issue CDs again, they let their Eurodollars run off.

NOTES: *Chart by FNCB.*

be some money-supply effect in Europe, because these transactions amounted to shifting reserves from banks with low (voluntary) reserve requirements to banks with higher reserve requirements.

The first-round effects of the gathering of Eurodollars by U.S. banks, therefore, were: In the United States bank credit went up by $7.5 billion and money supply was unchanged. In the Eurodollar market Eurodollar credit was reduced by $7.5 billion and the supply of Eurodollar money was unchanged.

But other things did happen. The reduction in supply of Eurodollar loans at a time when the demand for credit was very strong in Europe, as well as in the United States, pushed Eurodollar interest rates up. The rise of interest rates then drew dollars into the reserve base of the Eurodollar system from several sources.

According to estimates of the Bank for International Settlements,

U.S. residents transferred $2 billion into Eurodollars in 1969; private non-U.S. residents transferred $0.5 billion of dollar balances from banks in the United States to banks in the Eurodollar market; and foreign official agencies (including central banks) transferred about $1.5 billion from U.S. banks to banks outside the United States.[10] The high Eurodollar rates also induced many banks, traders, and investors to buy dollars from central banks, in exchange for other currencies, in order to put them into the Eurodollar market. About $3.5 billion of new reserves (BIS estimate) was drawn in from central banks in this way.

The central banks obtained some of the dollars they deposited in Eurodollar banks or sold in exchange for their own currencies by selling U.S. Treasury bills or other short-term assets in the United States. This had the interesting effect of reducing the U.S. money supply—not the money supply as reported in Federal Reserve statistics but the money supply actually held by U.S. residents. When the proceeds of the bill sales were transferred from American buyers of bills to the accounts of foreign central banks at Federal Reserve banks and then to the accounts of Eurobanks at U.S. banks, the domestic money supply held by U.S. residents declined. Because the U.S. money-supply statistics include foreign deposits, however, the transactions did not reduce the reported money supply. Furthermore, there was no reserve-multiplier effect —the reduction in (U.S.-owned) money supply was no greater than the amount of the central-bank sales of bills to Americans. Nevertheless, this is an intriguing example of how open-market operations conducted in the United States by foreign central banks (through the Federal Reserve Bank of New York) can influence the money holdings of Americans.

The expansion in volume of Eurodollars tended to inflate world money supply. As we saw in Chapter 11, however, when a central bank sells dollars in exchange for its own currency it contracts the domestic money supply of its country. The sale of dollars by central banks to people who then put them into the Eurodollar market, therefore, had a contractive effect on the supplies of other currencies.

Worldwide inflation in 1969 was ample reason for most countries to follow restrictive monetary policies. Of ten countries heavily involved in the Eurodollar market—the eight countries that report Eurodollar transactions to the BIS plus Japan and Canada—eight had substantially slower money-supply growth in 1969 than in 1968. Only two—Italy and Japan—had more monetary expansion in '69 than in '68. By pulling dollars out of central banks the Eurodollar expansion reinforced the efforts of central banks to curb money-supply growth. However, it increased the supply of substitutes for domestic currencies (including dollars in U.S. banks). We have no way of knowing which of these effects was the more important as an influence on the world price level.

In 1970 and 1971, as credit demands and interest rates fell in the United States, U.S. banks reduced their liabilities to foreign branches; some dollars that had been placed in the Eurodollar market by U.S. residents and others returned to the United States; and central banks again absorbed dollars in their official reserves. This might have been expected to contract the volume of Eurodollars outstanding; but, as we saw earlier, the incentive for borrowing Eurodollars to convert them into European currencies—especially the Deutschemark—was so great that the stock of Eurodollars grew. The Eurodollar-creating process was compounded when central banks obligingly redeposited dollars in Eurobanks.

This discussion has not settled the question of how big the Eurodollar multiplier is. But it should make one thing clear: the Eurodollar market can increase the supply of dollars *outside* the United States without reducing the supply of dollars *inside* the United States. Therefore, it can increase (or reduce) the total world supply of dollars. Furthermore, the supply of Eurodollars is largely demand-determined. When the demand for Eurodollars increased from 1966 through 1969, the stock of Eurodollars increased; when the demand fell in 1970, the stock contracted for a time, and then increased again in early 1971.

CENTRAL BANKERS WRESTLE THE WHIRLWIND

Thus far I have emphasized the moneyness of Eurodollars. But the Eurodollar market is viewed in most discussions more as a credit market—a market in dollar bank loans—and as an important accessory to the Eurobond market—an international capital market for bonds denominated mainly in dollars. Eurodollar interest rates, moreover, have fluctuated widely in recent years; and changes in the demand for Eurodollars have made it difficult for central banks to maintain fixed exchange rates.

The credit and interest-rate and exchange-rate implications of the Eurodollar have probably concerned world central bankers much more than its money-supply implications. In any case, they have been groping for ways to bring the market under control or somehow to insulate their domestic money markets from some of its effects. These efforts open up some surprising complications. Most interesting of all, they reveal how interdependent the monetary systems of the world have become.

Although no one central bank tries to regulate the stock of Eurobank reserves in the way the Federal Reserve controls reserves in the U.S. banking system, several do try to influence the Eurodollar market by adding or withdrawing dollars. The U.S. Federal Reserve System has for several years cooperated with other central banks and the Bank for International Settlements in attempting to stabilize exchange rates and interest rates in the Eurodollar market.[11] However, these operations are sporadic attempts to counter short-run pressures on interest rates or exchange rates. They are not intended to be a continuous effort to manage the volume of Eurodollars or Eurodollar interest rates.

Neither the data nor the management techniques are now available for controlling the volume of Eurodollars. Consequently, national efforts to isolate domestic economics from the market are proliferating.

In his survey of national policies with respect to the Eurodollar market, Donald Hodgman, of the University of Illinois, found that not one of the six major countries he studied has been willing to let its residents participate in the market without some form of official intervention.[12] The interventions ranged from comprehensive exchange controls to various devices intended to influence the profitability of banks' Eurodollar activities. Nevertheless, he says, none of these countries has found it possible to isolate its domestic economy from the effects of changing conditions in the Eurodollar market.

There has been much confusion about whether the raising of funds in the Eurodollar market by U.S. banks in 1966 and 1969 frustrated Federal Reserve attempts to fight inflation. Use of the Eurodollar market did not impair the Federal Reserve's control of the U.S. money supply. It merely affected the distribution of bank reserves within the United States, not the amount of reserves, by drawing bank reserves to banks in the larger money centers, such as New York City, Chicago, and San Francisco. By converting deposits subject to reserve requirements into liabilities to foreign branches—which were free from reserve requirements—these transactions did have the effect of reducing the average reserve-requirement ratio. But this effect was easily offset by Federal Reserve open-market operations.

Through its control over total member-bank reserves, however, the Federal Reserve was successful in restricting domestic money-supply growth. Furthermore, as other central banks placed dollars in the Eurobanks, the sale of Treasury bills in the United States by these central banks reinforced the restrictive effects of the Federal Reserve's own open-market operations.

Use of the Eurodollar market by U.S. banks did partially frustrate Federal Reserve credit policy—the Federal Reserve's attempt to restrict bank lending to businesses through restricting the access of large city banks to time-deposit funds. However, credit policy, as distinguished from money-supply policy, is an ineffective instrument at best. The central bank cannot control the total supply of credit in the economy because its direct control is limited to bank credit.

The Federal Reserve would have been better advised in 1966 and 1969 not to have attempted to restrict credit availability to businesses as such and to have paid more attention to the effects of restricting the growth of the money supply. By foregoing the use of Regulation Q ceilings as a selective control over credit, furthermore, it could have avoided most of the distress and disruption its policies caused in the Eurodollar market.

European central banks, too, have found that the Eurodollar market makes it more difficult for them to restrain credit availability. Businesses that cannot get mark or franc loans from West

German or French banks, for example, borrow Eurodollars instead. In this case, however, there is a money-supply effect. If businessmen convert borrowed Eurodollars into local currencies, to pay wages and dividends, for example, and if the central banks buy some of these dollars to maintain fixed exchange rates, the restraint policies are undermined by increases in the domestic money supply, as we saw in Chapter 11. Most frustrating of all to the Continental central banks was the role of the Eurodollar market in the exchange-rate speculation that led to the revaluations and floating exchange rates of May, 1971.

Not all of the national efforts to intervene in the Eurodollar market are aimed at isolation, however. Some central banks use the Eurodollar market to good effect in controlling their domestic money supply and volume of bank credit. In a technique pioneered by the Bank of Italy, a central bank that wants to restrain expansion of its domestic money supply and bank credit "swaps" dollars for its own currency with an agreement to buy back the dollars at some time in the future on terms that are more favorable than those available in the forward-exchange market.[13]

The swaps reduce domestic bank reserves and the banks use the dollars to buy earning assets in the Eurodollar market. In effect, these transactions amount to using the Eurodollar market for conducting open-market operations that would otherwise be difficult or impossible because of the limited size of the domestic securities market.

Despite all the worries about the instability of the Eurodollar market, the Eurodollar is now too big and too deeply rooted in world financial markets to be done away with. The alleged instability, moreover, comes more from the volatility of national policies than from characteristics of the market itself. By all odds the most disturbing influence in the market in the past decade has been the United States.

Selective controls in the United States, such as the interest-equalization tax and the "voluntary" restrictions on lending and investing abroad by U.S. corporations and banks, have made the market larger than it otherwise would have been. Without these controls much of the market's activity would instead be carried on in the

New York money market. Regulation of interest paid on U.S. bank time deposits has also made the Eurodollar market larger and less stable.

Rather than do away with the controls that created much of the problem, the Federal Reserve imposed special reserve requirements on part of the U.S. banks' liabilities to foreign branches in 1969. This step was intended to reduce the incentive for U.S. banks to take in Eurodollars. When the Eurodollars began to flow back in 1970, the Federal Reserve revised these reserve requirements to reduce the return flow, which, by then, was embarrassing European central banks by making it difficult for them to peg exchange rates and to keep their interest rates high. In 1971 the U.S. Treasury offered special issues of securities at attractive rates to U.S. banks that would hold Eurodollars at their branches instead of letting them run off. More patches were thus applied on top of an already unreasonable accumulation of controls.

The full potential of the Eurodollar market for good will not be realized until central bankers of the world bring domestic money supplies under stable and dependable control. As the First National City Bank observed in its July, 1970, *Monthly Economic Letter:*

> The spreading of controls on a market that was, until only a year ago, one of the freest in the world is disconcerting. The controls are rationalized by reference to the strains and stresses that mark Eurodollar banking in a world that is becoming increasingly sensitive to differentials in interest rates and exchange rate risks. These strains and stresses are, of course, symptoms—not causes—of domestic monetary difficulties and uncertainties.[14]

Despite the many advantages of the Eurodollar as a "vehicle currency" for carrying on world trade, there remains the unsettling prospect of a machine controlled by no one that can add to the world's money supply by creating dollars. As Milton Friedman has said, "the Eurodollar market has almost surely raised the world's nominal money supply (expressed in dollar equivalents) and has thus made the world price level (expressed in dollar equivalents) higher than it would otherwise be."[15]

four
___

WHY MONEY MATTERS

WHAT'S IN THE BLACK BOXES?

> The peculiar effects during transition periods
> are analogous to the peculiar effects in starting or
> stopping a train of cars. Normally the caboose
> keeps exact pace with the locomotive, but when
> the train is starting or stopping this relationship
> is modified by the gradual transmission of effects
> through the intervening cars. Any special shock
> to one car is similarly transmitted to all the others
> and to the locomotive.
> Irving Fisher, *The Purchasing Power of Money*,
> 1922[1]

To Irving Fisher the train analogy was an appealing way to explain lags in the transmission of money-supply effects through the
economy. In our more sophisticated, although not necessarily more
enlightened, age, however, everything must be more complicated.
The image of the "black box" full of electronic circuitry that guides
jet planes or missiles seems more appropriate.

Although one might expect "black box" to connote the latest and
best in transmission mechanisms, the term has been used to suggest deliberate concealment, almost deception, as when J. Dewey
Daane, member of the Federal Reserve Board of Governors, de-
scribes the Friedman approach to money:

At one end of the black box the supply of money is fed in, and out of
the other end emerges a stream of spending for goods and services—or
GNP. Since the actual conversion of the money supply into demands
for goods and services takes place within that closed box, one never
knows how the conversion was made or what is really going on inside.
And Professor Friedman and his supporters generally exhibit all too

little interest in the conversion process—in other words, in what goes on inside that box.[2]

Governor Daane's implied criticism of the monetary approach should, however, apply equally well to two other black boxes that are commonly used to explain the working of fiscal and monetary policies: the fiscalist black box (mainly Keynesian) and the credit-availability black box (an old central-bank apparatus with Keynesian embellishments). As a matter of fact, much is still unknown about the internal circuitry of all three of these mechanisms for transmitting the effects of fiscal and monetary policies to incomes and prices. With all three of them connected to the economy at once, it is difficult to determine which one is really carrying the load. Furthermore, as can be seen from the research to be reviewed in the next chapter, there is ample reason to question the reliability of some basic elements in these transmission mechanisms that formerly were taken on faith.

Comparing these black boxes is much like the problem U.S. and Russian intelligence agencies would have if they listened to the radio signals sent by each other's satellites and tracked them by radar but were never able to capture any of them to see how they were put together. By assuming that both countries employ many of the same basic components in their space vehicles, rival intelligence agencies could build models with which to simulate the performance of the other's satellites. Various models might approximate the performance of the satellites, but no model could exactly duplicate a real satellite orbiting overhead.

So it is with the models that are used to explain economic policy transmission mechanisms in the real world. Theoretical preconceptions or biases of the modelers may lead them to include components that should not be there or to reject components that should have been included. In viewing the real world transmission mechanisms, or black boxes, we must work with greatly simplified approximations at best.

Preconceptions about what the black box is supposed to do are extremely important in determining what the modeler will put into his model. For example, if one starts by assuming that a satellite has the task of gathering weather data, the model will be very different than if the satellite is assumed to be searching out missile sites. In the case of economic-policy black boxes, the crucial distinction is between models designed to explain how a government can exercise discretionary powers to stabilize an unstable economy and models designed to explain how to avoid destabilizing an otherwise stable economy. A model that is effective in one of these tasks might fail utterly at the other.

The fiscalist and credit-availability black boxes are viewed as discretionary instruments for stabilizing an unstable economy. Monetarists view their black box as more like a gyroscope: when running smoothly it contributes to the stability of a stable system; but it can cause havoc if it gets out of order. Most descriptions of the monetarist transmission mechanism, therefore, are concerned with what happens to an otherwise stable system when the monetary gyroscope gets out of order, rather than with how it might be used for discretionary fine-tuning in an unstable system.

THE FISCALISTS' BLACK BOX—KEYNESIAN VERSION

William Wolman has said that when Friedman and Meiselman opened the Keynesian black box they found it empty.[3] That is almost true. What they did was to cast doubt on the reliability and predictability of certain key components of the Keynesian transmission mechanism that had previously been taken for granted. In particular, they challenged the Keynesian assertion that fluctuations in investment and government spending have predictable multiplier effects on total income and spending. The multiplier is still a central part of Keynesian doctrine.

Investment (and any autonomous schedule shift) [says Paul Samuelson] has a multiplier effect on income. When investment changes, there is an equal *primary* change in national income. But as these primary income receivers in the capital-goods industries get more earned income, they set into motion a whole chain of additional *secondary* consumption spending and employment.

If people always spend about ⅔ of each extra dollar of income upon consumption, the total of the multiplier chain will be . . . 3. The multiplier works forward *or backward,* amplifying either increases or decreases in investment [italics in original].[4]

To offset a decline in investment, the government is supposed to increase its spending or to reduce taxes. In the terminology of Governor Daane, an increase of government expenditures or a reduction in taxes is fed in at one end of the black box and out of the other end emerges an increase of spending for goods and services—or GNP—that is several times as large as the change in fiscal measures. Keynesians have built models or theories in which this multiplier effect occurs, but they have not demonstrated that there is a transmission mechanism in the real world that behaves like the models.

Because Keynes wrote in a great hurry and did not have the wealth of statistics and computers we enjoy today, he might be excused for not verifying his statements empirically. This indulgence, however, should not extend to his followers, who, until recently, did not bother to test his theory either. The acceptance of Keynesian theory was not based upon rigorous testing, says Alan Walters of the London School of Economics.

The remarkable thing about Keynesian theory [he says] was that almost everyone swallowed it. Powers of persuasion, ridicule for the monetary "old fogeys," elegance of exposition won the day. No one thought it necessary to test such an obvious truth until the 1950s. Then Friedman and others not only suggested but also carried out comparative tests of the Keynesian model to see whether it predicted better than the simple monetary hypothesis for the United States. It did not, except for the period of the Great Contraction.[5]

The statistical tests performed by Friedman, Meiselman, and others found that the multiplier is neither prompt in working nor predictable in size.[6]

The most important circuit in the Keynesian black box, therefore, may fail the policy makers and the forecasters just when they count on it most. As we saw in Chapter 3, this was dramatically illustrated by the failure of tax increases in England and the United States to influence consumer spending significantly in 1968, despite the confident expectations of many forecasters that the effects would be both substantial and virtually immediate.

Robert Eisner, of Northwestern University, argues that the U.S. income-tax surcharge should not have been expected to have much influence on consumer spending in the second half of 1968.[7] In effect, he charges advocates of a tax increase in 1968 with having failed to apply a major improvement that had been made in their own analytical framework about fifteen years earlier—the permanent-income hypothesis of Milton Friedman.[8]

Although elementary textbook versions of Keynesian income-expenditure theory treat consumption expenditures as being determined closely by current measured income, more sophisticated versions add assets or wealth to the explanation and use *expected* or *permanent* income instead of *current* income. Therefore, both sudden windfalls and short periods of below-normal income have less-than-proportional effects on consumption spending.

If a household's assets and expected income are unaffected [says Eisner], we can expect little in the way of a change in consumption from a temporary reduction in income brought on by an increase in tax rates.[9]

In this case the tax increase was widely advertised as temporary. Eisner refers to some who opposed combining expenditure reductions with the tax increase as "mesmerized by simplistic application of the lessons of Economics/1—before the permanent income theory took hold."[10] I must say it was extremely refreshing to see the word "simplistic" applied to the thinking of nonmonetarists for a change.

The so-called "marginal propensity to consume" is the Achilles' heel of the Keynesian system. For if consumption does not in fact behave as the theory assumes, changes in the government budget and other autonomous variables such as exports and business investment will not have the multiplier effects on income that the theory predicts. Axel Leijonhufvud concludes that, "Professor Milton Friedman's permanent income hypothesis and the Modigliani-Brumberg-Ando 'life cycle hypothesis' alike imply such a low value for the multiplier that it would not be worth bothering about."[11] That is quite a comedown for the kingpin in the fiscalists' system.

Considering the disappointing record of fiscal policy in attempting to counter inflation and recession, it is curious that popular faith in the efficacy of budget deficits or surpluses is so strong all over the world. As Herbert Stein has pointed out, the fiscal revolution, or upsurge of faith in fiscal policy, preceded the Keynesian revolution; was more widely accepted; and may well outlast it.[12] This may be due at least partly to a tendency to mistake monetary effects for fiscal effects. The monetary black box does the work, but the fiscal box gets the credit or blame.

David Fand argues that even such large and sophisticated econometric models as the one built by the Federal Reserve Board and Professors Ando and Modigliani overestimate the fiscal multiplier by not adjusting properly for monetary effects.

There is general agreement that we need to distinguish between a deficit that is financed entirely through the capital market (and) involving no creation of money [says Fand] and a deficit that is financed through money creation by the banking system. In the first case the increase in GNP is entirely due to the deficit; in the second case, the multiplier must be adjusted to allocate part of the increase in the GNP to the monetary stimulus. Yet this simple difference between a multiplier adjusted for the monetary effects and a multiplier that includes both fiscal and monetary effects can easily be overlooked.[13]

The popular association of budget deficits with inflation and surpluses with deflation stems from the common tendency of central banks to increase money-supply growth when their host governments have deficits to finance. Budget deficits are, therefore, associated with inflationary rates of money-supply growth and surpluses are associated with low rates of money-supply growth or contraction. This is the elementary fact of life for which Fand says the econometric models fail to adjust. But central banks do not always have to behave in the traditional way. Central banks can, and do, refuse to finance government deficits at times; and so the effects of the two black boxes should be more carefully distinguished.

When Leonall Andersen and Jerry Jordan tested the two principal fiscal instruments—tax receipts and government expenditures —by a method that did adjust for the accompanying monetary effects, their results did not agree at all with the popular view of the fiscal black box.[14] For example, changes in tax receipts, which are almost universally believed to influence economic activity strongly, appeared to have insignificant effects. Andersen and

Jordan said this result was consistent with theories that the influence of government spending will not necessarily be greater if the funds to finance it are borrowed from the public rather than obtained through taxation. Milton Friedman has often argued that the common belief in stimulative effects of government borrowing is based on overlooking what investors in government securities would otherwise have done with their funds.[15]

Also extremely damaging to confidence in the effectiveness of fiscal policy was the Andersen-Jordan finding that an increase in government expenditures increases gross national product only temporarily. After six months of being mildly stimulative, an increase in government expenditures causes offsetting reductions during the following six months. The over-all effect, when distributed over a year, therefore, is small and not statistically significant. This surprising result, however, is consistent with a classical notion that was jettisoned along with money in the Keynesian mutiny long ago. Pre-Keynesian classical economists believed that an increase in government spending would be offset by a decrease in private spending; that fiscal policies could change the way total income is divided up but should not be expected to have much influence on the size of the pie. We saw this "crowding out" effect of fiscal policy in the GNP forecasting model of Chapter 6.[16]

Destructive testing of the main circuits in the fiscal black box may seem to have been overdone by the critics, but advocates of fiscal policy have had ample opportunity for rebuttal. They have not yet produced the evidence to back up their claims that fiscal measures have strong, prompt, independent effects on income. If we compare the input of fiscal actions with the output of changes in GNP at the other end of the black box, we do not find the simple, reliable relationship that Keynesian theory and most economic textbooks would lead us to expect. And if we look at the individual key components, such as the propensity to consume, we find little reason for expecting the fiscal black box to be a dependable instrument of public policy. Worst of all, the results of fiscal-policy experiments in the sixties did not live up to their advance advertising.

Since comparative testing of the transmission mechanisms began, says Karl Brunner, the views of the fiscalists have undergone a fascinating evolution.[17] At first fiscal policy was said to be a powerful and reliable instrument for stabilizing the economy and for accelerating its growth rate, while monetary policy was of minor importance as a complement to fiscal policy. After the Friedman-Meiselman study, fiscal and monetary policies were both said to have important independent effects; but fiscal policy was preferable because it was faster than monetary policy.

After monetary policy demonstrated the ability to overpower fiscal policy in 1966–1967 and 1968, it was conceded that fiscal policy also operated with long time lags while monetary policy was more powerful and operated with shorter lags than had been thought before. But some of the side effects of monetary policy were said to be so damaging to home building and some financial intermediaries that it was still preferable to use fiscal policy for stabilization purposes. Like the proverbial Russians in the sleigh, the fiscalists have been fleeing a wolf pack of facts, sacrificing one doctrinal brainchild after another as they go.

An even more basic objection to the fiscalist black box is that it was designed for a different world than the one of today—the world of the depressed 1930s. As Axel Leijonhufvud, David Fand, and others have argued, attempting to apply a depression theory to the fully employed economies of the post-World War II world has led to an inflationary bias in policies.

Though Keynesianism, born in the depression, was associated with stagnation and unemployment [says Fand], many modern Keynesians have switched their allegiance to the currently fashionable objectives of expansion and higher economic growth rates. But these Jet Age objectives are still linked to the 1930s Keynesian stagnationist-type model— an analytic structure with sticky prices, unused resources, and considerable output elasticity. The inflation since 1965 is just one example of a period where actual price level movements could not be handled satisfactorily by this model. It is this combination of expansionist objectives with depression-oriented theory that imparts an inflationary bias to Modern Keynesianism.[18]

As we saw in Chapter 4, the stagnationist antecedents of modern fiscalism showed through clearly in the early forecasts of a sluggish recovery in '71 that were made by prominent American Keynesians.

The fiscalist black box did not, until recently, include linkages between the fiscal levers in the hands of the authorities and prices. This is because the theory was originally meant to be a short-run analysis of an underemployed economy in which a large increase in output could occur without any impact on prices. Furthermore, the monetary theory in the fiscalist black box, such as it was, stressed money-supply effects on interest rates but omitted any direct effects of money-supply changes on spending and prices. The price level was determined outside the system by the past history of prices and the bargaining power of various interest groups. In recent years there have been attempts to bring prices into the model through relationships between actual and potential output—the "gap"—and between unemployment and the rate of rise of wage rates—the "Phillips curve."

Because of the cultural lag in adapting a depression theory to the problems of high-employment economies, fiscalists have concentrated on the difficult—largely political—problems of putting their fiscal policies into effect. They have relied on guideposts and incomes policies to contain inflation while pursuing expansion. But, most important, they have overlooked the inflationary risks of high rates of monetary expansion, to their sorrow, as we saw of American fiscalists in Chapter 3. They should have paid more attention to what was happening in the monetarists' black box.

THE CREDIT-AVAILABILITY BLACK BOX

Probably the least thoroughly tested of the three transmission mechanisms is the credit-availability one, although it unquestionably is highly regarded by central bankers nearly everywhere. Its appeal is commonsensical, for it seems perfectly obvious that an individual or a business will spend more if credit is easily available than if it is not.

In using this policy-transmission mechanism, the central bank tries to influence the total supply of credit in the economy by influencing the growth of bank credit, generally through the same measures—open-market operations and discount-rate changes—that are used to control money supply or interest rates. In addition, it is generally believed that certain kinds of credit, bank loans to corporations, for example, have more influence on economic activity than, say, bank credit in the form of government bonds.

Belief in the efficacy of credit availability has two main roots: a centuries-old concern of central banks over the amounts and kinds of credit and the more recent Keynesian emphasis on investment spending (amplified by the multiplier discussed above) as a major influence in business fluctuations. Originally, Keynesians emphasized interest rates as the key transmitter of central-bank policy; but surveys of businessmen's attitudes with respect to the influence of interest rates on their investment expenditures in the thirties had discouraging results. Businessmen did not seem to pay much attention to interest rates if other considerations told them it was a good time to invest or not to invest. Soon thereafter central banks were preoccupied with pegging interest rates for World War II, in any case, and had no scope for altering interest rates.

Economists of the U.S. Federal Reserve System, led by Robert V. Roosa, triumphed over the apparent disability of interest rates, or thought they did, by developing a new theory of monetary control soon after World War II—the credit-availability doctrine.[19] According to the new theory, monetary policy works much more through influencing the availability of credit than through influencing its cost. Therefore, it should be possible to curb spending through restricting the availability of bank reserves, without raising interest rates very much.

It was easy to see why the new theory should be eagerly seized as the rationale for Federal Reserve policy, said James Tobin several years later, "For it offers the hope that monetary policies can be effective without the large fluctuations of interest rates which used to be considered essential."[20] Then, as now, most people viewed interest-rate fluctuations with the enthusiasm usually reserved for outbreaks of hoof-and-mouth disease.

However, the credit-availability transmission mechanism is an extremely difficult one to apply. Its principal weakness is that the central bank, through the commercial banks, influences only a small part of the total supply of credit. If anyone fears that the money supply is not closely enough controlled by the central bank to be a reliable instrument of policy, he should be much more skeptical about the ability to control credit availability.

Any individual or firm, whether normally engaged in financial business or not, can become a supplier of credit. We saw this in the loan to an impecunious son-in-law in Chapter 1. Therefore, in some years in which growth of bank credit has been severely restricted, total credit has grown much faster than usual.

Although total bank credit can be controlled by the central bank, the allocation of that total among various kinds of borrowers is virtually impossible to control. Given the prevailing belief that some forms of bank credit are more stimulative than others, the difficulty of controlling allocation of bank credit can be a source of great frustration to central bankers, as could be plainly seen in the United States in the restraint periods of 1966 and 1969. It is all too easy at such times for the government and the central bank, often with strong support from businessmen who should know better, to yield to the temptation to employ selective controls. In many ways this is the most damaging result of adherence to the credit-availability doctrine, for the controls divert attention from the real problem and impair the efficiency of the capital markets.

The difficulty of trying to control credit availability in times of economic instability and inflation, furthermore, leads to questioning the long-run effectiveness of capital markets and to recommendations for changes in market structure and for new control instruments. Sherman Maisel, member of the Federal Reserve Board of Governors, says, for example, "The general problem is that of how to insure a more even-handed credit availability for individual sectors of the economy."[21] In case monetary policy is again required to curtail demand substantially, he "would feel far more confident of the eventual results if policies were based on increased knowledge and included possible improved techniques of distributing credit." As to new tools, he savs, "It seems to me that to curtail excess demands, a graduated 'charge' against increased borrowing by nonpreferred sectors would be a logical addition to the kit of stabilization tools."

Installing these new levers in the credit-availability black box, with their vastly increased data requirements and strains on the decision-making capacity of the authorities, might be warranted if there were no better means for stabilizing the economy. But there is a superior alternative at hand—the monetarist black box.

The illusion of success in applying credit-availability controls as policy instruments is another example of confusing the effects of the monetary black box with those of other policy instruments. Because most of the money supply consists of bank deposits, an effort to restrict growth of bank credit will also restrict growth of the money supply. However, the results will not be as good as if money supply itself were used as the guide. By focusing on credit availability, the central bank may permit money supply to grow too fast, or not fast enough, to achieve the desired effects on income and the price level. This happened in the United States in 1966 and 1969, when Federal Reserve efforts to curb growth of banks' business loans caused monetary policy, as measured by money-supply growth, to be too restrictive. The resulting instability in economic activity, prices, and interest rates then caused the damaging side effects on "preferred sectors," such as home building, that were so much deplored. These could have been avoided by keeping the money supply from growing too fast in 1965, 1967, and 1968.

About all a central bank that relies on the credit-availability transmission mechanism can do is "lean against the wind" until the economy appears to have responded in the desired direction. The central bank has only a poor idea of how much action is required because the linkages between central-bank actions and total credit and those between total credit and income are loose and poorly calibrated. In their attempts to improve their understanding of the mechanism, several countries have built elaborate flows-of-funds accounting systems. Unfortunately, these flows-of-funds accounts are more useful for explaining what has happened after it has happened than for predicting the results of central-bank actions in advance.

THE MONETARISTS' BLACK BOX

Arguments between Keynesians and monetarists over what should be included in the monetary policy black box wax loud and long. The Keynesian version, presented in many textbooks, stresses the effects of money-supply changes on market interest rates and the subsequent effects of these interest-rate changes on business spending for plant and equipment and on consumers' purchases of durable goods and housing. Expenditures on capital goods and new housing induced by a fall of interest rates increase the incomes of capital-goods producers who, in their turn, feed this income back into the economy in spending for consumer goods and services, raising the incomes of still more people through the multiplier process. Arthur Okun says, for example:

The Keynesian model of short-run income determination provides a clear specification of the way in which central bank instruments affect the level of output. A change in the volume of money alters the rate of interest so as to equate the demand for cash with the supply; the change in interest affects the level of investment; the change in investment has a multiplied effect on equilibrium income.[22]

Keynesian efforts to represent the monetary transmission mechanism in econometric and other models concentrate, therefore, on a small set of yields on financial assets, such as bonds and mortgages, which are then related to particular types of expenditures. Because of their strong preconceptions about the role of interest rates, Keynesians find it difficult to accept a view of the monetary transmission mechanism in which observable market rates of interest are not the main linkages between money and income.

Modeling the monetary transmission process according to their preconceptions about the role of interest rates, Keynesians can find only weak and long-delayed effects of money-supply changes in a few interest-sensitive activities, such as home building and business investment. Like the aeronautical engineers who proved from accepted principles of aerodynamics that bumblebees can't fly, therefore, they reject monetarists' evidence that what could not happen does happen. Somehow, what has happened again and again—as when money-supply changes overpowered fiscal measures in Chapters 2, 3, and 4—must not have happened because monetarists have not explained it in Keynesian terms.

Monetarists believe the link between money-supply changes and spending is more direct than the roundabout transmission mechanism of Keynesian models. The central bank buys securities from the public or lends through the discount window. The resulting increase in banks' holdings of high-powered money in the form of cash reserves induces them to buy securities or to make more loans, which in turn increases the money supply by some multiple of the original increase in high-powered money, as we saw in Chapter 9. This link in the monetary transmission mechanism has been well verified and calibrated. Although decisions of the banks and the public influence the money supply, this influence is much less than the influence of the monetary authorities. The nominal money supply is under the effective control of the central bank and therefore is a policy instrument, whether or not central banks fully exploit its potential or realize that they can.

The monetarists' version of the transmission mechanism uses a simple but powerful idea from capital theory—the idea that people try to eliminate any discrepancy between the actual stock, or amount, of an asset they hold and the amount they would like to hold. To understand how it works, imagine a water tank in which a municipal water company tries to keep enough water to meet, say, two months' normal demand. If the water level falls below the desired level, the managers pump water in faster; if the level goes above the desired level, the company slows down the pumps. The greater the discrepancy between the actual level and the desired level the larger is the change in rates of inflow. This simple notion has many applications in economics, such as in explaining changes in rates of home building or sales of consumer durable goods.

According to the monetarist credo, people want to hold some command over real purchasing power in the form of money. When the central bank pours more money into the economy than people want to hold they try to get rid of the excess by speeding up the velocity of turnover. They try to erase any discrepancy between the nominal quantity of money demanded and the nominal quantity supplied.

The key insight of the quantity theory approach [says Milton Friedman] is that such a discrepancy will be manifested primarily in attempted spending, thence in the rate of change of nominal income. Put differently, money holders cannot determine the nominal quantity of money (though their reactions may introduce feedback effects that will affect the nominal quantity of money), but they can make velocity anything they wish.[23]

(per cent change)

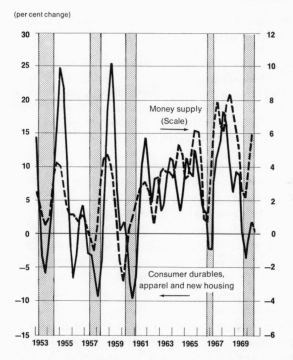

Chart 13-1. Consumer spending for postponables hinges on the money supply.

NOTES: Changes at annual rates, seasonally adjusted, smoothed by a weighted three-quarter centered moving average. Shaded areas represent recessions and the minirecession of 1967. For additional discussion see "How Money Can Fuel Revival," First National City Bank, *Monthly Economic Letter*, January 1971, pp. 5–6. *Chart by FNCB.*

The increase in spending induced by a discrepancy between actual nominal money supply and desired money supply is by no means confined to securities, as it is in the Keynesian model, nor to business investment. On the contrary, as can be seen in Chart 13-1, there evidently is a strong relationship between changes in money supply and household expenditures for durable goods, apparel, and new housing. This is extremely useful information for business forecasters, although it seems upsetting to economists who stick to the Keynesian convention of rigidly distinguishing between investment and consumption expenditures, as in the $C+I+G$ $=Y$ in the first chapter.[24]

The analysis of the substitution and wealth adjustment processes set in motion by monetary impulses [says Karl Brunner] yields no systematic priorities with respect to investment and consumers expenditures. This depends on a host of specific circumstances. Monetarist analysis would however not expect that investment expenditures lead in the average the impact of monetary impulses.[25]

The large econometric model of the Board of Governors—the FRB-MIT model—incorporates money-supply effects on consumption spending through changes in stock prices. This is a special case of the general Keynesian idea that the public attempts to exchange excess cash for securities until the yield on securities falls so low that there is no more incentive to buy securities. When stock prices rise or fall, stockholders feel wealthier or poorer and adjust their consumption spending accordingly. But this is still not the direct substitution of goods for cash that monetarists believe many people make when adjusting their cash balances.

At this point, however, many economists stop being satisfied with the explanation, for it seems much too simple. Unfortunately, we do not have the data necessary for examining the transactions of different kinds of money holders in much detail. For example, there are no reliable, current data on how much money is held by individuals, corporations, nonprofit organizations, financial institutions, farmers, retailers, and others that could be used to test how these various groups in the economy react to changes in their cash balances. At best, it is necessary to work with crude estimates. However, simplicity itself can be a virtue in analytical work.

In truth, no one can see everything that happens in any of the three black boxes. Economists of all persuasions must substitute theory and simplifying assumptions for what they cannot see, like the intelligence agencies building models of the spaceships they cannot see. But they disagree on how complicated and realistic the models should be. The monetarists tend generally to employ the simplest theory or model that yields good predictions because a simple theory requires less information and fewer assumptions than a complex one. Therefore, they use a simple direct relationship be-

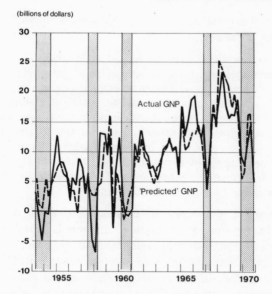

(billions of dollars)

Chart 13-2. Changes in the money supply can predict GNP changes.

NOTES: Quarterly dollar changes in GNP (seasonally adjusted) predicted from lagged quarterly change in money supply and a strike variable. Shaded areas represent recessions and the minirecession of 1967. For additional discussion see "What Really Shakes the Money Tree," First National City Bank, *Monthly Economic Letter*, February 1971, pp. 5–9. *Chart by FNCB.*

tween money and income, like the one in the simple forecasting model of Chapter 6 and the even simpler model of Chart 13-2. These provide better forecasts of short-run income fluctuations than the more complicated econometric models. The principal justification for faith in the simple money-income black box is that it works.

HOW COMPLICATED SHOULD IT BE?

The debate between the Keynesians and the monetarists is complicated by the fact that both want to make the comparative tests by their own rules. Harry Johnson has pointed out that the early replies by Keynesians to the Friedman-Meiselman tests failed to understand the principle Friedman-Meiselman applied in judging both bodies of theory:

The crucial principle is that the test of good theory is its ability to predict something large from something small, by means of a simple and stable theoretical relationship; hence the essence of the quantity theory was specified to be the velocity function relating income to money, and the essence of the income-expenditure theory was specified to be the multiplier relationship relating income to autonomous expenditure. . . . This principle is in sharp contrast to the more common view that the purpose of theory in this context is to lay out the full structure of a general equilibrium model in the detail necessary to produce an adequately good statistical "fit."[26]

The simple model, however, may not answer all the questions a policy maker may want to have answered. Governor Daane, for example, argues that attention should be given not only to the impact of monetary policy on over-all GNP but also to effects on specific sectors of the economy, such as the banking system, small businesses, state and local governments, or home builders. The FRB-MIT model, therefore, is an attempt to simulate a fiscal-monetary black box in great and costly detail in order to study the pattern of effects stemming from monetary and fiscal policies as they spread through the economy. This is a laudable enterprise.

But there is some risk that a model loaded down with enough equations to answer all questions could be like the F-111 that was supposed to meet the requirements of both the U.S. Air Force and the Navy and ended up satisfying neither. We might well question the utility of models that predict a great many financial flows and other aspects of economic activity yet mislead the authorities with regard to the course of total income, as did the econometric models consulted by the Federal Reserve in 1968.

Keynesians think monetarists oversimplify their explanation of the monetary transmission mechanism by not stressing the role of market interest rates. Monetarists counter by arguing that stressing observable rates on financial instruments oversimplifies the explanation by overlooking a vast panoply of implicit yields on real assets, such as machinery, automobiles, and inventories. These implicit yields influence decisions of consumers and businessmen, even though they cannot be observed directly. The importance of this distinction can be seen by contrasting the two views about how monetary policy might influence the demand for business plant and equipment.

In the Keynesian explanation an increase in money supply would be expected to reduce interest rates. To the business manager the fall of interest rates is taken as a reduction in the cost of capital, giving him incentive to buy more machinery. In the monetarist explanation the fall of market interest rates caused by an increase in money supply is only temporary and unimportant. More important is the effect of the money-supply increase on expenditures for all kinds of goods and services and securities as people try to get rid of excess cash. The increased demand for goods and services—including the services of the businessman's machinery—increases the implicit yield on real capital assets. The increase in yields on assets then induces businessmen to add new plant and equipment.

More important than the distinction in treatment accorded investment by the two schools, but related to it, is the relative emphasis they give to expectations of price changes. Keynes focused on short-run relationships in his *General Theory* and, in order to simplify, assumed that prices were stable over the period covered. Consequently, he did not have to consider the effects of price expectations on interest rates, on the demand for money, and on other important influences on economic behavior. Although this assumption was not inappropriate during the depression, it has been since World War II. Nevertheless, the followers of Keynes, until very recently, continued to assume stable prices, and hence no bothersome price-expectations effects, in their analyses. Monetarists, with the long quantity-theory concern over the purchasing power of money behind them, are not likely to overlook price changes and price expectations in their work.

If the assumption of stable prices is dropped, it is no longer possible to use market interest rates as a measure of the cost of capital in analyzing investment decisions, for example. It is the real rate of interest that influences decisions, and this cannot be observed directly. From the standpoint of the practicing central banker or business forecaster, furthermore, dropping the Keynesian assumption of stable prices means that high market interest rates can no longer be taken as evidence that monetary and fiscal policies are restrictive. High rates may merely mean that earlier policies have been so expansive that expectations of further price inflation have pushed rates up. In 1970 the effects of inflationary expectations became all too real.

There is a view that, unless all or most complications existing in the real world are grappled with in models, the modeler is not being properly realistic. John V. Deaver, an economist with the Ford Motor Company, who has had much experience with monetary forecasting models, takes sharp issue with this argument:

In models, complexity is the enemy of reliability . . . The term "structural richness" applied . . . to [the FRB-MIT] model is, therefore, misleading: richness implies that the structure is correct, for which there is little evidence, and gives reliable forecasts, which it is unlikely to do. . . . Remember, the behavioral equations of . . . elaborate models represent assumptions, not facts, about the real world. Fitting the data to them in no way verifies their accuracy. The model is a massive representation of how the author views the economic machinery. That is all.[27]

One thing is very clear. When a central bank changes the money supply, or allows it to change, changes in national income and prices will follow. Although we do not know as much as we would like to know about how these monetary impulses are transmitted from person to person and firm to firm, we can see from careful observations that there are strong and dependable linkages among money, income, and prices within the monetary black box. Furthermore, the quantity theory explains why we should expect to find those linkages; they are not just casual, unexplained correlations.

This does not make the monetarists' black box into a precise control system with which discretionary authorities can guide an economy through the updrafts and downdrafts of a turbulent world. There is no such control system, nor is one needed. The theory and the evidence do mean that a central bank cannot overlook what happens in the monetary black box while relying on one or both of the other two to maintain economic stability. That way lies inflation or unemployment. The transmission mechanisms of fiscal policy and credit availability are fully as mysterious as those of monetary policy but not as dependable. Therefore, there is no escape from the necessity of keeping the money supply under control.

14

MEANWHILE, BACK AT
THE LABORATORY . . .

In monetary matters, appearances are deceiving;
the important relationships are often precisely the
reverse of those that strike the eye.
   Milton Friedman and Anna Jacobson Schwartz,
   A Monetary History of the United States,
   1867–1960, 1963[1]

When Milton Friedman and Anna Schwartz thus summed up
the findings of their *Monetary History* in 1963, money was well
on its way back from limbo. Although the upsurge of inflation
in the sixties undoubtedly accelerated it, the upsurge of the new
monetarism could not have happened without the patient work
of researchers in the universities of many countries, the U.S. Federal Reserve System and other central banks, and business economics departments. This research, furthermore, was not performed
in serene isolation from worldly problems. Instead, much of it was
stimulated by policy disputes and by the challenge of trying to
make sense out of swift-moving events or to find out why forecasts went awry.

The full impact of this intellectual explosion is yet to come,
for it has hardly begun to be reflected in economics textbooks and
the press. It has, however, influenced public policies in the United
States and other countries and has had a powerful impact on business forecasting, where slow learners have more at stake than
their pride.

THEORY AND EVIDENCE

In a recent survey of developments in monetary theory Harry Johnson, of the London School of Economics and the University of Chicago, said:

> The Keynesian Revolution left the quantity theory thoroughly discredited on the grounds either that it was a mere tautology (the quantity equation) or that it "assumed full employment" and that the velocity factor it emphasized was in fact highly unstable. The revival of a quantity theory that could claim to rival the Keynesian theory required a restatement of it that would free it from these objections and give it an empirical content. Such a restatement was provided by Milton Friedman's classic article, which redefined the quantity theory as a theory of the demand for money (or velocity) and not a theory of prices or output.[2]

The tautology to which he referred was Fisher's $MV = PT$ equation that we discussed in the first chapter as the quantity-theory equation (transactions version). The classic article was "The Quantity Theory of Money—A Restatement," which Friedman wrote as the first essay in *Studies in the Quantity Theory of Money*, published by the University of Chicago, Workshop in Money and Banking in 1956.[3] It is characteristic of the "Chicago School" approach that this theoretical essay was part of a volume of empirical studies that examined various issues raised by the theory. Rigorous testing and careful observation have consolidated each advance in the evolution of the new monetarism.

It is also characteristic of Milton Friedman that he called his essay merely a restatement of an oral tradition at the University of Chicago rather than the crucial, original contribution that it actually was.[4] In any case, stating the quantity theory as the theory of demand for money provided the framework for an enormous volume of research. *Studies in the Quantity Theory* was the first of four volumes produced by students in the Workshop in Money and Banking that he conducts at the University of Chicago.[5] Let us hope there are more to come.

The Workshop studies and much of the work done elsewhere

focus on various parts of three major issues posed by Friedman in the initial essay: (1) the stability and importance of the demand function for money; (2) the independence of the factors affecting demand and supply; and (3) the form of the demand function or related functions.

As David Meiselman has explained in his introduction to *Varieties of Monetary Experience,* the fourth Workshop volume, all the monetarist studies are empirical analyses of the role of monetary behavior in shaping economic events. "All seek the greatest explanatory power," he says, "for the fewest variables and relationships by systematic search for stable, invariant, and simple relationships consistently applicable over a broad range of different circumstances."[6]

An alternative research strategy followed by others is to construct and test complex models employing many variables, rather than systematically tracing the behavior of a small number of variables. The two strategies can be complementary. However, the large size and cost of more complex models like the econometric models of the United States and Italy at the Federal Reserve Board and the Banca d'Italia necessarily limit them to a small range of experience.

In his "Restatement," Milton Friedman listed the following influences on the demand for money: interest rates, the expected rate of change of prices, real income, and holdings of various forms of wealth. The many studies of the demand for money in the United States and other countries since 1956 have attempted to measure the relative importance of these variables or, in some cases, to focus on one in particular, such as interest rates or the expected rate of price inflation. Essential as these studies are, many of them are not easy for laymen to grasp because they deal with fine nuances of econometrics technique and the selection and preparation of variables.[7]

The key research issue is the stability of the demand for money. If the demand for money proved to be highly unstable or volatile or if it was a simple function of interest rates alone, as some theories have asserted, changes in the supply of money would not have a predictable influence on income, employment, and prices.

I believe we can fairly say now that tests over a great variety of circumstances and for all the countries that have been examined demonstrate that the demand for money does have the stability and other properties required for making reliable predictions. This means, therefore, that what happens to the money supply is critical to the success of economic policies and business forecasting.

But are money supply and the demand for money independent? A long-standing criticism of the quantity theory, as Harry Johnson has pointed out, is that "the theory is irrelevant because the quantity of money supplied responds passively to the demand for it—the 'Banking School' position which remains strong in popular thinking on monetary policy."[8] For example, if a recession starts with liquidation of business inventories, firms would pay off bank loans as they reduce their inventories. If banks were willing to hold in cash or excess reserves the reserves thus freed up, this would in turn reduce bank deposits and money supply. Any conclusions one might draw about business fluctuations from observing changes in money supply, therefore, would be suspect if it could be demonstrated that the changes in money supply merely reflected changes in the demand for money. But banks are not indifferent about the amounts of cash they hold. If cash is freed up by a fall in business loans, they usually will buy securities, or make other loans, thus keeping the supply of deposits from falling.

However, there are some feedback effects of business on money, as we saw earlier, because of the influence of business conditions on central-bank operations. In mild business cycles a tendency of central banks to accommodate changes in credit demands makes it difficult to determine whether changes in money supply initiate the changes in business activity or if the changes in business activity affect the money supply.

Nevertheless, there are many reasons for believing that the direction of influence is primarily, although not exclusively, from money to business. One of the main kinds of evidence is historical. The massive work of Milton Friedman and Anna J. Schwartz, *A Monetary History of the United States, 1867–1960,* and a companion study by Phillip C. Cagan, *Determinants and Effects of Changes in the Stock of Money, 1875–1960,* demonstrated two things.[9] They demonstrated that money supply was determined independently from money demand, because the money supply of the United States has been controlled by a wide variety of institutional arrangements and forces, many of which could not conceivably have been much influenced by the state of demand for money. They also demonstrated the powerful influence of money-supply changes on U.S. economic history by relating them to all of the business cycles that have been identified by the National Bureau of Economic Research. The findings of Friedman and Schwartz and Cagan have been reinforced by the work of others, especially Clark Warburton.[10]

Furthermore, research on central-bank operations—much of which is reflected in Chapters 9, 10, and 11—demonstrates clearly that central banks and the governments they serve exercise a powerful independent influence through their power to issue or to extinguish high-powered money. Although they may, on occasion, plead innocence of responsibility for such embarrassing phenomena as inflation, the control of money supply is in their hands.

Development of money-supply theory has proceeded along two main tracks. The first, a University of Chicago tradition, is the application of capital theory to explain the amount of reserves desired by banks. It is this stable demand for cash reserves as an inventory to protect against cash withdrawals that induces the banks to respond promptly and predictably to any action of the central bank that expands or contracts total reserves. This approach is used in my own *Free Reserves and the Money Supply,* by George R. Morrison in his *Liquidity Preferences of Commercial Banks,* and by Adolfo C. Diz in Argentina, and Antonio Fazio at the Banca d'Italia.[11]

The other approach, which is specifically aimed at designing procedures by which central banks can control the money supply, has been developed largely by Karl Brunner and Allan Meltzer and their students.[12] Sometimes called the Brunner-Meltzer Non-Linear Money Supply Hypothesis, it has been the subject of intensive study, especially at the Federal Reserve Bank of St. Louis. Incidentally, the two approaches are not contradictory; they reinforce one another. Both, furthermore, demonstrate that the money supply is a policy instrument that can be managed for good or ill.

MONEY IN BUSINESS FLUCTUATIONS

The most convincing evidence that money-supply changes cause changes in output, income, and prices is presented in the voluminous works of Milton Friedman and Anna Schwartz, Phillip Cagan, Karl Brunner and Allan Meltzer, and Clark Warburton.[13] If monetarists are right, substantial changes in the rate of growth of money should be followed by changes in income and prices. Furthermore, their theory should hold over a wide variety of circumstances. Therefore, tracing the role of money in business fluctuations has been one of the most valuable ways of testing the theory. The accompanying charts contain a small sample of this evidence.

This work also has had valuable by-products in the form of improvements in ability to forecast turns in the business cycle, as we saw in the section on forecasting. Forecasting methods based on Keynesian income-expenditure theory have not done well in predicting the turns in U.S. cycles since World War II, beginning with the forecast that there would be eight million unemployed in the United States after the war.

The emphasis of modern monetarism on short-run fluctuations of income and output, in addition to the traditional quantity-theory emphasis on prices, is of immense practical importance. Professor Harry Johnson has charged monetarists with being interested mainly in controlling inflation. This would make them virtually irrelevant and doomed to lose influence, he says, because controlling inflation is not politically popular—in his opinion. Without conceding that controlling inflation is politically unpopular, I would argue that the monetary explanation of business fluctuations may well be the greatest contribution of the monetarist school. It leads to far more reliable means for minimizing unemployment than any the fiscalists have yet devised.

Chart 14-1, covering 1914 into 1971, compares behavior of money supply, defined as demand deposits and currency, with wholesale prices, industrial production, and stock prices. The shaded areas represent business contractions identified by the National Bureau of Economic Research and the '67 minirecession. The ratio scale is used to facilitate comparisons of the relative amplitudes

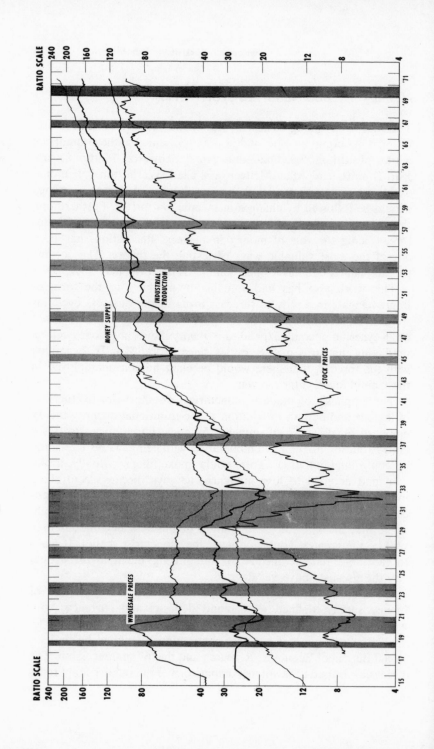

of fluctuation. Chart 14-2 shows the rates of money-supply growth over the same period.

Over the period covered there were thirteen contractions, two of which were brief reconversion periods following the World Wars and perhaps could be excluded. The money stock contracted sharply in each of the three major contractions—1920–1921, 1929–1933, and 1937–1938. In the worst contraction, 1929–1933, money supply declined by fully one third; and more than one third of this country's banks disappeared through failure or merger. Major price inflations occurred during and after both World Wars and during the Korean War, when war financing policies sharply expanded money supply.

Since World War II fluctuations in all of these measures have been much more moderate than those between the two World Wars. The postwar increase in economic stability has been variously attributed to structural changes in the economy, the so-called built-in stabilizers, and to skillful application of the New Economics. Monetarists argue, however, that the improvement actually stemmed more from the absence of major monetary disturbances. Monetary growth was much steadier between 1945 and 1965 than in any other period of comparable length in U.S. history. What can be seen, therefore, is evidence of how stable the economy can be when it is not subjected to wide and erratic swings in money supply. Even so, contractions in money supply in 1947–1948 and 1959–1960 were followed by the recessions of 1948–1949 and 1960–1961.

From 1964 on, money-supply growth increased and became

Chart 14-1. Industrial production, wholesale prices, stock prices, and money supply were more stable after World War II than they were between the wars.

NOTES: Money supply includes demand deposits adjusted and currency, average of daily figures, seasonally adjusted. 1915–1946, from Milton Friedman and Anna Jacobson Schwartz, *A Monetary History of the United States 1867–1960*, NBER, 1963, Table A-1, Col. 7. Since 1946, Board of Governors of the Federal Reserve System. Wholesale Price Index, 1957–1959 = 100, U.S. Department of Labor, Bureau of Labor Statistics. Stock Price Index, Standard & Poor's 500 Common Stocks, monthly average of weekly indexes from 1918–1927, monthly averages of daily indexes from 1928 to date, 1941–1943 = 10. Industrial production, 1915–1918 annual from G. Warren Nutter, *Growth of Industrial Production in the Soviet Union*, NBER, 1962, Appendix "A," p. 382. Since 1918, Board of Governors of the Federal Reserve System, seasonally adjusted. Shaded areas represent business contractions identified by National Bureau of Economic Research, Inc. *Chart by FNCB.*

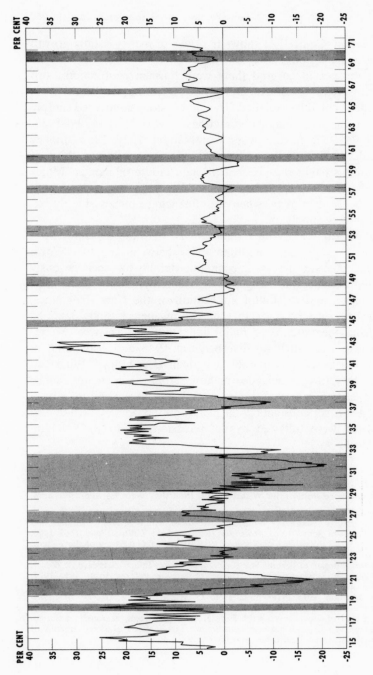

Chart 14-2. Rates of money-supply growth were also more stable after World War II than they were between the wars.

NOTES: Shaded areas represent business contractions identified by National Bureau of Economic Research, Inc. Money supply includes demand deposits adjusted and currency, seasonally adjusted. 1915–1963, six-month moving average computed by Beryl W. Sprinkel, *Money and Stock Prices*, 1964, Appendix more volatile. The noticeable increase in monetary growth after 1964 coincided with a rise in the wholesale price index that culminated in the worst price inflation since the Korean War. Money-supply contractions in 1966 and 1969 were followed by the mini-recession of 1967 and the full-blown recession of 1969–1970.

EXORCISING THE GHOST OF THE GREAT DEPRESSION

The historical evidence that money-supply changes cause business fluctuations is impressive. Get control of money, it implies, and the business cycle will be under control. But, for many people, the memory of the depression blocks acceptance of belief in the influence of money or in the effectiveness of monetary policy. At some future day of reckoning, IT might happen again.

According to some of the witnesses and principal actors at the scene, the Federal Reserve struggled valiantly against a massive collapse in the willingness of consumers and businesses to spend but was overwhelmed by forces far too powerful for any human agency to withstand. Clearing away this myth to reveal what really happened in the depression has been one of the greatest accomplishments of economic research since World War II.[14] Like military historians, the researchers who combed through depression annals found that reports of commanders are not always the most reliable accounts of battles, especially when defeats must be explained. In the revised view, it is clear that the monetary authorities fell into an almost inexplicable torpor after the stock market crash of 1929 and did virtually nothing to resist the monetary breakdown that the Reserve banks had been expressly designed (and expected) to prevent.

Clear understanding of the business cycle was not essential for coping with the problems of the banks and the securities markets. Central-bank tactics for dealing with a banking crisis had been explained by Bagehot long before in England. Some students of this period believe that Benjamin Strong, the first Governor of the Federal Reserve Bank of New York, would surely have taken strong action, had he been alive, and might have been able to carry the rest of the System with him.

The Federal Reserve Bank of New York did take timely and effective action at the time of the stock market crash, buying government securities and keeping its discount window wide open so that New York banks could borrow. For various reasons, however, it could not persuade the other Reserve banks and the Board to accept its many recommendations over the next several years for the additional purchases of securities that could have averted catastrophe. Not until pressed hard by Congress to do so in 1932 did the System make large open-market purchases. When Congress adjourned in July of that year the System slipped back into its policy of utter passivity. The contraction in money supply between 1929 and the end of 1933 can be clearly seen on Charts 14-1 and 14-2.

In their *Monetary History of the United States,* Milton Friedman and Anna Schwartz concluded:

The monetary collapse was not the inescapable consequence of other forces but rather a largely independent factor which exerted a powerful influence on the course of events. The failure of the Federal Reserve System to prevent the collapse reflected not the impotence of monetary policy but rather the particular policies followed by the monetary authorities and, in smaller degree, the particular monetary arrangements in existence.

The contraction is in fact a tragic testimonial to the importance of monetary forces . . . different and feasible actions by the monetary authorities could have prevented the decline in the stock of money. . . . Prevention or moderation of the decline in the stock of money, let alone the substitution of monetary expansion, would have reduced the contraction's severity and almost as certainly its duration. The contraction might still have been relatively severe. But it is hardly conceivable that money income would have declined by over one-half and prices by over one-third in the course of four years if there had been no decline in the stock of money.[15]

Although there is no time here to trace developments month by month, it is fair to say that the banks were under almost incessant pressure to contract their loans and investments from 1929 through 1933. One of these pressures, initially, was a contraction of the stock of high-powered money as foreigners drew down their deposits in U.S. banks and bought gold from the Treasury. As the business decline progressed and interest rates fell, the member banks reduced their borrowing at Reserve Banks, thus further reducing the stock of high-powered money. Because of the money-multiplier process explained in Chapter 9, the reduction in the stock of high-powered money forced a much larger reduction in money supply and total bank credit. Furthermore, with banks failing on all sides, the public tried to convert bank deposits into currency. This, too, forced a multiple contraction of bank deposits. And banks, fearing for their own safety, increased their ratios of reserves to deposits, further reducing the supply of money that could be supported by any given volume of high-powered money. After 1931, the supply of high-powered money actually rose as the Fed provided currency. But, by then, banks were in such a state of shock that they used the high-powered money to build up their reserves; the multiplier fell.

It is inconceivable that the Federal Reserve would not try to offset such a conjuncture of contractive forces today. Even then, Winfield Riefler had already devised a system of bank reserve accounting, much like the one used in Table 10-1 of Chapter 10. So it should have been possible to see what was happening to the reserves of the member banks. And the currency drain was a not unfamiliar form of crisis, for which vigorous counteraction might have been expected.

Friedman and Schwartz, for example, cite Bagehot's description of Bank of England actions in the panic of 1825:

The way in which the panic of 1825 was stopped by advancing money has been described in so broad and graphic a way that the passage has become classical. "We lent it," said Mr. Harman on behalf of the Bank of England, "by every possible means and in modes we have never adopted before; we took in stock on security, we purchased Exchequer bills, we made advances on Exchequer bills, we not only discounted outright, but we made advances on the deposit of bills of exchange to an immense amount, in short, by every possible means consistent with the safety of the Bank, and we were not on some occasions over-nice."[16]

If the Federal Reserve did nothing, why do so many people believe that it waged a valiant fight? One reason, it seems to me, stems from the same reserve-position doctrine that was to delay the Federal Reserve's response to an incipient recession thirty years later, in 1960, as we saw in Chapter 10. Although Bagehot would have interpreted a rise of member-bank borrowing between 1929 and 1933 as evidence that the Federal Reserve was doing something to keep the banks afloat, the reserve-position doctrine interpretation would have been just the reverse. Discount rates were reduced (raised again in 1931 to counteract a gold outflow), but market rates fell faster. The banks, consequently, had incentive to get out of debt and did so.

The Federal Reserve interpreted the fall in borrowings as a sign that its policy of ease was working. This false impression was reinforced by the fall in market interest rates. There are many statements in the records from Federal Reserve governors that the policy was easy; indeed some governors thought the policy was too easy. The Federal Reserve had done all it could, or so they thought, and few people outside of the Federal Reserve Bank of New York and the Congress saw it differently at the time.

This massive delusion has been enshrined in economic theory as the "liquidity trap," a monetary Sargasso Sea in which monetary policy is believed to be completely ineffective. The liquidity trap, as usually described, has two compartments, one for banks and one for the general public.

In the bank compartment it is argued that interest rates can become so low that the banks will not lend or invest any additional cash they get. The central bank, under such conditions, would be powerless to increase the money supply because banks simply would not lend. The principal evidence that such a condition can exist was the accumulation of excess reserves by U.S. banks when gold flowed into the country after 1933. Bankers, furthermore, remember that credit-worthy borrowers were few and far between.

George R. Morrison exploded the myth of the bank liquidity trap in his study, *Liquidity Preferences of Commercial Banks*.[17] According to him, excess reserves in the thirties became large; but they were not larger than the banks wanted them to be. The shock of seeing banks fail while the Federal Reserve "lender of last resort" stood by without attempting to save them stirred the survivors to look to their own salvation by holding more cash, if they were fortunate enough to get any. Canadian banks, whose nationwide branching system protected them from the failures that bedeviled their neighbors to the south, did not build up excess reserves, although the Canadian economy was depressed too.

Even while accumulating excess reserves, the banks also expanded loans and investments in 1934, 1935, and 1936, as can be seen from the high rates of money-supply growth for those years on Chart 14-2. Believing that the banks were out of control unless they were borrowing, and fearing that inflation might recur, the Federal Reserve tried to eliminate part of the banks' excess reserves by sharply increasing reserve requirements in 1936 and again in 1937. This egregious blunder led to frantic attempts by the banks to restore their lost liquidity, a sharp contraction of the money supply, and the 1937 recession, one of the worst in U.S. history.

In the public compartment of the liquidity trap, it is argued that at extremely low interest rates people will absorb unlimited amounts of money without increasing their spending. Therefore, an increase in money supply—if the central bank could achieve it—would have no effect. That nothing like this actually happened in the thirties can be seen in the behavior of wholesale prices, industrial production, and stock prices, on Chart 14-1, in 1934–1936 when the money supply was growing rapidly. The economy evidently was recovering at a fast pace, although it still had a long way to go when the recovery was aborted by the Federal Reserve's raising of reserve requirements in 1936.

Despite the contradictions in the conventional account that have recently been exposed, it is still widely believed that the depression was the fault of bankers, who wouldn't lend; businessmen, who wouldn't borrow and invest; and consumers, who wouldn't spend. And this misreading of events has been built into Keynesian income-expenditure theory.

THEORIES PUT TO THE TEST

The idea that swings in business investment and government spending dominate the business cycle, or are the cycle, is a plausible one because these types of spending fluctuate more widely than most other types of spending. Consequently, these so-called autonomous expenditures have played prominent roles in theories of the business cycle before and after Keynes. Nevertheless, income-expenditure theory had been subjected to surprisingly little empirical testing by its proponents before they were challenged to do so by Milton Friedman and David Meiselman in a study for the Commission on Money and Credit.

As we saw earlier, Friedman and Meiselman found that the quantity theory outperformed the Keynesian income-expenditure theory over most of six decades of U.S. experience. The one exception was the thirties subperiod in which the Keynesian theory had originated. The Friedman-Meiselman study stimulated much more testing of the two theories with the interesting result that even some of those tests that are believed to be most favorable to the Keynesian view attribute considerable significance to money-supply changes.

The Friedman-Meiselman findings were powerfully reinforced in 1968 by work of Leonall Andersen and Jerry Jordan at the Federal Reserve Bank of St. Louis.[18] Concerned with choosing public-policy instruments for economic stabilization, Andersen and Jordan tested propositions that the response of economic activity to fiscal actions is (1) larger, (2) more predictable, and (3) faster than the response to monetary actions. The results of their tests were not consistent with any of these commonly accepted propositions. Their results were consistent instead with propositions that monetary actions produce larger, more predictable, and faster responses than fiscal measures.

The Andersen-Jordan tests, and much of the discussion of them, covered only the period 1953–1968. Michael Keran, also at the St. Louis Federal Reserve Bank, applied similar tests in 1969 to a much longer period, 1919–1969, and to selected subperiods.[19] He found that for the whole period and for each of the subperiods (except the war years 1939–1946),

Changes in the money stock (the indicator of monetary influence) have consistently had a larger, more predictable, and faster impact on changes in economic activity than have changes in Federal Government spending (the indicator of fiscal influence).

... in every case where the monetary variable and the fiscal variable moved in opposite directions, economic activity moved in the direction of the monetary variable and opposite in direction to the fiscal variable.[20]

Still later Keran extended the tests to other countries, with results similar to those for the United States.[21] Alan Walters, of the London School of Economics, has been one of the leaders in conducting such tests in England.[22]

MONEY AND INTEREST RATES

The monetarist view of how money-supply changes influence interest rates is one of the most remarkable developments in economics in many years. Actually, this new view is largely a restatement of ideas that were worked out by Irving Fisher as early as 1896. He spent much of the rest of his life combating confusion about how interest rates are determined:

Probably the great majority of unthinking businessmen [he said] believe that interest is low when money is plentiful, and high when money is scarce.

This view, however, is fallacious, and the fallacy consists in forgetting that plentiful money ultimately raises the demand for loans just as much as it raises the supply, and therefore has just as much tendency to raise interest as to lower it.[23]

The gist of the revived Fisherian view is that money-supply changes influence interest rates in three ways. The first effect, which occurs very quickly, is a liquidity effect. This is the one that has been emphasized the most in central-bank practice and in the money-and-banking literature, especially since Keynes popularized his concept of liquidity preference. Until recently people who work in the money market believed it was the dominant effect, possibly because market traders take a very short view.

A central bank can drive rates down temporarily through purchasing securities and increasing the money supply. But the influence of a money-supply change does not stop there. Within six to nine months the increase in money supply will have induced a rise in income which, in turn, increases the demands for credit and money. This income effect brings rates back up to the original level, or higher, unless it is offset by additional money-supply injections. Somewhat later still, if money-supply growth causes price inflation and if people expect the inflation to continue, the expected rate of price inflation will be added to interest rates. This is the effect that was most emphasized by Irving Fisher in his work of distinguishing the nominal rates of interest, which can be observed in the market, from the real rates, which cannot be observed directly.

This new view is well supported by research done at the Federal Reserve Bank of Chicago, the Federal Reserve Bank of St. Louis, and elsewhere, some of which was reported in Milton Friedman's Presidential Address to the American Economic Association in December, 1967.[24] Furthermore, it was widely accepted in the financial markets within two years of the first publication of studies on the subject by William Gibson and George Kaufman, of the University of Chicago and the Federal Reserve Bank of Chicago. Investors and lenders observed for themselves that the restrictive policy of 1966 brought lower rates and that the extraordinarily expansive policies of 1967 and 1968 drove interest rates to record levels. It is not at all uncommon now to hear a bond dealer say that the one hope for higher bond prices (lower yields) lies in a restrictive monetary policy, not in easy money.

The first people to check Fisher's findings with data for the period since the twenties found, as he had, that price changes influenced interest rates with a very long time lag, twenty years or more, by some estimates. This implied that people's expectations about price inflation change very slowly. In the early years after World War II, for example, the actual rate of price inflation was high; but people acted as though they expected prices to fall again, as they had after World War I. Fisher believed there was a general tendency for interest rates to reflect price changes only partially.

A practical implication of the long price-expectations lag, therefore, was that a forecaster could ignore price influences and concentrate on the liquidity effect and the income effect when trying to forecast rates. This approach worked splendidly until 1968 and 1969, when rates went higher than seemed possible. The inflation that was not foreseen by many inhabitants of the capital markets in

1965 was reflected in market interest rates much sooner than Fisher would have predicted.

Working independently, two research groups in 1969 demonstrated what bond investors had already painfully discovered: price expectations affect interest rates much more quickly than the earlier research had indicated. William Yohe and Dennis Karnosky, at the Federal Reserve Bank of St. Louis, concluded that most of the effects of price-level changes on both long- and short-term interest rates occur within two years and that price changes accounted for nearly all of the increase of interest rates in the 1960s.[25] Shigeyuki Fukasawa, of Columbia University and First National City Bank, found slightly longer lags.[26] Both found the price effects to be more important in the sixties than in the fifties.

Fukasawa's explanation for the shortening of the time lag in adjustment of interest rates to price changes is that the formation of price expectations is influenced by how variable the rate of inflation is. If people have experienced short periods of inflation followed by periods of deflation, they will not expect a particular rate of price change to persist and so market interest rates will not reflect it fully. This is consistent with Fisher's observation that interest rates adjust only partially for price appreciations or depreciations when the cost of living is not stable.

In the 1960s there was a steady rise in the rate of inflation, which affected the public's expectations much more strongly than did the short inflation episodes of the fifties, according to Fukasawa. Institutional changes, such as an increase in the flow of information and opinion about economic conditions, may also have shortened the lags.

In addition to being extremely important for explaining the behavior of interest rates, this recent research on price expectations throws a great deal of light on the role of expectations in the determination of prices and wages. Prices and wages were slow to respond to monetary restraint in 1969 and 1970 for the same reasons that interest rates were slow to fall.

The practical implication of the new view of rates is that central banks cannot control interest rates, at least they cannot in the traditional way. If a central bank tries to keep rates down through buying securities or lending freely through its discount window, it can succeed for only a short time before the income effect and price-expectations effect push rates up again. In sum, easy money policies bring high interest rates and tight money brings low rates.

In addition to studying what determines the level of interest rates, several researchers have tried to find out why long-term rates are usually higher than short-term rates but are sometimes lower than short rates. Because long-term rates have been higher than short rates for most of the time since World War II, there is a common tendency to attribute the "upward-sloping yield curve" to a belief that short-term securities are more liquid and less risky than long-term securities and so command a lower rate. Although there is something to this idea, it cannot explain why short rates were higher than long rates in U.S. markets for many years during the nineteenth century, for substantial periods in the twenties, and for several months at a time near business-cycle peaks since World War II.

Changes in the relative quantities of short-term and long-term debt outstanding are another popular explanation for changes in the relationship of short rates to long rates. According to this explanation, if a government issued long-term securities in place of its short-term securities, it would raise long-term interest rates in relation to short-term rates.

The explanation that has been best supported by recent research, however, is that the term structure—the pattern of rates on obligations of different maturities—is determined primarily by expectations about what rates will be in the future.[27] According to the expectations hypothesis, a long-term interest rate is, in effect, an average of expected future short-term rates. Therefore, if lenders and borrowers expect rates to be higher in the future than they are today, lenders will try to avoid committing long-term funds at lower rates than they may be able to obtain later. Borrowers, on the other hand, will try to borrow funds for the future at today's lower levels. The interaction of the two will make long-term rates higher today than short-term rates. If rates are expected to be lower in the future, long-term rates will be lower than short-term rates.

The practical implication of the term-structure research is that central banks and governments not only cannot control the level of interest rates; they cannot control the term structure either. It had become fashionable after World War II among some economists and policy makers to recommend manipulating the term structure of rates through altering the maturity composition of the public debt, or debt management, as it was called.

In "operation twist," for example, U.S. authorities in the early sixties alleged that they were keeping long-term rates low to encourage investment while keeping short-term rates up to reduce capital outflows that would aggravate the balance-of-payments deficit. One of the more curious aspects of the operation was that the actual change in maturity of the public debt achieved by the Treasury was exactly opposite to what was called for by debt-management advocates; the average maturity was increased, which should have raised long-term rates relative to short-term rates. Long rates apparently declined in spite of the Treasury's debt-management operation—not because of it. Although it was not recognized at the time, the decline of long rates in relation to short rates between 1960 and 1964 probably reflected a change from expecting inflation, as in the fifties, to expecting price stability.

Monetarists have always stressed price changes and expectations of price changes, while Keynesians have not. As we saw earlier, that can create serious difficulties for Keynesian forecasters when price inflation causes nominal interest rates to depart from the real rates that influence expenditure decisions. In addition, Keynesian theories and policies have encountered difficulties by failing to guard sufficiently against price inflation.

Monetarists have not had a fully satisfactory explanation of the process of price adjustments either. The early quantity theory of Irving Fisher predicted the effects of money-supply changes on the price level in the long run but did not say much about the process of adjustment in the short run. We are not too much better off today. Monetarist models predict the change in nominal income but have no peculiarly monetarist method for predicting how a change in nominal income will be divided between changes in real income and changes in prices. Here the Keynesian and monetarist schools seem to be coming together.

One of the most exciting and promising subjects for economic research today is the process by which individuals adjust to changes in their circumstances. The classical economists assumed that everyone in a market could get all the information he needed at zero cost and that adjustment too was costless. Under these assumptions there is no explanation for unemployment of any resources.

As is now becoming ever more apparent, everyone must make decisions on the basis of imperfect information and adjustments can be costly. Therefore, a businessman may hesitate to change his selling prices or a man may remain unemployed for months because he does not know where another job may be found or he may not be willing to move to another city. After being preoccupied with the macroeconomics of national income, employment, and price levels for years, economists are now studying the microeconomic foundations of the wage and price adjustments that eventually determine the global aggregates in a world in which economic information is costly.[28]

This new work may help to explain lags in the response of the economy to changes in fiscal and monetary policy. For example, when aggregate demand falls, why and when does output decline? Why don't prices fall enough to avert cuts in output? It also should be helpful in analyzing the troublesome trade-offs between inflation and unemployment that can turn governments and their advisers out of office. And it should clarify the role of expectations in prices and interest rates. This work should be vastly helpful in clearing up questions about what is in the black boxes of Chapter 13.

RESEARCH ON THE FRONTIER

Most of the research reviewed here is unusual in being almost immediately relevant and applicable to current problems of economic policy and forecasting. This is not to say that all of the results have been satisfactory nor does it mean that the majority of policy makers and economists have yet accepted their implications and begun to act on them. But in most sciences there is much research that is so far from being "useful" in any mundane sense of the word that only some mysterious inner devil of curiosity drives the researcher on his quest. A generation or more later, however, the speculations of a Newton or an Einstein are part of the basic equipment of any physicist and of most engineers. So it is in economics. Irving Fisher, for example, was so far ahead of the profession in his day that only now are the full dimensions of his accomplishment becoming recognized.

The farthest-out monetary researchers today are following up tantalizing questions about how the rate of growth of the money supply might influence economic growth. This is way beyond the now familiar problems of relating money-supply changes to short-run fluctuations in economic activity. And it is not the old idea that by engineering a price inflation the monetary authorities could reduce interest rates and thereby increase the rate of investment in (presumably) growth-increasing capital goods. That one has been tried and found wanting.

One of the questions pursued by the investigators of money and growth is what is the optimum rate of growth of the money supply? Maurice Allais, of the University of Paris, suggests that the optimum situation is one in which the price level declines at the same rate at which productivity is rising.[29] This might require a gradual reduction in the nominal money supply, instead of the increase to which the world has been accustomed in the twentieth century. Milton Friedman, although approaching the problem somewhat differently, has a similar answer.[30] By his rough estimates the optimum policy for the United States would be about a 4 to 5 percent annual rate of decline in prices, which would require a reduction of 2 or 3 percent per year in broadly defined money supply (including time deposits). Conceding that the transition to any such policy would be extremely painful in the short run, he would compromise on some intermediate position, such as a constant money supply or a 2 to 3 percent growth rate.

In view of our current difficulties in trying to stop price levels from rising, it is evident that the world is far from ready for a policy of reducing prices. Furthermore, there is so little agreement yet on growth theories, of the monetary or any other variety, that it surely will be a long time before the policy makers take such proposals seriously. Nevertheless, thirty years ago monetary policy was believed to be ineffective in maintaining stability of income and prices. Thirty years from now, with the stability problem mastered, policy makers may be ready to entertain ideas for increasing the contribution of monetary policy to economic growth.

five
_____

MONEY IN AN OPEN WORLD

15

INTERDEPENDENCE—REAL AND MONETARY

We trust with perfect security that the freedom of
trade, without any attention of government, will
always supply us with the wine which we have
occasion for: and we may trust with equal
security that it will always supply us with all
the gold and silver which we can afford to
purchase or to employ, either in circulating our
commodities, or in other uses.
  Adam Smith, *The Wealth of Nations*, 1776[1]

Nations, despite Adam Smith's counsel, often are afraid to allow
either goods and services or money to move freely in international
trade. Therefore, they frequently interfere with both. The historic
preoccupation with the balance of payments is good evidence of
this. When traders settle their accounts by shipping money from
one country to another, nations can find themselves in perplexing
monetary difficulties. Does this mean there is something perverse
about trade, or is there something wrong with the world's management of money?

Most countries want to have at the same time high employment
and stable prices at home and stable rates of exchange between
their currencies and those of other countries. But some effects of
their monetary policies spill over on to other countries, through
trade and capital flows, and the effects of other countries' policies
spill over on to them—in the form of unwanted inflation, deflation,
or exchange-rate changes. Consequently, a nation's efforts to achieve
high employment and stable prices may reduce its ability to maintain stable exchange rates, or vice versa; and its best efforts in
either direction may be frustrated by the actions of other countries.

Yet no country can avoid these annoying consequences of inter-dependence by withdrawing from the world. The benefits of trade and international investment are too great for that. Trade and investment, furthermore, necessarily involve money, and so we must move here from considering the role of money in a closed economy to its role in the international monetary system.

Discussions of international monetary matters have a deplorable tendency to slide into a mysterious realm of balance-of-payments deficits, devaluations, revaluations, exchange reserves, speculation, exchange crises, paper gold, capital flows, "hot money," articles of agreement, currency swaps, two-tier gold markets, credit tranches, crises of confidence, communiqués from finance ministers, multi-lateral surveillance, and pious admonitions to various countries to "get their houses in order." The resort to such language is a symptom of the intellectual torture suffered by experts faced with problems they do not fully understand.

The chapters in this section of the book, therefore, will attempt to cut through the veil of jargon to some basic truths about the purchasing power of national moneys, the rates at which one can be exchanged for others, and the purchasing power of total world money. All of these depend primarily on how stocks of money are regulated. Unstable exchange rates and balance-of-payments deficits or surpluses are but symptoms of a more fundamental problem, the failure to keep money creation under control in particular countries and in the world at large.

MERCANTILISTS AND THE CLASSICALS

Economists and governments have been wrestling for centuries with the problems of reconciling national economic policies with the fact of economic interdependence in a multination world. As far back as 1381, says Jacob Viner, a mint official named Richard Leicester explained that England was losing gold by importing more goods than she was exporting.[2] All through the sixteenth century mercantilists, as Adam Smith later called them, argued that it was vitally important for England to have an excess of exports over imports in order to increase its stock of gold and silver. In 1615 the term "balance of trade" was coined and customs officials in England were requested to compute the total values of exports and imports. By 1623 Gerard Malynes was already criticizing the balance-of-trade figures as likely to be highly inaccurate, thus inaugurating a sturdy tradition that persists to this day.[3]

Although criticized by Adam Smith and others for having too simple a view of gold and silver as the sources of national wealth and power, the mercantilists clearly perceived that trading with other nations had monetary effects within a country. They thought it necessary, therefore, for a nation to manage its international trade through controls of many sorts in order that the effects of trade upon the domestic money supply be favorable. In a sense their trade policies were rudimentary attempts to manage domestic money supplies.

England, for example, an island nation without gold or silver mines, had to acquire these monetary metals from overseas by exporting more goods and services than it imported. Through regulating trade, therefore, a nation regulated the inflow of gold and silver—its balance of payments.

Although the mercantilists did not associate price inflation with inflows of gold and silver, according to Viner, many of them believed that bullion inflows—or balance-of-payments surpluses, as they would be called today—stimulated trade and industry. "An increased amount of money in circulation, they believed [says Viner], meant (or caused) an increased volume of trade, and since men would produce only what they could sell, a quickening of trade meant an increase of production and therefore a wealthier country."[4] The converse was probably as clear to them: a country that lost gold, through a balance-of-payments deficit, would suffer declines in trade, production, and wealth. This view has a clear echo today in the determined efforts of some countries to maintain balance-of-payments surpluses come what may.

The early classical economists, led by Adam Smith, had a very different view. A nation did not need trade policy to regulate its balance of payments or a domestic monetary policy either, they believed. International payments were automatically kept in balance, and the money supply was regulated, by the gold standard specie-flow mechanism.[5] If a country imported more goods than it exported—if it had a deficit in its balance of payments—it would pay for the difference with gold. The gold movement would reduce the money supply of the deficit country and reduce prices there. The influx of gold in other countries would increase money supplies and prices there.

The deficit country would be a less expensive place in which to buy, so its exports would rise and its imports would fall. Through free trade, unfettered by the tariffs and other obstacles advocated by the mercantilists, nations could enjoy the benefits of international specialization and the economies obtained by reaching larger markets.

The classical theory of the gold standard adjustment mechanism was based squarely on the quantity theory of money. We can see now that it was an overly optimistic version of the quantity theory because it implied that virtually all of the effects of gold flows and the money-supply changes caused by them occurred in prices, rather than in trade, production, and wealth, as the mercantilists believed.

It is unlikely that price adjustments ever could have been as smooth and as free from short-run disturbances in national real income as the classical gold standard theorists believed.

The gold standard [said John H. Williams] endeavors to maintain at a fixed rate the external value of a currency through the effects of gold flow upon the internal value. In this way monetary systems are expected mutually to correct and control each other. . . . But there may be situations in which countries cannot or will not permit prices to fall.[6]

Surely this is why the governments and central banks of the world never were entirely willing either to ignore the domestic effects of gold flows or to reinforce these effects, as the so-called "rules of the game" would have them do.

Although their views on policy were very different, both the mercantilists and the classicals strongly emphasized the role of money in the domestic economy and in the transmission of changes in economic conditions from country to country. Writers of both schools focused on the effects of trade on the money stock of a country and the effects of net transfers of money from country to country. Consequently, monetary policies were strongly influenced, often dominated, by international considerations long before domestic objectives were given much weight. It is important for us to remember this because beliefs about the interaction of trade, money, and national welfare that were first expressed hundreds of years ago still influence policies today.

The history of the international monetary system may well be viewed as a long contest for dominance between the two schools of thought. On one side, the mercantilist school, impressed with the disruptive effects of international money flows on internal income and wealth, has been in favor of intervening to regulate the flows or to insulate domestic economies from their effects. On the other side, the classicals, impressed with the benefits of free world trade, have been in favor of accepting occasional short-run sacrifices of internal income and wealth for the sake of external stability.

I believe it is fair to say that the mercantilist view has probably had the greater influence with world policy makers, even while they may have been expressing their devotion to classical free trade ideals. It is natural for any unit of government to pay more heed to the desires of its particular constituents than to those of a broader public. We have only to consider U.S. policies to see how easily restraints that would not be applied domestically are endorsed for international transactions.

INTERNAL VERSUS EXTERNAL STABILITY

Looking back through the mists and myths of time it is easy to exaggerate the degree to which the discipline of the gold standard was ever willingly accepted.

Thus, we are commonly told [Arthur Bloomfield has said] . . . that the various gold standard countries faithfully played the "rules of the game"; that the adherence to such rules was a factor of major importance in the successful functioning of the system; that the system worked more or less "automatically," with a minimum of discretionary action by the authorities, except in the case of the Bank of England which is alleged to have skillfully "managed" the gold standard system as a whole; that there was a remarkable "smoothness" in the functioning of the mechanism; and so on.[7]

On the contrary, Bloomfield found through painstaking historical research that the gold-standard central banks frequently bowed to domestic considerations when these conflicted with their professed objective of maintaining the convertibility of their currencies into gold at fixed exchange rates. Under the "rules of the game," for example, a deficit country was supposed to reinforce the deflationary influence of a gold outflow by *raising* its discount rate, while a surplus country was supposed to reinforce the inflationary influence of a gold inflow by *lowering* its discount rate. Nevertheless, says Bloomfield, "I can find no clear-cut evidence that any central bank [between 1880 and 1914] ever lowered its discount rate following gold inflows from abroad because of an explicit desire to play, or even because of an awareness of, the 'rules of the game.' "[8] And, again:

Far from central bank action before 1914 tending characteristically to accentuate the effects of gold (and other reserve) flows on commercial bank reserves and on the money supply—as the rules of the game would seem to imply—there was a tendency for those effects to be counteracted.[9]

Ragnar Nurkse found the same pattern of behavior in central banks between World Wars I and II.[10]

Although the pre-1914 central banks did not acknowledge responsibility for maintaining stability in domestic economic activity and prices, they preferred, when they could, to minimize the disturbing effects of their actions on business activity at home. Large changes in Bank rate, for example, might have distressing repercussions in the City. They also noticed that when gold flowed out of the country there were apt to be panics in the money markets and slumps in business. Furthermore, with centuries of mercantilist tradition behind them, they had a natural inclination to do whatever they thought would attract or hold gold.

Keynes described the conflict of objectives in graphic language when he predicted the dangers Britain would face if it returned to the gold standard after World War I. Returning to the gold standard would oblige Britain to exchange pounds for gold at a fixed price and thus would make the British money supply rise or fall as gold flowed in or out.

With the existing distribution of the world's gold [he said] the reinstatement of the gold standard means, inevitably, that we surrender the regulation of our price level and the handling of the credit cycle to the Federal Reserve Board of the United States. Even if the most intimate and cordial cooperation is established between the Board and the Bank of England, the preponderance of power will still belong to the former. The Board will be in a position to disregard the Bank. But if the Bank disregards the Board, it will render itself liable to be flooded with, or depleted of, gold, as the case may be.[11]

He had seen, correctly, that the gold standard to which much of the world returned after the war would not be the impersonal, automatic system described in the textbooks. Gold itself had become a "managed" currency, he said, whose value would depend on the policies of three or four of the most powerful central banks. The Genoa Conference had recommended in 1922 that central banks should act together to stabilize the value of gold. Some of the world's leading economists, including R. G. Hawtrey and Gustav Cassel, had also suggested that the value of gold be stabilized.

The United States, Keynes thought, would have the most influence on the value of gold. But the attitudes of those inscrutable Americans toward gold were difficult to fathom and the Federal Reserve had not yet demonstrated its competence to deal with economic instability. Therefore, he did not want to see Britain dangle like a tail on the soaring, swooping American kite.

A gold standard means, in practice [he said], nothing but to have the same price level and the same money rates (broadly speaking) as the United States. The whole object is to link *rigidly* the City and Wall Street. I beg the Chancellor of the Exchequer and the Governor of the Bank of England and the nameless others who settle our destiny in secret to reflect that this may be a dangerous proceeding.[12]

That Keynes was a good prophet, at least on this occasion, was clearly demonstrated when the U.S. Federal Reserve System "exported" deflation between 1929 and 1931, with far more painful consequences for the world than those of the inflation supposedly exported after World War II. As Milton Friedman and Anna Schwartz describe the process, the initial U.S. deflation led to a gold inflow from other countries in gold-standard fashion.

The international effects were severe and the transmission rapid, not only because the gold-exchange standard had rendered the international financial system more vulnerable to disturbances, but also because the United States did not follow gold-standard rules. We did not permit the inflow of gold to expand the U.S. money stock. We not only sterilized it, we went much further. Our money stock moved perversely, going down as the gold stock went up. . . . The result was that other countries not only had to bear the whole burden of adjustment but also were faced with continued additional disturbances in the same direction, to which they had to adjust.[13]

The first major country to cut loose from this source of deflation was Britain, which "devalued," or stopped exchanging pounds for gold—and thus for dollars—at a fixed rate of exchange in 1931.

. . . the devaluation of the pound [says Ragnar Nurkse] . . . offered an opportunity for initiating almost immediately a large and deliberate monetary expansion at home. Early in 1932 the bank rate was reduced from 6% to 2% and the Bank of England made large security purchases in the open market, thereby expanding the cash base and inducing, in turn, an expansion of commercial bank credit. For domestic credit policy, an important consequence of the suspension of gold payments was that expansionist open market operations could be carried out effectively, without any fear of their being neutralized by losses of gold.[14]

In short, by cutting the golden cord between it and a foundering United States, England was able to get about the urgent business of reducing unemployment at home.

THE INTERNATIONAL MONETARY FUND

After World War II there was the usual tendency to build protection against the ills most recently experienced while failing to foresee others that lay ahead. With the memories of the thirties still fresh, the framers of the postwar international monetary system tried to develop something that would accommodate the evident determination of nations to avoid deflation and unemployment while still keeping exchange rates between currencies fixed, or nearly so.

There were two main features of the new system. First was a pool of currencies in the International Monetary Fund that member nations with balance-of-payments deficits could draw on to settle their international accounts if they became short of gold and wanted to avoid the deflation that would have been their fate under the old gold standard. The reserve pool and the countries' own reserves were to act as buffers that would limit or delay the impacts of balance-of-payments deficits and surpluses on domestic income and employment.

The ubiquitous Lord Keynes, probably the most visionary of the monetary architects who gathered at Bretton Woods, wanted the pool of reserves to be a large one because he did not want national economic stabilization policies to be inhibited by shortages of gold or other international reserves. John H. Williams, of Harvard University and the Federal Reserve Bank of New York, doubted that such a generous provision of exchange reserves would be a good policy in view of the danger of a postwar inflation. With respect to the United States in particular he said that "one would need to ask whether it is wise to encourage such an expansion of bank reserves and bank deposits as would ensue, and on top of the doubling and more likely the trebling of our money supply which is resulting from our financing of the war."[15]

The U.S. delegates, representing the holder of most of the world's gold at the time, preferred to keep the pool of gold substitutes small. Their view prevailed. Within a few years, however, U.S. delegations were to change their tune at international monetary conferences when the U.S. gold hoard melted away and other nations began to suggest that the United States should follow more restrictive domestic policies.

The second major new feature of the postwar monetary system was an agreement not to change exchange rates except by international consultation and approval. During the turbulent thirties nations had become convinced that unilateral devaluations by their neighbors inflicted unemployment on them. Consequently, there was a strong desire to bring the supposedly potent instrument of exchange-rate manipulation under international control. This later proved to be about as effective as the U.S. attempt during the twenties to deny the comforts of alcohol to the restless, convivial American public.[16]

The system served rather well until a few years ago when it began to creak and groan under the strain of exchange crises, its inflationary bias, and the evident lack of an effective adjustment mechanism to replace the one of the gold standard. The framers of the system had visualized international flows of gold and other reserves like the ebbing and flowing of the tides. There should be no need, they thought, for adopting hasty domestic policies or suffering unpleasant consequences because of a tide that would soon turn of its own accord. What they had not foreseen was that the tides might flow in one direction for years on end. The classical gold standard, as we have seen, would have reversed the flows automatically; and the mercantilists would have taken direct measures to curb them.

By 1971 fundamental changes were clearly needed. The greatest weaknesses of the present system, I believe, flow from the failure of its framers and of the people who have tried to operate it to understand adequately the role of money. The neglect of money occurred after centuries in which money and the quantity theory had prominent roles in explanations of international economic relations. This lack of understanding came largely from the same Keynesian Revolution that dethroned money in the realm of domestic economic policy. How the ousting of money from the international monetary system came about is the story of the next chapter. What the restoration of money implies for the future of the system will be taken up later.

16

AN INTERNATIONAL MONETARY SYSTEM SANS MONEY

It is the policy of an autonomous rate of interest, unimpeded by international preoccupations, and of a national investment programme directed to an optimum level of domestic employment which is twice blessed in the sense that it helps ourselves and our neighbors at the same time. And it is the simultaneous pursuit of these policies by all countries together which is capable of restoring economic health and strength internationally, whether we measure it by the level of domestic employment or by the volume of international trade.

John Maynard Keynes, *The General Theory of Employment, Interest and Money,* 1935[1]

In the early sixties there arose the briefly tantalizing hope that it might after all be possible for a country to satisfy *both* domestic and international objectives, with fixed exchange rates, by finding and applying the proper mix of monetary and fiscal policies. The idea became known as the "assignment problem" among the *cognoscenti* of international economics who convene in such thought-conducive environments as Bologna, Bellagio, Princeton, and Chicago.[2] It was an application of a principle developed by James Meade, of Cambridge University, and Jan Tinbergen, the eminent Dutch econometrician and winner of the first Nobel Prize in Economics. According to this principle, a policy maker who has two or more independent policy goals and the same number of independent policy instruments should assign one of the instruments to the pursuit of each of the goals. In this case, monetary policy was supposed to achieve balance-of-payments equilibrium while fiscal policy was used to maintain domestic stability.

The idea of the monetary-fiscal policy mix was recognized by Herbert Stein as an old one that had been reintroduced without proper credit to its author. In his book, *The Fiscal Revolution in America,* he traced it back to the Keynes of the early twenties, who, as we have seen, had been frustrated by Britain's going back on the gold standard against his advice.

The situation and the proposals in Britain in the 1920s were similar to those in the United States in the early 1960s. The United States was suffering from excessive unemployment and balance-of-payments deficits. It was widely believed that monetary policy could not be made more expansive in the effort to reduce unemployment without causing an outflow of funds and deterioration of the balance of payments. Therefore, it was suggested that reliance should be placed on expansive fiscal policy, notably the 1964 tax reduction, to raise employment while continuing a tight monetary policy for the sake of the balance of payments. This was called a shift in the "monetary-fiscal mix." The 1924 Keynesian antecedent was not recalled at the later date.[3]

The 1924 Keynesian antecedent is not just a bit of footnote *curiosa*. It marks an early stage in the transformation of Keynes, the monetarist, into Keynes, the fiscalist, a transformation that was to have incalculable effects on the evolution of world economic thought and policy. By drastically changing the way domestic and international economic problems were analyzed, the transformation of Keynes also transformed the problems, and not for the better.

Early in his career Keynes, like other early monetarists, believed economic activity could be stabilized by using money supply changes to stabilize the price level. But the restoration of the gold standard, he believed, would rule out the use of monetary policy for domestic objectives because central banks would be preoccupied with balance-of-payments problems. Yet he was still concerned with the problem of correcting excessive unemployment.

It was the international considerations [says Stein] that led Keynes to summon fiscal policy to the aid of monetary policy, rather than relying entirely on monetary policy as he apparently still would have done in the absence of the international restraints.[4]

By the mid-thirties Keynes had produced his *General Theory* to justify the use of fiscal policy for economic stabilization, and, as we have seen in earlier chapters, the theory soon swept the economics profession. Furthermore, his theory replaced the quantity theory not only in the analysis of national economies but in explanations of international payments adjustment as well.

The classical theory of the gold-standard adjustment mechanism was a monetary explanation that emphasized changes in money stocks and the influence of money-supply changes on prices. When Keynes' followers extended his theory to analysis of international payments problems, the emphasis shifted to flows of income, propensities to import, foreign-trade multipliers, and adjustments in levels of output and employment rather than in prices.

In more ways than one the extension of Keynesian economics to international monetary problems was a reversion to mercantilism.[5] Most price changes dropped out of the analysis because of the Keynesian assumption of price stability. When relative price changes were admitted, they were attributed not to the working of the adjustment mechanism but to autonomous influences, such as national traits of docility or intransigence in labor unions. Monetary policy was limited to discount-rate changes or open-market operations designed to influence capital flows through changing interest rates. Therefore, until the recent revival of monetarism, most analyses of international monetary problems said very little about prices or money. That was like staging *Hamlet* without the Prince of Denmark or his mother.[6]

THE ADJUSTMENT MECHANISM IN
A MONEYLESS SYSTEM

Economists led by F. W. Taussig of Harvard found during the twenties that the balancing process in international trade worked faster and more smoothly than could be explained by the classical mechanism of adjustments through changing money supplies and prices. They found that if a country's exports increased there would be a counterbalancing increase in imports without the price changes called for by the classical mechanism.

The smoothness and speed with which many countries' balances of payments seemed to adapt themselves to changing circumstances in the years before the First World War [says Lloyd A. Metzler] led Taussig to surmise that the classical theory might be an incomplete explanation of the adjusting mechanism. . . . Even before the [Keynesian] theory of employment was developed, historical studies thus indicated that the balancing of international payments and receipts might be attributable to economic forces not considered in the classical theory.[7]

Studies of the elasticities of demand for individual products added to the doubts about the adequacy of the classical explanation because the physical volume of imports appeared to be only slightly responsive to changes in prices.

With the appearance of Keynes' *General Theory,* says Professor Metzler:

. . . the missing link in the classical theory became almost self-evident: the rapid adjustment of a country's balance of payments which Taussig had observed, and which seemed to occur without the assistance of price changes or changes in central bank policy, was found to be largely the result of induced movements of income and employment.[8]

The gist of the income explanation, as developed by Professor Metzler and others, is that if country A increases its imports from country B, and thus incurs a balance-of-payments deficit, income and employment increase in the export industries of country B. The increase in export-industry income would then increase total income and employment in country B, through the Keynesian multiplier process, just as an autonomous increase in private investment or government spending supposedly would do. Country B would then increase its imports from A, thus offsetting part of the original rise in exports to A. The adjustment would be only partial, however, making it necessary for countries to complete the adjustment through discretionary policies influencing trade or capital movements.

The classical explanation, while focusing on prices, had indeed neglected short-run effects of money-supply changes on income and employment that the mercantilists had emphasized and that we now realize are extremely important. Unfortunately, the new idea was carried too far; it replaced, rather than supplemented, the classical explanation.

As a classical economist, Taussig was puzzled by the rapid adjustment of the balance of payments because it preceded any perceptible impact on prices. If prices did not move, there must have been something other than a monetary process at work. The essence of the Keynesian answer to the puzzle, according to Metzler, was "that an external event which increases a country's exports will also increase imports *even without price changes,* since the change in exports affects the level of output and hence the demand for all goods [italics in original]."[9] But the same effect on the demand for imports could be explained by the monetary process we discussed in Chapter 11 as "imported inflation" under the gold-exchange standard.

The exporters are paid with foreign currency, which they sell to their central bank. The central bank pays for the foreign currency with high-powered money, thereby increasing the money supply of the exporting country. The increase in money-supply growth then induces a rise in nominal income and an increase in demand for goods and services, including imports, as people try to get rid of excess balances. We have here once again the problem of determining which black box transmits the effects of an "autonomous" expenditure change that has a money-supply change associated with it.

In the more familiar case of distinguishing between effects of fiscal and monetary policies, a government-expenditure increase causes a budget deficit, which the central bank monetizes. Keynesians attribute the income increase to the expenditure increase, while monetarists attribute it to the money-supply increase.

In the trade case an increase in exports brings with it an inflow of foreign currency, which the central bank monetizes, i.e., converts into a somewhat larger equivalent value of domestic currency. Keynesians attribute the income increase to the export increase, while monetarists attribute it to the money-supply increase.

The basic flaw in this Keynesian approach to international payments problems, as in other uncritical applications of a simple Keynesian apparatus, is that it starts from an assumption of chronic underemployment of labor and other resources. An increase in the demand for a country's exports, therefore, was expected to stimulate an increase in total output by calling unemployed resources into use. The classical assumption, which obviously is much more appropriate to today's conditions, is that resources are fully employed.

An increase in demand for a country's exports under classical assumptions would change relative prices and wages within the country so that output of exports would increase and production for home markets would decrease. An increase in consumption of imports would be substituted for the additional output going into exports. There would be no increase in total real income other than that gained by achieving a more efficient allocation of world resources.

The classical price adjustment, however, is a long-run process, at least longer-run than the classical economists believed. As we saw in the monetarist credo of Chapter 1, an increase in the rate of growth of the money supply will cause an increase in the rate of growth of nominal income about six to nine months later. The increase in rate of growth of nominal income, furthermore, usually shows up first as a temporary increase in real output and hardly at all in prices. The effects on prices come about six to nine months after the effects on income and output—or a year or two after the initial change in money-supply growth. Therefore, much of the adjustment of imports and exports that Taussig observed could occur before prices and wages reach their equilibrium levels and yet still be part of a *monetary* adjustment process.

The underemployment assumption and the assumption of fixed prices in the Keynesian income-theory of trade-balance adjustment nurture belief in the fallacies of the growth-inducing export surplus and the "beggar-my-neighbor" devaluation. If total national income and employment could be increased by a rise in exports (or an export surplus), why not engineer one by subsidizing exports or restricting imports? Or why not accomplish the same end by devaluing the currency? Devaluation would reduce prices of exports in terms of other currencies and would raise prices of imports in home markets.

In his "Notes on Mercantilism," Keynes argued that an export surplus was a means by which a country that was growing in wealth could meet the problem of an insufficiency of inducements to new investment.

At a time when the authorities had no direct control over the domestic rate of interest or the other inducements to home investment [he said], measures to increase the favorable balance of trade were the only *direct* means at their disposal for increasing foreign investment; and, at the same time, the effect of a favorable balance of trade on the influx of the precious metals was their only *indirect* means of reducing the domestic rate of interest and so increasing the inducement to home investment [italics in original].[10]

There seems little doubt that such hardy mercantilist beliefs about the influence of export surpluses on economic growth persist today. How else can one explain the implacable determination of some countries to maintain large export surpluses even when to do so various controls must be endured and their central banks must amass dollars they say they do not want? The sometimes vehement denunciation of countries that seem likely to devalue their currencies flows from a fear that devaluing countries can thereby increase their exports and rob the others of real income.

If price changes and money flows are admitted to the adjustment process, however, it can be seen that the country that maintains an export surplus through tariffs or other interferences with trade flows—or that keeps its exchange rate at a level lower than it would be in a free exchange market—merely gives up real goods and services in return for the money of other countries. In effect, it lends real goods and services in return for the monetary liabilities of other countries and usually at lower rates of return than it could earn by investing in capital assets at home. In that way, it wittingly or unwittingly subsidizes real income and consumption for people in other countries.

This perhaps surprising proposition should be more clear after we discuss exchange-rate adjustments. However, the key to understanding it is that a country that pegs its exchange rate at a below-free-market level must buy dollars, gold, or other foreign exchange to do so. The purchases of foreign exchange by the central bank increase the country's money supply, as we saw in Chapter 11. This process appears remarkably similar to what I called earlier the monetary policy of the mercantilists, in which a surplus of exports over imports was designed to draw in gold in order to increase the domestic money supply.

A contrived balance-of-payments surplus increases the money supply and, in the short run, stimulates a rise in trade and production. However, the monetary aspect of this process may not be recognized at the time. The rise in economic activity is more likely to be explained by the common-sense observation that manufacturing automobiles, radios, or ships for export puts people to work and raises income.

The increase in money supply induced by a balance-of-payments surplus initially may stimulate a rise in real income. This is the germ of truth in the mercantilist doctrine. But when resources are fully employed, the money-supply growth induced by the payments surplus eventually raises the country's domestic price level, thereby reducing home consumption of home goods so that more goods can be exported to the countries that supply money. There is no such thing as a free lunch.

MERCANTILISM REVIVED

The most damaging consequence of the neglect of money in explanations of international monetary problems is that it has diverted attention from the real problem. Keynesian theory focuses on flows of income and expenditures and therefore directs policy makers to seek ways of influencing particular flows in the balance-of-payments accounts. Influencing the flows, moreover, seems to be eminent common sense and has a long tradition in mercantilist thought. In the monetarist view, however, balance-of-payments deficits or surpluses (with fixed exchange rates) are caused by differences in rates of growth of national money supplies. The ways to adjustment, therefore, are to regulate money stocks—not international payments flows—or to let exchange rates change.

The predominant view of the international payments problem has concentrated for years on the flows summed up in the balance of payments—imports, exports, and capital flows. The mercantilists, as we saw, stumbled onto the same approach long before. Strenuous efforts have been made by individual countries to control particular trade and capital flows, while very little has been done to control the differential rates of money creation in the system as a whole. Yet these are the principal reasons for the net flows of dollars and gold (balance-of-payments deficits or surpluses) among nations in a fixed-exchange-rate system. Most ironic are attempts to influence capital flows through manipulating interest rates, for these attempts can produce changes in money supply that make the problem worse instead of better.

If unwilling to let international payments flows influence domestic economic activity and prices and if unable to offset or to sterilize them, nations may adopt a last-resort policy option with fixed exchange rates; they can try to limit the flows with direct controls. John Exter, of First National City Bank, likens this approach to the attempt to dam a fast-running stream by throwing rocks into it. Each rock, or control, may be watertight; but the stream merely flows around and over it.

The United States, in a chronic state of embarrassment over its balance-of-payments deficit, but with domestic and other international problems that seem more pressing, has led an inglorious retreat from freedom in world markets since 1960. Others have not been far behind:

. . . we find [says Samuel Katz] general tendencies, both in Europe and outside, toward the use of direct controls to check international flows of capital and, thereby, to break the link between domestic and international financial markets in the major industrial countries. This process of economic fragmentation . . . reflects largely the absence of any agreed path of balance-of-payments adjustment among the countries of the Group of Ten. This absence can be attributed in part to the subordination of international to domestic economic objectives, both in Europe and elsewhere, and in part to the use of offsetting techniques which reduce the impact of "automatic" corrective forces in the world payments system.[11]

CHASING A CHIMERA—THE "MONETARY-FISCAL MIX"

The neglect of money in international economics reached perhaps its highest flowering in the discussion of the monetary-fiscal mix mentioned earlier. The idea was applied in U.S. economic policies, or in some rationalizations for them, in the early 1960s. In the U.S. case, monetary policy was supposed to keep short-term interest rates high in order to reduce capital outflows that would worsen the balance-of-payments deficit, while an expansive fiscal policy was used to stimulate economic expansion. The traditional dilemma of reconciling domestic and international objectives was thus neatly resolved, or so it seemed.

The prescription has been applied also in some of the countries with large balance-of-payments surpluses, including Germany, in the form of easy money to keep interest rates low and tax increases to restrain inflation. Such policies can sow a crop of trouble to be reaped for years afterward.

Although, in theory, the mix was plausible, its components had not been adequately tested. Most of the elegant treatises on the use of the monetary-fiscal mix for resolving conflicts in international payments problems were written before the explosion of empirical research on effects of monetary and fiscal policies reviewed in earlier chapters. In light of this research, the following points can now be made against the mix approach: (1) no one has demonstrated a strong enough independent influence of fiscal policy in any country to justify substituting fiscal policy for monetary policy as a stabilizing instrument; (2) there is no such thing as a monetary policy that influences interest rates alone. The money-supply changes produced by efforts to influence interest rates have powerful lagged effects on income and prices and, consequently, on the balance of payments in the opposite direction from the interest-rate effects assumed in the mix proposals.

Theorists were reconsidering the whole problem by the late 1960s. Harry Johnson, for one, chided economists working in the international monetary field for not using more adequate analytical tools.

. . . international monetary economists [he said] have built models of international adjustment and policy problems which have employed as building blocks quite naïve Keynesian models of the national economy, in which consumption has been made a simple function of income and investment a simple function of interest rates.[12]

Robert Mundell, of the International Monetary Fund and the University of Chicago, who was one of the leading exponents of the mix, said at a conference on international adjustment problems that he seemed to have created a lot of trouble by using, in his early papers, a definition of monetary policy that he no longer liked or accepted. He had used the traditional Keynesian concept of monetary policy as interest-rate policy. He had assumed that bank-rate adjustment was the instrument of monetary policy and that the money supply had to be adjusted to make that rate effective in the market.[13]

To me, the most vulnerable assumption is that central banks can control interest rates, for this conflicts with what many of us learned the hard way in the 1960s. Irving Fisher was right. We must distinguish between the real rate of interest, which influences saving and investing decisions, and the money rate (nominal rate), which has been used in Keynesian models for domestic and international analysis.

A more crucial reappraisal will probably take place in those countries that have actually tried to apply the mix. Attempts to hold interest rates down with monetary policy to encourage capital outflows while curbing aggregate demand with fiscal policy are bound to be frustrated. The resulting money-supply growth will cause a price inflation and consequent worsening of the balance of payments that fiscal policy cannot check.

Attempts to hold interest rates up with monetary policy to discourage capital outflows while stimulating aggregate demand with fiscal policy are also bound to be frustrated. Fiscal policy cannot stimulate expansion in the face of overly restrictive monetary policy, nor can interest rates be prevented from falling if an economy slips into recession. The monetary-fiscal mix has lost its magic as a cure for international payments problems, although, like the copper bracelet for arthritis, some people still believe in it.

A MONETARIST'S VIEW OF WORLD MONEY

What remedy is there if we have too little Money? Answer: We must erect a Bank, which well computed, doth almost double the Effect of our coined money: And we have in England Materials for a Bank which shall furnish Stock enough to drive the Trade of the whole Commercial World.
Sir William Petty, *Quantulumcunque Concerning Money,* 1682[1]

The international monetary system has become intolerably confusing. The terminology and discussions are increasingly prolix. New institutions are superimposed on old ones in a tottering structure that inspires little confidence in those who must embark on the seas of world trade. And anyone with a taste for demonology can find much to feed on in the sermons of its reigning clergy. The clamor of charges and countercharges rises to the deafening point when the system comes under special strain, as in 1971.

Yet the essence of the world's money problem can be grasped intuitively by any tourist in an airport or hotel outside his own country. Faced with the outstretched palm of a porter, he mentally converts a handful of unfamiliar coins into units of his own currency—say quarters of a dollar if he is an American. A Swiss franc was equivalent to an American quarter in 1970; a British two shilling piece was worth slightly less than a quarter; and one Deutschemark, slightly more. On a later trip these exchange rates might be quite different and so might be the prices of goods and services at home and abroad. What is our money worth when it goes abroad? How should we weigh the money of strangers?

These questions arise from the fact that more than a hundred separate entities pursuing innumerable combinations of domestic and international objectives have the power to issue high-powered money. With supplies of many different moneys growing at many different rates, exchange rates seem about to change somewhere in the world every day, despite elaborate and determined efforts to hold them fixed. But much more is at stake than exchange rates; prices and incomes, too, are disturbed when money creation gets out of order.

For much too long international payments problems have been viewed as the balance-of-payments problems of individual countries. And balance-of-payments problems have been viewed as the results of importing foolishly or living beyond one's means. Monetary policy, similarly, has been a private affair of each country. When the monetary nature of the international payments system is recognized, however, the need for a world monetary policy appears. But if there is to be a world monetary policy, who is to determine it and who is to carry it out?

The gold standard came close to being a satisfactory solution to the problem because it provided, for a brief time, a semiautomatic control over the total world money supply and a mechanism for making national currencies convertible into one another at stable exchange rates. But growth in the world supply of gold fluctuated as new mines were found and old ones became exhausted. And with increasing recognition of the effects of monetary policy came increasing determination to use monetary instruments to attain national objectives.

Despite the proliferation of international monetary institutions since World War II and the multitude of ingenious new instruments for international monetary cooperation, we are still far from a universally satisfactory system for managing the world's money. While officials and central bankers of the world have been negotiating with agonizing slowness their complicated arrangements and agreements, private arrangements for getting the world's money work done, such as the Eurodollar market, have been evolving with remarkable speed and effectiveness. These private arrangements are not always to the liking of the officials who are trying to manage the system because they have vastly increased the interdependence of nations and thus have reduced the scope for national autonomy in monetary policies.

THE QUANTITY THEORY REARS ITS BARELY DISGUISED HEAD

One of the earliest major attempts to repair the neglect of money in international monetary analysis was a perceptive paper by J. J. Polak of the International Monetary Fund in 1957. By then, of course, Keynesian income-expenditure theory had long since won the field so Polak viewed his work as an effort to integrate monetary and credit factors into the prevailing income analysis. Almost apologetically, he said:

. . . it might be asked whether, in the assumptions made about money, the Quantity Theory of Money does not rear its barely disguised head? . . . Suffice it to say at this stage, first, that the monster was never really slain; and second, that once it has been properly tied to income analysis it appears to be not only harmless but indeed quite useful.[2]

To simplify his analysis, Polak assumed that the income velocity of money (the ratio of money supply to income) was constant. Therefore, under his assumption, a doubling of money supply would produce a doubling of money income. To those who might think this an outrageous assumption he suggested that it was no worse than the then-common practice of assuming a constant propensity to consume out of income:

Surely, anyone who took seriously all of Keynes' objective (six) and subjective (eight plus four) factors affecting the propensity to consume, together with their variability over time, would shrink from thinking of this propensity as something even approaching a statistical constant (which, of course, Keynes never suggested it was). But empirical economics, taking its cue from Kahn's earlier dynamic multiplier approach, has tended to sweep away doubts and fears of this nature, at least "as a first approximation," and has managed to turn Keynes' formal multiplier into a usable tool of analysis and policy.[3]

Furthermore, Polak had evidence drawn from more than forty countries to show that there was in fact considerable year-to-year stability in income velocity or a tendency for movements in one year to be subsequently reversed.

Polak's most interesting conclusion, for our purposes, was that an increase in the rate of credit expansion in a country (read "money-supply growth") will gradually bring about increases in money income and imports and a loss in exchange reserves (balance-of-payments deficit). The converse would also be true: a slowing in money-supply growth would slow the growth of money income and imports and bring about a balance-of-payments surplus.

The speed of international payments adjustment that puzzled Taussig and others in the twenties is no longer such a mystery when a monetary analysis is applied. A money-supply change will induce changes in the demands for goods and services and securities, both domestic and foreign, and thus will influence international trade flows and capital flows, *before* much change in prices appears.

As we saw in Chapter 11, if the Federal Reserve System permits U.S. money-supply growth to accelerate, the rate of money income will rise in the United States, as Americans try to reduce their excess cash balances. But American purchases of foreign goods and services will also rise—the increase in imports cited by Polak—and the U.S. balance-of-payments deficit will increase—also as implied by Polak's analysis. I would add here that the increase in U.S. money supply would induce increased U.S. purchases of foreign capital assets and securities, as well as the goods and services usually included in the trade balance.

In other countries the increase of U.S. money supply would induce increases in exports and money income. Here I would change the order of causation in the Polak analysis. He posited a chain of effects from exports to income to money supply. The increase in exports, in his explanation, would increase income (the Keynesian view) and the increase of income would induce an increase of money supply. I would say instead that the increase in exports would increase money supply which, in turn, would increase income.

In the process described in Chapter 11, the increase in dollar holdings of people from whom Americans buy goods, services, and securities—amplified by central bank purchases of dollars (to hold exchange rates constant)—causes supplies of other currencies to grow when the U.S. money supply grows. Furthermore, it is not just the United States that can initiate expansion of world money supply. Any other country can do so, as its central bank helps the government to borrow on favorable terms, or tries to stabilize interest rates, or follows any one of many policies believed to be in the national interest.

The principal contribution of the Polak analysis, and of other monetary studies that have appeared more recently, is the finding that international payments influence income through changing money supplies. We know from individual country studies that money-supply changes, however caused, will change national income. These monetary influences on income may be more powerful and more rapid in some countries than in others, but there is good reason to believe that they exist in all countries. Moreover, the possibility that they may not be simple to predict in all countries does not mean that money-supply effects on income can safely be ignored. In fact, this is all the more reason for caution in domestic and international monetary policies.

By focusing on money income, furthermore, it is possible for a monetary analysis of international payments adjustment to bridge some of the difference between the mercantilists and the classical economists. The effects of a money-supply change on income are divided between short-run effects on real income—which were stressed in the observations of the mercantilists—and longer-run effects on prices—which were stressed by the classical economists and early monetarists. When the Keynesian apparatus was applied to international payments problems, as we saw earlier, price effects dropped out and income effects were assigned the principal role. The new monetarist approach puts the price effects of international transactions back in without losing sight of the effects on income.

Thus far we have seen how *a country may push money out to other countries by expanding its own money stock too rapidly* and how this money will stimulate income increases there. But there is another fascinating implication of the relationship between money and income: the *quantity* of money demanded grows as real income grows. *If growth of the domestic money stock slows down in a country in which real income is growing, the people of that country may pull in the money of other countries* to satisfy their demand for money.

All of this puts conventional ideas about balance-of-payments deficits or surpluses in a new light. According to the conventional wisdom, a country will have a deficit in its balance of payments— money will flow out—if its government persists in large foreign aid programs or military operations overseas; or its businessmen insist on building too many factories in other countries; or if its people have too strong a desire for wines and automobiles from abroad. By the same token, a country will have a balance-of-payments surplus —money will flow in—if its businessmen know how to sell abroad, its labor unions are responsible, and its people are hardworking and thrifty. These influences may be important but the primary cause of balance-of-payments deficits or surpluses, in the monetarist view, is the existence of differing national rates of money-supply growth in a world of differing national rates of growth of the demand for money.

Some years ago John Exter of First National City Bank suggested that the economies of the world were like:

. . . a system of reservoirs interconnected by innumerable channels, and each central bank like a faucet that could pour money into, or pull money out of, each reservoir. There are so many of these channels, as between Canada and the United States, for instance, that money flows as freely from Canada to Detroit as from New York to Detroit. Whether you think of Canada or Germany or Costa Rica or Vietnam, the channels are infinite. You put dollars into one or another of them whether you shop in Windsor, buy a Volkswagen, eat a banana, or pay taxes for Vietnam.[4]

However good the intentions of a particular government, as long as its currency is linked to others and the dollar through fixed exchange rates, it cannot control its balance of payments and its domestic money supply at the same time. The United States is no more exempt from this constraint than is anyone else.

The Federal Reserve can control the total volume of dollars in the world; it cannot control the shares of these dollars that are held inside and outside the United States. This is because anyone who gets his hands on a dollar is under no compulsion to spend it in the United States. Therefore, if the U.S. monetary authorities control the domestic money supply of the United States they cannot control the U.S. balance of payments that feeds dollars to the rest of the world. If they control the balance of payments, they lose control of the domestic money supply.

Clarification of these monetary interconnections and their implications for monetary policies in an open world has occurred virtually simultaneously in various parts of the world through empirical observation and theoretical work. For example, Pierre Berger and his colleagues at the Banque de France have discovered a remarkable alternation in the contributions of domestic and international influences on growth of the money supply of France from 1820 through 1968.[5] When domestic credit creation was unusually high, says M. Berger, there were compensating outflows of foreign exchange reserves (balance-of-payments deficits); and when there were inflows of foreign exchange (balace-of-payments surpluses), there were compensating reductions in the rate of domestic credit creation. M. Berger has extended his analysis to the other Common Market countries for the period since World War II.

In North America, elements of this new view appear in some promising theoretical work.[6]

THE DOLLAR-EXCHANGE STANDARD

In his characteristically prescient way, Irving Fisher anticipated the current discussion long ago.

. . . no great increase of money (M) in any one country or locality can occur [he said] without spreading to other countries or localities. As soon as local prices have risen enough to make it profitable to sell at the high prices in that place and buy at the low prices elsewhere, money will be exported. The production of gold in Colorado and Alaska first results in higher prices in Colorado and Alaska, then in sending gold to other sections of the United States, then in higher prices throughout the United States, then in export abroad, and finally in higher prices throughout the gold-using world.[7]

It is not difficult to recognize features of the old gold-exchange standard in the international payments system that prevailed until recently. The dollar served the role formerly played by gold. And the United States owned the world's dollar mines, except for those in the Eurodollar market. As long as exchange rates between dollars and other currencies were fixed, and other central banks used dollars for reserves, the Federal Reserve System of the United States was the principal determinant of world money supply. The rising and falling output of Colorado's and Alaska's gold mines similarly influenced total world money supply under the gold standard.

Changes in the ratios between holdings of dollars and holdings of other currencies, which people and central banks tried to maintain, influenced total world money supply just as changes of reserve ratios (or the money multiplier) do within a national monetary system.[8] This was true of the gold-exchange standard, too. As under the gold standard, furthermore, changes in the supplies of substitutes for dollars or gold in central-bank reserves—national currencies and the new Special Drawing Rights (SDRs) of the International Monetary Fund—are also important.

The automatic adjustment feature of the gold standard that survived in the international monetary system until August 15, 1971, was, at most, a tendency of dollar flows to produce differential rates of price inflation (and money-income growth) which, in time, influenced imports and exports of the United States and other countries. This differential-inflation tendency operated in the direction of restoring equilibrium only if other central banks passively bought or sold dollars whenever necessary to prevent changes in exchange rates. But they did not passively accept the discipline of the dollar flows as the key determinant of what their money supplies should be. Nor were there any overwhelming arguments that they should, in view of the erratic performance of the U.S. authorities in regulating the supply of dollars over the past decade. Changes of internal incomes and price levels for the sake of external stability were no more palatable under the dollar standard than they were under the gold standard.

Another outstanding difference between the gold standard and the dollar standard is that an outflow of dollars from the United States did not automatically reduce the U.S. money supply in the way a gold outflow would supposedly have done. Therefore, instead of an inflationary influence in dollar-gaining countries being matched by a deflationary influence in the dollar-losing country there can be price inflation on both sides. This was because the United States was never a dollar-losing country; it was a dollar-producing country. If the United States inflated, therefore, all inflated. The system had an inflationary bias.

Jacques Rueff, former economic adviser to President de Gaulle and eloquent advocate of a return to the classical gold standard, has excoriated this feature of the recent system more than once. For example:

> My friends in Washington agree that, because of the gold-exchange standard, there is no automatic contraction of credit in response to the payments deficit, but they say, "What money has not done, we can do by deliberate credit policy." I have told them, "Maybe you can do it, but there is no chance whatever that you will do it." In a year in which there has been a $3 billion deficit in the balance of payments, they could not reduce credit by such an amount. It may not be technically impossible, but it would certainly be politically impossible.[9]

He would remove from the system the power of deficit countries to choose whether or not to deflate.

THE INTERNATIONAL LIQUIDITY FLAP

Understanding the international monetary system is made more difficult by the existence of two major kinds of money demanders, whose tastes in money are very different. One type can be called *official*—the central banks and governments of the world; the other type, *private,* includes everybody else. The difference in preferences of the two groups accounts for the paradox of worldwide concern about a shortage of international liquidity at the same time that a worldwide price inflation indicates that the world economy is actually swamped in money. The officials fear there may not be enough of the kinds of money they prefer for their own use as reserves, but they have produced over the past generation far more than enough of the dollars, pounds, marks, francs, pesos, lire, yen, rupees, and so on that are used by the businessmen and ordinary citizens of the world.

To consider the official demand for money first, it should be remembered that the central banks of the world evolved from commercial banks or were modeled on other central banks that had evolved from commercial banks. Therefore, like commercial banks, they keep cash reserves of some sort. Within the United States commercial banks keep reserves in the form of deposits at Federal Reserve banks that can be transferred from bank to bank when a customer in New York, say, wants to pay someone in San Francisco. These "federal funds" are as acceptable to banks in San Francisco as they are to banks in New York.

Central banks, similarly, hold reserves in a form of money that is universally acceptable in order to make net payments to other countries when their countries have balance-of-payment deficits and to buy up their own currencies on foreign-exchange markets when necessary to prevent their exchange rates from falling.

Gold was long the most highly esteemed form of central-bank reserve because it was good anywhere. It was also believed to provide a natural check on the quantity of other forms of money within a country, as long as people were free to exchange other forms of money for gold (or silver in some countries) on demand. If a central bank maintained a constant ratio of gold reserves to its liabilities, the money supply of a country would automatically increase when gold flowed in and contract when gold flowed out, as we saw in the discussion of the gold-exchange standard.

In the gold-exchange standard, central banks supplemented their gold reserves with a "reserve currency," primarily the British pound for a long time. Sterling was a good instrument for settling international accounts because it was acceptable all over the world, was stable in purchasing power, could be exchanged at any time for a wide variety of British goods and services, and could be traded in the world's most highly developed money-and-capital market—the City of London.

After World War II the dollar gradually supplanted the pound as a reserve currency for central banks. It too demonstrated more stability in purchasing power in the postwar years than most other currencies; it could be exchanged at any time for a wide variety of American goods and services; and it could be traded in highly developed money-and-capital markets—New York at first and now London and the rest of the Eurodollar market. In addition, the

Bretton Woods Agreement made the dollar the official "intervention currency" to be used in buying and selling currencies to peg exchange rates; and the United States was the official custodian of the value of gold.

In view of the remarkable potential of the Japanese economy, the yen might well be the next major reserve currency. Or, if the European Economic Community develops a common currency, perhaps that too will win acceptance as a reserve currency. But all of the major central-bank reserve assets—gold, pounds, and dollars—first proved their worth in the world of markets. Their successors, if any, will have to do the same.

The worry about an international liquidity shortage grew out of recognition of the fact that world gold production could not keep up with growth in world demand for central-bank reserve assets, plus growth in private demands for gold, at the U.S. support price of $35 an ounce. Growth in central-bank reserves seemed likely to be mainly, if not entirely, in dollars; the dollars must come into central-bank hands through U.S. balance-of-payments deficits. Dollars, furthermore, were becoming less attractive to some central banks, as shrinking U.S. gold holdings made it obvious that the United States could not convert all central-bank dollars into gold.

The central bankers faced a dilemma of what to use for reserves if the United States were ever to succeed in eliminating its balance-of-payments deficit, as they were urging it to do.[10] It was somewhat as though when other wells in a town went dry the owner of the biggest well still flowing was urged to seal it because the townspeople did not want to become dependent on him for water.

The search was on for a new reserve asset that would be as good as gold and that would not be supplied at the will or whim of one country. According to an inside joke among economists a few years ago, any good economist could design a new international-reserve asset on the back of an envelope—and many of them had. The world watched with well-controlled excitement the unveilings of the Triffin Plan, the Bernstein Plan, the Stamp Plan, the Roosa Plan, the Medium for International Transactions—the handiwork of an MIT economist—the Mundell Plan, and the many more.

Each of these plans provided an institutional arrangement for creating a new central-bankers' money, deciding how much to produce, when and by whose decision to produce it, and how to distribute it. These raise extremely complicated questions, for no nation can treat lightly the prospect that it might some day have to honor with real wealth a liability levied on it by some outside organization. There has, furthermore, been an understandable reluctance by some countries to enter into arrangements that seemed designed to relieve the balance-of-payments difficulties of countries that might otherwise try harder to make adjustments.

Various multilateral and bilateral arrangements for lending reserves to one another were also negotiated by the central banks and international institutions during the sixties so that the existing stock of reserves could be used more efficiently and be quickly mobilized for use in emergencies. And, in 1970, the Special Drawing Rights, or SDRs, were inaugurated by the members of the International Monetary Fund.[11]

The SDRs are the first real money to be created by an international organization. In time they may be effectively used as substitutes for gold or dollars for settling accounts among central banks. However, it is unlikely that many central banks will consider SDRs more than a third-best reserve asset for a long time to come. What is more, SDRs and most of the exotic international moneys of the various plans are not designed to circulate except in a select circle of central banks. This may be a fatal weakness. For how is a money to be credible that has not been tested in the world's markets for goods and services?

Another proposed solution for the international liquidity problem, for which there was a flurry of enthusiasm in the sixties, and a stronger upsurge of support during the crises of 1971, was an increase in the price of gold. If the United States were to increase the price at which it supports gold, other central banks could write up the value of their gold-holdings accordingly. The growth rate of the stock also would be increased because gold producers would have more incentive to develop new sources. Peter Oppenheimer of Oxford University, for example, has estimated that doubling of the support price by the United States could produce an annual flow of $2 billion of gold into official reserves.[12]

Unfortunately for the people who favored raising the official gold price, public opinion in the United States never warmed to the idea. It has been too long since American citizens have had the privilege of owning gold for many of them to care what the price is. The many affirmations by U.S. Presidents of their devotion to the $35 price would make a change seem almost a national humiliation. But after gold convertibility was suspended by President Nixon in 1971, the mood changed. Now there is considerable support for the view that a modest increase in the official dollar price of gold would be a small price to pay for concessions in the bargaining over the realignment of exchange rates and the removal of barriers to trade.

The most substantial objection to an increase in the price of gold has been raised by Fritz Machlup, Robert Mundell, and Otmar Emminger, among others.[13] A large increase, such as doubling the price, would generate inflationary pressures if the sudden increase in the value of some central banks' reserves led them to follow more expansive policies. The increase in value of private gold-holdings, in countries whose citizens are permitted to hold gold, would also lead to an increase in spending and a rise in prices, unless the central banks promptly offset it by reducing supplies of their national currencies.

Despite the vast amount of attention that has been lavished upon it, the provision of reserves for central banks is not the most important problem in the evolution of the international monetary system. Fears that domestic deflation might result from a deficiency in international reserves have always seemed to me greatly exaggerated. A fall in the international reserves of a country may make it difficult to avoid changes of exchange rates, but it would not force domestic deflation on a nation that does not want to deflate. Central bankers surely are ingenious enough to find domestic assets they could monetize in a pinch, whatever the state of their international reserves. If anything, they are likely to err on the side of doing too much rather than too little.

Nor, in view of the pressure to exchange real goods and services, is there a serious danger that the growth of international trade and investment will be strangled by a deficiency in the supply of official reserves. The traders of the world will find the monetary instruments necessary to do their work, unless, of course, governments block their way with controls. Until recently, dollars served the needs of trade very well. To rephrase an old slogan: money follows trade; trade doesn't follow money.

IS THE FEDERAL RESERVE READY TO BE THE WORLD'S CENTRAL BANK?

One obvious approach to the problem of controlling world money supply would be an international organization, the International Monetary Fund, for example, that could create an international money. The Special Drawing Rights mentioned earlier are a step along that road. William McChesney Martin, former Chairman of the Federal Reserve Board, sees growing international cooperation as evolution toward a world central bank. Furthermore, he believes that nations will accept some limitations on their freedom of action out of enlightened self-interest.[14]

Attractive as the idea of a world central bank is in some ways, it is a matter of brute fact that hardly a nation in the world is any more willing to relinquish control over its money supply than it is to relinquish control of its armed forces to an international command. Given the widespread lack of agreement on matters of monetary theory and policy in the world today, the risks seem much too high. If anything, the turmoil in international exchange markets in 1971 probably pushed the world back several steps in the evolution toward a super central bank.

Another approach would be international coordination of national monetary policies, again through an international organization that could recommend appropriate policies. In fact, there already is a substantial degree of voluntary cooperation and coordination; but the problems of securing agreement are enormous when national interests diverge, as they often do.

Although the world may be working toward agreement on some sort of world central bank, there is sure to be a long time in which something else will have to do. That something else may be the Federal Reserve System of the United States. Several Americans have recommended that the Federal Reserve bow to the inevitable and accept the mantle graciously. One explicit step would be to add a world representative, perhaps several, to the Federal Open Market

Committee. However, there has been no welling up of acclaim for the idea in other countries.

The sheer bulk of the U.S. economy, the widespread use of the dollar by the businessmen of the world, and the fixed-exchange-rate linkage between the U.S. money supply and the world money supply—if the fixed-exchange-rate system survives—nevertheless make a large measure of world responsibility inescapable for the Federal Reserve. The only way out would be to abandon fixed exchange rates, as the United States in effect threatened to do when it suspended convertibility of the dollar into gold in August, 1971. But if one asks whether the Federal Reserve is ready for the job of world central bank in a fixed-exchange-rate system, the best answer is: No. What the Fed and other central banks can do we shall consider later.

six

TOWARD BETTER MONETARY AND FISCAL POLICIES

CONFLICTING TARGETS OF MONETARY POLICY

In the discount market, the Bank's stress on the desirability of steadiness in the Treasury bill rate compromises its control over the cash base; in the bond market, the more it cares about the price of bonds, the less control it has over the liquid assets basis of the clearing banks.
    R. S. Sayers, *Modern Banking,* 1964[1]

Because monetary policies affect the economy with long time lags, the monetary authorities cannot immediately see the effects of their actions upon such key variables as national income, employment, and prices. Therefore, they must use intermediate guides for their day-by-day operations to tell them if they are exerting their influence in the right direction and in appropriate amounts.

The current world debate over standards for guiding monetary policy focuses on two main possible guides, or groups of guides. On one side are interest rates, which are price measures. On the other side are the monetary aggregates, such as money supply, bank reserves, the monetary base, or total bank credit; these are quantity measures. Although central banks generally strive for a compromise between the two, both guides cannot be followed at the same time. If a central bank attempts to control interest rates, it must allow money supply to fluctuate. If it controls money supply, it must allow interest rates to fluctuate.

A good guide should have two main characteristics. First, it should be closely under the control of the central bank, so that the central bank can interpret a change in the guide as the result of its own actions rather than the result of outside forces. Second, changes in the guide should have a strong and predictable relationship to changes in ultimate policy variables, such as income, employment, and the price level. This involves the problem of understanding what is in the black boxes of Chapter 13.

Although no guide may be considered ideal, some meet the practical requirements of the policy makers better than others. Money supply is far superior to interest rates, which have traditionally been the preferred guide of central banks. Monetarists have compiled abundant evidence on this point for the United States and have recently begun to do the same thing for other countries.[2] In fact, the time-honored practice of trying to control interest rates while allowing the money supply to wander as it will can result in extremely serious and costly mistakes. It has fostered economic instability, price inflation, and large fluctuations of interest rates.

THE INTEREST-RATE GUIDE

In most popular textbooks today, changes in the rate of growth of money supply are assumed to influence the economy mainly through changing interest rates, which in turn influence business investment spending, and, finally, consumer spending. This orthodox, although perhaps oversimplified, Keynesian doctrine would justify the use of interest rates as monetary policy guides. A central bank might, therefore, try to stabilize the economy by changing interest rates.

In practice, however, central bankers seldom apply a consistently Keynesian approach to interest rates in the United States or anywhere else, although their explanations of their actions might suggest that they do. Most of the time the Federal Reserve and other central banks have been more concerned with stabilizing interest rates and money-market conditions than with manipulating them for contracyclical purposes. The practice of trying to minimize short-run changes in interest rates and availability of credit amounts to adding stability of financial markets and institutions as a fourth ultimate policy objective to the usual three—price stability, high employment, and balance-of-payments equilibrium.[3] The market-stability objective, moreover, conflicts with the others.

Nearly everywhere it is assumed that the central bank is "called upon to keep the financial structure on an even keel." Those words are borrowed from Britain's Macmillan Committee Report, written in 1931, not from the more recent discussion of Federal Reserve operations in the United States.[4] Stability in money-market conditions, or an even keel, is an elusive concept; but it has a high place among the goals of central bankers. It would probably be highly valued by most commercial bankers and other members of the financial community as well. At least they have become so accustomed to the daily presence of the central bank in the market that they find it difficult to imagine operating without it.

Central-bank pursuit of the widely extolled ideal of financial stability may now be a more important, though more subtle, threat to stability of income, prices, and interest rates than is the alleged propensity of governments to use their central banks as "engines of inflation." It is a more subtle danger precisely because it meets such widespread approval; official pressure on central banks to finance deficits is openly endorsed by almost no one.

A plausible rationalization for central-bank emphasis on interest rates and credit-market conditions is a belief that financial markets and institutions work better if interest rates are stable than if they fluctuate. Central banks, therefore, try to cushion money markets from sudden rate changes that might somehow impair market performance.

In the United States the Federal Reserve helps the Treasury to issue new securities or to refund existing ones by attempting to keep interest rates stable during Treasury financing operations. These so-called even-keel operations are especially important when budget deficits are large, as they were in 1967 and 1968. Even-keel operations during such periods can produce extremely large increases of money supply. Consequently, it is often assumed that the Federal Reserve is yielding to political expediency in helping the government to borrow on more favorable terms than it could otherwise. Although perhaps partly true, this is too simple an explanation.

Because the government is generally the largest and most disturbing borrower in the markets, it is the one most likely to trigger stabilizing operations by the central bank. Therefore, the borrowing of governments tends to be accommodated automatically by central banks. The Federal Reserve's solicitude, however, is intended more for the market than for the government.

A STABLE MONEY MARKET OR
A STABLE ECONOMY?

The principal objection to the practice of stabilizing interest rates is that supplies of bank credit and money will then be determined largely by changes in the demand for them. When the central bank intervenes in the markets, it uses high-powered money. This means that there will be changes in money supply several times as large as the central bank's purchases or sales, unless these operations are almost immediately canceled out by offsetting sales and purchases.

The paradoxical result of stabilizing interest rates or retarding their movement is that the central bank automatically becomes expansive when the government runs a deficit, instead of acting as a counterweight in the way indicated by most discussions of the appropriate fiscal-monetary policy mix. Because changes in money supply are induced also by increases or decreases in private demands for credit and money, a rate-stabilizing policy results in money-supply changes that amplify business fluctuations instead of countering them. This directly contradicts the usual textbook view that the central bank is a stabilizing influence in the economy.

Although fluctuations in the rate of growth of U.S. money supply since World War II—even those after 1964—have been much more moderate than those before the war, they have been enough, in the opinion of monetarists, to have caused each of the postwar recessions and the minirecession of 1967. To have kept money supply growing at a steady rate, therefore, would at least have removed a source of disturbance and thus would have increased the stability of income and employment.

Central banks are so sensitive to the possibility of economic recession today that they are not likely to be misled by falling interest rates into being too restrictive. A much more likely mistake is the one of resisting a rise of rates and thus causing price inflation. In the summer of 1965, for example, the Vietnam War buildup and an already booming private economy caused U.S. interest rates to begin rising, as we saw in Chapter 3. The Federal Reserve System's efforts to keep rates from rising led to an enormous expansion of money supply that contributed to the inflation that plagued the country for years afterward.

In effect, price inflation was part of the cost of attempting to moderate the rise of interest rates. The interest-rate policy, moreover, was unsuccessful, for interest rates soared in spite of the Federal Reserve's efforts. Again, a simple policy of keeping the money supply growing at a steady rate would have done more to maintain stability than what was actually done.

The monetarist view of how interest rates are influenced by money-supply changes that we discussed in Chapters 7 and 14 makes it clear that a policy of stabilizing interest rates in the short run makes them less stable in the longer run. Contrary to common belief, a restrictive monetary policy means lower rates and an expansive policy means higher rates. This view of interest-rate determination has truly ironic implications for central bankers because it demolishes the principal justification for their preoccupation with interest rates.

The bitter fruits of years of central-bank solicitude for investors can be seen in two representative long-term government bonds, one British and one American. British Treasury 2½s, redeemable after 1975, traded at less than 30 in 1970, or, in real terms, about 10 percent of their value at issue in 1946. U.S. Treasury 3s of 1995 traded as low as 60 in 1970, or at less than half their real value when they were issued in 1955. Holders of mortgages, long-term corporate bonds, and state-and-local government issues have similar capital losses to mull over.

It may seem that the deficiencies of the interest-rate guide are not in interest rates themselves but rather in the way the guide has been used by the central banks. It could be argued that if central banks aggressively changed interest rates in pursuit of more stable income and prices instead of stabilizing the rates, the results would be better. However, this argument is weak on two points: (1) central banks, as we have seen, have very little control over interest rates; and (2) the effects of changes in market interest rates on incomes and the price level are not easily predicted. Recognition of the effects of price expectations on market interest rates has weakened confidence in interest rates as a guide for both of these reasons.

The central bank has only a tenuous and temporary influence on market interest rates. Therefore, the monetary authorities cannot know whether a change of interest rates is a result of something they have just done, or a delayed result of actions taken many months earlier, or the result of forces completely out of their control.

Levels of market interest rates can be disastrously misinterpreted. In the thirties, for example, low interest rates were interpreted as evidence that U.S. monetary policy was expansive when, in fact, money supply was contracting. In the sixties high interest rates were interpreted as evidence that U.S. monetary policy was restrictive when, in fact, money supply was growing at an inflationary rate.

In Keynesian theory the rate that is important for influencing investment and saving is the real rate. Because Keynes assumed that prices were fixed over the period analyzed, market interest rates could be used as proxies for the real rate. Furthermore, money-supply changes could be used to manipulate interest rates without fear of inflationary consequences. But in the real world over-expansion of money supply does raise prices; and price expectations drive a wedge between the real rate that influences saving and investment and the nominal rates, or market rates, that we can measure. Therefore, changes in market rates cannot be assumed to be equivalent to changes in real rates. In fact, effects of central-bank actions on the real rate, if there are any, probably will be in exactly the opposite directions from the effects the central bank is trying to achieve on nominal market rates. Interest rates, therefore, are neither a reliable guide nor a policy instrument for the monetary authorities.

WHICH MONETARY AGGREGATE?

When a central bank turns from interest rates to the monetary aggregates as guides it is confronted with a bewildering number and variety of aggregates from which to choose. Indeed, critics of the monetary aggregates point to this variety as a major problem. I believe this criticism is a red herring.

The U.S. Federal Reserve System still attempts to follow several guides at once, although this can be confusing. The confusion is avoidable, however, because one guide would be enough. Each of the candidates can be tested with regard to two criteria: (1) controllability by the central bank and (2) predictability of the relationship between the aggregate and the ultimate policy goals, such as income and prices.

The following list covers some of the monetary aggregates proposed as monetary-policy guides in the United States and suggests the shortcomings and advantages of each. Not all of them have close counterparts in other countries.

1. *Free reserves,* excess reserves less borrowings of member banks. This old favorite of the Federal Reserve and of many money-market practitioners is by all odds the least useful and most misleading guide that has ever been proposed. It is neither controlled by the Federal Reserve nor dependably related to any important ultimate policy goal.

2. *Credit proxy,* total liabilities of U.S. member banks. This measure has the advantage of being available to the Federal Reserve on a weekly basis as an approximation for total bank credit. However, it has all the weaknesses of total credit in explaining changes of income and prices. The apparent closeness of its relationship to income stems from the fact that it closely approximates changes in broadly defined money supply (M_2) because total member-bank deposits are a large part of total M_2.

3. *Nonborrowed reserves* of member banks—probably the purest measure of what the Federal Reserve is doing to reserves of member banks. Looked at from the standpoint of the member banks, these are the reserves over which the banks have no control, but which the banks can supplement by borrowing from Reserve banks. Although closely controllable by the Federal Reserve through open-market operations, nonborrowed reserves are less closely related to income and prices than are other monetary aggregates.

4. *Total reserves* of member banks. More comprehensive than

nonborrowed reserves, they are more closely related to income and prices; but they are a little more difficult for the Federal Reserve to control.

5. *High-powered money, or monetary base,* total member-bank reserves plus currency in the hands of the public. This is a key variable in determining the money supply, as we saw in Chapter 9. Because it is determined partly by decisions of the public, however, it is not a pure measure of central-bank actions. Furthermore, it is less closely related to income and prices than is money supply. In some other countries, however, this may well be the best operating guide available.

6. *Money supply* (M_1, M_2, M_x). Money supply, in any of its variants, is the most closely related to income and prices of all the monetary aggregates and, on this account, is the best guide. Ordinarily, narrowly defined money (M_1) and money including time deposits (M_2) perform about equally well in models for forecasting gross national product. But the Federal Reserve's use of Regulation Q ceiling rates on time deposits has so badly distorted M_2 in recent years that it is not safe to rely on predictions made from relationships between M_2 and income that were estimated before Regulation Q was an important influence. Other versions of money supply, represented here as M_x, incorporate other variables, such as savings and loan shares or other liquid assets, or attempt to adjust for the distorting effects of Regulation Q by excluding negotiable certificates of deposit (CDs), for example. These are interesting refinements, but they are not essential for practical purposes.

The main objection to the use of money supply is that it is not completely within the control of the central bank. How important this objection is must be weighed against the alternatives available to the monetary authorities.

Perhaps the most extreme alternative to money supply as a guide for monetary policy was suggested by the Radcliffe Committee, an official body established to "inquire into the working of the monetary and credit system" of Britain in the late fifties.[5] In its 1959 Report, the Radcliffe Committee concluded that the quantity of money was virtually irrelevant because the velocity of circulation was unstable. The key variable, instead, was "total liquidity," to which money supply was only one of a great many contributors.

Because total liquidity was never clearly defined and because the relationships between it and the ultimate goals of income, prices, and the balance of payments were never empirically demonstrated, this concept could not serve as an operational guide. The Committee's endorsement of it did have the negative effect, however, of encouraging the Bank of England and other central banks to neglect the behavior of the money supply for a few years more.

At a tenth anniversary celebration of the Radcliffe Report, Professor A. A. Walters of the London School of Economics administered a less-than-merciful *coup de grâce* to the total-liquidity concept.

"Liquidity" [he said] . . . is an eternally elusive concept—a will-o'-the-wisp of monetary economics. Liquidity is "the amount of money which people *think* they can get hold of . . ." (para. 390) or "the lending behavior of an *indefinitely* wide range of financial institutions" (para. 394). It is impossible to grasp such a concept. Liquidity is a state of mind relative to an indefinite range of institutions. But even if one's intuition were to penetrate the mists to meaning it is clearly quite impossible *in principle* to measure "liquidity." No refutable theoretical propositions can be formulated in terms of liquidity. The pure Radcliffe theory can never be tested [his italics].[6]

A related criticism of money, the "Gurley-Shaw Thesis," became popular in the United States at about the time of the Radcliffe Report.[7] In the course of an original treatment of the role of financial intermediaries, Professors John G. Gurley and Edward S. Shaw of Stanford University argued that savings and loan shares and other liabilities of nonbank financial intermediaries were close substitutes for money. One implication, therefore, was that if the central bank restricted growth of the money supply, other financial intermediaries would create more liabilities for the public to hold and the central bank would be frustrated. With nonbank intermediaries growing faster than commercial banks, furthermore, central banks would have to find ways to extend their powers to the nonbank intermediaries or resign themselves to impotence.

Like many other initially promising ideas, however, both of these propositions foundered when confronted with facts. Although the "near-moneys" are substitutes for money in the long run, the nonbank intermediaries do not have the power to frustrate the monetary authorities in the short run by issuing more of their liabilities when the central bank restricts growth of money.[8] On the contrary, when growth of money supply is restricted, the nonbank intermediaries suffer a prompt and painful "disintermediation," as we saw in 1966 and 1969. Rather than viewing the nonbank intermediaries as a threat, the Federal Reserve System has been worried about how they can be shielded from the restrictive effects of its policies.

Still another vestige of the Radcliffe total-liquidity idea lingers in the "new view" of money that is associated with James Tobin and some of his students at Yale University.[9] The "new view" emphasizes the role of portfolio management by economic units, an idea with which monetarists are quite at home, as we saw earlier. It differs from the monetarist view, however, in arguing the necessity "to regard the structure of interest rates, asset yields, and credit availabilities rather than the quantity of money as the linkage between monetary and financial institutions on the one hand and the real economy on the other."[10] The quantity of money, moreover, is not an autonomous variable controlled by the monetary authorities but an endogenous or "inside" quantity determined by the banks and other economic units. Effective policies, in the "new view," would require a tremendous investment in measurement and analytical efforts by the authorities and intervention at many points in financial markets.

These may seem like minor differences in emphasis, but they are of the sort that can keep controversies among the experts alive for a generation or more. And they can cause doubts about the efficacy of monetary policy, especially when put forward by such an eminent and distinguished economist as James Tobin. Nevertheless, I find myself, as a monetary practitioner rather than a theoretician, in agreement with Professor Harry Johnson's comment:

. . . the "new view" is long on elegant analysis of theoretical possibilities, but remarkably short on testable or tested theoretical propositions about the way the economy works, and specifically how it responds to monetary impulses, when the interaction of the monetary and real sectors is taken into account.[11]

The performance of the economy would be improved, I believe, if central banks merely avoided gross changes in rates of money-supply growth. Fine tuning of the money supply day by day or week by week is not required. The monetary authorities have been overly sanguine about the consequences of the money-supply changes they produce while following guides they consider to be more important. But it is now clear that money matters. As I argued earlier, tolerance of large money-supply changes has increased economic instability, caused inflation, and made interest rates less stable in many countries. Worst of all, neglect of money supply has nourished beliefs that monetary policy is either impotent in the face of price inflation or too harsh in its effects on certain sectors of the economy. One result has been a proliferation of governmental intrusions in the marketplace.

WHAT SHOULD BE DONE?

Although it is unlikely that money supply will continue much longer to be neglected as a monetary-policy guide, increasing the emphasis on money supply does present some adjustment problems for the central banks and for market institutions. The Joint Economic Committee of the U.S. Congress recommended for several years that the Federal Reserve should keep money-supply growth within limits shown on Chart 18-1.[12] The System followed such a policy for a while in 1970. The International Monetary Fund made somewhat similar recommendations to the Bank of England in 1969.[13] In both countries, the monetary authorities thus made a start toward more direct control of the money supply. However, the traditional central-bank concern with money-market conditions was not entirely abandoned in either country.

Given the fact that financial institutions are so much accustomed to the old regime in which the central bank continually attempted to moderate interest-rate fluctuations, any change is likely to be gradual and will stir protests from market operators who will have to acquire new reflexes and new rules of thumb.

The Federal Reserve can make a gradual shift of emphasis be-

PER CENT CHANGE

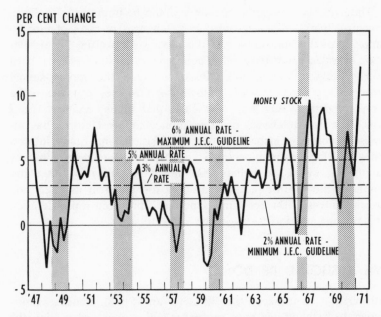

Chart 18-1. Whenever money-supply growth fell below the minimum 2 percent annual rate recommended by the Joint Economic Committee in 1969, a recession followed. When money-supply growth rose above the Committee's maximum guidelines in the 1960s, inflation followed.

NOTES: Money stock—quarterly changes at annual rates of money supply (demand deposits and currency). Shaded areas are recessions. *Chart by FNCB.*

tween interest rates and the monetary aggregates within the framework of its present operating procedures through changing the Open Market Committee's directive.[14] The directive formerly emphasized avoidance of short-run interest-rate fluctuations by instructing the manager of the Open Market Account to conduct open-market operations with a view to maintaining a particular set of money-market conditions, as described in Chapter 10. A proviso clause, added for the first time in 1966, was intended to guard against excessive fluctuations of bank credit and money supply. That is, if money supply or bank credit appeared to be increasing, or contracting, too much, the manager of the Open Market Account had authority to depart from the interest-rate targets.

With the new ordering of the guides after January, 1970, the Federal Open Market Committee instructed the manager of the Open Market Account to try to achieve some desired change in money supply and other monetary aggregates. The proviso clause then called for modifying operations if short-run changes in interest rates exceeded some specified range. If wide fluctuations of interest rates would impose costs and structural changes on the economy, the proviso clause could be a safety valve.

We actually do not know much about the costs of fluctuating rates or how wide the fluctuations would be if the Federal Reserve attempted to keep money-supply growth within narrow bounds. These characteristics of the system must be determined through experiment. I believe these potential costs of greater short-run variability of interest rates have been vastly overestimated for the United States.

Simulation experiments with the FRB-MIT econometric model reported by James Pierce, an economist at the Board of Governors, indicate that stability of the U.S. economy would increase as the bounds on money-supply growth are narrowed and the permissible range of variation of interest rates is widened. This is in line with the expectations of monetarists.[15]

As experience with the new techniques and new strategies accumulates, the range of fluctuation permitted in money supply should be narrowed while the range of fluctuation of interest rates is broadened. By making the changes gradually, central banks can permit money-market institutions to adjust their practices with minimum strain.

However, I would urge the central bankers of the world not to be too kind to their money-market friends. It would be far better to inconvenience securities dealers and banks with fluctuating interest rates than to risk instability in income, employment, and prices for whole countries, and their neighbors, as some central banks have done in the past. Financial institutions are flexible and have strong incentives for adapting to whatever operating guides the central banks follow. *The key step in improving monetary policy will be for central banks to renounce attempts to control interest rates,* once and for all. The Bank of England came close to this in announcing in May, 1971, that it would restrict the extent of its operations in the gilt-edged market. This step was in line with the Bank's earlier decision to increase its emphasis on controlling monetary aggregates.[16]

MEASURE, CONTROL, SIMPLIFY

Advice to central bankers about using money supply as a guide can be summed up in three words: measure, control, simplify.

Measurement is the essential first step. When the Federal Reserve System was not much interested in the money supply, it devoted very little effort to measuring it. Until the late 1950s the published money-supply series of the Federal Reserve was based on a one-day-per-month estimate. Because demand deposits in the United States sometimes fluctuate by several hundred million dollars per day, a one-day-per-month measure could be, and was, seriously misleading at times.

When the Federal Reserve Bank of St. Louis took on its now-legendary concern for the money supply around 1958, William J. Abbott, senior economic adviser, and his research assistant, Marie Wahlig, personally reconstructed the Federal Reserve's entire money-supply series.[17] They based their new series on daily-average deposit data for the member banks that the System had gathered for years in the course of enforcing reserve requirements but had not used in the money-supply series. This one project immensely improved the quality of U.S. money-supply data and was a significant step toward improving U.S. monetary policy. Their project has since been followed by other improvements in U.S. money-supply data by the staff of the Board of Governors.

Nevertheless, the U.S. money-supply data still had serious flaws in 1969 and 1970, years in which the Federal Reserve was trying to curb inflation and to facilitate a recovery from recession. In Chapter 4, I argued that the 1969–1970 recession was caused by too sharp a deceleration in money-supply growth in 1969. That error, however, should not be charged to faulty money-supply data, although there were substantial revisions of prior estimates during the year. In 1969 the Federal Reserve had not yet adopted money supply as a guide. Therefore, I would attribute the overly severe restrictiveness of that year's policies to Federal Reserve attempts to curb business investment spending while overlooking what was happening to the money supply.

But in 1970 the Federal Reserve was trying to learn how to control the money supply. Errors in the statistics did not make that task easier. Large upward revisions of the data after the fact revealed that money-supply growth between February and October had been appreciably greater than the Fed had intended.

In his *Newsweek* column, Milton Friedman said in March, 1971:

> The explanation of the major errors of the past two years is highly technical and cannot be spelled out here. I can only report my judgment that the errors would not have been anything like so large, and might not have occurred at all, if, years ago, the Fed had devoted to improving its measures of the money supply anything like the attention and research effort it has lavished on its index of industrial production, let alone on its surveys of liquid assets.
>
> The Fed neglected monetary statistics for years because it took interest rates rather than monetary aggregates as its criterion of policy. It has corrected the mistake in policy. But it has not corrected the mistake in statistics. As a result, its present estimates of monetary aggregates are still defective.[18]

Other central banks, like the Federal Reserve System, lavish resources on gathering and reporting financial and economic data of many kinds. Yet most of them lack good money-supply series. Obviously, this is something that can and will be corrected when they become serious about attempting to control the money supply.

There is still much to be learned about methods of money-supply control. The difficulty, however, stems mainly from attempting to do other things at the same time. The U.S. Federal Reserve System was still trying in early 1971 to control several monetary aggregates and interest rates simultaneously. The Federal Reserve, as we saw in Chapter 10, was attempting to control money supply through controlling interest rates (money-market conditions), possibly the most difficult approach that could be found.[19]

In the first half of 1971 this method of trying to control money-supply growth by controlling interest rates led to serious embarrassment for the Federal Reserve. The virtual explosion of monetary growth in that period revived fears of inflation that had been quieting down. It seemed to confirm press reports that the Nixon Administration had persuaded the Fed to abandon the fight against inflation. Long-term interest rates began to rise at once, despite the declared hopes of Administration and Federal Reserve spokesmen that they would continue to decline. Furthermore, it confirmed the fears of Europeans that the United States was indifferent to their problems of coping with large dollar inflows. Although the international monetary crisis of May, 1971, had many roots, there is no question that the upsurge of money-supply growth in the United States was one of them.

As we saw in 1959–1960, 1965, 1967, 1968, 1970, and 1971, the use of the "money-market strategy," or reserve-position doctrine, in guiding Federal Reserve open-market operations leads to changes in bank credit and money supply that the Federal Open Market Committee did not intend. And these inadvertent departures from the Committee's intentions have come at the most awkward times—at the onset of recessionary or inflationary swings in the economy.

More direct, more effective, methods for controlling the money supply will surely be developed. The key requirement is the will to do it. The will of the Federal Reserve should have been strongly reinforced by the furor stirred up by the monetary accident of early 1971.

A possible new procedure has been suggested by economists of the Federal Reserve Bank of St. Louis, which is an elaboration of the classic high-powered money and money-multiplier framework discussed in Chapter 9.[20] In essence, the suggested procedure requires the Open Market Committee to express a target in terms of a growth rate of money. This growth rate of money is then translated into a growth of "net source base"—nonborrowed reserves of the member banks plus currency held by the public plus vault cash of nonmember banks—that the trading desk is to achieve through open-market operations over the control period of a month or quarter at a time.

To determine the growth of monetary base needed to reach the money-supply target would require a forecast of the multiplier. There is good reason to believe this can be done well enough to keep money supply under much better control than is attainable with the money-market conditions approach.

Finally, there is a great need for simplifying central-bank techniques. In viewing themselves as required to intervene in a great many ways in a great many markets in pursuit of a great many objectives, central bankers have made it extremely difficult for anyone to appraise the effectiveness of their actions. By narrowing down to a single guide, money supply, they would concentrate on something they can do and they would be able to determine the relationships between their actions and the behavior of ultimate objectives, such as income, employment, and prices. It would be especially helpful to drop the traditional preoccupation with interest rates.

The Bank of England, the "mother of central banks," has led the way by announcing its withdrawal from the hallowed practice of supporting the gilt-edge market. In a truly remarkable effort, the Bank also has simplified and improved its procedures and regulations. The Federal Reserve has been retrogressing in recent years. The number and variety of reserve requirements have been increased. Furthermore, the proposals for the so-called reform of the discount mechanism would make it more difficult for the System to control the issue of high-powered money.[21] The number of reserve requirements should be cut to one, or none. The discount window could be abolished in the United States, for it has been rendered an anachronism by the development of open-market operations and the Federal Funds (interbank) market for rapidly transferring reserves within the System.

The most important, and currently most widely misunderstood, simplification would be to adopt a steady-growth rule for the money supply.[22] A not untypical example of the misunderstanding about monetarists' arguments for steady growth in the money supply was a 1970 statement of Alfred Hayes, president of the Federal Reserve Bank of New York:

I am applying that term ["monetarist"] to those who believe in a virtually assured mechanical relationship of a causal character between the money supply and economic activity, and who therefore tend to favor a very steady increase in the money supply and a minimum resort to discretionary policy by the central bank.[23]

Monetarists argue that it is precisely because there is *not* a "mechanical" one-to-one correspondence between changes in money and changes in income that they favor a steady growth-rate for money supply. Because of the slippage, we do not now know how to do better than to maintain a steady growth-rate. This does not rule out the possibility of adopting some other rule later when the linkages are better understood.

The wielders of discretionary powers seldom want to give them up. But the Federal Reserve and other central banks have treated the world economy as a "free-fire zone" in launching their discretionary measures at many visible and invisible targets. Among the unintended results of their discretionary measures have been economic instability, price inflation, and a growing uneasiness about the viability of the international monetary system. This is not a criticism of their intentions but is instead recognition of how limited is our knowledge of the linkages between actions and results. I believe it would be possible to do better by attempting less.

THE WAY OUT OF THE MONETARY-FISCAL MIXUP

The chief harm done by the balance-wheel theory
is . . . not that it has failed to offset recessions,
which it has, and not that it has introduced an
inflationary bias into governmental policy, which
it has too, but that it has continuously fostered
an expansion in the range of governmental activities at the federal level and prevented a
reduction in the burden of federal taxes.
  Milton Friedman, *Capitalism and Freedom,*
  1962[1]

In rejecting the idea that government spending and taxing serve
as an economic balance wheel, Milton Friedman was not suggesting
that fiscal policy is unimportant. He meant instead that fiscal policy
is much too important to be relegated for use as a short-run stabilizer. Furthermore, the balance-wheel theory need never have been
invented if central banks had kept the money supply growing during the early 1930s.

As we have seen in earlier chapters, the failure of central banks
and governments to provide a stable monetary framework for the
world economy has caused inflations, recessions, and instability in
exchange rates among currencies. If central banks fail to control
money-supply growth, however, what can be done about economic
instability? Attempts to find answers can be seen in a worldwide
resort to selective controls, incomes policies, wage-price guideposts,
price and wage freezes, and various tax and government expenditure measures intended to hold down demand or to increase it. The
wage-price freeze announced by President Nixon in August, 1971,
is only one instance among many of this sad process.

At best, these substitutes for a stable monetary framework suppress some of the symptoms of inflation; but if monetary expansion is excessive, prices rise and exchange rates change anyway. Expenditure programs intended to spur flagging economies usually have their main impacts long after the supposed need for them has passed, or they divert resources into activities whose contribution to economic growth is small or negative. In either case, as the Friedman quotation suggests, they rarely fail to become securely embedded in the permanent structure of government.

Controls cost a country dearly through impairing efficiency, abridging personal freedom, and misallocating resources, while failing to achieve their stated purposes. The warping of fiscal policy and the imposition of controls may well, in the end, be the most serious costs of neglecting to keep monetary growth within bounds.

BUDGETS DRAWN OFF COURSE

What then of fiscal policy? It is often charged that the irresponsible fiscal policies of politicians make it impossible for their more sober central-bank brethren to conduct proper monetary policies. It is true that wars and costly public ventures like the U.S. space program can hardly be blamed on central bankers. But it also can be argued that the failure of the monetary authorities to understand their instruments and to use them to best effect makes it extremely difficult for governments to maintain appropriate fiscal policies. By appropriate fiscal policies I mean spending and tax policies that are determined by the conscious choices of the electorate.

There has been a seductive notion for some time that monetary policy and fiscal policy are easily substituted for one another. Therefore, a country that would like to enjoy low interest rates and price stability at the same time could combine an easy monetary policy with a restrictive fiscal policy. Or if it wants to stimulate demand without depressing interest rates it could combine a restrictive monetary policy with an expansive fiscal policy. Unfortunately, it has not been demonstrated in any country that either of these mixes would work in the way intended.

As we saw in Chapter 13, key linkages in the fiscal-policy transmission mechanism either do not exist or do not perform in accordance with theory. Furthermore, the monetary authorities cannot control interest rates without affecting income and prices in ways that later push interest rates in the opposite direction from the one intended. This was clearly demonstrated by U.S. experience in 1965, 1967, 1968, and 1971, when Federal Reserve efforts to hold interest rates down actually drove them sharply higher by raising public expectations of price inflation.

Instead of the smoothly blended monetary-fiscal mix that is glowingly described to political leaders and the public by economists, most countries now have the monetary-fiscal mixup. Each policy is applied to the problem for which it is most poorly adapted. Applying fiscal policy to short-run economic stabilization is detrimental to its long-run function of allocating resources between public and private uses. Monetary policy is drawn into efforts to influence resource allocation through efforts to ration mortgage-loan funds and other credit flows while failing to provide the framework of economic stability that should be its principal concern.

Attempts to use fiscal policy for short-run economic stabilization, a task for which it is demonstrably unsuited, seriously distorts long-run allocational decisions. Pressure exerted by bureaucracies inside government and by special-interest groups outside make it highly unlikely that an expansion of public spending, undertaken to compensate for a shortfall in private spending, will ever be reversed. Consequently, governments become larger than they would be if the allocation of resources between public and private uses were approached more directly.

At the same time the effects of economic instability on various sectors of the economy tempt the monetary authorities more and more into trying to make allocation decisions, to impose penalties or extend special benefits in order to direct credit away from some users or toward others. As equivalents of taxes and subsidies, these actions are properly instruments of fiscal policy. Because monetary authorities often are shielded from the discipline and accountability of the electoral process by long tenure in office—the 14-year terms for members of the Board of Governors of the Federal Reserve System are much too long—their attempts to reallocate income and wealth should not be tolerated in a free society.

The business cycle, which is rooted in monetary mismanagement, results in a ratchet pattern of government expenditures. In each period of recession expenditures are increased. And, since their impact is not felt until the beginning of the subsequent business expansion, there is a reluctance to cut them back because that might endanger the recovery. Then, by the time policy has turned toward restraint again, the recession programs have become permanent additions to the government budget that must be financed through taxing or borrowing. The upshot is that taxes must then be raised to avert inflationary fiscal deficits.

The proposition, fundamental to conventional fiscal policy, that government expenditures must offset any temporary decline in total spending is a fallacy springing from the Keynesian dogma that economies cannot otherwise generate full employment. But the fact is that an increase in the government's absorption of goods and services—except in periods of deep and prolonged depression such as the 1930s—displaces private demands for those same goods and services. The decision to substitute government for private activities should be made on its own merits—whether goods and services can really be better provided collectively rather than by individual efforts—not to fill any shortfall in demand.

Instability also raises the average unemployment rate over time and reduces productivity because it confuses people in the labor markets and prevents them from finding the most productive use for their talents. Stop-and-go policies impose severe costs by causing labor to be preoccupied with job protection and security and by inhibiting businessmen from investing in more productive equipment or in the development of new products. Furthermore, instability raises the costs of unemployment compensation and the burden of welfare services.

Compensation of the injured becomes especially difficult in times of inflation and so it is no accident that costs of social-welfare programs have ballooned in the United States and other countries since the acceleration of price inflation in the mid-1960s. This is damaging enough to fiscal-policy-decision processes, but the impact of inflation on the real tax burden in countries with progressive tax systems is even worse in confusing the choices involved in fiscal policy.

This is well illustrated by the experience of the United States following the overexpansion of the money supply in the years 1965 through 1968. A little-noticed effect of the Vietnam inflation was to push people into higher tax brackets by raising money incomes. This sharply increased the tax burden falling on the mass of wage earners. Congress did not have to increase tax rates to extract a larger share of income from the electorate. Therefore, it was easier to approve increases in expenditures. Furthermore, the inflation increased the costs of all government programs, calling for still more dollars, such as the 7 percent increase in Social Security benefits approved in 1965, the 13 percent increase in 1968, the 15 percent in 1969, and the 10 percent increase approved in 1971.

The impacts of inflation on taxes can be seen in an example used in the April, 1971, *Monthly Economic Letter* of First National City Bank:

... if a man earned $10,000 in 1965 and his salary increased by 23% between 1965 and 1970, his income would have just kept pace with the cost of living. But if he took the standard deduction and claimed four personal exemptions, his tax payments would have risen from $1,114 in 1965 to $1,556 in 1970 (excluding the tax surcharge), or nearly 40%. Thus, his real income tax burden would have grown by 14%. For taxpayers who earned over $10,000 in 1965 and were therefore subject to the $1,000 maximum standard deduction, the federal income-tax bite has been progressively deeper as their incomes increased.[2]

Over the same period the Social Security tax paid by this sample wage earner rose from $348 in 1965 to $748 in 1970. Furthermore, he can look forward to further increases to $811 in 1971 and the tax of $1,102 proposed for 1972. I count the so-called employer's contribution as part of the tax on the wage earner for it is part of what the employer pays for his services and, therefore, enters into the decisions of whether to hire him or not and how much to pay him.

Between 1965 and 1970 the combined income tax and Social Security tax of our hapless taxpayer rose from $1,462 to $2,304 without counting in the surtax. That was an increase of 58 percent in current dollars or 28 percent in real terms. State and local taxes bit him sorely over the same period. These increases far exceeded any benefits he could have realized from the 1964 tax cut. It is no wonder that wage negotiations were somewhat tense in 1971.

As the same issue of the *Monthly Economic Letter* said:

Through inflation, in short, society has yielded a growing share of potential income to government without having made a conscious decision to do so. A growing tax burden—which voters had hardly intended to shoulder—coupled with inability to see the benefits of higher government spending is hardly a combination that is calculated to have a tonic effect on society.[3]

THE MONETARIST CASE FOR TAX CUTS

The United States had in 1971 a rare opportunity to reduce taxes. The program for ending the war in Vietnam had freed resources that could be returned to the taxpayers as a partial restitution for the accidental increase in real tax burden that had been caused by inflation. And the Federal Reserve had demonstrated that it could, if it wanted to, control the money supply and gradually reduce the rate of inflation. Furthermore, the strong economic recovery already under way promised to restore much of any revenue loss, even with lower tax rates.

A somewhat similar situation existed in England, where a restrictive monetary policy had much improved England's balance of payments, although it had not yet succeeded in slowing inflation very much. Her Majesty's government grasped the opportunity and made substantial cuts in taxes; the U.S. government did not.[4] President Nixon proposed some tax reductions in his August, 1971, program, but these were viewed more as special incentives for stimulating recovery from recession than as a reallocation of national income.

The argument for tax reduction in the United States would have been less compelling if the cost of the war had been met by reducing nondefense expenditures of the federal government, for there would have been justification for restoring vital public services that had been restricted. But the war did not mean cutting back on the total volume of services the voters had asked for and were willing to pay for. To the contrary, the war was accompanied by an extraordinary growth in federal nondefense programs, the costs of which are still ballooning upward like the cloud from a bomb explosion. This mushrooming of federal programs, whatever their individual merits might be, was disconcerting to many of the voters who must pay the bills.

The costs of the war and the accompanying expansion of non-defense expenditures had been met by cutting back on private expenditures through taxes, inflation, and the draft. The draft could be viewed as a special tax that deprived hundreds of thousands of young men of income they could otherwise have earned.

This argument for tax reduction was not based on the old Keynesian short-run fiscal multiplier. As we saw in earlier chapters, recent research and experience have demonstrated that there is no dependable fiscal multiplier. The argument was based, instead, on a long-run allocation argument. The Eisenhower tax reduction of 1954—a war-to-peace measure—yielded substantial benefits by increasing the relative share of national income employed in the private sector, where incentives for innovation and efficiency are more effective than they are in government. The 1971 tax reductions in England had similar objectives.

An implicit, and generally unexamined, assumption in most discussions in early 1971 of the "fiscal dividend" from ending the Vietnam War was that the dividend should be employed for "high-priority public objectives," as though there might be no high-priority private objectives worthy of consideration. Americans had endured an unrelieved diet of calls for sacrifice and more sacrifice for a mounting catalogue of public objectives since 1961. They had responded, but without the satisfaction of seeing much evidence that these objectives were being achieved. They need not apologize, therefore, if they welcome a tax reduction that would accommodate more of their personal objectives. They could change their minds later if they were to decide that public objectives were indeed being neglected.

To reduce taxes while trying to curb an inflation might seem an intolerable breach of the conventional wisdom that budget deficits are inflationary and surpluses are deflationary. But countries have had inflations while running budget surpluses and have stopped inflations while running large budget deficits. What matters is not whether there is a budget deficit, or how big it is, but how it is financed. If the Federal Reserve were to finance the deficit by buying the new Treasury securities, the deficit would be inflationary because this would mean excessive growth of the money supply.

The Federal Reserve has demonstrated that it can control expansion of the money supply in spite of budget deficits. In 1966 the Federal Reserve reduced the money supply in the face of rapidly growing expenditures; in 1970 it held money-supply growth to a moderate rate in the face of what, by past standards, was a substantial deficit (unified budget basis). With some improvements in technique the Federal Reserve can prevent accidental explosions of money supply such as those that accompanied the budget deficits of 1967 and 1968. Some increase in the deficit could have been incurred in 1971 without danger of stimulating an expansion of money supply larger than the monetary authorities consider to be appropriate. By not cutting taxes early in the recession, the Nixon Administration found unwanted expenditure programs forced on it by the Congress.

Effects of the 1969 and 1970 policies of the Administration and the Federal Reserve on the inflation rate should have moderated future deficits on the expenditure side as well, if these policies had been continued. As inflation slows down, interest rates should come down also, reducing interest payments on the public debt, which were about $18 billion in 1970. Wages and salaries of federal employees would also rise at a slower rate as the inflation moderates, much improving the prospects for controlling expenditures. Transfer payments, such as Social Security benefits, also should grow more slowly when cost-of-living adjustments are less necessary. Unfortunately, the Federal Reserve's abrupt swing to an inflationary course in 1971 seemed sure to draw future budgets off course by increasing the pressure for spending increases.

THE WAY TO A STABLE AND FREE ECONOMY

A tax cut early in 1971 would have been essentially an adjustment measure to repair some of the damage of earlier policy mistakes, just as was the restrictive monetary policy of 1969. I believe it also would have bought time for continuing to rely on monetary policy to curb inflation by convincing the public that they were benefiting from the Nixon Administration's program. The paucity of tangible benefits, visible to all, undoubtedly contributed to the crisis of public confidence that drove the Administration to the hastily improvised New Economic Program of fiscal stimulants and direct controls in August, 1971. A bolder, and more imaginative, fiscal policy earlier in the year, therefore, might well have enabled the Administration to avoid its distasteful, and dangerous, resort to direct controls.

For the future, however, we need to blend monetary and fiscal policies in a new way. Neither fiscal nor monetary policy is suitable for short-run stabilizing operations, despite the many recommendations that either or both be made more flexible. The ideal policy blend of the future should be made up of three main strands, all three of which had a partial trial in the United States during 1969 and 1970. The three are: a self-stabilizing budget, a policy of keeping the money supply growing steadily at a noninflationary rate, and the avoidance of controls or other interference with market processes.

In the new-style budget, expenditures are supposed to be held within the revenues that would be generated by the tax system when the economy is at high employment. Such a budget has an automatic tendency to stabilize private spending in that tax collections fall off in periods of recession and rise when the economy grows more rapidly. This is radically different from the fiscalists' approach of attempting to influence national income and employment by doing much more than that through short-run changes in taxes and expenditures. Budget decisions under the self-stabilizing budget approach, moreover, are concerned only with the long-run allocation of resources within the government and between the government and private sectors of the economy.

Both Herbert Stein, then at the Committee for Economic Development, and Milton Friedman wrote prescriptions for such a budget soon after World War II.[5] The time was not yet ripe for adoption of their idea then, but the results of the budgetary gyrations of the sixties have made it much more attractive. It has the great virtue of making the long-run consequences of budget decisions more clearly visible than they are when expenditures and taxes are frequently raised and lowered in an attempt to stabilize the economy.

Avoidance of federal deficits when the economy is fully employed and of sudden swings in expenditures vastly simplifies the problems of the monetary authorities. The central-bank practice of helping treasuries sell new debt even when this help seriously impairs monetary policy grew out of the fact that fiscal policies have been badly managed in most countries for longer than anyone can remember.

The second strand—steady growth of the money supply—is probably the most controversial of the three. There is a lurking fear in the minds of many people that the economy is so unstable that if the monetary authorities were bound by a rule of any sort they would be unable to respond to an emergency soon enough to prevent disaster. Others merely believe that central-bank efforts to stabilize the economy by "leaning against the wind" are beneficial on the whole and should not be discontinued. Whatever the intentions of the Federal Reserve may have been, however, their stabilizing efforts since World War II have increased instability in the U.S. economy rather than reduced it. In trying to suppress ripples, the U.S. monetary authorities have generated waves.

As we saw in Chapters 9 and 10, large changes in the growth rate of the U.S. money supply have not been so much intentional as inadvertent; they have resulted primarily from Federal Reserve efforts to do something else, usually to influence interest rates or credit flows. Much the same statement could be made about the behavior of money supply in most other countries. It is such *accidental* changes that central banks should try to avoid.

As Irving Fisher said, it is risky for a theory to become the subject of political dispute. Through its identification with the Nixon Administration, the quantity theory is obviously in a position of some peril. However, a theory that is supposed to explain movements in national incomes and price levels must be tested in use. In 1969 the new monetarism had not yet achieved the respectability in the press and the public mind that the Keynesian idea commanded in 1961, but it was otherwise ready for trial. And—at least in 1969 and 1970—the Nixon Administration placed it in the proper framework of a stable budget and reliance on free-market processes.

But in Washington conditions for the test were unlikely to be ideal. More important than politics, there was the fact that the monetary authorities were not as convinced of the need to control the money supply as were the Administration's economists. Although the quantity theory was tested under some of the most difficult conditions imaginable, however, no good monetarist would have wanted to avoid the test. Monetarists only regret that the test was abandoned just before the results would have come in.

The Federal Reserve badly needs to improve its techniques for controlling the money supply, perhaps along the lines discussed in Chapter 18. The 1970 performance was the best in years but was still spotty. The 1971 performance was much worse, when a relapse into trying to control interest rates again caused the money supply to soar out of control. Renouncing the use of interest-rate targets once and for all is the essential step that the Federal Reserve has, thus far, been reluctant to take.

In addition to the domestic harm done by volatility in money-supply growth is the impact of U.S. instability on the rest of the world. If the world is to have stable, not fixed, exchange rates, the United States will have to avoid wide gyrations in money-supply growth, such as those from 1964 through 1971. In fact, the world can no longer tolerate such volatile domestic policies in major nations.

As we saw in Chapter 11, central banks of other nations do not have the tools for smoothly offsetting the impacts of unstable U.S. monetary policies on their economies. The alternatives of widely fluctuating exchange rates and controls over international trade and capital movements are also objectionable to most countries. All of these considerations are powerful arguments for stable fiscal and monetary policies in the United States—and in the rest of the world.

The third strand—the renunciation of direct controls—is a re-affirmation of liberalism—a reliance on freedom of choice through freely functioning markets. One reason for the appeal of Keynesian economics is the popular belief that free-market economies are dangerously unstable and inequitable. It is no accident, therefore, that many proponents of the income-expenditure theory also favor government interventions of many sorts to correct the alleged deficiencies of the market system.

Many of the young men and women who flocked to the Keynesian banner immediately after World War II did so out of a sincere desire to reform the world. Deeply shaken by the depression of their childhood years and accustomed by the war to seeing governments manage economies, it was natural for them to concentrate on devising governmental instruments for solving problems rather than to seek market solutions. Much older now, some still hold to their youthful view of stagnant economies and starved public sectors—a truly remarkable example of cultural lag.

With more stable monetary and fiscal policies, it should be possible to place much more confidence in the ability of market adjustments and the free play of private incentives to advance the general welfare than have most economists since World War II.

But the Nixon Administration's record in pressing for freer markets is one of almost total failure. It has done little to dismantle the controls and subsidies that were in place when it came to power and would appease the textile industry with more protection from foreign competition. Farm-price supports, oil and other import-quotas, tariffs, and union barriers to entry into the building trades and other occupations—all government-sponsored or sanctioned impediments to freer markets—make it more difficult to slow inflation. Each of them is the property of a powerful interest group with vigilant defenders in the Congress and a serious effort to trim back this rank growth, especially when the opposition party has a majority of the seats in Congress, would probably encounter insuperable opposition.

Monetarist policies have not yet had a conclusive test. Monetarist theory, however, has been well tested since Milton Friedman reformulated it in 1956. It has shown its superiority in predicting the outcomes of fiscal and monetary policies. This has become especially clear to business forecasters, who do not make public policy but must help their employers react to it.

Monetary policy is the key to controlling inflation. But politicians of any party must keep an eye on the level of unemployment as well. It is illusory to accept an inflation rate of 4 or 5 percent per year in the hope of securing high employment. Even if the unemployment problem could thereby be resolved—and it cannot—inflation sorely aggravates already serious social problems in the United States by pitting group against group. It is unlikely, therefore, that the American people would passively adjust to perpetual inflation without a system of effective institutional safeguards. Moreover, if the attempt to restore price stability through monetary policy is abandoned, as it appeared to have been abandoned in 1971, pressures for a long night of direct wage, price, and profit controls would soon be irresistible. The resulting losses of freedom and productivity would be much greater than the United States and the world can afford. The United States went much too far down that road in 1971.

It is very difficult to conduct a critical experiment in an atmosphere so charged with partisan passions as the arena of national economic policy. There are powerful forces aligned against a fresh approach to money and the fisc, within the Executive branch of the government, in the Congress, and most important, within the Federal Reserve System. Yet some future year may see the completion of fair trial, the validation of alternative policies for economic stability and their rapid spread to other countries. Only then will the new monetarism have arrived.

20

THE WAY TO SOUND MONEY
AND STABLE EXCHANGE RATES

Now if a country is rapidly increasing its supply
of money, the same lack of confidence in the
future of the money which ultimately worms its
way into the skull of the thickest-headed citizen,
strikes like a flash upon the consciousness of the
well-informed and impressionable gentlemen whose
business it is to carry on dealings in foreign
money. They become highly willing to buy foreign
money and to sell the money of their own
country.

D. H. Robertson, *Money,* 1948[1]

The earlier chapters on world money abided by a polite fiction;
they assumed that exchange rates among world currencies were
fixed. If true, it would be a great convenience for those who travel
and trade in other countries. But it is not.

Between World War II and mid-1971, of twenty-one major industrial countries, only two—the United States and Japan—had
no change in par value. Twelve of the twenty-one devalued their
currencies more than 30 percent against the dollar, and four—Germany, the Netherlands, Switzerland, and Austria—had upward
revaluations. At mid-1971, four countries—Canada, Germany, the
Netherlands, and Belgium—had floating or semifloating exchange
rates. And in August, 1971, its largest member, the United States,
set the whole system adrift by suspending convertibility of the
dollar, and Japan allowed the yen to float a few days later.

Exchange rates in the developing countries have been even more
unstable.[2] The "well-informed and impressionable gentlemen whose

business it is to carry on dealings in foreign money" are always busy.

It is no longer enough to talk of national monetary policies. A better way must be found to put them together in a world monetary policy. The instability of exchange rates reveals a pervasive disharmony in national monetary policies.

JUMPING, CRAWLING, OR STABLE EXCHANGE RATES

Exchange-rate changes are inevitable if the purchasing power of national currencies for goods and services on world markets changes at different rates. Most exchange-rate changes since World War II have been devaluations forced by the more rapid depreciation in purchasing power of money in other countries than in the United States. But in 1969 and 1970 West Germany and Canada both let their exchange rates appreciate against the dollar, partially to insulate themselves against the U.S. inflation. In 1971, again to insulate themselves against inflation, Germany and the Netherlands let their currencies float; Belgium and France maintained a fixed exchange rate for some transactions and a floating rate for others; and Switzerland and Austria raised their par values in terms of the dollar.

To see how exchange-rate adjustments can insulate one country from inflationary or deflationary effects of monetary policies pursued by others, assume that central banks were not under any present obligation to buy or sell dollars to keep their exchange rates between 99 and 101 percent of an agreed parity. And assume that the world problem of the day is an inflationary monetary policy in the United States, like the one of 1965 or 1967. If the central banks did not step in to buy, the price of dollars in terms of other currencies would fall, when residents of their countries attempted to get rid of the excess dollar balances being pressed on them by the U.S. inflation. This would increase the incentive of people in other countries to spend the dollars in the United States because it would reduce the prices of American goods and services in terms of their currencies. It would also induce Americans to spend less abroad because prices of foreign goods and services would be higher in

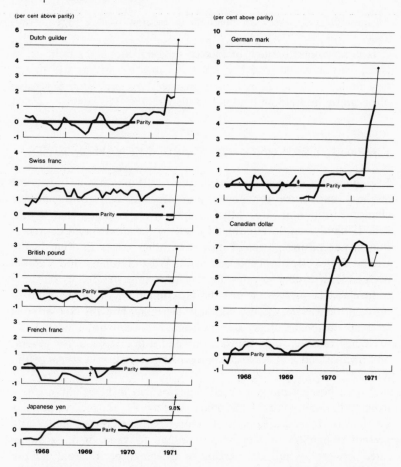

Chart 20-1. Major industrial nations kept their exchange rates generally within 99 percent and 101 percent of parity until the international monetary crises of 1969, 1970, and 1971 forced large changes.

NOTES: *Break represents parity change on May 10, 1971. †Break represents parity change on August 10, 1969. ‡Break represents parity change on October 26, 1969. Plottings are based on monthly averages of daily foreign-exchange rates in the New York market shown as the percentage above or below parity (or above former parity for currencies with floating exchange rates). Dots represent quotes in New York as of Monday, August 30. The dot for the French franc refers to financial transactions. *Chart by FNCB.*

terms of dollars. Both of these shifts in expenditures would work to offset the tendency of U. S. money-supply expansion to increase American demand for foreign goods, services, and securities.

With no exchange-rate pegging, domestic money supplies of other countries would not be increased by central-bank buying of dollars with high-powered money. An inflationary impulse from the United States would, therefore, be absorbed by a change of exchange rates without causing inflation abroad.

If countries could so easily insulate themselves from the monetary policy errors of their neighbors, why do they now try so hard to keep exchange rates fixed? The primary reason is the belief that stable rates of exchange among world currencies facilitate international trade and investment and thus help to integrate the world economy. That is an excellent reason.

Ideally, a single world money would accomplish for world trade and investment what the dollar has done for trade and investment among the fifty United States. Lacking this, a system of national currencies freely convertible into one another at stable rates of exchange is the next-best arrangement.

You will notice, however, that I said "stable rates" not "fixed rates." One of the principal aims of the Fund Agreement was "to promote exchange stability," not fixed rates. These stable rates should be comparable to what J. Marcus Fleming, of the International Monetary Fund staff, calls an "equilibrium rate":

To an economist, an equilibrium rate of exchange, even a long-term equilibrium rate, is something that is liable to change, gradually but continuously, with changing international relationships with respect to productivity, wage levels, normal capital exports, normal degree of employment, and so on.[3]

Attempting to fix the rates has not produced stability. Today, the world has not fixed rates, nor even stable rates, but jumping rates. Although there is little disagreement that some exchange-rate adjustments are unavoidable, there are wide disagreements about how frequently exchange rates should change, how much they should change, why they should change, and by whose decision. At one extreme are people who believe all exchange rates should be free to change every day in the foreign-exchange markets, without any intervention by governments or central banks. At the other extreme are people who believe exchange rates should almost never change, and then only after international consultation or other steps to be sure a change is unavoidable.

The International Monetary Fund was originally intended to provide a mechanism for making orderly changes in exchange rates so that nations would be free to use their monetary and fiscal policies for domestic objectives. As we saw earlier, Lord Keynes argued vigorously and with considerable success for a system that would not link countries rigidly together. Changes in parities were to be initiated by the governments concerned but were supposed to be approved by the IMF and were only to be for the purpose of correcting a "fundamental disequilibrium," which was not well defined. This is called the "adjustable-peg" system.

In practice, the adjustable peg has become a jumping peg. Parity changes usually have been too long postponed, have sometimes involved wrenching international crises, and have been large when they finally did occur. Because the conditions that eventually should make a change necessary are usually apparent long before anything is done, speculators buy or sell the currency in question, making it all the more difficult for the authorities to peg the rates.

Businessmen who have to deal in a currency that is under speculative pressure are subjected to intolerable risks and uncertainty because they have no way of knowing when, or if, or how far, the peg will jump. However, they usually are sure they know which way it will go, if and when it does. They most certainly do not want to find on a Monday that some currency they held in a bank on Friday had lost 10 percent or more of its dollar value over the weekend. Nor do they want to hold dollars if they can get some other currency that might suddenly appreciate in dollar value. In early 1971 the self-protective reflexes of corporate treasurers, who were faced with agonizing uncertainty about exchange rates, helped to swell the flood of dollars into the Deutschemark and other strong currencies. The treasurers were joined by other well-informed and impressionable gentlemen who believed there might be a quick profit in borrowing dollars in the Euro-dollar market; converting them into Deutschemarks or Swiss francs; and converting them back into dollars after a change in parities—if it occurred and if it went the way they expected.

International consultation to establish a new parity is virtually impossible because if the slightest hint of consultations leaks out, speculators and sober businessmen who would never dream of calling themselves speculators rush to buy or to dump the currency involved. These one-way options make the jumping-peg system as unstable at times as an overloaded ferryboat whose passengers rush en masse from one rail to the other.

Governments faced with pressure to change an exchange parity usually hesitate to do so because whichever way they eventually shift the peg a substantial part of the populace will be displeased: exporters in the case of a revaluation and importers and consumers in case of a devaluation. Infrequent, large jumps in exchange rates, however, are bound to be more upsetting to international trade and investment than slow, gradual changes to which businessmen could adjust.

Samuel Brittan, of the *Financial Times,* has explained very well the political and economic dilemmas in which procrastination on exchange-parity adjustment can mire governments.

. . . if an imbalance is allowed to persist too long, a deficit country acquires an excessively home-based industrial and commercial structure, while the surplus country becomes excessively export-oriented. . . . This makes adjustment needlessly painful and difficult when it does come, and there is a risk of high transitional unemployment while resources are being transferred. Shop assistants in Britain cannot be transferred overnight to engineering establishments which do not yet exist, while Volkswagen workers cannot move straight away into the German social services. These very facts themselves become ammunition for those who oppose parity changes, and the eventual adjustments are all the more sudden and severe, when at last they come.[4]

The country that is reluctant to change its own exchange rate may oppose change in its neighbors' rates, as well, for fear a neighbor may gain an advantage in world markets. We saw in Chapter 16 that many people believe a decline in exports would reduce total national income through the Keynesian multiplier process. This idea, furthermore, has firm roots in centuries-old mercantilist beliefs that export surpluses are essential to economic growth. In any case, workers in Volkswagen, or Toyota, or Fiat, or Volvo, or Citroën factories would naturally oppose any change in exchange rates that would seem to help the others to sell on more favorable terms in the U.S. market. Therefore, there are great internal and external pressures to keep rates fixed long after they would have changed in a free market.

There can be little question, however, that the international monetary system is now evolving toward allowing more flexibility in exchange rates, in order to replace the jumping peg with a hopping or crawling one that would move more frequently and by smaller steps. This is true despite the agreement by members of the European Common Market in 1970 to narrow the bands within which they permit their exchange rates with one another to vary. The form the new flexibility will take, however, is still uncertain.

Just as a few years ago there was a worldwide contest to suggest plans for increasing international liquidity, there now is a contest in devising exchange-rate adjustment plans.[5] Most of these provide for more latitude in short-run fluctuations around parity—"broadening the bands"—or a gradual crawl or glide of the peg in the direction indicated by market forces. The various rate-adjustment plans, however, require negotiation and agreement that may be a long way off.

Although conceding the need for more flexibility in exchange rates, the Executive Directors of the International Monetary Fund have taken a dim view of outsiders' proposals for changing the par-value system. In their Report on the *Role of Exchange Rates in the Adjustment of International Payments,* the Executive Directors did, however, suggest three improvements in the system: prompt adjustment of parities in "appropriate" cases, a slight widening of the margin around parity, and temporary deviations from par-value obligations. The old concept of "fundamental disequilibrium" was described once more as justification for a change of parities but, again, was not well defined.

The Report's definition of fundamental disequilibrium [says George Halm] is not, and cannot be, precise enough to help member countries find the correct moment for, and the correct amount of, changes in par values. Repeated study of the Report leaves the reader with the impression that the Executive Directors consider it safer to err in the direction of delay. If, occasionally, a different interpretation seems to be justified, this hope is always dashed by a postscript that harps on the dangers of any substantial deviation from the par-value system.[6]

Although contrary to the Articles of Agreement of the International Monetary Fund, the actions of West Germany and Canada in letting their currencies float to new levels in 1969 and 1970 probably were a more reliable indicator of how rates will be adjusted in the future than all of the widely discussed gliding-crawling-peg plans. Instead of announcing a shift to a new parity, both countries simply stopped trying to peg their exchange rates for a time when large inflows of U.S. dollars threatened to aggravate inflation. Their exchange rates "floated" upward, that is, the price of U.S. dollars in Deutschemarks and Canadian dollars sank when the governments of Germany and Canada stopped supporting it with purchases. The new rate-adjustment method gained in acceptance in '71 when more countries joined.

The final blow to the old fixed-rate system came when the United States suspended convertibility of the dollar into gold. The parities in the IMF system are defined in dollars and gold. Pulling the pin, as the United States did, put the world on a floating-rate system, at least temporarily.

Advocates of floating (free-market) exchange rates have been frustrated, according to Samuel Brittan, by the lack of empirical evidence on the behavior of market-determined rates in advanced industrial countries.

The supporters of fixed rates [he says] seem extremely anxious that such evidence should not become available. When the Germans floated the mark for a short period in the autumn of 1969, every conceivable pressure was brought on them to bring the experiment to an end as soon as possible before it could yield useful data.[7]

The German experiment in 1969 was flawed, in Brittan's view, because it had been made clear that the authorities would soon fix another parity. Furthermore, the Bundesbank did not refrain completely from buying or selling marks during the "transitional float," which lasted from September 30 to October 26, 1969. Nevertheless, the German experience did show that a floating, or nearly floating, rate could be maintained without producing chaos in the markets.

The Canadian experiment that began in June, 1970, ran much longer and also produced an agreeable stability in the exchange rate between the two dollars. W. Earle McLaughlin, chairman and president of the Royal Bank of Canada, has argued that the government had three options when the decision to let the Canadian dollar float was made:

(1) *to defend the old undervalued parity, with a corresponding increase in the money supply and, therefore, a much higher rate of inflation;*
(2) *to revalue to another parity, with no certainty that it would not be too low and ineffective in curbing upward pressure on the rate or too high, thereby creating an exchange crisis of the opposite sort—in either case, condemning us to defend a new, but still indefensible, rate of exchange; or,*
(3) *to float as we did, thus avoiding a massive inflation as well as the twin evils of guessing too low or too high* [italics in original].[8]

A temporary float to a new parity, when it becomes obvious that an exchange rate is too high or too low to be held any longer, at least prevents or halts disruptive speculation and may help to overcome the economic and political obstacles to a parity change. What is more, as the McLaughlin argument indicates, it provides a practical answer to the difficult question of what parity level to set. In effect, the market sets the new parity level so that the government is less likely to be criticized for going too far or not far enough.

There were good reasons for Canada not to hurry back to the fixed-parity system because when the Canadian dollar floated during the decade of the 1950s the results were favorable. The exchange rate was stable and was not disturbed by the speculative movements of funds that cause so much trouble for the fixed-exchange-rate system. Furthermore, says Earle McLaughlin, "In the 1950s Canada did not have to resort to foreign-exchange controls of any kind and had a better record in fighting inflation than she had under the fixed exchange rate in the 1960s."[9]

The move toward greater exchange-rate flexibility will be beneficial in permitting rate adjustments to be made in gradual degrees that can be more easily predicted and hedged against by businessmen and traders than the large arbitrary jumps that characterize the present system. Greater flexibility should lead to the dismantling of many controls that have been installed as substitutes for real adjustment. It should also reduce the volume of official reserves that central bankers believe they need to operate the system.

Moving to a completely free market in exchange, which seems to me to be a desirable ultimate goal, is said by some authorities to be out of the question now because central bankers and governments are unable, or unwilling, to refrain from intervening in the markets. For example, the Executive Directors of the IMF have said that "national authorities could not be expected in modern conditions to adopt a policy of neutrality with respect to movements in an economic variable of such importance to the domestic economy as the exchange rate, with its effects on prices, incomes, employment, and the structure of industry as between domestic and foreign sectors."[10]

Under present conditions, with the money supply essentially out of control in many countries, that may be so; but it need not always be so. Before attempting to predict how exchange rates will be determined in the future, however, we should understand clearly why they change now.

How nearly stable exchange rates can become under any system for determining them, I believe, will depend ultimately on how well money is managed in individual countries. For the monetary chaos of the thirties that led to distrust of exchange-rate flexibility did not come from a weakness in the international monetary system. It came from domestic instability brought on by catastrophic mismanagement of the money supply, especially in the United States.[11]

THE BALANCE OF PAYMENTS IS NOT THE PROBLEM

In early 1971, Gottfried Haberler of Harvard and Thomas Willett of Cornell stirred a flurry of indignation abroad by recommending that the United States follow a passive attitude toward the balance of payments, an attitude they characterized as one of "benign neglect."[12] Other Americans made similar remarks at about the same time. Despite protestations to the contrary from high officials in the U.S. Treasury and the Federal Reserve, furthermore, it did indeed look from the other side of the Atlantic as though the U.S. attitude was one of neglect, although hardly benign. At about the same time the Administration announced its 1971 forecast of a $1,065 billion GNP, which indicated renewed inflation to the worried observers abroad. Worst of all, the Federal Reserve permitted the money supply to leap upward in February and March and U.S. interest rates fell. Continental central banks were at the time absorbing dollars at what seemed to them an unconscionable rate. Soon even that rate was to seem small compared with the flood of late April and early May.

It had also been fashionable in the United States for some time to say, as I did in earlier chapters, that the world was on a dollar standard. Squirm though it might, the world was hooked on dollars and could not get off because there was no alternative. It was argued, too, that central banks with more dollars than they wanted to keep would find the window dropped on their fingers if they tried to exchange more than token amounts for gold at the U.S. Treasury. If they wanted to stem the inflow of dollars they could revalue their currencies, a step we have seen would be extremely unpopular with their own constituents, although pleasing to American manufacturers of automobiles, shoes, steel, textiles, chemicals, and other products. Here we have the ingredients of ugly, but needless, quarrels that could delay progress in the integration of the world economy for years to come.

It is certainly understandable that countries suffering what they believe is the fallout of inflationary U.S. policies would be infuriated by American indifference to their complaints. For the United States to "do something about its balance-of-payments deficit," however, is not the best way to begin healing the rents in the international monetary fabric. As I argued earlier, the balance of payments itself is not the problem. Balance-of-payments deficits and surpluses are but the symptoms of international differences in rates at which money is being created.

If national moneys continue to grow at widely different or fluctuating rates there will continue to be deficits and surpluses in international payments. But, much more important, domestic price levels and exchange rates will be under irresistible pressures to change. Unless the sources of money are brought under control, trying to maintain price stability and fixed exchange rates by inter-fering with the flows of money among nations—the balance-of-payments deficits and surpluses—means choking vital flows of goods and services and capital. This is treating a nosebleed with a tourniquet around the neck.

The solution, therefore, is not for the United States to curb its balance-of-payments deficit or for other nations to curb their balance-of-payments surpluses. Both of these might be done if nations were willing to endure enough deflation or inflation or to change their exchange rates. But it is by now obvious that all of these courses are unpalatable, probably unacceptable. The problem, therefore, is to find a way for all nations to achieve domestic price stability and exchange-rate stability at the same time. This blissful state I call "world monetary equilibrium"—sound money and stable exchange rates.

DISTASTEFUL OPTIONS

In the disturbed conditions of early 1971 the countries that were concerned about excessive dollar inflows and over-all balance-of-payments surpluses were considered to have several options: They could curb the inflows by raising their exchange parities, that is, appreciate their currencies against the dollar. They could continue to absorb dollars while waiting for the United States to curb its outflow. They could adopt more expansionary monetary policies, thus reducing their surpluses. Or they could loosen restrictions against U.S. imports and reduce export subsidies.[13]

The first and fourth of these options were the same, in effect, for changes in trade restrictions or in restrictions on investment transactions amount to partial depreciation or appreciation of currencies. For the reasons mentioned earlier, taking either of these options would be distasteful to most governments. Some of the effort to secure agreement on a European common currency in 1970 and 1971 may well have been intended to make it possible for the Continental bloc countries to appreciate against the dollar together. That way no country would have to risk awarding a competitive advantage to its neighbors by being the only one to appreciate its currency.

The second and third options also were roughly equivalent to one another in the end. If a central bank buys dollars, and does not offset the dollar purchases with sales of something else, it increases the domestic money supply. That is an expansionary policy. As we saw in the chapter on central banks outside the United States, few central banks are equipped to conduct offsetting open-market operations when they buy or sell dollars. That is the reason for the common complaint that central banks cannot control the money supply.

One of the more durable illusions of international monetary discussions is that a country can avoid painful adjustments to changes in the outside world if it keeps its official exchange rate fixed by buying or selling an international-reserve asset, be it gold, dollars, or SDRs. That is one of the main reasons countries hold exchange reserves. However, all that is avoided by this means is adjustment of the exchange rate. The economic adjustment then takes place through changes in domestic money supply, incomes, and prices. The illusion of escape is strengthened by the Keynesian emphasis on net exports as a key determinant of national income that we discussed in Chapter 16.

The terms of the trade-off can be more clearly seen if we imagine there were only two countries in the world, A and B, with an official exchange rate of one unit of A's currency for one unit of B's currency. If country A suddenly doubled its money supply, incomes and prices would begin to rise there. But people there would soon realize they could buy more goods and services by converting their depreciating currency into money of country B, at the official exchange rate, and spending it there. To keep the exchange rate from changing, B's central bank would have to buy the currency of A, which would increase the supply of money in B, raising incomes and prices there.

At some point there would no longer be any advantage in converting from currency A into currency B because a unit of either one would buy the same amount of goods and services in either country. But the same adjustment could have been accomplished earlier, by letting the exchange rate change, without any change in money supply and prices in country B.

The old monetarists, or classical economists, believed the price adjustment occurred rapidly. We realize today, however, that prices adjust very slowly to changes in money supply, both domestically and internationally. Therefore, countries do not avoid adjusting to the monetary policies of other countries by accumulating or using reserves to peg exchange rates; they merely substitute a slower form of adjustment—changes in their own money supplies, incomes, and price levels.

At the new world equilibrium—after the world has fully adjusted to the doubling of country A's money supply—prices would be higher in both countries; real income would be the same as it would have been without the changes in money supplies (because it is limited in the long run by availability of real resources and technology); and there would no longer be a tendency for the exchange rate to change.

A confirmation of this thesis was recently provided by Henry J. Gailliot in his study, "Purchasing Power Parity as an Explanation of Long-Term Changes in Exchange Rates." He tested the proposition, originally expounded by Gustav Cassel, that "in the long run, important changes in the domestic price level have a much greater influence on the exchange rates than any other change in the real conditions of international trade." He compared average prices and exchange rates in the period 1900–1904 with average prices and exchange rates in the 1963–1967 period for the United States, Canada, Japan, the United Kingdom, France, Italy, Switzerland, and Germany.

Gailliot concluded that, although changes in prices were not the sole determinant of exchange rates, they certainly accounted for the largest part of the changes in exchange rates. "Perhaps the most striking result," he said, "is the tendency toward equilibrium values of currencies even when one is forced to use observations that have been influenced by two wars and a great depression."[14]

What I am arguing is the converse. If exchange rates are fixed, with the system out of equilibrium, price levels will eventually move so that the real purchasing power of currencies will be equal at the official exchange rates.

After the return to equilibrium, however, the B central bank might have a political problem in justifying its holding of the A currency (or some international reserve asset) that it accumulated while pegging the exchange rate. This is why some central banks would like to convert their dollars into something more solid and defensible like gold, if they could. And the people of country A would be richer by the amount of B's real goods and services that they received in exchange for the currency they sold to the B central bank. Looking at it one way, this can be viewed as the price paid by the people of B for the convenience of maintaining a fixed exchange rate. Looked at in a more cynical way, however, the transfer of goods and services from B to A suggests that *an inflationary member of a fixed-exchange-rate system can extract real wealth from the others, as long as they choose to maintain fixed exchange rates rather than to stabilize the domestic purchasing power of their currencies.*

In the real world of 1971 there were additional complications; but the basic characteristics of our simple example still applied. Because prices adjust so slowly to changes in money supply, prices were still rising in the United States even though money-supply growth had slowed down. Inflation in the surplus countries, furthermore, had not yet proceeded far enough to bring about a new equilibrium (absence of pressure on exchange rates) at the official parities.

Surplus countries were also experiencing large inflows of dollars, possibly because exchange parities were out of line but possibly because speculators merely *thought* they were out of line. The only way to find out what exchange rates would be stable (require no central-bank intervention) would be to let their currencies float. Canada had stopped the U.S. dollar inflow by letting the Canadian dollar float.

At this juncture, therefore, the surplus countries had only two options: they could appreciate (or float) their currencies or they could continue to permit inflation until there was no longer any advantage for people to convert dollars into their currencies at the official exchange rates. If they adopted the first course, their central banks could concentrate on curbing inflation at home because it would again be possible for them to control their domestic money supplies. By, in effect, bottling up the U.S. inflation within the United States they could put back on the American public more of the inconvenience of bringing the inflation under control.

If they adopted the second option—holding to 1971 parity levels and letting domestic inflation bring their currencies back into equilibrium with the dollar—the surplus countries might have to wait a long time for sound money and stable exchange rates. That would be true even if the United States were to continue its anti-inflationary policies. Price stability in the United States, although attainable, was three years or more away in 1971, at best. At the eventual new equilibrium, furthermore, central banks of the surplus countries would hold even more dollars than they had in 1971.

By suspending convertibility of the dollar into gold and by imposing a 10 percent surcharge on imports in August, 1971, the United States government evidently hoped to press other countries to revalue their currencies against the dollar. The import surcharge was a bargaining device to stir countries to take actions that they were extremely reluctant to take. Within a short time, there were substantial changes in exchange rates, as can be seen on Chart 20-1.

Nevertheless, these changes were only a temporary solution to the problem. The new exchange rates were not stable, nor are they likely to become so unless there are some basic changes in the international monetary system and a new approach to domestic monetary policies the world over. Without stable monetary policies, there will continue to be international monetary crises and a proliferation of direct restraints on international trade and investment.

A WORLD MONEY-GROWTH RULE

When a definitive history of monetarism comes to be written, it will probably characterize the intellectual process by which the monetarist position on international monetary affairs came to be almost solely identified with flexible exchange rates as unfortunate. Flexible exchange rates are obviously a key to a rational system of international monetary coordination. But even more so is the monetarist emphasis on stable monetary-growth rates. Moreover, the kind of monetarist analysis that has made headway in the United States, through pointing out the irrationality of the conventional targets of macroeconomic policy, has an equal bearing on the conventional wisdom about the proper scope and content of rules for the international coordination of economic policy. It is unfortunate that this emphasis is only now coming to the attention of policy makers and the public.

It is a dogma among economists that most of the world's ills spring from the malfeasance, misfeasance, or nonfeasance of politicians. But comfortable as this view may be, it can be argued equally cogently that much of the trouble with the world monetary system today springs directly from the tendency of politicians to do what economists tell them to do.

If world monetary equilibrium can be roughly defined as reasonably stable exchange rates, reasonably full employment, and reasonable stability of world prices, it would describe a state that clearly did not exist in 1971. Everywhere prices were rising. Some exchange rates had been jumping, while others were held at parity only by large central-bank operations in foreign-exchange markets. Therefore, countries had neither stable prices nor stable exchange rates. And economists have to bear a good share of the responsibility for this state of affairs.

Any short statement about the sources of the malaise is an oversimplification. But it is perhaps not unrealistic to attribute most of the disturbance to the excessive money-supply growth in the United States between 1964 and 1968. Although the United States was by no means responsible for all of the world's price inflation, there is no question that the burst of U.S. money-supply growth between 1964 and 1968 accelerated it. Nor are the hands of economists entirely clean in any analysis of why this occurred. It is true that the weight of U.S. economic opinion did favor a tax surcharge to pay for the Vietnam War—and favored it before it was recommended by the Administration and long before it was enacted into law. But many economists argued for low interest rates in late 1965. The weight of economic opinion favored the rapid reversal of monetary policy in the 1967 minirecession. Furthermore, the pessimistic forecast that led to a burst of money-supply growth in 1968, when the tax surcharge was enacted in the United States, was widely shared in the economics profession.

It is also true that insofar as the Federal Reserve again turned to rapid monetary expansion in 1971, its actions were supported by the analysis of those economists who persist in ignoring the direct effects of money-supply growth on income and prices and who continue to identify a stimulative monetary policy with the deliberate pursuit by the central banks of low nominal interest rates.

Clearly, then, one requirement for movement toward a better world money system is better economic analysis. And, as in the case of domestic policy, monetarism clearly has an important role to play. A number of maxims can be drawn from the monetarist view of world money in Chapter 17. The first series will be prohibitions, a series of statements of what not to do if world monetary coordination is to be achieved. I will then state two positive rules that I believe would promote world monetary equilibrium.

The most important of the negative rules is one for the U.S. Federal Reserve: *If the Federal Reserve is to contribute to world monetary equilibrium, it will have to give up its attempts at contracyclical policies at home or in the world as a whole.* As the discussion of Federal Reserve actions has already indicated, much of the monetary acceleration of the years from 1964 to 1968 was the result of attempted contracyclical actions. Coping with bad forecasts and with the lags between policy actions and their effects in the U.S. economy is difficult enough. When the additional transmission lags of international payments are considered, it should be obvious that managing world contracyclical policies from Washington and New York exceeds the capacities of the Fed—or of any other agency for that matter. *The Federal Reserve cannot be the world's central bank, nor is one needed.*

Given the tendency of economists to tinker and prescribe, this is a difficult anti-maxim to follow. When money-supply growth in the United States accelerates, the U.S. balance-of-payments deficit increases and the world money supply grows more rapidly. This has suggested to some economists, including Robert Mundell of the University of Chicago and Richard Cooper of Yale, that the Federal Reserve System should try to stabilize the world economy by supplying more money at some times than at others. Mundell, for example, said in 1968 that the Federal Reserve had completed a full cycle of tight money and easy money during 1966–1967 that was consistent with the requirements of the world economy.[15] That was far too generous an appraisal, for the volatile U.S. monetary policies of those years had markedly increased economic instability and price inflation not only in the United States but in the rest of the world.

The idea of steady growth in the U.S. money supply should appeal to the reluctant partners of the United States in the international monetary system, although it runs counter to a deep-seated central-banker aversion to being constrained by rules. Gyrations in U.S. policies, which other countries have seen as balance-of-payments problems, have been deeply unsettling to them in recent years, and with good reason. If they must live with the dollar—and there does not appear to be a ready alternative if they want fixed rates, too—other countries should prefer a predictable, stable dollar to one that incessantly bounces to the latest beat in the U.S. economy.[16]

A corollary of this rule, of course, is that other countries too should avoid contracyclical policies. It is worth noting that the conventional analysis that ascribed the most recent monetary crisis to a difference in cycle phases between countries was correct. But most commentaries failed to point out that the cycles at issue could hardly be described as resulting from the inherent instability of any private economy. Instead, they were cycles caused by the character of contracyclical policies in the United States. Essentially, they were reverberations of the initial disturbance caused by the hyper-expansive U.S. policies of 1964–1968. Nothing could do more to mitigate business cycles than the abandonment of contracyclical monetary policies around the world.

All attempts at international interest-rate coordination should be abandoned, as should the attempts to affect the term structure of rates. Those officials and economists who have called on the United States to raise interest rates to affect the flow of funds across the exchanges have asked U.S. authorities to do the impossible. *Are higher interest rates to be achieved by a deceleration of monetary growth?* If so, the policy would be self-defeating in the long run, which might not be a very long run either, given the tendency of U.S. capital markets to behave increasingly as monetarists say they should. *Or are higher rates to be achieved by an acceleration of monetary growth?* This policy might achieve the expected results; but surely it is not what Europeans, who would have to cope with another wave of dollars, have in mind.

A desire to manipulate interest rates is deep-seated among those who worry about balance-of-payments equilibrium. Its antecedents reach all the way back to the early mercantilists. But it is to be doubted that interest-rate manipulation can make even short-run contributions to stability, particularly given the enhanced tendency of markets to act on monetarist expectations.

The so-called international liquidity problem should be recognized for what it is—essentially a side issue. Much attention has been focused on the seeming paradox of worldwide concern about a shortage of international liquidity at the same time a worldwide price inflation indicates that the world is actually swamped in money.

The international-liquidity problem would fade away into richly deserved obscurity if stable domestic monetary policies and flexible exchange rates were adopted. For these two reforms would do away with the need for a reserve asset for central bankers to use in pegging exchange rates.

Controls are not the way to deal with the so-called Eurodollar problem. The Eurodollar market at its present size is a function of controls, including U.S. balance-of-payments policies, such as the interest-equalization tax, the "voluntary" restraint on bank loans to foreigners and the mandatory restraints on direct foreign investment. All of these controls could and should be abandoned. If they were, and if the regulation of bank time-deposit rates in the United States were abolished, the Eurodollar market would wither to a shadow of its former self. It would not be a great offshore, out-of-control creator of dollars. *Removal of controls—not another layer of controls—is the way to deal with the Eurodollar problem.*

WORLD MONETARY EQUILIBRIUM IS LIKE HAPPINESS

If these particular anti-maxims add up to one grand anti-maxim, it is this: *the goal of world monetary equilibrium should not be pursued directly.* In the Aristotelian view, he who pursues happiness directly will find it elusive. Happiness, instead, is an unsought reward for doing other things well. So it is with economic policy.

The positive monetarist maxim for international equilibrium is for central banks of the world to concentrate on doing what they can do—controlling money supply—and to abandon attempts to do what they cannot do—controlling interest rates and balance-of-payments deficits or surpluses. By following a steady-growth policy, furthermore, they would have the best chance of enjoying both price stability and stable exchange rates.

If the world stays with the fixed-exchange-rate system, with the dollar as the key reserve currency, the system would resemble the gold standard but with steady gold (dollar) production. The rate of growth of the world money supply would be determined primarily by the United States. The steady rate of dollar production, however, would enormously simplify the world's monetary problems.

The rate of dollar inflow is a determinant of money-supply growth in surplus countries; but, as we have seen, it is not—and certainly need not be—the sole determinant. Central-bank purchases of domestic assets (or loans through their discount windows) usually are even more important than their purchases of foreign exchange as sources of high-powered money. This is obviously true also of the deficit countries because they have no net dollar inflows to force money-supply expansion. *Controlling their purchases or sales of domestic assets,* therefore, *will permit central banks to control domestic money supply in a fixed-exchange-rate system, if exchange parities are reasonably close to equilibrium levels and if no major country upsets the system by expanding its money supply too fast.* To initiate such a system, however, will require adjustments in parities. In a sense, the turmoil in the international monetary system in 1971 was primarily an attempt to adjust exchange parities to the changes in purchasing power of currencies that had occurred over the preceding near-decade.

If a particular country lets its money supply grow slightly too fast (in relation to the rate of growth of the supply of dollars), it will lose dollars from its reserves. This suggests a way by which central banks could get rid of the dollars they accumulated in pegging rates after the U.S. inflation began in 1965. If a country expands its money supply at slightly more than the equilibrium rate (with relation to the dollar), it could feed dollars into world exchange markets without altering its exchange rate or the price level. If a country lets its money supply grow at less than the equilibrium rate (with relation to the dollar), it would gain reserves. In either case, little harm would be done either to exchange-rate stability or to price stability if the money-supply growth rates were stable and if the United States did not let the world supply of dollars grow too rapidly.

One of the principal advantages of the steady-growth rule from the standpoint of the international monetary system is that it would greatly reduce pressures to change exchange rates. The question of whether to have fixed rates or free rates, therefore, would become less important because exchange-rate stability could be maintained under either system. Volatility of national monetary policies has overwhelmed attempts to achieve exchange-rate stability under the fixed-exchange-rate system in the past.

Exchange rates would be more stable if they were allowed to float in a world in which individual nations followed steady-growth monetary policies than they would be with a system of adjustable pegs. This is because there would not be the incentive for destabilizing speculation that the one-way options of the peg system provide now. The small residual adjustments in exchange rates that might be necessary if central banks follow a steady money-growth rule should occur slowly and gradually enough that businessmen could allow for them as they now allow for changes in the purchasing power of domestic currencies.

Another advantage of the steady-growth rule (especially with floating rates) is that elaborate arrangements for international coordination of policies would not be required. If agreement on policies is sought, it is far easier to agree on something simple that can be carried out entirely at home by each country.

By floating their exchange rates, furthermore, those countries that agreed to follow steady, noninflationary monetary policies would be protected from disruptions caused by countries that were not willing to go along. The world would then have sound money and stable exchange rates within the group of steady-growth countries and unstable rates between these countries and the outsiders.

The advantages of free trade and investment should provide incentive for more countries to join.

A country that avoids rapidly increasing its supply of money, and avoids being tied through fixed exchange rates to those that do not observe the same restraint, need not worry about confidence in its currency. There would no longer be incentive for "well-informed and impressionable gentlemen" or anyone else to be "highly willing to buy foreign money and to sell the money of their own country."

NOTES

CHAPTER 1

1. Irving Fisher, *The Purchasing Power of Money* (New York: Reprints of Economic Classics, Augustus M. Kelley, 1963), preface to 1st ed., 1911, p. viii.

2. Arthur M. Okun, *The Political Economy of Prosperity* (Washington, D.C.: The Brookings Institution, 1970), pp. 71–72.

3. Harry G. Johnson, "The Keynesian Revolution and the Monetarist Counter-Revolution," *American Economic Review*, LXI, No. 2 (May, 1971), 12.

4. *Ibid.*, pp. 7–8.

5. For issues involved in the definition of money see Milton Friedman and Anna J. Schwartz, *Monetary Statistics of the United States; Estimates, Sources, Methods* (New York: National Bureau of Economic Research, distr. by Columbia University Press, 1970), pp. 89–198; and David Laidler, "The Definition of Money: Theoretical and Empirical Problems," *Journal of Money, Credit and Banking*, I, No. 3 (August, 1969), 508–525.

6. Jean Bodin, *Réponse au Paradoxe de Malestroit Touchant l'Enchérissement de Toutes Choses*, in Henri Hauser (ed.), *La Réponse de Jean Bodin à M. de Malestroit* (Paris, 1932). English version in A. E. Monroe (ed.), *Early Economic Thought* (Cambridge, Mass., 1924), pp. 123–141.

7. Richard A. Radford, "The Economic Organization of a Prison Camp," *Economica*, November, 1945, pp. 189–201.

8. Fisher, *The Purchasing Power of Money*, pp. 55–73, 159–162.

9. Irving Fisher, "The Business Cycle Largely a 'Dance of the Dollar,' " *Journal of the American Statistical Association*, December, 1923, pp. 1024–1028.

10. Irving Fisher, *100% Money* (New Haven: The City Printing Co., 1935), pp. 123–124.

11. For one of the earliest published reports of the Friedman-Schwartz work on money and business fluctuations see U.S. Congress, *Compendium of Papers Submitted by Panelists Appearing Before the Joint Economic Committee, March 31, 1958*, Milton Friedman, "The Supply of Money and Changes in Prices and Output," pp. 241–256.

12. Clark Warburton, "The Misplaced Emphasis in Contemporary Busi-

ness-Fluctuations Theory," *Journal of Business of the University of Chicago,* 19 (1946), 199–220. Reprinted in *Readings in Monetary Theory,* Blakiston Series of Republished Articles on Economics, (New York: The Blakiston Co., 1951), V, pp. 284–318.

13. Milton Friedman, "Money: Quantity Theory," *International Encyclopedia of the Social Sciences,* 1968, p. 434.

14. See "Key Propositions of Monetarism" in Milton Friedman, "The Counter-Revolution in Monetary Theory," published for the Wincott Foundation by the Inst. of Economic Affairs (London), 1970, pp. 22–26.

15. Nicholas Kaldor, "The New Monetarism," *Lloyds Bank Review,* July, 1970, p. 1.

16. Paul A. Samuelson, *Economics, An Introductory Analysis* (8th ed.; New York: McGraw-Hill Book Co., Inc., 1970), p. 208. Earlier editions were more categorical on this point. The 4th (1958), for example, said: "*All modern* economists are agreed that *the* important factor in causing income and employment to fluctuate is investment" (p. 222).

17. John Maynard Keynes, *The General Theory of Employment, Interest and Money* (New York: Harcourt, Brace and Co., 1935), p. 96.

18. Samuelson, *Economics* (8th ed.), p. 195.

19. *Ibid.,* pp. 195–196.

20. Keynes, *General Theory,* p. 116.

21. See, for example, Samuelson, *Economics,* pp. 295–296, 313–316.

22. Lawrence R. Klein, *The Keynesian Revolution* (New York: The Macmillan Co., 1947), p. 31; Herbert Stein, *The Fiscal Revolution in America* (Chicago: Univ. of Chicago Press, 1969), pp. 151–156.

23. Stein, *Fiscal Revolution,* p. 465.

24. Milton Friedman and David Meiselman, "The Relative Stability of Monetary Velocity and the Investment Multiplier in the United States, 1897–1958," *Stabilization Policies,* A Series of Research Studies Prepared for the Commission on Money and Credit (Englewood Cliffs, N.J.: Prentice-Hall, 1963), pp. 167–268.

25. *Ibid.,* p. 187.

26. *Ibid.,* p. 188.

CHAPTER 2

1. Herbert Stein, *The Fiscal Revolution in America* (Chicago: University of Chicago Press, 1969), pp. 379–380.

2. Walter W. Heller, *New Dimensions of Political Economy,* The Godkin Lectures at Harvard University (Cambridge: Harvard University Press, 1966), p. 51.

3. Arthur M. Okun, *The Political Economy of Prosperity* (Washington, D.C.: The Brookings Institution, 1969), p. 45.

4. Committee for Economic Development, Research and Policy Committee, *Taxes and the Budget: A Program for Prosperity in a Free Economy* (New

York: Committee for Economic Development, 1947); Milton Friedman, "A Monetary and Fiscal Framework for Economic Stability," *American Economic Review*, XXXVIII (June, 1948), 254–264; reprinted in Friedman, *Essays in Positive Economics* (Chicago: University of Chicago Press, 1953), pp. 133–156.

5. See First National City Bank, *Monthly Economic Letter*, February, 1960, pp. 14–15.

6. Richard M. Nixon, *Six Crises* (Garden City, N. Y.: Doubleday & Co., 1962), pp. 309–310.

7. Federal Open Market Committee Minutes (National Archives of the United States Microfilm Publications), Microcopy No. 591, Roll No. 15, January 12–May 24, 1960.

8. First National City Bank, "The Scarcity of Money," *Monthly Economic Letter*, February, 1960, pp. 20–23.

9. *Economic Report of the President* and the *Annual Report of the Council of Economic Advisers* (Washington, D.C.: United States Government Printing Office, 1962), p. 81.

10. Stein, *The Fiscal Revolution*, p. 369.

11. Paul W. McCracken, "An Elder Statesman Looks at the New Economics," *Michigan Business Review*, 19, No. 4 (1967), 15.

12. Stein, *The Fiscal Revolution*, p. 369.

13. Board of Governors of the Federal Reserve System, *Forty-Sixth Annual Report, Covering Operations for the Year 1959* (Washington, D.C., 1960), pp. 2–3.

14. For an excellent retrospective review of the Radcliffe Report see David R. Croome and Harry G. Johnson (eds.), *Money in Britain, 1959–1969*, the Papers of the "Radcliffe Report—Ten Years After" Conference at Hove, Sussex, October, 1969 (Oxford University Press, 1970). The Gurley-Shaw thesis appears in their *Money in a Theory of Finance* (Washington, D.C.: The Brookings Institution, 1960).

15. Milton Friedman, "The Supply of Money and Changes in Prices and Output," *The Relationship of Prices to Economic Stability and Growth, Compendium of Papers Submitted by Panelists Appearing Before the Joint Economic Committee*, March 31, 1958 (Washington, D.C., U.S. Government Printing Office, 1958), p. 250.

16. Stein, *Fiscal Revolution*, p. 371.

17. CEA *Annual Report*, January, 1962, pp. 83–84.

18. Heller, *New Dimensions*, p. 32.

19. *Ibid.*, pp. 61–62.

20. CEA *Annual Report*, January, 1962, p. 85.

21. "Operation Twist" was recommended to the Kennedy Administration by a task force headed by Paul Samuelson in a report, "Prosperity and Policies for the 1961 American Economy." For an early review, see First National City Bank, "The Samuelson Report," *Monthly Economic Letter*, February, 1961, pp. 14–18.

22. Heller, *New Dimensions,* p. 43.
23. CEA *Annual Report,* January, 1962, p. 189.
24. Heller, *New Dimensions,* p. 37.
25. *Ibid.,* p. 34.
26. *Ibid.,* p. 35.
27. Samuelson, *Economics* (4th ed., 1958), p. 245.
28. Okun, *Political Economy of Prosperity,* p. 52.
29. Heller, *New Dimensions,* p. 113.
30. *Ibid.,* pp. 70–71.
31. CEA *Annual Report,* January, 1963, p. 17.
32. *Board of Governors Forty-Ninth Annual Report,* Covering 1961, p. 8.
33. *Ibid.,* p. 77.

CHAPTER 3

1. *Economic Report of the President together with the Annual Report of the Council of Economic Advisers,* January, 1965 (Washington: U.S. Government Printing Office, 1965), p. 3.
2. CEA *Annual Report,* January, 1966, p. 34.
3. William McChesney Martin, "Does Monetary History Repeat Itself?" Address before the Alumni Federation, Columbia University, June 1, 1965. Walter Heller, too, reports that just before the Vietnam escalation in July "many observers of the U.S. economic scene were expressing doubts about our ability to sustain prosperity into 1966." See his *New Dimensions of Political Economy* (Cambridge: Harvard University Press, 1966), p. 86.
4. *Economic Report of the President,* January, 1965, p. 11.
5. CEA *Annual Report,* January, 1965, p. 88.
6. *President's Economic Report,* January, 1965, p. 13.
7. CEA *Annual Report,* January, 1965, pp. 57–59.
8. William McChesney Martin, testimony before Hearings U.S. Congress, House Ways and Means Committee, *President's 1967 Tax Proposals,* Hearings 90th Cong., First Sess., Part 2, September 14, 1967, p. 697.
9. Heller, *New Dimensions,* pp. 85–86.
10. Okun, *Political Economy of Prosperity,* p. 71.
11. CEA *Annual Report,* January, 1967, p. 60.
12. Sherman J. Maisel, "The Effects of Monetary Policy on Expenditures in Specific Sectors of the Economy," *Journal of Political Economy,* 76, No. 4, Part II (July-August, 1968), 796–814; and Jean Crockett, Irwin Friend, and Henry Shavell, "The Impact of Monetary Stringency on Business Investment," *Survey of Current Business,* 47 (August, 1967), 10–27.
13. CEA *Annual Report,* January, 1967, p. 60.
14. More contraction than staff estimates had projected was reported at the meetings of September 13, November 1, November 22, and December 13. The Board of Governors, *Fifty-Third Annual Report Covering Operations for the Year 1966,* pp. 174–201.

15. Okun, *Political Economy of Prosperity*, p. 80.

16. Peter H. Crawford, "Monetary Policy and Household Liquidity," *Financial Analysts Journal*, January–February, 1967.

17. Bond yields peaked in late August and Treasury bill yields peaked in the third week of September. The first definite statement of an intention to ease was the decision at the November 22 meeting of the Open Market Committee to conduct operations "with a view to attaining somewhat easier conditions in the money market . . .," Board of Governors, *Annual Report* for 1966, p. 194.

18. See First National City Bank, "The Turnaround in World Interest Rates," *Monthly Economic Letter*, February, 1967, pp. 21–23.

19. Board of Governors, *Annual Report for 1967*, p. 133.

20. Board of Governors, *Annual Report for 1968*, p. 161.

21. *Ibid.*, pp. 165–166.

22. Alfred Hayes, "Inflation: A Test of Stabilization Policy," Federal Reserve Bank of New York, *Monthly Review*, February, 1970, p. 21.

23. First National City Bank, *Monthly Economic Letter*, June, 1968, p. 65.

24. *Ibid.*, July, 1968, p. 75.

25. Board of Governors, *Annual Report for 1968*, pp. 182–183.

26. *Ibid.*, p. 184.

27. *Ibid.*, p. 184.

28. *Ibid.*, p. 219.

29. *Ibid.*, p. 224.

30. *Ibid.*, p. 225.

31. See H. I. Liebling and J. M. Russel, "Forecasting Business Investment by Anticipation Surveys and Econometric Models in 1968–1969," American Statistical Association, *1969 Proceedings of the Business and Economic Statistics Section*, pp. 250–260. They reported that three government models, whose forecasts were not available for analysis, also predicted overkill. These three were the Council of Economic Advisers Dernberg-Hymans-Lusher model, the Department of Commerce OBE model, and the MIT-FRB model, which was not fully operational. "To our knowledge," they say, ". . . and we would like to stand corrected—no well-known large-scale econometric model would have provided the proper economic advice in the last half of 1968" (p. 251).

32. Okun, *Political Economy of Prosperity*, p. 92.

33. A. A. Walters, *Money in Boom and Slump*, 2nd ed. Hobart Paper 44 (London: Institute of Economic Affairs, 1970), pp. 47, 48. For an account of the fiscal measures, see "Chancellor's Budget Speech," text of the speech by the Chancellor of the Exchequer, the Rt. Hon. Roy Jenkins, M. P., in the House of Commons, March 19, 1968.

34. Board of Governors, *Annual Report Covering 1968*, p. 326.

35. Leonall C. Andersen and Jerry Jordan, "Monetary and Fiscal Actions: A Test of their Relative Importance in Economic Stabilization," Federal Reserve Bank of St. Louis, *Review*, November, 1968, pp. 11–24.

36. U.S. Congress, Senate, *1968 Joint Economic Report,* Report of the Joint Economic Committee on the January, 1968, Economic Report of the President, 90th Cong., 2nd Sess., 1968, Report 1016, pp. 15, 16.

37. CEA *Annual Report,* January, 1969, p. 42.

CHAPTER 4

1. Richard M. Nixon, *Economic Report of the President, together with the Annual Report of the Council of Economic Advisers,* February, 1970 (Washington, D.C.: U.S. Government Printing Office, 1970), p. 9.

2. *Ibid.,* p. 10.

3. *Ibid.,* p. 6.

4. *Ibid.,* p. 58.

5. *Ibid.,* p. 23.

6. Paul W. McCracken, "The Game Plan for Economic Policy," American Statistical Association, *1969 Proceedings of the Business and Economic Statistics Section,* p. 298.

7. CEA *Annual Report,* February, 1970, p. 33.

8. First National City Bank, "A Turn in Monetary Policy," *Monthly Economic Letter,* January, 1969, p. 6.

9. Milton Friedman, "The Inflationary Fed," *Newsweek,* January 20, 1969.

10. Milton Friedman, "Money and Inflation," *Newsweek,* May 26, 1969.

11. Dean S. Ammer, "The Side Effects of Planning," *Harvard Business Review,* May–June, 1970, p. 34.

12. Among the most effective defenders of the Federal Reserve in this period were: Alan R. Holmes, "Operational Constraints on the Stabilization of Money Supply Growth," in *Controlling Monetary Aggregates.* Proceedings of the Monetary Conference held on Nantucket Island, June 8–10, 1969 (Federal Reserve Bank of Boston); Sherman J. Maisel, "Controlling Monetary Aggregates," in *Controlling Monetary Aggregates,* pp. 152–174 and pp. 65–77; Richard G. Davis, "How Much Does Money Matter? A Look at Some Recent Evidence," Federal Reserve Bank of New York, *Monthly Review,* June, 1969, pp. 119–131; J. Dewey Daane, "New Frontiers for the Monetarists," remarks before the Northern New England School of Banking, Dartmouth College, September 8, 1969; Andrew J. Brimmer, "United States Monetary Policy in 1969," a paper presented at the Sixteenth Annual Bankers' Forum, Georgetown University, October 4, 1969; Alfred Hayes, "Inflation: A Test of Stabilization Policy," an address before the forty-second annual midwinter meeting of the New York State Bankers Association, January 26, 1970 (Reprinted in Federal Reserve Bank of New York *Monthly Review,* February, 1970, pp. 19–24); George W. Mitchell, "A New Look at Monetary Policy Instruments," remarks at the Conference of University Professors, Milwaukee, Wisc., September 10, 1969, "Bank Lending Practices and Change in the Monetary Environment," remarks at the Robert Morris Associates Conference, San Juan, Puerto Rico, October

27, 1969, "New Standards for Credit and Monetary Policy," delivered before the *Business Week* Conference on Money and the Corporation, December 8, 1969.

13. Paul W. McCracken, "The Game Plan," p. 296. At the same meeting Otto Eckstein, former member of the Kennedy-Johnson CEA and no monetarist, made somewhat similar remarks in his "The 1961–69 Expansion: Programs and Policies," (ASA *Proceedings,* pp. 325–332). In arguing against extreme swings in fiscal and monetary policies, he said, "Periods of extreme advance or no advance in the money supply have been mistakes without exception" (p. 331).

14. J. Dewey Daane, "New Frontiers for the Monetarists."

15. Alfred Hayes, "Inflation: A Test of Stabilization Policy."

16. Robert V. Roosa, "Controlling Inflation and the Inflationary Mentality," Papers and Proceedings of the Twenty-Eighth Annual Meeting of the American Finance Association, December 28–30, 1969, *Journal of Finance,* XXV, No. 2 (May, 1970), 236, 237. At the time of this address he was Partner, Brown Brothers Harriman & Co.

17. Board of Governors of the Federal Reserve System, *56th Annual Report,* 1969, p. 204.

18. *Ibid.,* p. 206.

19. In statements to Congressional Committees, Chairman Burns spoke of monetary policy having to tread a narrow path "between too much restraint and too much ease" in a year of transition (statement before the Joint Economic Committee, February 18, 1970, and statement before the Senate Committee on Banking and Currency, March 18, 1970). He also spoke critically of excessive variability in monetary policy: "We have lived through a period in which the disadvantages of marked changes in the degree of monetary restraint or ease have been all too evident" (to Joint Economic Committee, February 18, 1970). Monetarists probably read too much into these cryptic remarks at the time and should have paid more attention to the remarks in the same statements about how "monetary policy must stand ready to adapt quickly to unanticipated developments in the economy and in financial markets" (to Joint Economic Committee, February 18).

20. Joseph R. Slevin, "Friedman Theory Kayoed," Washington *Post,* June 9, 1970.

21. According to estimates by the Council of Economic Advisers, changes in tax rates occurring during 1970 reduced revenues by roughly $9 billion. CEA *Annual Report,* February, 1971, p. 70.

22. *Congressional Record, Senate,* September 23, 1970, "Memorandum for the Senate Democratic Policy Committee," p. S 16292.

23. Walter W. Heller, *New Dimensions of Political Economy* (Cambridge: Harvard University Press, 1966), p. 51.

24. *Congressional Record, Senate,* September 23, 1970, p. S 16295.

25. *Ibid.,* p. S 16293.

26. *Ibid.*

27. Leonard S. Silk, "The Accord of 1970," *New York Times,* December 9, 1970.

28. U.S. Congress, Joint Economic Committee, *The 1971 Economic Report of the President,* Hearings Before the Joint Economic Committee, 92nd Cong., 1st Sess., Part 2, February 22, 23, 24, 25, and 26, 1971. Paul Samuelson said, "I have to respectfully submit that no responsible jury of informed persons can agree that the Nixon team forecast of money GNP for 1971 in the neighborhood of $1,065 billion is warranted" (p. 454). Otto Eckstein had recently revised his forecast down to $1,045 billion (p. 491).

29. Sam Nakagama, *Argus Weekly Staff Report* (Argus Research Corporation), March 2, 1971.

30. "Milton Friedman: An Oracle Besieged," *Time,* February 1, 1971.

31. Richard F. Janssen, "Nixon's Flight from Friedmanism," *Wall Street Journal,* February 1, 1971.

32. Council of Economic Advisers, "Inflation Alert," Report to the National Commission on Productivity, August 7, 1970 (pp. 1–6).

33. Arthur F. Burns, Statement before the Joint Economic Committee, February 19, 1971 (Board of Governors release).

34. In its *Annual Report,* February, 1971, the CEA had said: "In the past year monetary policy has moved towards a greater degree of stability in the rate of increase of the monetary aggregates, notably the stock of currency plus demand deposits. This is, as was stated in last year's *Economic Report of the President,* a desirable direction. The financial and economic system is thus given a more stable monetary framework within which to operate" (p. 85).

35. For a critical view of 1971 monetary policy and the 1966–1967 mistake, from inside the Federal Reserve System, see Darryl R. Francis, president, Federal Reserve Bank of St. Louis, "The Road to Accelerating Inflation is Paved with Good Intentions," lecture to School of Banking of the South, Louisiana State University, June 1, 1971. Reprinted in Federal Reserve Bank of St. Louis *Review,* July, 1971.

36. Paul A. Samuelson, "Plague and Problem of Monetarism," The Washington *Post,* August 1, 1971.

37. Herbert Stein, *The Fiscal Revolution in America* (Chicago: The University of Chicago Press, 1969), pp. 379–380.

CHAPTER 5

1. U.S. Congress, House Ways and Means Committee, *President's 1967 Tax Proposals,* Hearings, 90th Cong., First Sess., Part 1, August 14, 1967, p. 66.

2. Victor Zarnowitz, *An Appraisal of Short-Term Economic Forecasts,* Occasional Paper 104 (New York: National Bureau of Economic Research, Distributed by Columbia University Press, 1967), p. 7.

3. *Ibid.*, p. 6.

4. Papers presented at this seminar appear in *Business Economics,* IV, No. 4 (September, 1969), 13–35.

5. Beryl W. Sprinkel, *Money and Stock Prices* (Homewood, Ill.: Richard D. Irwin, 1964).

6. William F. Butler and Robert A. Kavesh (eds.), *How Business Economists Forecast* (Englewood Cliffs, N.J.: Prentice-Hall, 1966).

7. Paul A. Samuelson, *Economics* (4th ed.; New York: McGraw-Hill Book Co., 1958), p. 211. In the 8th ed., 1970, the sentence has been modified to "the laissez faire system is without a *good* thermostat (italics added), p. 195.

8. Karl Brunner, "The Monetarist Revolution in Monetary Theory," reprinted from Weltwirt Schaftliches Archiv, Vol. 105, No. 1, 1970, research project Monetary Theory and Monetary Policy at the University of Konstanz, Reprint No. 1.

9. Milton Friedman, "The Monetary Studies of the National Bureau," National Bureau of Economic Research, Inc., *Forty-Fourth Annual Report,* June, 1964, pp. 17, 18.

CHAPTER 6

1. Milton Friedman and Anna Jacobson Schwartz, *A Monetary History of the United States, 1867–1960.* A Study by the National Bureau of Economic Research, New York (Princeton: Princeton University Press, 1963), p. 676.

2. The Friedman, Schwartz, Cagan work was in the National Bureau business-cycle analysis tradition; see F. and S. *Monetary History* and "Money and Business Cycles," *Review of Economics and Statistics,* XLV, No. 1, Part 2 (Supplement: February, 1963), 32–78; Phillip Cagan, *Determinants and Effects of Changes in the Stock of Money, 1875–1960,* Studies in Business Cycles, No. 13 (New York: National Bureau of Economic Research, Distributed by Columbia University Press, 1965). Much of Clark Warburton's work on money and business fluctuations has been collected in his *Depression, Inflation, and Monetary Policy, Selected Papers, 1945–53* (Baltimore: Johns Hopkins Press, 1966).

3. Geoffrey H. Moore and Julius Shiskin, *Indicators of Business Expansion and Contractions,* Occasional Paper 103 (New York: National Bureau of Economic Research, distributed by Columbia University Press, 1967), table 6, pp. 36–39.

4. Moore and Shishkin, *Indicators of Business Expansion and Contraction,* p. 19, n. 9.

5. Friedman and Schwartz, "Money and Business Cycles," pp. 38–43; and Friedman, "The Monetary Studies of the National Bureau," National Bureau of Economic Research, *Forty-Fourth Annual Report,* pp. 14–18.

6. Zarnowitz, *Appraisal of Short-term Economic Forecasts,* pp. 36–40.

7. Leonall C. Andersen, "Money and Economic Forecasting," *Business Economics,* IV, No. 4 (September, 1969), 16–20.

8. Milton Friedman and David Meiselman, "The Relative Stability of Monetary Velocity and the Investment Multiplier, 1897–1958," *Stabilization Policies,* A Series of Research Studies prepared for the Commission on Money and Credit (Englewood Cliffs, N.J.: Prentice-Hall, 1963), pp. 167–268.

9. Michael W. Keran, "Economic Theory and Forecasting," Federal Reserve Bank of St. Louis *Review,* March, 1967.

10. Leonall C. Andersen and Jerry L. Jordan, "Monetary and Fiscal Actions: A Test of their Relative Importance in Economic Stabilization," Federal Reserve Bank of St. Louis *Review,* November, 1968.

11. First National City Bank, *The United States Economic Outlook for 1970,* Special Economic Study, the Foreign Information Service, February, 1970.

12. Phillip Cagan, "Monetary Policy Choices in the First Year of Recovery," paper before American Statistical Association, New York Area Chapter, Forecasting Conference, April 23, 1971.

CHAPTER 7

1. Irving Fisher, *The Theory of Interest* (New York: The Macmillan Co., 1930, reprinted by Augustus M. Kelly, Publishers, 1967), p. 505.

2. Irving Fisher, "Appreciation and Interest," Publications of the American Economic Association, August, 1896, reprinted in Fisher, *Mathematical Investigations in the Theory of Value and Price (1892), Appreciation and Interest (1896)* (New York: Reprints of Economic Classics, Augustus M. Kelly, Publishers, 1967), p. 505.

3. Fisher, *Theory of Interest,* p. 37.

4. *Ibid.,* p. 43.

5. Survey of Institutional Investors, Financial Research Center, Princeton University, 1971.

CHAPTER 8

1. *Wall Street Journal,* November 19, 1969.

2. *Ibid.,* November 20, 1969.

3. J. Dewey Daane, "New Frontiers for the Monetarists," remarks before the Northern New England School of Banking, Dartmouth College, September 8, 1969, p. 13.

4. Geoffrey H. Moore and Julius Shiskin, *Indicators of Business Expansions and Contractions,* Occasional Paper 103 (New York: National Bureau of Economic Research, distributed by Columbia University Press, 1967), pp. 36–39.

5. Beryl W. Sprinkel, *Money and Stock Prices* (Homewood, Ill.: Richard D. Irwin, Inc., 1964).

6. Michael W. Keran, "Expectations, Money, and the Stock Market," Federal Reserve Bank of St. Louis *Review,* January, 1971, pp. 16–31.

7. Milton Friedman and Anna Schwartz, "Money and Business Cycles," *Review of Economics and Statistics,* XLV, No. 1, Part 2 (Supplement: February, 1963), 61.

8. J. H. Lorie and Lawrence Fisher, "Rates of Return on Investments in Common Stocks," *Journal of Business of the University of Chicago,* January, 1964.

9. George M. Lingua, "Equities 1970: The Return to Reality," comments at First National City Bank's 1970 Insurance Forum, October 22, 1970.

10. Albert E. Burger, "The Effects of Inflation (1960–68)," Federal Reserve Bank of St. Louis *Review,* November, 1969, pp. 25–36.

CHAPTER 9

1. John Maynard Keynes, *A Treatise on Money,* Vol. 2 (London: Macmillan and Co., 1930, reprinted 1960), p. 225.

2. Sherman J. Maisel, "Controlling Monetary Aggregates," *Controlling Monetary Aggregates,* Proceedings of the Monetary Conference Held on Nantucket Island, June 8–10, 1969 (Boston: Federal Reserve Bank of Boston), p. 61.

3. Board of Governors of the Federal Reserve System, *The Federal Reserve System: Purposes and Functions,* 3d ed., 1954, p. 27.

4. "Record of Policy Actions of the Federal Open Market Committee: Meeting Held on January 15, 1970," *Fifty-Seventh Annual Report of the Board of Governors of the Federal Reserve System,* pp. 96, 97.

5. Milton Friedman and Anna J. Schwartz, *A Monetary History of the United States, 1867–1960* (Princeton: Princeton University Press, 1963), see especially Appendix B, pp. 776–808; Phillip Cagan, *Determinants and Effects of Changes in the Stock of Money, 1875–1960* (New York: National Bureau of Economic Research, distributed by Columbia University Press, 1965); Allan H. Meltzer, "The Behavior of the French Money Supply: 1938–54," *Journal of Political Economy,* LXVII, June, 1959, 275–296.

6. Jerry L. Jordan, "Elements of Money Stock Determination," Federal Reserve Bank of St. Louis *Review,* October, 1969, pp. 10–19.

7. Leonall C. Andersen, "Three Approaches to Money Stock Determination," reprint from Federal Reserve Bank of St. Louis *Review,* October, 1967, p. 8.

8. Alan R. Holmes, "Operational Constraints on the Stabilization of Money Supply Growth," *Controlling Monetary Aggregates* (Monetary Conference, June, 1969, Federal Reserve Bank of Boston), p. 75.

9. Phillip Cagan, *Determinants and Effects of Changes in the Stock of*

Money, 1875–1960 (New York: National Bureau of Economic Research, 1965, distributed by Columbia University Press), pp. 18–21.

10. The Brunner-Meltzer results are reported in Allen H. Meltzer, "Controlling Money," Federal Reserve Bank of St. Louis *Review,* May, 1969, pp. 16–24.

11. *Ibid.*

12. Cagan, *Determinants and Effects,* p. 43.

13. Lauchlin Currie, *The Supply and Control of Money in the United States* (2nd ed., rev., Cambridge: Harvard University Press, 1935), pp. 69–82.

14. George J. Benston, "An Analysis and Evaluation of Alternative Reserve Requirement Plans," *Journal of Finance,* XXIV, No. 5 (December 1969), 849–870.

15. *Ibid.,* p. 865.

16. W. F. Crick, "The Genesis of Bank Deposits," reprinted from *Economica,* 1927, in *Readings in Monetary Theory,* Friedrich A. Lutz and Lloyd W. Mints (comps.) (New York: Blakiston Co., 1951), pp. 52–53.

17. Jordan, "Money Stock Determination," p. 19.

18. Richard G. Davis, "How Much Does Money Matter? A Look at Some Recent Evidence," Federal Reserve Bank of New York, *Monthly Review,* June, 1969, p. 124. For a reply to this argument, see: Leonall C. Andersen, "Additional Empirical Evidence on the Reverse-Causation Argument," Federal Reserve Bank of St. Louis *Review,* 51, No. 8 (August, 1969), 19–23.

19. Crick, "Genesis of Bank Deposits," p. 51.

CHAPTER 10

1. Henry Thornton, *An Enquiry into the Nature and Effects of the Paper Credit of Great Britain,* 1802.

2. Milton Friedman and Anna Jacobson Schwartz, *A Monetary History of the United States, 1867–1960* (Princeton: Princeton University Press, 1963), pp. 196–239.

3. *Tenth Annual Report of the Federal Reserve Board Covering Operations for the Year 1923,* pp. 3–16.

4. Lester Chandler has a good account of the early days of reserve-position doctrine in his *Benjamin Strong, Central Banker* (Washington, D.C.: The Brookings Institution, 1958), pp. 237–240. Perhaps the earliest discussion in a Federal Reserve publication appeared in the *Tenth Annual Report of the Federal Reserve Board Covering Operations for the Year 1923,* pp. 3–16. Winfield W. Riefler made the most complete early statement of the doctrine and subjected its hypotheses to careful testing in his *Money Rates and Money Markets in the United States* (New York: Harper & Brothers, 1930). Other early writers on the doctrine were W. Randolph Burgess, *The Reserve Banks and the Money Market* (rev. ed., New York: Harper & Brothers, 1936); and Irving Fisher, *The Theory of Interest* (New York: Kelley & Millman, 1954),

pp. 444–451. See also my *Free Reserves and the Money Supply* (Chicago: University of Chicago Press, 1962), pp. 7–23, for account of the origin of reserve-position doctrine.

5. Burgess, *The Reserve Banks and the Money Market*, p. 239.

6. Meigs, *Free Reserves and the Money Supply*, pp. 14–19.

7. John Maynard Keynes, *A Treatise on Money*, Vol. II of *The Applied Theory of Money*, 6th ed. (London: Macmillan and Co., 1960), pp. 238–239.

8. Minutes of the Federal Open Market Committee, National Archives of the United States Microfilm Publications, Microcopy No. 591, Roll No. 15, Jan. 12–May 24, 1960. Meeting of February 9, 1960.

9. *Ibid.,* meeting of March 1, 1960.

10. *Ibid.,* meeting of March 22, 1960.

11. *Ibid.,* meeting of April 12, 1960.

12. C. A. Phillips, *Bank Credit* (New York: Macmillan Co., 1921).

13. E. A. Goldenweiser, *American Monetary Policy* (New York: McGraw-Hill Book Co., 1951), pp. 109–130.

14. Federal Reserve float arises in the process of clearing checks for member banks when banks presenting checks for collection are credited with the proceeds (in their reserve account) before the banks on whom the checks were drawn have had their reserve accounts debited. The volume of this float can rise or fall by hundreds of millions of dollars from one day to the next.

15. Record of Policy Actions of the Federal Open Market Committee, meeting held on March 9, 1971, *Federal Reserve Bulletin,* June, 1971, p. 509. FOMC had decided to "maintain prevailing money market conditions" also at the February 9 meeting (*Federal Reserve Bulletin,* May, 1971, p. 397).

16. Paul Meek and Rudolf Thunberg, "Monetary Aggregates and Federal Reserve Open Market Operations," Federal Reserve Bank of New York, *Monthly Review,* 53, No. 4 (April, 1971), 83.

17. Alan R. Holmes, "Operational Constraints on the Stabilization of Money Supply Growth," *Controlling Monetary Aggregates,* Federal Reserve Bank of Boston Monetary Conference, June, 1969, p. 73.

18. *Ibid.,* p. 74. George G. Kaufman, then at the Federal Reserve Bank of Chicago, was one of the few within the System who argued in writing when the rule change was proposed that the lagged reserve plan would make it more difficult to control money. The answer was, "So what?" It was adopted primarily to make life easier for the small banks and to keep them from withdrawing from the System. A revised version of his memorandum is available from the author as "Federal Reserve Inability to Control the Money Supply: A Self-Fulfilling Prophecy" (College of Business Administration, University of Oregon, Eugene, Oregon).

19. *Ibid.,* p. 75.

20. Harry G. Johnson and John W. L. Winder, *Lags in the Effects of*

Monetary Policy in Canada, Canada, Royal Commission on Banking and Finance, November, 1962, pp. 140–141. J. A. Galbraith and Anna L. Guthrie of the Royal Bank of Canada pointed out some of the difficulties caused by lagged reserve requirements in their "Cash Reserve Ratios and Banking Reserve Behavior," *Journal of Political Economy,* 78, No. 1 (January–February, 1970), pp. 82–83.

21. Meek and Thunberg, "Monetary Aggregates," p. 82.

22. W. Randolph Burgess, *The Reserve Banks and the Money Market* (rev. ed.; New York: Harper & Brothers, 1936), p. 239.

23. Holmes, "Controlling Monetary Aggregates," p. 75.

24. The original target, borrowings, was modified in the 1950s to include the influence of excess reserves. "Free reserves" consisted of excess reserves minus borrowings. If borrowings were larger than excess reserves the number would be negative, or "net-borrowed reserves."

25. Winfield W. Riefler, *Money Rates and Money Markets in the United States* (New York: Harper & Brothers, 1930), pp. xi–xii.

26. Meigs, *Free Reserves.*

27. For example, William G. Dewald, "Free Reserves, Total Reserves, and Monetary Control," *Journal of Political Economy,* 71 (April, 1963), 141–153; and Karl Brunner and Allan H. Meltzer, *The Federal Reserve's Attachment to the Free Reserve Concept:* A Staff Analysis for the Subcommittee on Domestic Finance of the House Committee on Banking and Currency, 88th Cong., 2d sess., May 7, 1964.

28. Sherman J. Maisel, "Controlling Monetary Aggregates," *Controlling Monetary Aggregates,* Federal Reserve Bank of Boston Monetary Conference, June, 1969, pp. 152–174.

29. See, for example, Albert Burger, Lionel Kalish, and Christopher Babb, "A Procedure for Money Stock Control and Its Implications for Monetary Policy," Federal Reserve Bank of St. Louis *Review,* October, 1971. See also Chapter 14, n. 12.

CHAPTER 11

1. J. Zijlstra, Chairman of the Board of Directors, Bank for International Settlements, *Annual Report for 1969.*

2. Karl Brunner, "Controlling the Money Supply," *The Times* (London), Sept. 7, 1970.

3. Allan H. Meltzer, "The Behavior of the French Money Supply: 1938–54," *Journal of Political Economy,* LXVII, No. 3 (June, 1959), 275–296.

4. *Ibid.,* p. 288.

5. Bruno Brovedani, *Bases Analíticas de la Política Monetaria* (Mexico: Centro de Estudios Monetarios Latinoamericanos, 1961), and *Un Modelo de Análisis Monetario y de Programación Financiera* (Mexico: Centro de Estudios Monetarios Latinoamericanos, 1969).

6. Joachim Ahrensdorf and S. Kanesathan, "Variations in the Money

Multiplier and their Implications for Central Banking," International Monetary Fund *Staff Papers,* VIII, No. 1 (November, 1960), 126–149.

7. The volume of work in this field is growing so rapidly that I have undoubtedly missed some valuable studies, especially among the unpublished works. Among those I have seen are: Manfred J. M. Neumann, "Bank Liquidity and the Extended Monetary Base as Indicators of German Monetary Policy," unpublished paper for Konstanzer Seminar on Monetary Theory and Monetary Policy, June 24–26, 1970 (Konstanz University, Konstanz, West Germany); J. Siebke, "An Analysis of the German Money Supply Process: the Multiplier Approach," unpublished paper for Konstanzer Seminar, June 24–26, 1970; Manfred Willms, "Monetary Targets and Economic Stabilization Policy of the Deutsche Bundesbank," unpublished paper for Konstanzer Seminar, June 24–26, 1970; Willms, "Controlling Money in an Open Economy: the German Case," Federal Reserve Bank of St. Louis *Review,* April, 1971, pp. 10–27; Homer Jones, *Korean Financial Problems* (Seoul: Agency for International Development, United States Operations Mission to Korea, 1968); Adolfo Cesar Diz, "Money and Prices in Argentina, 1935–62," in David Meiselman (ed.), *Varieties of Monetary Experience* (Chicago: University of Chicago Press, 1970), pp. 69–162; Michael W. Keran, "Monetary Policy and the Business Cycle in Postwar Japan," *Varieties of Monetary Experience,* pp. 163–248; Bruno Brovedani, "On the Implementation of Monetary Programs: the Italian Case," Banca Nazionale del Lavoro *Quarterly Review,* No. 69, June, 1964, pp. 130–156; Brovedani, "Italy's Financial Policies in the Sixties," Banca Nazionale del Lavoro *Quarterly Review* No. 89, June, 1969; Antonio Fazio, "Monetary Base and the Control of Credit in Italy," Banca Nazionale del Lavoro, *Quarterly Review* No. 89, June, 1969.

8. Heinrich Irmler, "The Deutsche Bundesbank's Concept of Monetary Theory and Monetary Policy," unpublished paper for Konstanzer Seminar on Monetary Theory and Policy, June 24, 1970, p. 16.

9. Ira O. Scott and Wilson E. Schmidt, "Imported Inflation and Monetary Policy," Banca Nazionale del Lavoro, *Quarterly Review,* December, 1964, pp. 390–403.

10. Paolo Baffi, "Western European Inflation and the Reserve Currencies," Banca Nazionale del Lavoro, *Quarterly Review,* March, 1968. Manfred Willms agrees that the monetary authorities in Germany have in fact been able to offset the effects of foreign-exchange flows and thus to maintain effective control in the short run over the money stock. See his "Controlling Money in an Open Economy: the German Case," Federal Reserve Bank of St. Louis *Review,* April, 1971.

11. U.S. Congress, House Subcommittee on Domestic Finance of the Committee on Banking and Currency, *The Federal Reserve System After Fifty Years,* 88th Cong., 2nd Sess., 1964, Vol. 2, p. 1163.

12. Harry G. Johnson, "Alternative Guiding Principles for the Use of Monetary Policy in Canada," prepared for the Royal Commission on

Banking and Finance; published as Essays in International Finance No. 44, International Finance Section, Princeton University, November, 1963; and in Johnson, *Essays in Monetary Economics,* 2nd ed. (London: George Allen and Unwin Ltd., 1969) pp. 198–199.

13. For a convenient survey of central-bank instruments outside the United States, see Peter G. Fousek, *Foreign Central Banking: The Instruments of Monetary Policy* (New York: Federal Reserve Bank of New York, 1957).

14. George Garvy, *The Discount Mechanism in Leading Countries Since World War II,* prepared for the Steering Committee for the Fundamental Reappraisal of the Discount Mechanism Appointed by the Board of Governors of the Federal Reserve System (Washington: Board of Governors, 1968), p. 15.

15. See Michael W. Keran, "Monetary Policy and the Business Cycle in Postwar Japan," David Meiselman (ed.), *Varieties of Monetary Experience* (Chicago: University of Chicago Press, 1970), pp. 176–177.

16. *Ibid.,* p. 200.

17. Garvy, *The Discount Mechanism,* pp. 30–31.

18. *Ibid.,* pp. 32–33.

19. Frank Tamagna, *Central Banking in Latin America* (Mexico: Centro de Estudios Monetarios Latinoamericanos, 1965), pp. 129–133.

20. For a review of some of these recent innovations, see Samuel I. Katz, *External Surpluses, Capital Flows, and Credit Policy in the European Economic Community, 1958 to 1967,* Princeton Studies in International Finance No. 22 (International Finance Section, Princeton University, 1969).

CHAPTER 12

1. Fritz Machlup, "Eurodollar Creation: A Mystery Story," Banca Nazionale del Lavoro, *Quarterly Review,* No. 194, September, 1970, p. 237. Available also under same title from International Finance Section, Princeton University, *Reprints in International Finance* No. 16, December, 1970.

2. Although some Eurodollar deposits have a maturity of over one year, Eurodollar deposits are predominantly a short-term instrument.

3. Geoffrey L. Bell, "Credit Creation through Eurodollars?," *The Banker* (London), August, 1964, pp. 494–502; Ernest Bloch, *Eurodollars: An Emerging International Money Market,* C. J. Devine Institute of Finance *Bulletin* No. 39 (New York University, April, 1966); Alexander K. Swoboda, *The Eurodollar Market: An International Interpretation,* International Finance Section, Princeton University, *Essays in International Finance* No. 64, February, 1968; Jehan Duhamel, "Les Caractéristiques des Euro-Marches," in *Colloque d'Information sur les Problèmes de Balance des Paiements,* 19, 20, 21 Mai, 1969 (Paris: Banque de France, 1969), pp. 49–66; Federal Reserve Bank of Chicago, "Eurodollars—An Important Source of Funds for American Banks," *Business Conditions,* June, 1969;

Milton Friedman, "The Eurodollar Market: Some First Principles," *The Morgan Guaranty Survey*, October, 1969; Helmut W. Mayer, *Some Theoretical Problems Relating to the Eurodollar Market*, International Finance Section, Princeton University, *Essays in International Finance*, No. 79, February, 1970; Federal Reserve Bank of Cleveland, "The Eurodollar Market: The Anatomy of a Deposit and Loan Market," *Economic Review*, March, 1970; Charles J. Scanlon, "Definitions and Mechanics of Eurodollar Transactions," in *The Eurodollar*, Herbert V. Prochnow (ed.) (Chicago: Rand McNally and Co., 1970); Fritz Machlup, "The Magicians and their Rabbits," *The Morgan Guaranty Survey*, May, 1971.

4. Michele Fratianni and Paolo Savona, "The International Monetary Base and the Eurodollar Market," in Karl Brunner (ed.), *Konstanz— Symposium I on Monetary Theory and Monetary Policy*, Proceedings of the Seminar held at Konstanz University (West Germany) on June 24–26, 1970. See also their "Eurodollar Creation: Comments on Professor Machlup's Propositions and Developments," Banca Nazionale del Lavoro, *Quarterly Review* No. 97, June, 1971; and "Una struttura formale per l'analisi della capacità moltiplicativa del mercato dell'eurodollaro," *L'Industria*, September, 1970, pp. 345–356.

5. Guido Carli, "Eurodollars: A Paper Pyramid?" Abstract of speech presented in Naples, March 24, 1971, at the Istituto per lo sviluppo economico (Printing Section of the Bank of Italy).

6. Fred Klopstock, *The Eurodollar Market: Some Unresolved Issues*, International Finance Section, Princeton University, *Essays in International Finance*, No. 65, March, 1968; and "Money Creation in the Eurodollar Market—A Note on Professor Friedman's Views," Federal Reserve Bank of New York, *Monthly Review*, January, 1970, pp. 12–15.

7. Scanlon, "Definitions and Mechanics of Eurodollar Transactions," p. 18.

8. In his remarks before the International Banking Conference, Munich, West Germany, on May 28, 1971, Arthur Burns mentioned steps that had been taken in March and April "to check the creation of Eurodollars by European central banks which had inadvertently, but on a disconcertingly large scale, added to the dollar reserves that resulted from the balance-of-payments deficit of the United States" (p. 5). He also suggested to the central banks that their stabilizing functions should not be influenced by considerations of profit or loss: "If central banks do respond to the same factors that motivate private entities, they are likely to aggravate their own problems, as happened during the past year when a significant volume of central banks reserves was placed in the Eurodollar market" (p. 7) (Board of Governors press release).

9. Friedman, "The Eurodollar Market," p. 11.

10. Bank for International Settlements, *Annual Report*, June, 1970, pp. 145–147.

11. For an early report of these operations see Charles A. Coombs,

"Treasury and Federal Reserve Foreign Exchange Operations." Federal Reserve Bank of New York, *Monthly Review,* March, 1968.

12. Donald R. Hodgman, *Eurodollars and National Monetary Policies,* an Irving Economic Study, Economic Research Department (New York: Irving Trust Co., 1970). See also *Regulations and Policies Relating to Euro-Currency Markets.* Monetary and Economic Department, Bank for International Settlements, Basle, December 6, 1969.

13. Francesco Masera, "International Movements of Bank Funds and Monetary Policy in Italy," Banca Nazionale del Lavoro, *Quarterly Review,* No. 79, December, 1966. See Samuel I. Katz, *External Surpluses, Capital Flows and Credit Policy in the European Economic Community, 1958 to 1967,* Princeton Studies in International Finance No. 22 (International Finance Section, Princeton University, 1969), pp. 18–22; and "Eurodollar Banking Today," First National City Bank, *Monthly Economic Letter,* July, 1970, p. 81.

14. "Eurodollar Banking Today," First National City Bank *Monthly Economic Letter,* July, 1970, p. 81.

15. Friedman, "The Eurodollar Market," p. 11.

CHAPTER 13

1. Irving Fisher, *The Purchasing Power of Money* (2d ed. rev., 1922; New York: Reprints of Economic Classics, Augustus M. Kelley, 1963), p. 161.

2. J. Dewey Daane, "New Frontiers for the Monetarists." Remarks before the Northern New England School of Banking, Dartmouth College, Sept. 8, 1969.

3. He was referring to their study, "The Relative Stability of Monetary Velocity and the Investment Multiplier in the United States, 1897–1958," *Stabilization Policies,* A Series of Research Studies Prepared for the Commission on Money and Credit (Englewood Cliffs, N.J.: Prentice-Hall, 1963), pp. 167–268.

4. Paul A. Samuelson, *Economics, An Introductory Analysis* (8th ed.; New York: McGraw-Hill Book Co., 1970), p. 219.

5. Alan Walters, "Kaldor on Monetarism," *The Banker* (London), October, 1970, p. 1053.

6. For example, Friedman and Meiselman, "The Relative Stability of Monetary Velocity and the Investment Multiplier"; Leonall C. Andersen and Jerry Jordan, "Monetary and Fiscal Actions: A Test of their Relative Importance in Economic Stabilization," Federal Reserve Bank of St. Louis *Review,* November, 1968, pp. 11–24; and Michael W. Keran, "Monetary and Fiscal Influences on Economic Activity—The Historical Evidence," Federal Reserve Bank of St. Louis *Review,* November, 1969, pp. 5–23.

7. Robert Eisner, "Fiscal and Monetary Policy Reconsidered," *American Economic Review,* LIX, No. 5 (December, 1969), 897–905.

8. Milton Friedman, *A Theory of the Consumption Function,* National Bureau of Economic Research (Princeton: Princeton University Press, 1957).

9. Eisner, "Fiscal and Monetary Policy," p. 899.

10. *Ibid.,* p. 900.

11. Axel Leijonhufvud, *Keynes and the Classics,* Occasional Paper 30 (London: The Institute of Economic Affairs, 1969), p. 42.

12. Herbert Stein, *The Fiscal Revolution in America* (Chicago: University of Chicago Press, 1969), pp. 1–5 and 454–468.

13. David I. Fand, "The Monetary Theory of Nine Recent Quarterly Econometric Models of the United States," *Journal of Money, Credit and Banking,* III, No. 2, Part II (May, 1971), 450–460.

14. Andersen and Jordan, "Monetary and Fiscal Actions: A Test of Their Relative Importance."

15. For example, in Milton Friedman and Walter W. Heller, *Monetary vs. Fiscal Policy,* The Seventh Annual Arthur K. Salomon Lecture, New York University (New York: W. W. Norton & Co., 1969), pp. 53–54.

16. Roger W. Spencer and William P. Yohe, "The 'Crowding Out' of Private Expenditure by Fiscal Policy Actions," Federal Reserve Bank of St. Louis *Review,* October, 1970, pp. 12–24.

17. Karl Brunner, "The 'Monetarist Revolution' in Monetary Theory," *Weltwirtschaftliches Archiv,* 105, No. 1 (1970), reprinted by Research Project in Monetary Theory and Monetary Policy at the University of Konstanz, Konstanz, West Germany.

18. David I. Fand, "Keynesian Monetary Theories, Stabilization Policy, and the Recent Inflation," *Journal of Money, Credit and Banking,* I, No. 3 (August, 1969), 561.

19. See Robert V. Roosa, "Interest Rates and the Central Bank," in *Money, Trade and Economic Growth,* Prepared in honor of John H. Williams (New York: Macmillan, 1951); Ira O. Scott, Jr., "The Availability Doctrine: Theoretical Underpinnings," *Review of Economic Studies,* 25 (October, 1957), 41–48; and Board of Governors of the Federal Reserve System, "The Influence of Monetary Policy on Lenders and Borrowers," *Federal Reserve Bulletin,* 39, No. 3 (March, 1953), 219–226.

20. James Tobin, "A New Theory of Credit Control: The Availability Thesis," *Review of Economics and Statistics,* XXXV, No. 2 (May, 1953), 118–127. Reprinted in Lawrence S. Ritter (ed.), *Money and Economic Activity, Readings in Money and Banking* (Boston: Houghton Mifflin Co., 1961), p. 170.

21. Sherman J. Maisel, "Credit Allocation and the Federal Reserve," remarks at a lecture sponsored by the Banking Research Center at Northwestern University, Chicago, Ill., April 22, 1971.

22. Arthur M. Okun, "Monetary Policy, Debt Management and Interest Rates: A Quantitative Appraisal," *Stabilization Policies,* A Series of Research Studies Prepared for the Commission on Money and Credit (Englewood Cliffs, N.J.: Prentice-Hall, 1963), pp. 167–268.

23. Milton Friedman, "A Theoretical Framework for Monetary Analysis," *Journal of Political Economy,* April, 1971, p. 100. Also available under the same title as Occasional Paper 112, National Bureau of Economic Research (New York: Distributed by Columbia University Press, 1971), p. 51.

24. See First National City Bank, "What Really Shakes the Money Tree," *Monthly Economic Letter,* February, 1971, pp. 5–9; and David Meiselman and Thomas Simpson, "Monetary Policy and Consumer Expenditures: The Historical Evidence," paper for the Second Nantucket Monetary Conference of the Federal Reserve Bank of Boston, June 20–22, 1971. The reader may properly object that the categories of consumer expenditures in Chart 13–1 should be called household investment, for they are purchases of capital goods. In that sense all purchases of goods that are not to be consumed immediately can be defined as investment expenditures.

25. Karl Brunner, "The 'Monetarist Revolution' in Monetary Theory."

26. Harry G. Johnson, "Recent Developments in Monetary Theory—A Commentary," David R. Croome and Harry G. Johnson (eds.), *Money in Britain 1959–1969,* The Papers of the Radcliffe Report—Ten Years after Conference at Hove, Sussex, October, 1969 (London: Oxford University Press, 1970), pp. 86–87.

27. John V. Deaver, "Monetary Model Building," *Business Economics,* September, 1969, p. 29.

CHAPTER 14

1. Milton Friedman and Anna Jacobson Schwartz, *A Monetary History of the United States, 1867–1960* (Princeton: Princeton University Press, 1963), p. 676.

2. Harry G. Johnson, "Recent Developments in Monetary Theory—A Commentary," *Money in Britain 1959–1969,* David R. Croome and Harry G. Johnson (eds.) (London: Oxford University Press, 1970), p. 85.

3. Milton Friedman, "The Quantity Theory of Money—A Restatement," *Studies in the Quantity Theory of Money* (Chicago: University of Chicago Press, 1956), pp. 3–21.

4. Don Patinkin argues that the "reformulated quantity theory" presented by Friedman actually is an "elegant exposition of the modern portfolio approach to the demand for money which, though it has some well-known (though largely underdeveloped) antecedents in the traditional theory, *can only be seen as a continuation of the Keynesian theory of liquidity preference* [italics added]." He also says that the Friedman restatement is very different from the "oral tradition" he remembers from his own days as a

student at Chicago. See his "The Chicago Tradition, The Quantity Theory, and Friedman," *Journal of Money, Credit and Banking,* I, No. 1 (February, 1969), 46–70. Friedman would be the first to acknowledge the debt of monetarists to Keynes; the so-called counterrevolution is more against Keynesians than against Keynes. But the "Restatement" and the empirical verification that follows it are quantum leaps from either the Keynesian theory of liquidity preference or the Chicago oral tradition.

5. The others, all from the University of Chicago Press, are: Meigs, *Free Reserves and the Money Supply* (1962); George R. Morrison, *Liquidity Preferences of Commercial Banks* (1966); and David Meiselman (ed.), *Varieties of Monetary Experience* (1970).

6. Meiselman, *Varieties of Monetary Experience,* p. 4.

7. For some examples, see Allan H. Meltzer, "The Demand for Money: The Evidence from the Time Series," *Journal of Political Economy,* June, 1963; Gregory Chow, "On the Long-Run and Short-Run Demand for Money," *Journal of Political Economy,* April, 1966; Edgar Feige, *The Demand for Liquid Assets: A Temporal Cross Section Analysis* (Englewood Cliffs, N.J.: Prentice-Hall, 1964); Milton Friedman, "The Demand for Money—Some Theoretical and Empirical Results," *Journal of Political Economy,* June, 1959; M. J. Hamburger, "The Demand for Money by Households, Money Substitutes and Monetary Policy," *Journal of Political Economy,* December, 1966; David Laidler, *The Demand for Money: Theories and Evidence* (Scranton, Pa.: International Textbook Co., 1969); H. A. Latané, "Cash Balances and the Interest Rate—A Pragmatic Approach," *Review of Economics and Statistics,* November, 1954; R. Teigen, "Demand and Supply Functions for Money in the United States," *Econometrica,* October, 1964; N. J. Kavenaugh and A. A. Walters, "The Demand for Money in the U.K.," *Bulletin of the Oxford Institute of Statistics and Economics,* 1966.

8. Johnson, "Recent Developments in Monetary Theory," pp. 87–88.

9. See also Friedman and Schwartz, *Monetary Statistics of the United States: Estimates, Sources, Methods,* Studies in Business Cycles No. 20 (New York: National Bureau of Economic Research, distributed by Columbia University Press, 1970).

10. Clark Warburton, *Depression, Inflation and Monetary Policies, Selected Papers, 1945–53* (Baltimore: Johns Hopkins Press, 1966).

11. Adolfo Cesar Diz, "Money and Prices in Argentina, 1935–1962," in David Meiselman (ed.), *Varieties of Monetary Experience;* and Antonio Fazio, "Monetary Base and the Control of Credit in Italy," Banca Nazionale del Lavoro, *Quarterly Review,* No. 89, June, 1969.

12. Karl Brunner and Allan Meltzer, "Some Further Investigations of Demand and Supply Functions for Money," *Journal of Finance,* May, 1964, pp. 247–248; Brunner and Meltzer, *An Alternative Approach to the Monetary Mechanism,* for Committee on Banking and Currency, House of Representatives, Aug. 17, 1964 (Washington: U.S. Government Printing

Office, 1964); Meltzer, "Controlling Money," Federal Reserve Bank of St. Louis *Review,* May, 1969, pp. 16–24; Leonall C. Andersen, "Three Approaches to Money Stock Determination," Federal Reserve Bank of St. Louis *Review,* October, 1967, pp. 6–13; Andersen, "Federal Reserve Defensive Operations and Short-Run Control of the Money Stock," *Journal of Political Economy,* 76, No. 2 (March–April 1968), 275–88; Albert E. Burger, *An Analysis of the Brunner-Meltzer Non-Linear Money Supply Hypothesis,* Working Paper No. 7, Federal Reserve Bank of St. Louis, May, 1969; Jerry L. Jordan, "Elements of Money Stock Determination," Federal Reserve Bank of St. Louis *Review,* October, 1969, pp. 10–19; Lionel Kalish III, *A Study of Money Stock Control,* Working Paper No. 11, Federal Reserve Bank of St. Louis, 1970; and Kalish, "A Study of Money Stock Control," *Journal of Finance,* September, 1970, pp. 761–776.

13. Especially Friedman and Schwartz, *Monetary History;* Cagan, *Determinants and Effects of Changes in the Stock of Money;* Brunner and Meltzer, *Federal Reserve Monetary Policy* (forthcoming); and Warburton, *Depression, Inflation, and Monetary Policy.* Friedman and Schwartz have at least two more volumes in preparation.

14. Chapter 7 of the Friedman and Schwartz *Monetary History* has been reprinted as *The Great Contraction, 1929–1933* (Princeton: Princeton University Press, 1965). See also Brunner and Meltzer, "What Did We Learn From the Monetary Experience of the United States in the Great Depression?" *Canadian Journal of Economics/Revue Canadienne d'Economique,* I, No. 2 (May, 1968), 334–348; Elmus R. Wicker, "Federal Reserve Monetary Policy, 1922–33: A Reinterpretation," *Journal of Political Economy,* LXXIII (August, 1965), 325–343; Lester Chandler, *American Monetary Policies, 1928–1941,* (New York: Harper & Row, 1971); Clark Warburton, "Monetary Theory, Full Production, and the Great Depression," *Econometrica,* April, 1945, pp. 124–128, and other articles in his *Depression, Inflation, and Monetary Policy.*

15. Friedman and Schwartz, *Monetary History,* pp. 300–301.

16. *Ibid,* p. 395.

17. George R. Morrison, *Liquidity Preferences of Commercial Banks,* pp. 21–78. See also Karl Brunner and Allan H. Meltzer, "Liquidity Traps for Money, Bank Credit, and Interest Rates," *Journal of Political Economy,* 76, No. 1 (January–February, 1968) 1–37.

18. Leonall Andersen and Jerry Jordan, "Monetary and Fiscal Actions: A Test of their Relative Importance in Economic Stabilization," Federal Reserve Bank of St. Louis *Review,* November, 1968, pp. 11–24.

19. Michael W. Keran, "Monetary and Fiscal Influences on Economic Activity—the Historical Evidence," Federal Reserve Bank of St. Louis *Review,* November, 1969, pp. 5–23.

20. *Ibid.,* p. 23.

21. Michael Keran, "Monetary and Fiscal Influences on Economic Activity: The Foreign Experience," Federal Reserve Bank of St. Louis *Review,*

February, 1970, pp. 16–28; and "Selecting a Monetary Indicator—Evidence from the United States and Other Developed Countries," Federal Reserve Bank of St. Louis *Review*, September, 1970, pp. 8–19.

22. See his *Money in Boom and Slump*, Hobart Paper 44 (2d ed.; London: Institute of Economic Affairs, 1970).

23. Irving Fisher, *Elementary Principles of Economics* (New York: Macmillan Co., 1919), p. 356.

24. Milton Friedman, "The Role of Monetary Policy," *American Economic Review*, LVIII, No. 1 (March, 1968), 10–17; William E. Gibson and George G. Kaufman, *The Relative Impact of Money and Income on Interest Rates: An Empirical Investigation*, Staff Economic Studies, No. 26 (Federal Reserve Board of Governors, 1966); William Gibson, *Effects of Money on Interest Rates*, Staff Economic Studies, No. 43 (Board of Governors, 1968); Gibson, "Interest Rates and Monetary Policy," *Journal of Political Economy*, 78, No. 3 (May–June 1970), 431–455, and reprinted in Gibson and Kaufman (eds.), *Monetary Economics: Readings on Current Issues* (New York: McGraw-Hill Book Co., 1971), pp. 311–329; First National City Bank, "Central Banking and Interest Rates," *Monthly Economic Letter*, June, 1967, pp. 63–66; and David Meiselman, "Bond Yields and the Price Level: The Gibson Paradox Regained," in *Banking and Monetary Studies*, Deane Carson (ed.) (Homewood, Ill.: Richard D. Irwin, Inc., 1963), pp. 112–133.

25. William P. Yohe and Dennis S. Karnosky, "Interest Rates and Price Level Changes," Federal Reserve Bank of St. Louis *Review*, December, 1969, pp. 19–36. Reprinted in Gibson and Kaufman, *Monetary Economics: Readings*, pp. 352–374.

26. Shigeyuki Fukasawa, "A Variable Lag Pattern in the Formation of Expected Price Changes" (unpublished Ph.D dissertation, Columbia University, 1970).

27. See David Meiselman, *The Term Structure of Interest Rates* (Englewood Cliffs, N.J.: Prentice-Hall, 1962); Reuben A. Kessel, *The Cyclical Behavior of the Term Structure of Interest Rates*, Occasional Paper 91 (New York: National Bureau of Economic Research, distributed by Columbia University Press, 1965); Burton G. Malkiel, *The Term Structure of Interest Rates: Expectations and Behavior Patterns* (Princeton: Princeton University Press, 1966). All of these treatments of the expectations hypothesis owe a considerable debt to Friedrich A. Lutz, "The Structure of Interest Rates," *Quarterly Journal of Economics*, 55 (November, 1940), 36–63, reprinted in American Economic Association, *Readings in the Theory of Income Distribution* (Homewood, Ill.: Richard D. Irwin, 1946), pp. 499–529. For reports of research on interest rates at the National Bureau of Economic Research, see Joseph W. Conard, *The Behavior of Interest Rates*, No. 81, General Series (NBER, 1966), and Jack M. Guttentag and Phillip Cagan (eds.), *Essays on Interest Rates*, No. 88, General Series (NBER, 1969), both distributed by Columbia University Press.

28. For an excellent collection of papers in this field see Edmund S. Phelps (ed.), *Micro-Economic Foundations of Employment and Inflation Theory* (New York: W. W. Norton & Co., 1970).

29. Maurice Allais, "Growth and Inflation," *Journal of Money, Credit and Banking,* I, No. 3 (August, 1969), 355–426.

30. Milton Friedman, *The Optimum Quantity of Money and Other Essays* (Chicago: Aldine Publishing Co., 1968), pp. 1–50.

CHAPTER 15

1. Adam Smith, *An Enquiry Into the Nature and Causes of the Wealth of Nations* (ed. by Edwin Cannan; New York: Modern Library, 1937), p. 404.

2. Jacob Viner, *Studies in the Theory of International Trade* (New York: Harper & Brothers, 1937), p. 6.

3. *Ibid.,* pp. 9, 10.

4. *Ibid.,* pp. 36, 37.

5. David Hume is generally credited with being the originator of the classical theory of the specie-flow mechanism in his *Political Discourses* (1752) and *Essays, Moral, Political and Literary,* 1875 edition, I, 330–345. Viner says, "His main objective in presenting his theory of the mechanism was to show that the national supply of money would take care of itself, without need of, or possibility of benefit from, governmental intervention of the mercantilist type." (*Studies in the Theory of International Trade,* p. 292.)

6. John H. Williams, *Postwar Monetary Plans and Other Essays* (3d ed. rev.; New York: Alfred A. Knopf, 1947), p. 193.

7. Arthur I. Bloomfield, *Monetary Policy Under the International Gold Standard,* 1880–1914 (New York: Federal Reserve Bank of New York, 1959), p. 10.

8. *Ibid.,* p. 24.

9. *Ibid.,* p. 50.

10. League of Nations, *International Currency Experience* (League of Nations, 1944, reprinted by United Nations, 1947), pp. 66–112.

11. John Maynard Keynes, *Essays in Persuasion* (New York: W. W. Norton, 1963), p. 210.

12. *Ibid.,* p. 233.

13. Milton Friedman and Anna J. Schwartz, *A Monetary History of the United States* (Princeton: Princeton University Press, 1963), pp. 360–361.

14. League of Nations, *International Currency Experience,* p. 127.

15. Williams, *Postwar Monetary Plans,* p. 13.

16. One of the best concise histories of the IMF that I have seen is a thoughtful lecture by J. Marcus Fleming of the IMF Research and Statistics Department: "Developments in the International Payments System," International Monetary Fund *Staff Papers,* X (1963), 461–482. See especially the section on "The Postwar Orthodoxy," pp. 461–467.

CHAPTER 16

1. John Maynard Keynes, *The General Theory of Employment, Interest and Money* (New York: Harcourt, Brace and Co., 1935), p. 349.

2. Development of the theoretical basis of the monetary-fiscal policy mix in international payments adjustment was done largely by Robert A. Mundell. See his "The Appropriate Use of Monetary and Fiscal Policy for Internal and External Stability," International Monetary Fund *Staff Papers*, 9 (1962), 70-77.

3. Herbert Stein, *The Fiscal Revolution in America* (Chicago: University of Chicago Press, 1969), n. 11, pp. 481–482.

4. *Ibid*, p. 137.

5. Keynes thought the mercantilists viewed some problems more clearly than did the classical economists who followed them. See his "Notes on Mercantilism" in Chap. 23 of his *General Theory*, pp. 333–351.

6. After I wrote this I found the same thought expressed by Arnold Collery: "the confusion is so great that balance-of-payments adjustment and exchange-rate variation are even analyzed in models without money. Since the foreign-exchange rate is the price of one money in terms of another, how can anything be said about the behavior of such a price in a world without money? In a world of barter, what possible meaning can be given to a balance-of-payments deficit?" *International Adjustment, Open Economies, and the Quantity Theory of Money*, Princeton Studies in International Finance No. 28 (Princeton: International Finance Section, Princeton University, 1971), p. 1.

7. Lloyd A. Metzler, "The Theory of International Trade," in Howard S. Ellis (ed.), *A Survey of Contemporary Economics*, published for the American Economic Association (Homewood, Ill.: Richard D. Irwin, 1948), Vol. I, p. 214.

8. *Ibid.*, p. 215.

9. *Ibid.*, p. 213.

10. Keynes, *General Theory*, p. 336.

11. Samuel I. Katz, *External Surpluses, Capital Flows, and Credit Policy in the European Economic Community, 1958 to 1967*, Princeton Studies in International Finance No. 22 (Princeton: International Finance Section, Princeton University, 1969), pp. 43–44.

12. Harry G. Johnson, "The 'Problems' Approach to International Monetary Reform," in Robert A. Mundell and Alexander K. Swoboda (eds.), *Monetary Problems of the International Economy* (Chicago: University of Chicago Press, 1969), p. 398.

13. Robert A. Mundell, in Mundell and Swoboda, *Monetary Problems of the International Economy*, pp. 262–265.

CHAPTER 17

1. Sir William Petty, *Quantulumcunque Concerning Money*, Vol. II, (1682). In Charles Henry Hull (ed.), *The Economic Writings of Sir William Petty* (Cambridge: Cambridge University Press, 1899), pp. 446–447.

2. J. J. Polak, "Monetary Analysis of Income Formation and Payments Problems," International Monetary Fund *Staff Papers*, Vol. 6 (1957–1958), pp. 8–9.

3. *Ibid.*, pp. 2–3.

4. John Exter, "Financing Freedom's Future—Can We Moderate the Boom?" address before the Economic Club of Detroit, April 25, 1966.

5. Pierre Berger, "Rapports Entre l'Evolution de la Balance des Paiements et l'Evolution de la Liquidité Interne," in *Colloque d'Information sur les Problèmes de Balance des Paiements*, 19, 20, 21 mai, 1969 (Paris: Banque de France), pp. 132–180.

6. Some of the people cited here would not want to be called monetarists, but their work points clearly toward a much greater emphasis on money in explanations of international payments adjustment. For example, see Gottfried Haberler, *Money in the International Economy*, Hobart Paper 31 (London: Institute of Economic Affairs, 1965); Charles P. Kindleberger, *Balance of Payments Deficits and the International Market for Liquidity*, Essays in International Finance No. 46 (Princeton: International Finance Section, Princeton University, May, 1965); Ronald I. McKinnon, "Portfolio Balance and International Payments Adjustment," in Robert A. Mundell and Alexander K. Swoboda (eds.), *Monetary Problems of the International Economy* (Chicago: University of Chicago Press, 1969); McKinnon, *Private and Official International Money: The Case for the Dollar*, Essays in International Finance No. 74 (Princeton, April, 1969); George N. Halm, *International Financial Intermediation: Deficits Benign and Malignant*, Essays in International Finance No. 68 (Princeton, June, 1968); Arthur B. Laffer, "The U.S. Balance of Payments—A Financial Center View," *Law and Contemporary Problems*, Winter, 1969, reprinted as Reprint Series, No. 179, Center for Mathematical Studies in Business and Economics, Graduate School of Business, University of Chicago; Thomas J. Courchene, "General Equilibrium Models and the World Payments System," *Southern Economic Journal*, XXXVI, No. 3 (January, 1970), 309–322; Robert A. Mundell, *Monetary Theory* (Pacific Palisades, Calif.: Goodyear Publishing Co., 1971); Arnold Collery, *International Adjustment, Open Economies, and the Quantity Theory of Money*, Princeton Studies in International Finance No. 28 (Princeton, June, 1971); Alexander K. Swoboda, "Monetary Policy in the Open Economy; Some Analytical Notes," preliminary draft prepared for the Second Konstanz Seminar on Monetary Theory and Policy, June 24–26, 1971.

7. Irving Fisher, *The Purchasing Power of Money* (new and rev. ed.;

New York: Reprints of Economic Classics, Augustus M. Kelley, 1963), p. 7.

8. For an extension of the high-powered money-multiplier framework to determination of world money supply see Michele Fratianni and Paolo Savona, "The International Monetary Base and the Eurodollar Market," in Karl Brunner (ed.), *Konstanz—Symposium I on Monetary Theory and Monetary Policy*, Proceedings of the Seminar held at Konstanz University (West Germany), June 24–26, 1970.

9. Jacques Rueff, "The Rueff Approach," in Randall Hinshaw (ed.), *Monetary Reform and the Price of Gold* (Baltimore: Johns Hopkins Press, 1967), pp. 38–39.

10. For an excellent guide through this problem, see Fritz Machlup, "The Need for Monetary Reserves," Banca Nazionale del Lavoro *Quarterly Review*, No. 78, September, 1966, reprinted in Reprints in International Finance No. 5 (Princeton, October, 1966).

11. See First National City Bank, "A Quarter Century of International Currency Experience," *Monthly Economic Letter*, September, 1969, pp. 104–107; and "The World's Money on the Eve of the IMF Meetings," *Monthly Economic Letter*, September, 1970, pp. 100–103; Michael W. Keran, "A Dialogue on Special Drawing Rights," Federal Reserve Bank of St. Louis *Review*, July, 1968, pp. 5–7; Martin Barrett, "Activation of the Special Drawing Rights Facility in the IMF," Federal Reserve Bank of New York, *Monthly Review*, February, 1970, pp. 40–46.

12. Peter M. Oppenheimer, "The Case for Raising the Price of Gold," *Journal of Money, Credit and Banking*, Vol. I, No. 3 (August, 1969), pp. 649–665.

13. See, for example, Otmar Emminger, "The Gold-Exchange Standard and the Price of Gold," in Hinshaw (ed.), *Monetary Reform and the Price of Gold*, pp. 97–107.

14. William McChesney Martin, "Toward a World Central Bank," paper prepared at the request of the Per Jacobsson Foundation, presented at Aula Der Universitat, Basle, Switzerland, Sept. 14, 1970.

CHAPTER 18

1. R. S. Sayers, *Modern Banking* (6th ed.; Oxford: Clarenden Press, 1964), p. 122.

2. See, for example, Karl Brunner (ed.), *Targets and Indicators of Monetary Policy* (San Francisco: Chandler Publishing Co., 1969), and Michael W. Keran, "Selecting a Monetary Indicator—Evidence from the United States and Other Developed Countries," Federal Reserve Bank of St. Louis *Review*, September, 1970, pp. 8–19.

3. Michael W. Keran and Christopher T. Babb, "An Explanation of Federal Reserve Actions, 1933–68," Federal Reserve Bank of St. Louis *Review*, July, 1969, pp. 7–20; Robert V. Roosa, *Federal Reserve Operations in the Money and Government Securities Markets* (New York: Federal Re-

serve Bank of New York, 1956), pp. 10–17, 64–65, 100–103; Sayers, *Modern Banking,* pp. 101–123; Paul Meek and Jack W. Cox, "The Banking System—Its Behavior in the Short Run," Federal Reserve Bank of New York, *Monthly Review,* April, 1966, pp. 84–91; "Monetary Aggregates and Money Market Conditions in Open Market Policy," *Federal Reserve Bulletin,* February, 1971, pp. 79–104; and *Open Market Policies and Operating Procedures—Staff Studies* (Washington: Board of Governors of the Federal Reserve System, 1971).

4. *Committee on Finance and Industry Report Presented to Parliament by the Financial Secretary to the Treasury by Command of His Majesty* (London: HMSO, June, 1931), p. 15. For a definition of even keel in American idiom, see First National City Bank, *Monthly Economic Letter,* September, 1967, p. 99.

5. See David R. Croome and Harry G. Johnson (eds.), *Money in Britain 1959–1969* (Oxford: Oxford University Press, 1970).

6. A. A. Walters, "The Radcliffe Report—Ten Years After, a Survey of Empirical Evidence," in Croome and Johnson, *Money in Britain,* p. 40.

7. John G. Gurley and Edward S. Shaw, *Money in a Theory of Finance* (Washington: Brookings Institution, 1960).

8. See David I. Fand, "Intermediary Claims and the Adequacy of Our Monetary Controls" in Deane Carson (ed.), *Banking and Monetary Studies* (Homewood, Ill.: Richard D. Irwin, 1963), pp. 234–253; N. J. Gibson, *Financial Intermediaries and Monetary Policy,* Hobart Paper 39 (2d ed.; London: Institute of Economic Affairs, 1970); David Meiselman, "The Impact of Monetary Policy on Commercial Banks: Gurley-Shaw Revisited," paper presented at annual meeting of the American Statistical Association, Dec. 30, 1970; Allan H. Meltzer, "Money, Intermediation, and Growth," *Journal of Economic Literature,* VII, No. 1 (March, 1969), 27–56.

9. Much of the new view is collected in Donald D. Hester and James Tobin (eds.), *Financial Markets and Economic Activity,* Cowles Foundation Monograph 21 (New York: John Wiley & Sons, 1967.)

10. *Ibid.,* p. 3.

11. Harry G. Johnson, "Recent Developments in Monetary Theory—A Commentary," in Croome and Johnson, *Money in Britain,* p. 105.

12. In its report of March 17, 1967, the JEC urged the monetary authorities to adopt a policy of moderate and relatively steady increases in the money supply, "generally within a range of 3–5 percent per year," U.S. Congress, Senate, *1967 Economic Report,* Report of the Joint Economic Committee on the January, 1967, Economic Report of the President, 90th Cong., 1st Sess., 1967, Rept. No. 73, p. 14. The minority members of the Committee (Republican) suggested a range of 2 to 4 percent (p. 60). In 1968 the JEC broadened the range of recommended growth rates to 2 to 6 percent per year. U.S. Congress, Senate *Standards for Guiding Monetary Action,* Report of the JEC 90th Cong., 2d Sess., 1968, p. 17. After the severely restrictive monetary policy of 1969, the JEC majority did not mention the

money-growth rule again. The minority, however, recommended a growth rate of 2 to 3 percent with a possible range of 2 to 6 percent if the state of the economy changed drastically; *1970 Economic Report,* Report of JEC 91st Cong., 2d Sess., 1970. In 1971 the JEC, apparently influenced by the recession, did not specify a monetary growth rate but, instead, recommended a policy of affecting "the term structure of interest rates in order to bring about a decline in the long-term rate"; *1971 Economic Report,* Report of JEC, 92d Cong., 1st Sess., 1971, Report No. 9249, p. 29. The minority members did not specify a monetary growth rate either, saying, "we must rely heavily on the judgment of the Federal Reserve, operating in close consultation with the Administration and reporting regularly to the Congress, to follow a sufficiently flexible course to stimulate growth toward the hoped-for goal without rekindling inflation and sacrificing real growth to the specific total figure goal" (p. 93). This was said on the eve of the monetary explosion of first-half 1971 that we discussed in Chapter 4.

13. In a Letter of Intent to the IMF on May 22, 1969, the Chancellor of the Exchequer indicated that it would be the Government's policy to maintain a satisfactory rate of domestic credit expansion (DCE). DCE was approximately equal to the change in money supply plus certain adjustments for changes in money balances directly caused by a balance-of-payments surplus or deficit. See "Domestic Credit Expansion," Supplement to the Bank of England *Quarterly Bulletin,* September, 1969.

14. See First National City Bank, "Operating Guides for Monetary Policy," *Monthly Economic Letter,* June, 1969, pp. 64–67. For an orthodox Federal Reserve discussion of the directive, see Stephen H. Axilrod, "The FOMC Directive as Structured in the Late 1960's: Theory and Appraisal," in *Open Market Policies and Operating Procedures—Staff Studies.*

15. James L. Pierce, "Some Rules for the Conduct of Monetary Policy," in *Controlling Monetary Aggregates* (Federal Reserve Bank of Boston, 1969).

16. "Competition and Credit Control," Bank of England, May, 1971.

17. The Abbott-Wahlig series was first published, with a technical description, in "A New Measure of the Money Supply," *Federal Reserve Bulletin,* October, 1960, pp. 1102–1123.

18. Milton Friedman, "Money—Tight or Easy," *Newsweek,* March 1, 1971, p. 80. For other articles on money-supply revisions and the reasons for them see Albert E. Burger, "Revision of the Money Supply Series," Federal Reserve Bank of St. Louis *Review,* October, 1969, pp. 6–7; First National City Bank, "Money Data—Ideal and Actual," *Monthly Economic Letter,* October, 1969, pp. 112–114; Irving Auerbach, "International Banking Institutions and the Understatement of the Money Supply," Federal Reserve Bank of New York *Monthly Review,* May, 1971, pp. 109–118; Albert E. Burger and Jerry L. Jordan, "The Revised Money Stock: Explanation and Illustrations," Federal Reserve Bank of St. Louis *Review,* January, 1971, pp. 6–11; "Revision of the Money Stock," *Federal Reserve Bulletin,* December, 1970, pp. 887–909.

19. For Federal Reserve explanations of the procedures see "Monetary Aggregates and Money Market Conditions in Open Market Policy," *Federal Reserve Bulletin,* February, 1971, pp. 79–104; Paul Meek and Rudolf Thunberg, "Monetary Aggregates and Federal Reserve Open Market Operations," Federal Reserve Bank of New York *Monthly Review,* April, 1971, pp. 80–86; and *Open Market Polices and Operating Procedures—Staff Studies.*

20. Albert Burger, Lionel Kalish, and Christopher Babb, "A Procedure for Money Stock Control and its Implications for Monetary Policy," Federal Reserve Bank of St. Louis *Review,* October, 1971. For other St. Louis studies of money-stock control procedures, see Chapter 14, n. 12. A major part of the research that has been done anywhere in the world on methods of controlling the money stock has been done at the Federal Reserve Bank of St. Louis.

21. See Robert C. Holland and George Garvy, *The Redesigned Discount Mechanism and the Money Market,* prepared for the Steering Committee for the Fundamental Reappraisal of the Discount Mechanism Appointed by the Board of Governors of the Federal Reserve System, July 1968; and "The Federal Reserve Discount Policy: A Symposium," *Journal of Money, Credit, and Banking,* II, No. 2 (May 1970), pp. 135–165. For an analysis of how changes in Federal Reserve regulations have made it progressively more difficult for the System to control the money supply, see George G. Kaufman, "Federal Reserve Inability to Control the Money Supply: A Self-Fulfilling Prophecy," unpublished paper available from the author at College of Business Administration, University of Oregon, Eugene, Oregon.

22. For an excellent summary of the arguments for the steady-growth rule, see Milton Friedman, *A Program for Monetary Stability,* the Millar Lectures Number Three (New York: Fordham University Press, 1959), pp. 84–99. Although Milton Friedman is popularly identified with the steady-growth rule, he never has claimed to be its originator. Clark Warburton was advocating such a rule soon after World War II, when Lloyd Mints, Friedman, and others of the "Chicago School" were in favor of stabilizing the price level or other rules that would require fluctuations in money-supply growth. See his "Rules and Implements for Monetary Policy," *Journal of Finance,* VIII, No. 1 (March, 1953), 1–21. Reprinted in Warburton, *Depression, Inflation and Monetary Policy* (Baltimore: The Johns Hopkins Press, 1966).

23. Alfred Hayes, "Recent Developments in Banking Structure and Monetary Policy," Federal Reserve Bank of New York *Monthly Review,* June 1970, p. 121.

CHAPTER 19

1. Milton Friedman, *Capitalism and Freedom* (Chicago: University of Chicago Press, 1962), p. 76.

2. First National City Bank, "The Case for a Tax Cut—Now," *Monthly Economic Letter,* April, 1971, pp. 4–6.

3. *Ibid.,* p. 5.

4. For the details of tax reform in England, see *Reform of Personal Direct Taxation,* presented to Parliament by the Chancellor of the Exchequer by Command of Her Majesty, April, 1971 (London: HMSO, Cmnd. 4653).

5. Committee for Economic Development, Research and Policy Committee, *Taxes and the Budget: A Program for Prosperity in a Free Economy* (New York: CED, 1947); Milton Friedman, "A Monetary and Fiscal Framework for Economic Stability," *American Economic Review,* XXXVIII (June, 1948), 254–264, reprinted in Friedman, *Essays in Positive Economics* (Chicago: University of Chicago Press, 1953), pp. 133–156.

CHAPTER 20

1. D. H. Robertson, *Money,* Cambridge Economic Handbooks—II (4th ed.; London: Pitman Publishing Corp., 1948).

2. Richard N. Cooper, taking in a broader population of countries, counts over 200 devaluations between 1947 and 1970 and 5 upvaluations, or revaluations. See his *Currency Devaluation in Developing Countries,* Essays in International Finance No. 86 (Princeton: International Finance Section, Princeton University, June, 1971), p. 3.

3. J. Marcus Fleming, "Developments in the International Payments System," International Monetary Fund *Staff Papers,* X (1963), 463.

4. Samuel Brittan, *The Price of Economic Freedom: A Guide to Flexible Rates* (London: Macmillan and Co., 1970), p. 18.

5. For surveys of the proposals see George N. Halm, *Approaches to Greater Flexibility of Exchange Rates: The Burgenstack Papers* (Princeton: Princeton University Press, 1970); and Halm, *Toward Limited Exchange-Rate Flexibility,* Essays in International Finance No. 73 (Princeton: International Finance Section, Princeton University, March, 1971), p. 19.

6. George N. Halm, *The International Monetary Fund and Flexibility of Exchange Rates,* Essays in International Finance No. 83 (Princeton: International Finance Section, Princeton University, March, 1971), p. 19.

7. Brittan, *Price of Economic Freedom,* p. 54.

8. W. Earle McLaughlin, "1971—A Year of Unanswered Questions," an address delivered at the 102nd Annual Meeting of Shareholders, Royal Bank of Canada, Jan. 14, 1971.

9. W. Earle McLaughlin, "Lessons on Floating from Canada," *American Banker,* Special Supplement for World Bank—IMF Meetings, Sept. 21, 1970.

10. Executive Directors of the International Monetary Fund, *The Role of Exchange Rates in the Adjustment of International Payments* (Washington: IMF, 1970).

11. The clearest explanation of flexible exchange rates that I know of is by

Milton Friedman, "The Case for Flexible Exchange Rates," in Friedman, *Essays in Positive Economics* (Chicago: University of Chicago Press, 1953), pp. 157–203. See also Egon Sohmen, *Flexible Exchange Rates: Theory and Controversy* (Chicago: University of Chicago Press, 1961); and Milton Friedman and Robert V. Roosa, *The Balance of Payments: Free Versus Fixed Exchange Rates* (Washington, D.C.: American Enterprise Institute for Public Policy Research, 1967).

12. Gottfried Haberler and Thomas D. Willett, *A Strategy for U.S. Balance of Payments Policy* (Washington: American Enterprise Institute, February, 1971).

13. *Ibid.*, pp. 10, 11.

14. Henry J. Gailliot, "Purchasing Power Parity as an Explanation of Long-Term Changes in Exchange Rates," *Journal of Money, Credit and Banking,* II, No. 3 (August 1970), pp. 348–357.

15. Robert A. Mundell, "Toward a Better International Monetary System," *Journal of Money, Credit and Banking,* I, No. 3 (August, 1969), pp. 630–631.

16. Clark Warburton was perhaps the first to extend the steady-growth rule to international monetary problems. See his "How Much Variation in the Quantity of Money Is Needed?" *Southern Economic Journal,* XVIII, No. 4 (April, 1952), 495–509; and "Rules and Implements for Monetary Policy." *Journal of Finance,* VIII, No. 1 (March, 1953), 1–21. Both of these are reprinted in his *Depression, Inflation, and Monetary Policy* (Baltimore: Johns Hopkins Press, 1966). He told the House Committee on Banking and Currency in 1964 that adoption of his proposal for a 3 percent per year growth rate for money, "would signify to residents of other countries the determination of our Government to avoid policies leading either to inflation or to deflation. This would reduce the incentive for foreign holders of dollars to convert them into gold." U.S. Congress, House Committee on Banking and Currency, *The Federal Reserve System After Fifty Years,* Hearings, 88th Cong., 2d Sess., Vol. 2, 1964, p. 1325. Others to recommend the rule are Ronald McKinnon, *Private and Official International Money: The Case for the Dollar,* Essays in International Finance No. 74 (Princeton, April, 1969); and Arthur B. Laffer, "The U.S. Balance of Payments—A Financial Center View," *Law and Contemporary Problems,* Winter, 1969, reprinted as Reprint Series No. 179, Center for Mathematical Studies in Business and Economics, Graduate School of Business, University of Chicago.

Index